The Philosophical Aesthetics of Dance:

Identity, Performance and Understanding

'ϱ

The Philosophical Aesthetics of Dance:
Identity, Performance and Understanding

Graham McFee

DANCE BOOKS

Published by Dance Books Ltd.,
Charwell House
Wilsom Road
Alton
Hampshire
GU34 2PP

© 2011 Graham Mc Fee
ISBN 978 1 85273 149 6

A CIP catalogue record for this book is available from the British Library

Printed and bound in Great Britain by Latimer Trend & Co. Ltd., Plymouth

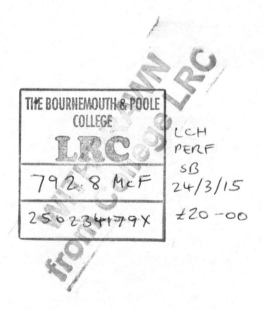

Contents

Preface

§1. Preamble

This text is an exposition of themes in the philosophical aesthetics of dance: as such, it attempts (in its body) both to motivate and to explain questions of the sort typically raised when one discusses those danceworks that are also artworks. My concerns here reflect sets of long-standing commitments in my personal life as well as my professional one. Hence I shall comment briefly, first, on the intersection of those lives (§2) and, second, on the contents of my professional contributions (§3). Those wishing to get on with this book can safely ignore these sections, especially the second, not least because autobiographical elements recur in Chapter One.

This work also satisfies to some degree another plan of mine; namely, the composition of what, following my wife's insightful suggestion, I call *The Muscular Aesthetic* — of which this is volume two! (*Artistic Judgement* [McFee, 2011 = AJ (see below)] is the first volume, elaborating the framework sketched below.) For here we consider some distinctive features of the philosophical aesthetics of dance within the framework of general aesthetics. And those distinctive features will at least reflect in some way the distinctly physical embodiment of dance-ideas in the danceworks themselves.

§2. My own history: Past work and this one

Some of the back-story to this text lies in the history of my writing about dance. So autobiographical remarks here, relating this text specifically to my book *Understanding Dance* (McFee, 1992a = UD), may prove helpful. In the 1980s, students of the aesthetics of dance needed an introductory book to present key themes from philosophical aesthetics in relatively non-technical language, giving dance examples, and reflecting the fact that dance was a performing art. I wanted (and students needed) these discussions in the context of a more general philosophical aesthetics, even if some chapters would reflect issues *distinctive* of the performing arts — and some, perhaps, issues distinctive of dance. Thus *Understanding Dance* was written, chiefly in the late 1980s, as a kind of textbook for a course on the aesthetics of dance I was teaching to an audience of comparative beginners in philosophy. One critic complained that the book was basically a general text on aesthetics with dance examples: this summary is fair enough at least for *some* chapters — although, since that is what I intended, I do not see it as a criticism!

In my past work some features familiar (to me) from the practice of dance did not feature, or feature extensively. By contrast, a new and more direct focus is apparent here, locating the foundations of our enquiry more clearly within dance practice: in particular, the dependence of the dances one sees on the activities taking place in the rehearsal rooms and dance studios. In that sense, this text reflects more powerfully (than the previous one) the foundations of the aesthetics *of dance*, as well as recording the progress of my thought since that time.

Bob Sharpe (1983: Preface) has suggested that many philosophers are:

> ... constitutionally incapable of writing textbooks since, through training and inclination, they are unable to avoid their own opinions from intruding at every corner in the argument.

For the same reason, they find it difficult to write books offering a synoptic view of the issues, arguments and positions in a particular area of philosophy; say, the philosophical aesthetics of dance. But, having already attempted it once, I am making a second attempt here. Yet now I need not avoid my own opinions and arguments, given the role, for better or worse, that those opinions and arguments — especially those from my book *Understanding Dance* (UD) — have played in shaping this area. If some of what follows seems rather self-referential and self-absorbed, that is the reason.

Another advantage of looking back on work completed twenty years ago is to acknowledge both passages I wrote less well than I might have, and passages where I have changed my mind (these last are surprisingly few).

§3.   The structure of this book

This book is in four main parts, after an introductory chapter has set the scene. In Part One, I consider what follows for the understanding of danceworks from the fact that dance is a performing art (or, at least, that the danceworks of concern here are artworks in a performing art). This simple-sounding idea — that danceworks are *performables* — sets the scene for what follows, by clarifying what is involved in danceworks being multiples; and hence in the dance *itself* being an abstract object. This discussion is one way to expand the commonsense realisation that, in a performing art, the very same artwork (here, dancework) can be performed at different times and places, with different casts: hence, one performance can differ quite substantially from another, although both are the very same dancework. Some of this discussion becomes fairly technical, in an attempt to display the options before selecting one. (And a further level of technicality is introduced here by the Appendix.)

Then Part Two addresses the making of danceworks by raising issues (standard in philosophical aesthetics generally) concerning authorship, as well as exploring the role of improvisation. The outcome clarifies the role of the choreographer as author of the dancework; and connects a proper understanding of the choreographer's activities with a revitalised view of what it is to have *intended* the particular work.

Further, Part Three contains a discussion of the role of the dancer, around two key questions: first, what is the dancer's contribution to the performance; and, second, how is that contribution best theorised? Under the first heading, the dancer's role is explored — how should we give it due weight, neither overrating nor underrating it? A key thought will differentiate dancer from choreographer (as roles, even if instantiated by the same person): that will help to clarify — and hence to properly applaud — the dancer's contribution to the performance. Under the second heading, some puzzling claims made on behalf of dancers are explored, and set aside.

Finally, in Part Four, the understanding of dances is considered by first investigating the project of reconstructing dances of the past — for that involves elucidation of project of such reconstruction: how does it relate to simply aiming to retain in the repertoire a dance that has disappeared? Or to return to the repertoire a dance that has not been performed for some time? To explore these matters involves investigating the conception of continuity, and its importance, deployed here. Moreover, a fuller discussion of understanding danceworks reconsiders the place of a narrative of dance history in the identification of those *categories of art* in terms of which danceworks can be made sense of. For only then is misperception to be avoided. Elaborating the recognitional capacities here sketches the kinds of 'ideal observers' whose judgements represent the informed understanding of danceworks.

The work concludes with a discussion which returns us to the beginning, in exploring the question of defining *dance*: once we have surveyed the field, we can put aside that project in a principled fashion.

Throughout, the aim is to provide the reader with as wide a view of the range of options open to philosophical aesthetics as is consistent both with a work of a realistic length and with presenting my own preferred resolutions (or dissolutions) of the difficulties identified. And, as this account should make plain, one focus is the place of the *dancer* in the *performable*.

§4.   A philosophical framework for aesthetics

Although this text is intended to be free-standing, it is of course continuous with my other writing. Hence it rests (if somewhat implicitly) on a framework for philosophical aesthetics elaborated elsewhere (AJ). Outlining its four main pillars here offers a global overview of the conceptual backdrop to this text. Since discussion moves us away from this book's main themes, readers keen to think only about dance need not consult these issues unless they recur.

The first 'pillar' is a contrast (sketched in Chapter One §7) central to our articulation of the distinctiveness of the concept *art*: that between artistic interest and judgement and (mere) aesthetic interest and judgement. This contrast follows from the *transfiguration* inherent in objects becoming artworks: when *this* snow shovel, or *this* pile of fire bricks, counts as a work of art, things are true of it that were not true before — and are not true of other snow shovels. or fire bricks. For comments in art appreciation are, effectively, comments about the works themselves, reflecting what is (now) true of them. And, taking an artistic interest in an object already involves seeing it (defeasibly) as having some value, of a (non-monetary) kind characteristic of artworks. In this context, that recognises the force of the artistic; and hence artistic value. Again, our engagement with the artistic is essentially perceptual: that is, perceptual and not, for example, inferential. Indeed, as Richard Wollheim (1993a p. 142) puts it, "... perception of the arts *is* ... the process of understanding the work of art". Those who conflate actors with the characters they portray are right to the degree that we do *see* the character (which is why, say, one goes to the theatre, rather than just reading a play). But, also, as Thomas Reid ([1785] 2002 p. 574) urged, "[t]his excellence [of an air in music] is not in me; it is in the music. But the pleasure it gives is not in the music; it is in me." For granting that our concern is with the properties of the artworks, not simply our responses to them, recognises those properties as themselves response-reliant.

So, in summary, such judgement has, at least, a perceptual *base*: one's critical remarks about a painting would be rightly dismissed if one had never seen the painting (at best, this would just be someone else's judgement that one was repeating). And the judgement must take the work to be a work of art: in terms of the previously drawn distinction, it must be artistic judgement *rather than* (mere) aesthetic judgement — this will involve, at the least, granting both the object's having been intended as art and its meaning-bearing character. Moreover, artistic judgement involves seeing works in the appropriate *category of art*; categories both supplying the concepts through which the perception is mediated, and importing the distinction between standard, non-standard and irrelevant properties for artworks of that kind. Again, reference to *categories of art* implies that, in artistic judgement, the artwork in question is located in its appropriate history or tradition. Further, what judgements one can make centrally depends on what one can *see* in the work — as we might say, what one has learned to see. Finally, there is an essentially affective element in artistic judgement. As Peter Kivy (1975 p. 210) once put the point:

> To describe something in artistic terms *is* to *describe it*; but it is to savour it at the same time: to run it over your tongue and lick your lips; to 'investigate' its pleasurable possibilities. (Rectified for the artistic/aesthetic contrast.)

So the essential sensuousness of artistic appreciation need not be denied.

Crucially, the *distinctiveness* of the arts is recognised through noting the possibility of misperceiving an object as either (a) an artwork, when it is not (or vice versa); or (b) as in artistic category X (say, cubist painting) what was more properly a work in a *different* category. Drawing this distinction means that terms in their *artistic uses* (or the properties thereby ascribed) amounted to something different from that in the *aesthetic uses* of those same terms (or, again, the properties thereby ascribed). So that, for instance, what counted as *beauty* or *gaudiness* amounted to something different when the beautiful object, or gaudy object, was an artwork than when it was some other object of aesthetic interest or judgement. Further, since taking an artwork for a (merely) aesthetic object was *mis*taking it, misperceiving it, the contrast clarified the argumentative centrality of the idea of misperception. Misperception must be avoided if our experience is to be *of art*. So these ideas are at the heart of *art*.

But how should such facts be explained? Replying identifies the second pillar of my framework: the occasion-sensitive account of meaning and understanding. In fact, this feature is really yet more fundamental — a kind of foundation for much of the other work, resting on an occasion-sensitive picture of philosophy in general (and hence of philosophical aesthetics). So our claims, reflecting the features which make them true or false, should always be seen as answers to specific questions, importing a concern with those features, here. Then some other answer would be likely were a different question raised, since the same concern could not be assumed.

Accepting the occasion-sensitivity of understanding is a key step both to rejecting some assumptions about exceptionlessness in philosophy and to suggesting how to deal with exceptions; say, in the form of (putative) counter-examples. When John Wisdom (1953 p. 222) first wrote of the *dullness* or *dreariness* of aesthetics, he complained that general or abstract books about art had no role: that they offered nothing but platitudes. At the heart of this complaint was the need to treat artistic value case-by-case. And Wisdom compared that position with the ways in which, for instance, novels could be revealing without producing exceptionless generalisations about human flourishing. On some occasions, "all" and "every" (and similar terms) are not used exceptionlessly: hence analysing their use as (always) exceptionless may mislead. (This is the specific topic of McFee, 2010a = EKT pp. 179-193.) As Paul Ziff (1972 p. 128) remarked, cheetahs can outrun men: but what exactly was said, in saying that on a particular occasion? One did not mean any particular men or any particular cheetahs — nor were cheetahs encumbered with weights, or the slow horned cheetah, at issue. Certainly it did not amount to *some* cheetahs being able to do so (for then we could ask, "Which?"). Hence a kind of generality without exceptionlessness is identified. In a context, it makes sense to assert that (say) everything goes with beer or everyone likes Chinese food and, if pressed, to grant the truth of what was asserted. Of course, on some occasions (perhaps in natural science), the terms "all", "every" should be read exceptionlessly. But there are other contexts, and other occasions. As this suggests, recognising that, on some occasions, the terms "all", "every" are not used exceptionlessly could have great importance within philosophy.

Our commitment to occasion-sensitivity explains this effect. For, in approaching the other key topics, our discussions must be seen as answering specific questions as they arise in their specific contexts — hence, putting aside any demand that our account of art be exceptionless. Thus, only a broad account of the connection of art to the rest of our lives (the 'life-issues' connection) need be sketched, before identifying how to meet apparent counter-cases. Further, the meanings of artworks are thereby tied to the judgements offered of the meanings of those works: as a slogan: *meaning in art is what is explained by explanations of the meanings of artworks* (UD pp. 113-116). In thus connecting artistic meaning to explanation, this picture permits that an artwork's meaning might be mutable in the light of changes in how it should (appropriately) be explained: that is, in terms of the current *narrative* of art-making.

That takes us to the third pillar. It is that, in certain circumstances, the meaning-features of an artwork can be changed by later conceptual events: changes in how the *narrative* of art should be written at some later time can amount to changes in what properties can (truly) be ascribed; and hence in how those works should be understood, on an appropriate occasion. So the framework grants this *forward retroactivist* picture of the historical character of art. This results partly from recognising that artistic properties are necessarily available to humans (in principle). As Jerrold Levinson (1990 p. 197) characterises it:

Adopting the perspective of *forward retroactivism*: ... involves construing ... [a later artwork] in the light of ... [an earlier artwork], which is just traditional historicism, and then projecting this understanding back onto [the earlier work].

So this is a through-going recognition that one's historical position can (in principle) affect the meaning of artworks of the past, as well as those of the future — where the changes are in how the works are (appropriately) understood. And, if the interrogation of artistic practice by philosophical aesthetics is occasion-sensitive, later generations may also be asking different questions: hence, at least sometimes, different answers (reflecting conceptual changes) will be appropriate.

Finally, the framework's fourth pillar is our institutional account of art, connecting the reality of our experience of art with the preconditions for an audience for art. For the possibility of art requires that people be able to recognise artistic properties, but also that they be inclined to do so. In this way, it requires the traditions of art-making and art-understanding. Further, at least for performing arts, there will also be training in performance: as we might say, in *art-instantiating*! Moreover, there are traditions of performance; and venues (of various sorts) for its presentation. Such institutionalism also offers a reply to specific questions about the limitations of candidate artworks (putting aside 'wishing makes it so' and 'the unintended artist'): for it posits an *authoritative body* ("the Republic of Art"), employing phases of self-election and other-acclamation. Here, this "Republic" will be composed of choreographers, producers, dance theatre owners and so on: and, in particular (other) dance-critics and dance-theorists. On our two-stage theory, any movement sequence put forward as dance (self-election) and accepted by others (other-acclamation by the Republic) is indeed an artwork (in this case, a dance), at least defeasibly.

My institutionalism, in particular, is easily misunderstood, since the prospects for an institutional account of art have become entangled with the fortunes of George Dickie's (putative) institutional *definition* of art (Dickie, 1974). The literature on institutional accounts of art typically accepts features of Dickie's version as identifying all (or anyway most) of the requirements for institutionalism about art. But, as sketched above, my account differs radically from Dickie's: most importantly, it does not offer a *definition* of art, and it discusses an expressly *evaluative* conception (or denies Dickie's sharp contrast between classification and evaluation). Finally, its emphasis on, and account of, an *authoritative body* is distinctive.

On this institutional picture, both *art-status* and *artistic value* are in the gift of the Republic: that a 'decision' on the part of the Republic could down-grade an artist's work or simply eject it from the canon of artworks. Hence this account is not merely classificatory, since it bears on artistic value as well as art-status.

However, very little in this text depends directly on my institutional account of dance (or of art more generally). Still, this is one way in which the account here is realistic, reflecting some features of the *actual* Republic of Dance, as it might be encountered. And it supports the practice, within philosophical aesthetics, of taking what goes on the artworld as the 'test bed' for our claims (just as it is not philosophers of science who give us the list of scientists). So we do not have complete freedom here: our claims must be tested against central practices in the artworld. Perhaps some examples are peripheral; but not all are. And most of what is wanted from institutionalism in this text should be accepted by anyone who notices that; and sees it as a framework for debate about cases or examples.

§5. Acknowledgements

Material from, or versions of, the following papers and presentations (revised) is incorporated here:

- "Cognitivism and the Experience of Dance" in A. C. Sukla (ed.) *Art and Experience*. Westport, CT: Praeger, 2003b pp. 121-143 (in Chapter Ten)

- "The Artistic and the Aesthetic" *British Journal of Aesthetics* Vol. 45 No 4, 2005a pp. 368-387 (in Chapter One)

- "The Friends of Jones' Painting: A Case of Explanation in the Republic of Art" *Contemporary Aesthetics*, Vol. 6, 2008 (in Chapter Eleven)

- "Dance, Identity and Performance" — versions or segments of this material were presented at the meeting of the Pacific Division of the America Society for Aesthetics, Asilomar, March, 2007; at University of Washington, Seattle, January, 2008; and at a conference, *The Aesthetics of Dance: Ontology, Cognition, Emotion*, University of Nancy, France, 22nd-25th May, 2008; and published as McFee, 2010b (in Chapter Three)

- "Dance, Dancers and Subjectivity: Some Questions about Subjectivity and the Performing Arts" presented to *The Expression of Subjectivity in the Performing Arts*, International Conference, held at Universidad Politecnica de Valencia, Spain, 23rd-26th November, 2008; and published as McFee, 2010c (in Chapters Seven and Eight)

- "'Admirable Legs'; or, The Dancer's Importance for the Dance" Keynote address to "Thinking Through Dance: The Philosophy of Dance Performance and Practices", University of Roehampton, 26th February 2011 (in Chapters Four and Seven)

The presentations benefited from the contributions of those present, who are hereby thanked.

This work has also benefited from discussion with many colleagues, in many contexts. While I cannot formally thank each one, let the following alphabetical list of those who made specific contributions, through discussion of ideas or papers or through reading parts of the text, stand for them all:

Sally Banes, Noël Carroll, Renee Conroy, Terry Diffey, Cecilia Hynes-Higman, Jeff Mason, Katherine Morris, Anna Pakes, Bonnie Rowell, Charles Travis, Andrea Woody.

My thanks also to:

- Department of Philosophy, University of Washington, Seattle for the kind invitation to visit in January, 2008; and for support and hospitality while I was there. And likewise the organisers of the three conferences mentioned above, in Nancy, Valencia, and Roehampton.

- Department of Philosophy, California State University Fullerton and Chelsea School, The University of Brighton, both of which supported me in various ways while I was writing this.

- The reader for Dance Books, whose suggestions have clarified aspects of the structure and content.

- Paul McNaught-Davis, and the village of Joncelets, France (completing the trilogy).

This book would not have been finished without the support and assistance of my long-suffering wife, Myrene: who contributed at all stages of the processes of thinking and writing, and also taught me how to make the index.

And, of course, my thinking here — as elsewhere — is indebted to the late Gordon Baker.

§6. Abbreviations
(a) to my own works:
McFee, 1992a — "UD";
McFee, 2004a —"CDE";
McFee, 2000b — "FW";
McFee 2004c — "SRV";
McFee, 2010a — "EKT";
McFee, 2011 — "AJ".
(b) to works of Wittgenstein:
Wittgenstein, 1953/2001 — "PI"
Wittgenstein, 1969 — "OC"

Wittgenstein, 1980 — "CV"
Wittgenstein, 1993 — "PO"
(c) to works of Goodman:
Goodman, 1968 — "LA"
Goodman, 1972 — "PP"

Chapter One

Dance, art and philosophy:

A personal introduction

§1. Thinking about authenticity in dance performances

An article in the *LA Times*, entitled "Five things I hate about ballet", included the suggestion that ballet "... falsifies its present" (Segal, 2006 p. E36 [a]), by presenting as 'the classics' what were really new works:

> ... the so-called traditional versions of *Swan Lake* danced by the New York City Ballet and American Ballet Theatre were premiered more recently than the radical Matthew Bourne modern-dance adaption — the one with the male swans.

In part, this author's critique is that what one *takes* for traditional danceworks — the standard fare of these big ballet companies — are in fact far more modern, having "premiered ... recently". As a result, the danceworks one sees are "... compromises between the look of then and the technique of now" (Segal, 2006 p. E36 [a]).

One aspect of this author's objection to the state of ballet today is directed at the *repertoire* of many ballet companies today — really a way to criticise some of the stale or out-dated material still performed[1]. It is easy to sympathise with these complaints especially — as I first wrote this — with another *Nutcracker* season in prospect! But two points set a stronger course. First, many of the criticisms of ballet apply equally to modern dance companies; and especially, say, Martha Graham's (at least in some of its moments). So the culprit is not really ballet as such. Second, at any time, most of the dance being performed, and being choreographed, is not good — as most of the painting or poetry at any time is not good!

So are works performed as 'the classics' really new, as our author implies? To answer, one really needs a clear sense of what is and what is not a particular dancework (say, *Swan Lake*). This question might seem easy to answer. But any clear basis for resolving what is and what is not *the very same dancework* faces difficulties, given the diversity among performances which are still of *Swan Lake*. For one performance of *Swan Lake* can differ from another, without the second becoming the performance of a different dancework. What changes here (say, to cast, costume or staging) are consistent with our (rightly) still seeing that same dancework? And which go too far? On the face of it, no clear reply is forthcoming. So one cannot readily identify dances in the way our author assumed. But, without resolving such issues, it seems difficult to comment accurately on the properties of particular dances. When did I see that dance? And when not? Hence the real and abiding topic concerns when the performance one observes is of a particular dance (say, *Swan Lake*). Further, these issues arise whether one thinks about *staging* a particular dance; whether our perspective is that of the choreographer or that of the dancer; whether our concern is with *appreciation* (or, more generally criticism) of a particular dancework; or, again, whether one seeks to 'reconstruct' a dancework from the past. Each of these contexts will be addressed in this text, since this is (among) the stuff of the philosophical aesthetics of dance.

Perhaps the author of the "Five things I hate about ballet" would not be placated by the discussion that follows. But this text's argument shows that the issue is not centrally *theoretical*; not a problem for *ballet* (nor for dance), but only a problem for ballet*s* or for ballet companies. Those who pursue the topic in practice *can* resolve whether or not such-and-such a dance is being performed in so-and-so (putative) revival — or anyway have a public, reasoned debate about it. These matters cannot typically be open, or arbitrary, despite the difficulty in resolving them. For (at least primarily) the difficulty in resolving the issue *really* resides in assumptions about the form taken by such a resolution: theoretical worries disappear once it is recognised as case-by-case, at best, rather than exceptionless. But a great deal of discussion is required to establish such a conclusion. And, of course, that leaves the practical issues of having the debate about *this* dancework, and staging the work, in this context, with these resources.

As such cases suggest, the interest in dance here is localised to those danceworks that are artworks — these will usually be performed in theatrical contexts (such as theatres or other auditoria), and typified by ballets and works of modern dance. No doubt there are many other kinds of dance, not considered here; and this sketch does not draw our boundaries very closely. Still, a rough (and temporary) account here identifies the danceworks that concern us here as "ballets and similar-ish dances", setting this topic aside for later (see Chapter Eleven).

This Chapter identifies some main contours of the problems around which this text is constructed. Its focus is on "work-identity"; or, more transparently, issues concerning whether or not two performances are of the same dancework. For those danceworks that are also artworks are typically *performables* (a fundamental thought here!): they can be re-performed on another occasion or in another place. As well as presenting a set of dance-related conclusions, this work offers a comprehensive account of central issues in the development and articulation of the philosophical aesthetics of dance: that is, the philosophy of dance for those danceworks that are artworks. Thus concerns with *performing* arts unite with those of *art-making* more generally.

Often, describing the field of philosophical esthetics as it presently exists involves confronting my arguments and opinions — at least my former arguments and opinions, since those opinions and arguments (especially the ones from *Understanding Dance*: hereafter "UD") have been instrumental in shaping this area[2]. Indeed, many positions of others are most easily understood by contrast with mine. On most topics I am here going beyond my earlier work, but sometimes that has involved citing that work or rehearsing its arguments or conclusions.

§2. Performables, (numerical) identity questions, and philosophy

The discussions throughout are motivated by ordinary, everyday concerns: we need to be clear (literally) *what* we are talking about. And that issue can arise for dances. When I ask what we are discussing, your first response is unlikely to be some kind of 'definition' of *dance*. Rather, you indicate the object of our concern, pointing to a particular dance performance, and saying, "we are talking about *that*!". Well, yes ... but (typically) not that *performance* exactly — although that *can* be our topic: instead, we are talking about the *dance* of which it is a performance. (This would be especially clear were we judging a choreographic competition.)

All this is common knowledge, I take it: that, for typical danceworks, the very same dancework can be performed on more than one occasion — that dancework is a *performable*. So, needing to view the dancework again, you might note that the same company is performing it again next week — although, of course, in a different kind of performance-space. And, since one lead dancer was injured tonight, that role will be danced by someone else. And so on. Although performances of *the very same dance*, these performances differ in their details. In this sense, then, our concern is with 'the dancework as object': the kind of thing one could return to on another occasion. And *that* is what we are talking about. But what *exactly* is that? What exactly are *performables*? And when does one confront the very same one again?

Philosophy sometimes raises such issues are under the general heading of (numerical) *identity*: that is just a concern with *the very same one*. Familiar examples[3] introduce most of the basic issues of numerical identity as they apply to danceworks. For instance, suppose someone claims to inherit under so-and-so's will — claims he is so-and-so's grandson. This is a (numerical) *identity* claim: he is claiming to be the very same person as identified in the will of the 'grandfather'. Were he not that person, he *should* not inherit: he has no right to inherit. Thus the numerical-identity issue here is not trivial. Also, it clearly cannot depend on obvious properties of the claimant: he is six feet tall, slim, with long hair. The person 'the grandfather' saw was a baby: small, bald and chubby. But that is irrelevant. In fact, such changes in the intervening twenty five years are the norm. His looking now just as he did (say) at the will's witnessing would be *prima facie* evidence of his not being the legitimate heir: change is rightly *expected*. Moreover, such change typically bears on his opinions, views, and beliefs as well as his appearance.

Just as, there, one hunts for the *very same person* despite these differences, so the dance case involves identifying the very same dancework despite the differences between one performance and another. This is (roughly) a kind of *identification* of the dances (as of the people), rather than showing anything profound about them — as other uses of the term "identity" might suggest. For instance, one incarnation of a particular dance can still be preferred to another (or valued over another); and for good reasons — just as one might say that, in growing up, he had become a nicer person. Clearly, danceworks are not spatio-temporal continuants, in the way that chairs or watches (or, arguably, people) *are*: the very same dance can be performed in different places at the same time, as well as at different times. So part of our discussion engages with the distinctiveness of dance in these respects (especially in Part One).

Since this book is about *dance*, philosophy must not overstep its bounds. For instance, if the dance community recognises such-and-such as dance, philosophy cannot gainsay that view — at least usually. For example, it will not be the task of philosophy to decide *if* it counts as dance to have:

> ... merely walked around a space. Following straight, diagonal, or slightly curving paths, he slowly lifted one foot, then the other, going continuously except for a few brief rest stops. (Siegel, 1977 p. 314)

In the same vein, when the status of a particular movement sequence is problematic (is it dance or not?), philosophy's project cannot require making *clear* the status of that sequence — either clearly dance or clearly not. In this sense, faced with the dictates of the danceworld, philosophy "leaves everything as it is" (PI §124[4]). Then danceworld practice provides a number of uncontentious cases (and also of borderline cases) to provide a 'test bed' for one's claims; and to ground one's reasoning. And more than just the conclusions are relevant. Due weight must be given to the *practices* of the danceworld themselves. For it seems implausible that, say, the fact that dances typically require long and demanding rehearsals is a mere contingency, which might well have been different. Indeed, to my thinking, far more than is normally supposed here counts as conceptually-connected — it is towards the 'necessary' (rather than contingent) end of the continuum. (This drives me towards an institutional account of the arts: see Preface §4; Chapter Eleven §§3-5.)

Another factor points in the opposite direction, for there is no reason to *do* the philosophy unless it has potential to help practitioners: roughly, to clarify their claims. So, were the claims of philosophy *irrelevant* to the concerns of practitioners — as merely abstract concerns with work-ontology[5] might be — my interest in doing philosophy here would wane. On my view, philosophy should be *therapeutic* in the sense of answering the perplexities of particular individuals, by offering *"objects of comparison"* (PI §130). Clearly, some engagement with practitioners' activities is required: either they are the perplexed individuals or their activities are what leave others perplexed.

§3. Locating the philosophical aesthetics of dance

The philosophical aesthetics of dance partly involves the presentation of general themes from philosophical aesthetics with dance *examples*: points from those discussions are not distinctive of dance, although of course they are true of danceworks. It also contains material *distinctive* of dance. But a few topics, addressing instead the performing arts (of which dance is one), are neither generally applicable across the arts nor exclusive to dance — even though accounts of 'the performing arts' often need modification for dance. Thus a three-fold categorisation roughly locates the philosophical aesthetics of dance (McFee, 2000a): it involves (i) general themes from philosophical aesthetics with dance *examples*; (ii) themes from philosophical aesthetics as they apply to dance *and to similar* art forms; but also (iii) as they apply to dance only. But aspects (i) and (ii) mean that examples (and even arguments) from outside dance will be considered if they are clearer, or more informative.

The foundations of our current enquiry, located more clearly (than previously) within dance practice, offers a more direct focus here. So that, in this work, only the latter elements of that three-fold division feature strongly (with the discussion of artist's intention, in Chapter Five, the big exception). Some chapters present for discussion alternative answers to the questions posed (especially those offered by various philosophers — often those the text cites). Other chapters aim simply to identify and clarify an issue for philosophy of dance.

Even some issues broached here for the philosophical aesthetics of dance, being really issues for philosophical aesthetics more generally, cannot be completely and conclusively resolved in this text! (Our contextualism precludes it: in another part of philosophical aesthetics, perhaps things must be done differently.) But this work addresses the majority of issues for the aesthetics of dance that are specific to dance.

Since philosophical aesthetics of dance reflects philosophical aesthetics more generally, positions in the first should mirror positions in the second. Sometimes no attempt to be specific here is required, beyond what is granted by the idea of making the *corresponding* changes (in the jargon, *mutatis mutandis*). This attitude can be right (roughly reflecting the three-fold categorisation above); but not always. For many issues do not, in this way, generalise across the arts. The distinctiveness of philosophical aesthetics of dance typically follows from the distinctiveness of dance itself from within the arts. So, when an issue arises because we are dealing with a performing art, answers for dance should parallel those for music. But with the distinctiveness of dance — say, as physical — to the fore, the account for dance will typically differ from that for music; and any accounts failing to acknowledge such differences could be criticised (for that reason). What distinctiveness should be acknowledged? That question asks us to reflect on the experience of dance (as art) in all its variety.

At one period in my life, a large amount of time was spent waiting outside rehearsal rooms. While this would also doubtless be true of those waiting for actors, it seems especially true for dance. A typical play, it seems to me, begins with a script; and much rehearsing consists in *getting right* how the words are to be said, with what movements (and what business). Yet the reality of the preparation for typical dance performances is very far from this. In a sense, the rehearsal time, even for a familiar dance, often amounts to a kind of reconstructing of the dance for this cast and this performance space. For (as I will bewail later) most dances with a history do not begin from notated scores, but — at best — from someone's memory. Or, if there is a score, its status too is contestable since (in all likelihood) it records only one past performance, rather the work itself (see Chapter Three). Moreover, many dances are made, more or less from scratch, in this 'rehearsal' process.

Further, that I stood *outside* (at least of the process) is significant: for elements of the typical dance-rehearsal process (as with some theatre) would be 'for the dancer', not the kind of thing to share even with someone trying to understand the place of rehearsal in dance-making. Of course, some time will typically be taken by 'class'; by working on the technical aspects of the dance *style* of the (projected) performance; some will bear directly on the choreography. But some (and sometimes part of the 'class') typically involves exercises aimed at preparing the dancers: perhaps exemplified by a place for (say) contact improvisation in building one's dance company. This might be thought the iceberg's hidden percentage — not actually part of the work, but central to grasping the nature of dance as experienced, since a dancer's life incorporates a great deal of such rehearsal.

Much writing on the philosophical aesthetics of dance (as on philosophical aesthetics generally) rightly begins from the artwork itself: concerns with, say, the artist's psychology have no place in such deliberations. (Considering them involves looking away from the art-object itself to the process that created it. But fruitful processes may result in poor art.) If it has seemed to some critics that, like other aestheticians, my writings ignoring the rehearsal idea, that would explain the misapprehension. For some features familiar from the practice of dance did not appear, or anyway loom large, in my past work: in particular, the dependence of the dances one sees on the activities taking place in the rehearsal rooms and dance studios. Anything like an *accurate* or *full* account of the aesthetics of dance should reflect these features.

The rehearsal was always central to my thinking: it was a key to my expounding the idea of works in performing arts as *performables* — that one rehearsal could apply to the whole week's performance was indicative that there was a single artwork here. Further, the importance of the rehearsal process in setting the dance should be recognised: that process involves setting what should or must be done to instantiate the work in our troupe's performance version (which may, of course, also coincide with some performer's interpretation — say, Nureyev's; or we may be doing something quite different). But the normativity here proscribes differently for different styles of dance, for different companies, and so on. Still it facilitates clarifying what is involved in doing *this* dance; or, at least, in *our* doing it. If little more is heard *directly* on this topic here, its impact is still pervasive.

As related example, suppose that, as in the film *The Boy Friend* (1971), a young ASM goes on for the injured star — and much of what happens subsequently (and much of the impact on the audience, as one might imagine it) derives from that ASM actually *feeling* the emotions, and such like, that she portrays. Certainly, were she to go on the following night, she could not be expected to replicate this performance. In that sense, she is not *acting* at all. In particular, although she has no doubt previously 'blocked out' the patterns of movement for the part (like any good understudy), she can hardly be said to have *rehearsed* it. Again, the 'performance' we see her give, as the film portrays it, was certainly not rehearsed. Whatever one makes of her 'performance', it is a *one-off*: as such, it functions oddly in a performable — something capable of being re-performed! And we can comment on this specifically both in respect of dance-identity (Chapter Three) and of dancer's importance (Chapter Seven).

§4.   The account of dance (and dance-understanding)

So this work's starting point engages two specific features of much dance-making: the first of these — that typical danceworks are *performables* — returns us to the *re-performance* of dance; and hence to questions of dance identity raised above. To explore *this* topic, the possibility of notation of dances is recognised, and some concerns with notationality for dance are reprised, together with a re-evaluation of the contribution of the choreographer (in Chapters Three, Four and Five). The second of the features mentioned above concerns the place of *the dancer* in such processes (discussed in Chapters Six, Seven and Eight). Then, to move beyond these features, the place of dance reconstruction is addressed; and to reflect the possibility of making sense of danceworks — as intentional, meaning-bearing 'objects' — I turn to the role of dance history (in Chapters Nine and Ten).

To elaborate, this work approaches a general account of the philosophical aesthetics of dance through a consideration of what being a *performable* requires of the nature of dance: a topic sometimes called "the identity of danceworks" — although that title can be confusing (since it refers to *numerical identity* only). In the context of this text, dance is centrally a *performing* art; and, given its particular relation to performing, an essentially *physical* art form. In effect, three features must receive credit:

(i) That dance is an *art form* — that partly limits our investigation (to those dances that *are* art forms, which ever those turn out to be) and partly acknowledges the nature of art here; and for me that, in turn, involves granting the artistic/aesthetic contrast (McFee, 2005).

(ii) That dance is a *performing* art — that raises sets of questions about confronting the same work on two occasions. And the very idea of a performing art (and hence of one that can be performed on more than one occasion — a *re-performable* art) requires that, in principle, a performance *is*, or is *not*, an instantiation of the dancework in question, for performances on two such occasions (say, Tuesday's performance and Wednesday's).

Further, thinking about how to guarantee that possibility of re-performing will intersect with our concerns with the notation of the dancework.

(iii) That fundamental to dance is (bodily) *action*; that dance is *physical* in at least that sense — the contrast is with music, where the players movements typically *brings about* the music, rather than *instantiating* it. So music is not bodily, not physical, in this sense.

The primary concerns here are with the second of these three aspects. Yet some fundamental connections between the second and third of these play a role — connections visible when improvisation is considered, for instance. For one must enquire precisely what *movements*, and what *actions*, are required to instantiate such-and-such a dancework.

But the *force* of the idea of danceworks as *performables* — and hence (at least typically) re-performable on another occasion — is clear. First, the artwork is only encountered when one encounters a *performance* of it, thereby recognising the concreteness or specificity of dance. (One might quibble about the status of, say, video recordings, but the moral is straightforward: if watching the video recording counts as watching the dance, it is a *performance*, albeit an indirect or recorded one. If, by contrast, watching the video recording does not count as watching the dance, we can regard it as slightly less than a performance [Sparshott, 1995 pp. 448-451].)

Second, the dancework itself is always *under-determined*, relative to any particular performance of it, since each performance makes concrete in particular ways features of the dance which might have been concretised in other ways — indeed, those *other ways* might figure in another performance of that very dance, even one by the same company. This aspect of dance is also reflected in dance notation (see Chapter Three). For dancers making concrete the dance, instantiating it, might be conceptualised as giving substance to the notation for that dance. In doing so, they implicitly emphasise some of the features of the dance, at the expense of others. This is, of course, to produce a performer's interpretation.

Dancers' actions, which (along with, say, music, costume and the like — where appropriate) bring the dance into being, might be regarded as the following of a *recipe* (Urmson, 1976 p. 246), to generate "... those things ... of which the witnessable work consists" (Urmson, 1976 p. 243). Similar things might be said of any performing art (see Part One of this work).

Yet, before beginning elaboration of this picture, we must clarify what follows from our concern with dances that are artworks: that is, to begin from the idea of dances as artworks (idea 1. above). Here, as often, my aim is to arrive at a defensible view by considering, and setting aside, the alternatives most regularly raised; and in that way arriving at my preferred outcome.

§5. Are dances just aesthetically pleasing movement?
Danceworks might be thought simply passages of aesthetically pleasing movement. If this account appears unduly simplistic, that might only be

because it leaves out other elements of typical dances, as one sees them —
the music, the costume, the stage-setting perhaps. But these might be
thought just ways to intensify the aesthetic appeal of the whole event, given
the familiar thought of the beauty, grace, elegance (and such like) of fellow
human beings when they move. For one might well be struck by the grace of
a sportsplayer, or even someone performing a relatively straightforward task,
such as sweeping the street.

Although such an account does not require undue elaboration, two of its
features deserve emphasis. First, the concern here is *aesthetic* in precisely the
same sense in which a beautiful sunset might provide aesthetic pleasure, or
aesthetic enjoyment. As a sloganised version of such aesthetic enjoyment or
appreciation, it could be thought of as the appreciation of *beauty*. While that
may not fit every case exactly, it gives a broad sense of what is at issue: grace,
and line, and fluency, and such like are recognised in the world around us.
(In fact, the catalogue of aesthetic properties or qualities should more
properly include also the negative ones; but these are rarely mentioned in
this context.) So, turning to a parallel account, the appreciation of a painting
would be, in effect, the appreciation of a graceful design in the world. Then,
second, such features could equally be naturally-occurring or man-made.

A slightly different account (see UD pp. 51-52) regards dance as
"aestheticised movement": that is, movement in which an aesthetic interest
is taken. But then the two views come to the same thing — that we are struck
by the grace, line, and so on, of the world around us. At best, the dance might
be marked-out from the rest of those things in which an aesthetic interest is
taken, or aesthetic pleasure derived, in being made with this in mind.

Such an account of dance is widespread (like the parallel one for art more
generally). Yet this view cannot offer what is needed to move forward in the
aesthetics of dance, for it does not match our account of the value of
danceworks. Consider the idea that dance is just (one kind of) human
movement in which an aesthetic interest is taken. Of course, we should then
want to know *what* kind: what are the features of dance, as opposed to (say)
gymnastic floor-work, that allows us to contrast them? But, even if that point
were put aside, something here obviously remains unexplained. Imagine
some people "... enthusing how beautiful or interesting the movement is,
how skilled or extraordinary the dancers, but muttering that they've no idea
what it all means" (Mackrell, 1997 p. 1). Yes, they are clearly missing
something; but this fact casts a shadow over their admiration of, say, the
dancers' skill — since they do not know what is going on, they cannot know
whether a particular movement is crucial or not: they would equally applaud
a dancer performing the wrong movements, as long as there was virtuosity.
As these people cannot see this movement's relation to others, and to the

whole, they cannot judge the skill in *dance*, but only technical virtuosity of the kind one might applaud in, say, tightrope walking. A parallel with painting makes the point sharply. On this view, a painting — even an artistic masterpiece — is just an elaborate wall-covering in which an aesthetic interest is taken. Of course, it is *designed* to elicit such interest; but so is much wallpaper. What is missing, of course, is precisely that one is, and the other is not, an artwork (in the 'fine art' sense). Now, elaboration of this category of *fine art* must be put off until later: but our recognition of it can begin here[6]. The same is true for dances — whatever one says positively of the grace of the road-sweeper, his activity is not a fine art (even when we admire the craftsmanship with which he accomplishes it). Once that is seen, a more adequate account must be sought. That returns us to the second feature of this account, described above. For clearly a feature of *art* (in that 'fine art' sense) is that it is *meant*; that there is a human intelligence behind it, where this amounts to more than simply that it was designed. Hence it cannot be naturally-occurring in the way typified by the sunset, contrary to this account. For, in speaking of the meaning of danceworks (as of artworks generally), one grants a sense — sometimes described in terms of the communicative potential of artworks — in which the work speaks to its audience.

Further, such "speaking to its audience" must have a certain generality: it can be contrasted with associations a certain dance performance or painting might have — it was at that performance or by that painting that I first met so-and-so. This fact, no doubt profound in my life, does not speak to the quality of dancework or painting. Similar indifference to quality applies for social significance; and again the case of painting provides a powerful example. Picasso's *Guernica* was (a) painted by probably the most important painter of his day (and a Spaniard); (b) originally planned to go on the wall of the Spanish Pavilion at 1937 World's Fair in Paris; (c) altered when, as part of Franco's uprising against the Republican government, German aircraft bombed the town of Guernica; and (d) given to the Spanish people, but not to return to Spain while Franco lived and while Spain was not a republic. This catalogue of facts, ensuring the social significance of the painting, has no bearing, one way or the other, on whether it is a good painting. For those facts could be granted by someone who had never seen the painting. Here too significance is divorced from the merit of the work *as art*. In a similar vein, the reason that Rick, the Humphrey Bogart character in the film *Casablanca*, has instructed his pianist, Sam, never to play the tune "As time goes by" is that tune's association with his lost-love, Ilse — it was 'their song'. Hence its prohibition has nothing to do with the song's merit or other direct properties. Again, similar things can be said (if perhaps less poignantly) for various danceworks. Even if we met at a performance of *Swan Lake* (indeed, even if we met as principal dancers in some performance), that fact is irrelevant to the quality of the ballet: it is not a fact *about the ballet* at all. So that artistic meaning should be contrasted with both association and (social) significance.

Further, recall that artistic meaning is certainly not confined to works that we aesthetically appreciate in some *positive* fashion — as beautiful, graceful, and such like. Artworks can be grotesque (say, Goya's painting *Saturn Eating his Children*) without that counting against our (justified) high regard of them. Indeed, those critics of Graham's early dances who complained that the flexed feet and cupped hands had *given up* the graceful lines of ballet were falling into precisely this trap. For, if there is beauty there (as I am sure there is), it is not something grasped simply by looking. Perhaps those critics were right that the works lacked what was *standardly called* "beauty": but, as with other art forms, that simply opens the door to other forms of beauty — the beauty of art. Thus Siegel (1979 p.37) quotes a description of Graham's work as "... purged ... of the superficial prettiness of the past". But to focus on *aesthetic* appreciation here would involve attention to such "prettiness".

So, instead, the appreciation of danceworks (as of other artworks) must begin from a recognition of them as *art*, for this allows attention to be draw to their relations to other danceworks, and to the tradition of composing and performing dances. In that sense, thinking of dances merely as movement viewed aesthetically misses something crucial to them.

§6. Are dances considered aesthetically and artistically?

What might this suggest? Perhaps, after all, from the perspective of its beauty (or aesthetic interest), whether or not the movement sequence, the dance, is *art* is beside the point: it would be just as *beautiful* (or whatever other aesthetic property one is ascribing) whether or not it was art.

This position has something to recommend it, allowing the recognition that such-and-such a movement pattern is a dancework (and hence bringing to bear on it whatever follows from its being dance) while *also* treating it as an object of aesthetic interest. The thought, then, that its beauty does not depend on its art-status — that it would be equally beautiful (or whatever) even if it were not art — *seems* appealing. For it seems that what one sees, in seeing the dancework, cannot be altered by knowing, or failing to know, that this movement sequence is in fact a dancework (that is, an work of art, in the 'fine art' sense).

So this position, as well as recognising the aesthetic interest of this movement sequence, also gives weight to the art-status of our candidate dancework. But, it gives it the *wrong* weight, in three related ways. First, it seems as though the craft-based aspect of our artwork — if there is one — is irrelevant to its aesthetic impact; as though its beauty, or whatever, is independent of how it comes about. We know that is false for the case of naturally-occurring objects, where the beauty precisely lacks being *crafted*. That is why the sculpture could be expressive, witty, and so on, while such concepts could not apply to the meteorite (see Ground, 1989 pp. 25-26) — even when one could be mistaken for the other. So the fact that the object was *made* cannot be beside the point. Equally, artistic admiration will not be *reducible* to an admiration of craft: some artworks do not have craft *as such* as a major element (people say, with some justice, "a child could have done that" — if he could have thought of it!); further, praise for the work as art does not seem praise for its craft (when there is craft), since (say) *virtuosity* here need not be something one can specify independently. And this would be as true for danceworks as for other artworks.

Second, the importance already assigned to its *being* art seems misplaced if our central appreciation of the movement-sequence neither recognises, or nor depends on, its being art. In that way, on this view, its being art would be a fairly unimportant fact about the movement sequence. That seems wrong. For it suggests that the informed judgement of, say, the dance critic has nothing to recommend it over the judgement of anyone else who is struck by the movement sequence's grace or beauty. Yet to distinguish mere preferences towards or away from a particular dance from evaluations or appreciations of that dance is to concede that the evaluations require justifications: that reasons for or against such evaluations must be offered (see Carroll, 2008 p. 193). And then informed judgements seem at least a *desirable* base from which to justify one's appreciations. So informed judgement cannot function on the model permitted by this picture of appreciation.

Third, failing to recognise that what one sees is a *dance*, one will typically mis-describe it, which may be a basis for mis-judging it. In the simplest case, we might mistake for something designed or planned what was in fact merely a naturally occurring movement sequence — one that had no meaning, but was simply my passage from point A to point B. This tells us that, in the imagined example, whether or not the sequence is dance is not irrelevant to our appreciation of it. Again, painting offers a simpler case: if, looking out of my window, I am struck by the grace and line of the sunset, or the moon on the lake, my appreciation is of the sunset, or the moon on the lake. Then it will be crucial to my appreciation that this *is indeed* a sunset, or moon on the lake. If, instead, I mistake a painting of the moon on the lake for the real thing, I am drawing the wrong comparison — I am not seeing it in terms of the kinds of beauty appropriate to other *paintings*. Yet that is the appropriate way to regard the painting.

In fact, here two points overlap. The first recognises that perception is concept-mediated; and then identifies misperception when inappropriate concepts are brought to bear. This in turn is reflected in our perceptual powers and capacities. So, if one lacks the concept "oak tree", there is a sense in which one cannot see oak trees: one cannot distinguish them perceptually from other kinds of trees. And, famously (UD p. 216), from the discussions of radiologists, one can learn to see detail in X-rays that were previously opaque to one: here is one is *learning to see* — one's perceptual experience is modified in this experience. Further, and for that reason, merely having knowledge of certain facts or concepts will not be enough here; one must be able to mobilise those concepts in one's experience of the dance (UD p. 173). For only then does the fact of having the concept bear on one's experience. Then, second, a particular role here should be assigned to one class of concepts — often called "categories of art" (Walton, 1978 [2008]: elaborated Chapter Ten). They allow us to recognise the dance before us as of this or that kind or genre: hence without the appropriate *category*-ascription, our (mis)perception of the dancework will be based on inappropriate expectations. For knowing that our painting is cubist, or that our music is atonal, sets up expectations: and those expectations will be misplaced if the wrong *category of art* is deployed. Thus, taking the music to be tonal in design, one thinks very badly of it. Yet that judgement draws on the category; and hence can be often reversed *in one's experience* once the error is recognised.

In these ways, then, the centrality of the concept *art* here must be granted — it underpins one's actual judgements of dancework. But what are the implications of that revelation?

§7. Dance and transfiguration

The thought here, then, is that correctly regarding danceworks *as danceworks* involves seeing them differently from how one would in thinking of them merely as aesthetic objects: that becoming an artwork is a *transformative* process — that there is a real sense in which, if the movement sequence really is a dancework, then things are potentially true of it that simply could not be true were it not an artwork. Here a sharp contrast between *the artistic* and *the aesthetic* is being drawn[7]. To clarify these intuitions, Arthur Danto (1981 p. 1) offers an example from visual art: a 'gallery of indiscernibles', composed of four objects, each consisting of a canvas with a large square patch of red pigment. As Danto describes them, the elements from the gallery are:

(a) "a minimalist exemplar of geometrical art ... [entitled] ... 'Red Square'" (Danto, 1981 p. 1);

(b) "a still-life executed by an embittered disciple of Matisse, called 'Red Table Cloth'" (Danto, 1981 p. 1);

(c) "a canvas grounded in red lead, upon which, had he lived to execute it, Giorgione would have painted his unrealized masterpiece 'Conversazione Sacra'" (Danto, 1981 p. 1): here, I imagine the preparation done by workers in the studio — this *would have* become an artwork, although presently it is not;

(d) "a surface painted ... in red lead" (Danto, 1981 p. 1): although Danto does not explain this, I imagine its being a kind of window blind, the red pigment being especially suitable in a certain climate. As with (c) above, Danto would call this a 'real thing': we can adopt this terminology.

In the example, any of these objects ('real' or artwork) might be mistaken for any other ('real' or artwork).

Much ink has been expended contesting the conditions of indiscernibility here (see Wollheim, 1993b; Wieand, 1994). Yet the simplest version (you don't know which one you are looking at) probably motivates the cases, once it is conceded that they *are* distinct in ways that bear on their proper appreciation. Further, it is *relative* indiscernibility: as Danto (2000 p. 132) notes, "a photograph ... [of Warhol's *Brillo Box*] would be indiscernible from one taken of the commonplace containers in which the soap pads were shipped to supermarkets". So objects with differences whose significance is either not transparent until the art-status issue is resolved, or within limits of, say, mechanically produced 'versions', should count as indistinguishable — the concern is always with *relevant* differences.

Moreover, these comments in art appreciation are, effectively, comments about the works themselves. As Bob Sharpe (2000 p. 40) put it, "... the music itself is sad, not the composer, performer, or listener." This too follows, of course, from the *transfiguration* inherent in objects becoming artworks: when *this* snow shovel, or *this* pile of fire bricks, counts as a work of art, things are true of it that were not true before — and are not true of other snow shovels, or fire bricks.

These cases suggest (surely correctly) that the objects in Danto's gallery differ: different things can (truly) be said of each. Hence, one can misperceive any of them by (mis-)taking it for another one, or treating one as though it were another. Further, Danto's gallery of indiscernibles rightly shows that the 'transfiguration' into artwork is important just because it brings with it a critical vocabulary of the kind appropriate to art — the kind of *artistic valuing* from which we began. That is precisely what both the artworks have, and the 'real things' lack, even when, as in case (c), the 'real thing' has some connection to the world of art. That it is not (yet) transfigured into art means that the requisite critical vocabulary for art (of that type) is inapplicable to it. Further, this clearly articulates how the artworks — cases (a) and (b) — differ: a different critical vocabulary is appropriate to each, since each has a place in a different 'narrative' of art-history, or in a different tradition; a different *category of art* applies to each, and a different critical discourse follows.

What is implied for our concern with dances that are artworks? Beginning, as above, from dances as artworks involves beginning from movement 'transfigured' into dance. Suppose, coming late to my dance performance, you see a lone figure on the stage, sweeping it: you are struck by the grace and line (and such like) of this stage-sweeping. You are making *aesthetic* judgements concerning that movement-sequence (using the artistic/aesthetic contrast above). But you are *mistaken* so to do, since this is a section of my dancework: being a literalist choreographer, I included the broom as a prop from the dancer. So you *misperceived* the movement-sequence, seeing as 'ordinary' movement (however graceful) what was in fact a segment of a dancework: that is, a segment of an artwork. In misperceiving the movement in this way, you attribute to it properties it lacks. And this is true *even if* the stage ends up clean(er). Now, various things are true of the movement-sequence viewed (correctly) as part of my dance — that is, viewed under *artistic* concepts; or, as an *artwork* — that could not be true of it were it merely an aesthetic object: for example, it is *witty*. Of course, things would be true of it as an aesthetic object that would not be true of it as an art-object, *if it were* merely an aesthetic object (that is, if you were *correct* so to view it). Yet, in failing to recognise it as (part of) an artwork, you are *not* correctly viewing it: to repeat, you are misperceiving it. As Danto (1994 p. 384) puts it, "[t]he aesthetic difference [better, *artistic* difference] presupposed the ontological difference." But *this* kind of misperception — mistaking artwork for 'real thing' — attributes to the artwork the properties it *would have*, were it a 'real thing'; and hence the properties that a "confusable counterpart" (Danto, 1981 p. 138) 'real thing' does have.

Indeed, such a point could be reinforced by consideration of a sequence from Yvonne Rainer's *Room Service* (1963) in which "... two dancers [are] carrying a mattress up an aisle of the theatre, out one exit, and back through another" (Carroll and Banes, 1982 reprinted in Banes, 1994 p. 11). Suppose that:

[t]he point of the dance is to make ordinary movement qua ordinary

movement perceptible. The audience observes the performers navigating a cumbersome object, noting how the working bodies adjust their muscles, weights, and angles. (Banes, 1994 p. 11)

And, of course, real furniture movers might have done exactly the same movements: that would have been a 'confusable counterpart' of the dance. Yet the two cases differ. Thus, the primary objective for the furniture movers — the key feature of their project — is that the bed should be moved from A to B; if they do not achieve that, they have failed. But that is not so for the Rainer piece: if, one night, the dancers are too tired (or too weak from lack of food, given their prevalent anorexia) and the bed does not make it, that does not undermine the piece — at least not automatically.

As a simpler example, consider the literalist choreographer described above who builds his dance from the movements of a stage-sweeper; and (being a literalist) gives his soloist a broom. Perhaps, as a result, the stage will end up cleaner after a performance of the work, but that is irrelevant; for the genuine stage-cleaner, though, it is his *raison d'être*. So one cannot uniquely characterise a 'way of looking' or 'way of seeing' here, without saying that one is (and the other is not) the seeing of an artwork. Thus, suppose once again that someone comes into my performance space and sees the person in the raised performance area busily at work with his broom. *Of course*, in this case someone can misperceive what is going on — as above, it is a Danto-esque confusable counter-part: one needs to know if this is my stage-sweeper or my soloist (the dance having been so boring that the audience has gone home). But there seems no way to articulate the *kind* of attention one takes to each, divorced from the kind of activity it is; and especially from the primary goal of each activity. (Floor-cleanliness should be mentioned in the first case; and the term "art" in the second.) The appropriate kind of regard cannot be identified independently of the objects so regarded. That these are confusable counterparts — and hence misperceived when mis-identified — supports my contention that the art-status cannot depend on a distinctive, independently-specifiable kind of regard.

So, crucially, the *distinctiveness* of the arts is recognised through noting the possibility of misperceiving an object as either (a) an artwork, when it is not (or vice versa); or (b) as in artistic category X (say, cubist painting) what was more properly a work in a *different* category. Drawing this distinction between the artistic and the aesthetic had three important corollaries: first, terms in their *artistic uses* (or the properties thereby ascribed) amounted to something different from that in the *aesthetic uses* of those same terms (or, again, the properties thereby ascribed). For instance, what counted as *beauty* or *gaudiness* amounted to something different when the beautiful object, or gaudy object, was an artwork than when it was some other object of aesthetic interest or judgement. And, since artistic judgement draws on categories of art, we should more exactly have spoken of *gaudy for a Fauve*, and so on.

Then, second, taking an artwork for a (merely) aesthetic object was *mis*taking it, misperceiving it. So the contrast clarified the argumentative centrality of the idea of misperception: misperception must be avoided if our experience is to be *of art*. And classic modes of misperception involved both taking an artwork for a (mere) aesthetic object, or vice versa; and mobilising an inappropriate category of art in one's appreciation of an artwork. The object must be seen aright. Then the third corollary was that the value of artworks, a value of a non-monetary kind not (in principle) shareable with (mere) aesthetic objects, was best characterised in terms of a kind of *meaning* appropriate to artworks. Here, too, the emphasis was on not 'getting it wrong' in trying to make sense of an artwork. And only an account of art sharing these corollaries would be drawing the contrast on which I have insisted. These are at the heart of our account of art.

But how are these corollaries, and especially the first, to be explained? My strategy involves recognising a profound contextualism here, reflecting an occasion-sensitive account of meaning and understanding. On it, as Austin (1970 p. 130) noted, "[t]he statements fit the facts always more or less loosely, in different ways on different occasions for different intents and purposes." So our claims about dances, reflecting the features of those dances which make the claims true or false, should always be seen as answers to specific questions, importing a concern with those features. Then some other answer would be likely were a different question raised, since the same concern could not be assumed[8].

This transfiguration of movement patterns into works in the art form of dance has crucial implications sketched above, reflected in our dance-aesthetics. First, different sets of qualities (or properties) are truthfully ascribed to the movement (etc.). In our example of 'sweeping', the dance might be (for instance) *witty* in ways the mere sweeping cannot. Recognising the dancework as *art* brings with it a vocabulary of the art-critical, ascribing artistic properties to that movement sequence. These are arguably then *real* properties of the dances, despite requiring a suitably sensitive 'recogniser'. As noted earlier, even when the same term is used to ascribe properties both to artwork and to 'ordinary' movement (say, the term "graceful"), it amounts to something different in each case — roughly, one is the grace of *danceworks*, in such-and-such a genre, and so on. Thus, recognition of the grace of the artwork appeals implicitly to the history and traditions of dance, in that genre, and so on (even when rejecting aspects of those traditions, or of that narrative of art history, or whatever: Sparshott, 1998 p. 94).

Second, this transfiguration brings with it kinds of *understanding* not available for the mere sweeping: in both cases, some causal mechanisms may be shared — but the dance involves something different to understand, a "something" picked-out in speaking of the arts in terms of *communication*. For the dance is created or intended to be understood (when it attracts a suitably knowledgeable audience): this recognition is integral to recognising the dance as art (or the movement sequence as dance). Disputes about cognitivism in dance (the idea that dances are fit objects of understanding) will parallel discussions for *music alone* (Kivy, 1993: 360-373; McFee, 1997). At the least (as before), whatever follows about understandability from art-status (if anything does) will apply to dances also. For the special case of music, as Stephen Davies (1994 p. ix) puts it:

> ... I am not embarrassed to use the term 'meaning' here because I think both that music can and should be understood to be appreciated and that it is created to be so.

Something similar might be said for dance. Whatever one's reservations about the term "meaning" here (Carr, 1997), this dimension is precisely how 'real things' — and especially aesthetically pleasing 'real things' — differ from artworks: thinking otherwise *reduces* art, treating artworks as merely aesthetically-pleasing (or perhaps aesthetically-relevant) 'real things'. In our case, it dissolves the conceptual differences between the dance and the (mere) sweeping.

A third implication relates that movement sequence's art-status (associated with its meaning-bearing character) with the dance's *value*. So, the transfiguration into dance brings not merely a critical vocabulary, reflecting what (following Davies [above]) we call "meaning," but also *value* (of a non-monetary sort). For any argument for that movement sequence's art-status is simultaneously an argument for its value; and such an argument refers (perhaps implicitly) to the past of the art of dance.

Suppose, with Noël Carroll, that addressing the relation of Isadora Duncan's dances to those of the ballet tradition contemporary with her activity leads to confrontation with someone who denies art-status to Isadora's "barefoot prancing and posing" (Carroll, 2001 p. 91). In reply, Carroll (2001 p. 91) sketches a narrative to show that "Duncan was able to solve the problem of the stagnation of theatrical dance by repudiating the central features of the dominant ballet and by reimagining an earlier ideal of dance". But, as Carroll illustrates, that narrative also shows what advantages Duncan saw in this revitalised dance (and hence what values she brought to it): both her pronouncements and her actions constitute an 'argument' for a modification of practices of art-making and art understanding. That this 'argument' succeeded in changing taste (to the degree that it did) also reflects the state of the art-minded community at the time: in that artworld, Isadora's strategies were appropriate — we know that because we know they worked! Thus, to compose such a *narrative* in respect of (in this case) Isadora's achievement, so as to render it intelligible, requires consideration both of the values challenged and of what Carroll (2001 p. 91) has called "the lay of the artworld". In this way, the transfiguration into dance is captured by concepts (including value-concepts) from the history of dance through the relevant *narrative* of dance history.

§8.   Examples A: *Swan Lake* and the history of 'art'

When writing about danceworks, examples illuminating one's points must be provided: but the nature and role of examples in philosophy is often contentious. At one extreme, all examples given should be replaceable by a reader who finds them unconvincing — such that the replacement examples *would* be convincing to this reader! At the other extreme, one uses the examples that one finds convincing. In different contexts (say, if giving a talk to two different groups) different examples might be chosen. But clearly contextualism of that kind is not possible in a book. As a result, some examples here reflect what are convincing to me as danceworks, in addition to making some philosophical point. Readers critical at such moments should focus on disputing the points, not (just) the examples.

My past use of examples, in UD, aimed to make clear both that knowledgeable and respected writers on dance *did* say the things I *claimed* they said; and also that none of my conclusions depended on my judgements of particular works. To these ends, the judgements of dance critics, and primarily of Marcia Siegel, were used. Her judgements resonated with my own: but my attitude, then as here, is that — if readers will grant the point — the *example* may be given up.

This book follows broadly the same procedure, depending chiefly on the claims of dance critics, and for the same reasons, although others' dissatisfactions with my examples, and tendency to focus on the example *only*, have combined with pressure of space to leave fewer examples here than one might like. But one particular example, *Swan Lake*, requires comment, since its use in this context has been challenged. So is *Swan Lake* a good example here?

Other writers happily use this example: discussion of their writing would typically already involve repeating it. Thus, the example recommends itself as a matter of mere convenience. That offers one reason to stick with it in some places. Another comes when we recognise that it is *only* an example. For an objection to the example *only* is not philosophically revealing — at most, it suggests looking for other examples. If the points are clear, those worried on *this* issue only can supply their own examples.

But the root objection to *Swan Lake* bear directly on this text's concerns. It is, roughly, that the concept of a *dancework*— and the associated concept of a *choreographer* as maker of that work — did not, when *Swan Lake* came about, reflect the sets of social roles they now occupy. Thus, as Judith Mackrell (1997 p. 7) puts it, *Swan Lake* may date from a time "... when works were passed on to new dancers, individual steps, and even whole dances, were altered ... the choreography is now danced differently." In particular, does *Swan Lake* have an author, in the required sense?

Of course, the issues for dance here are intricately connected with those for the fine arts generally. Arguably, the beginnings of philosophical aesthetics as we understand it roughly coincides with the articulation of a distinctive concept of *art* (as 'fine art'), and with a distinctive *valuing* of both such a concept and the objects to which it applies — a valuing distinct from its beauty, monetary worth, and so on. For instance, Roger Scruton (1990 p. 98) writes that:

> ... aesthetics, conceived as a systematic branch of philosophy [what I call 'philosophical aesthetics'], is an invention of the eighteenth century. It owes its life to Shaftesbury, its name to Baumgarten, its subject-matter to Burke and Batteux, and its intellectual eminence to Kant.

On such a view, then, philosophical aesthetics begins in the period where a concern with a distinctive conception of *the artistic* makes sense: then, the appreciation of nature and of craft-work is implicitly contrasted with that of *art*. Not, of course, that philosophical aesthetics was (always) primarily interested in art — Kant, for instance, certainly was not! But his interest in, say, natural beauty must be understood against a back-drop provided by art: the contrast between free and dependent beauty is, in effect, one tool here (see McAdoo, 2002). Further, to argues that the philosophy of art has enough problems of its own, and can therefore be treated independently of the philosophy of natural beauty (as perhaps Hegel did), is also to mark such a contrast.

Since the concern for *dance* here is with 'fine art' cases, the history of this idea is important. Trying to plot the contours, within western thought (?), of the concept *art*, requires confronting at least the following two difficulties. First, of the term "art", it is certainly true that *the (classical) Greeks did not have a word for it* — that their word *techne*, for example, covers crafts as well as (fine) arts. But also in the tragedies of Euripides, the lyrics of Archilochos of Paros, and the sculptures of Praxiteles, Classical Greek culture embraced many great artworks. So, although (as a general rule) one should insist that artworks can only be made (or indeed attempted) in cultural contexts where there *is* the concept "art", the application of that rule will be complex — as this case shows. As Kivy (2001b p. 9) remarks, "Plato had no a concept of the fine arts, at least as we understand that concept. It had to await formulation in the eighteenth century." For the Greeks lacked a way to stress both the unities within (or between) various arts, *and* the differences from other (non-art, or artistically different) activities. I made the (strategic) mistake of urging this point at a job interview — only to be told that the Greeks *must* have had a word for *dance*, since they had a muse for it (Terpsichore). But that simply reiterates the point here: for of what *exactly* was Terpsichore the muse? (I would deny that the concept at issue matches at all closely our concept *dance*, especially in its 'fine art' use.) A similar point is visible when, later, the art-status of music with words was transparent while that of *music alone*, "... without text, title, program, or plot" (Kivy, 1993 p. 361), was problematic: again, this contrast is not one within the *art* of music.

Then, second and relatedly, a distinctive fine art is "... of comparatively recent origin" (Kristeller, 1965 p. 165): that "... the fine arts as we know them, as a system of related practices, came into being in the first half of the eighteenth century" (Kivy, 2001a p. 19). And we refer to *that* concept, given some codification by Batteux perhaps (Kristeller, 1965 p. 199), when talking of (fine) art. But here too there will be cases of proto-art, or seeming-art, or ... however we are to categorise it. At least some of these will *now* be seen as art, as any satisfactory account must grant. Thus, our case intersects with the so-called problem of *first art*: that is, of objects produced in societies either definitely or arguably lacking the concept *art* (see Chapter Eleven §5). At least arguably, then, the concept *art* (as fine art) appeared in western Europe relatively recently.

Yet this *seems* like the identification of *one* concept of art, one among many; as though offering a (misplaced) contrast between, say, *your* concept of art and *mine*. In fact, debates here often concern the *extension* of the concept "art" (or what things are, or constitute, artworks), and we can differ on *that* topic while deploying the same understanding of art. Further, accounts which range too far from central cases or issues are (for that reason) not discussions of *art*. Thus, in my favourite case (UD p. 286), 'dances' designed to actually remove the white man from the plains of America are, for that reason, not *dances* in our sense: *whatever* dance does, it is not this.

Of course, no simple answer can be expected to the question, "When did *dance* begin?", as our earlier discussion indicated. For the 'history' of *dance* will always be contentious, especially given the variety of dance (even within the western world): what counts and what does not? In our specific context, recognising its connection to the previous discussion, the term "dance" means (fine) *art-type dance*. Yet the question remains. Traditional histories of dance (see Mackrell, 1997; Quirey, 1976) rightly locate the beginnings of ballet in the courtly dance of France — that, if not uncontentious, will suffice for our purposes: we are not historians. But how do we move from *there* to *here?* From the Baroque ballets, with "... complex patterns which the steps traced across the floor, enabling large groups of dancers to move together in an intricate human geometry" (Mackrell, 1997 p. 16) where the main participants joined in (including "Queen Louise and her ladies": Mackrell, 1997 p. 16); then becoming attractive patterns as *divertissement* in opera or similar; to *dance* the (relatively) self-contained art form? Even that question is far too big: and, at its root, is chiefly a question for dance-historians. Certainly, "... towards the end of the (eighteenth) century dancers and choreographers were beginning to explore ballet's dramatic potential ..." (Mackrell, 1997 p. 17). Since the historical issues seem vexed and conceptual questions are more clearly my brief, I will concentrate on one aspect of the concept *art*, at least as I would articulate it; namely, the place of *authorship* (see Chapter Five). For with the modern (fine) arts came *artists* (eventually).

§9. Examples B: *Swan Lake* and authorship

Where does this leave *Swan Lake* as an example? Certainly, by the time Batteux's categorisation applies, the arts — or, anyway, *most* of the arts, including architecture — had *artists* as authors or creators. By contrast, only quite *late* in the development of ballet in the modern period did the *achievements* of the choreographers come to be regarded as *appropriately* sacrosanct (as Mackrell, 1997 pp. 36-37 grants).

Nor is this requirement trivial. One key factor distinguishing natural beauty from the beauty of art is that art is *meant, intended* — hence, not accidental (except perhaps where someone chooses to use accident as a compositional tool). Here, at least, what goes for beauty goes for other artistic properties. Indeed, such a connection to human intention is one aspect of any plausible artistic/aesthetic contrast (see above). Similarly, the possibility (for an artwork) of a *meaning* distinct from its social or cultural significance (as above) is easily regarded as a contribution of the *author* — one for which he or she is responsible (in both senses of the term).

To simplify at this point, let us assume the author is *male* (reflecting the gender of the author of this work) and *singular*: that is, putting aside the obvious case of multiple authorship, given that (say) most dances are collaborations of choreographers with composers and costume/stage designers; and most films are even larger collaborations. Yet, while multiple authorship can be an interesting topic, we have enough on our plate without it. Our author, then, will typically be *he* (male and singular) — but only as a matter of convention, for simplicity's sake, not reflecting any biases or preoccupations.

Then the question, "When did *dance* begin?" becomes, "When did dances acquire *authors*?" Here, too, one must go slowly. What is needed is an author in something like the sense in which Reubens is the author of his paintings: that is, his is the primary *responsibility* for the painting (even if much of the 'grunt work' is provided by others: say, from his studio), and where Reubens working as he does is recognised as a reputable model of art-making. Of course, works of art that are individual objects differ crucially from those that are multiples. It is much easier to see how 'the master's hand' might provide the *final* (yet crucial) touch to a painting.

Central here is the location of *this* artist's achievement within what we might call "a narrative of art history" in the relevant art form (following Carroll, 2001 pp. 63-74; 75-99). In this light, then, the suggestion that, roughly, Carl André does for *texture* (as embodied, in this case, in his collection of fire bricks, *Equivalent VIII*) what Turner did for *colour*[9] offers a way to discuss André's *Equivalent VIII*: to make sense of it in terms broadly familiar. The comparative aspect is crucial to making out this case, as is the connection to the past of the art form. Our treatment of works *there* explains our treatment of the new case — if only as rebellion against the past! Thus, as André (quoted Fuller, 1981 p. 117) suggests, perhaps "... the *Venus de Milo* would just be a stone woman if nobody knew about sculpture." (This topic recurs in Chapter Ten.)

Then, turning to dances, the importance of works as *responsible productions* is key, since there could be no full-blown *artists* here if what they produced were (rightly) regarded as of little worth. And one index of this kind of regard is that the work cannot be changed willy-nilly: that would conflict with the *author's* being the responsible one. Now we come to the nub of our case. For, as Mackrell (1997 p. 30) grants, it is only quite *late* in the development of ballet in the modern period that the *achievements* of the choreographers came to be regarded as *appropriately* sacrosanct.

But what is meant by "appropriately sacrosanct"? Well, the term "sacrosanct" here should imply that any changes must be *motivated* or *explained* changes: that one would need a good *reason* here. And that, typically, only the work's authors could provide such reasons — for only they could be seen as *revising* (as opposed to merely changing) the works. After all, these works are their *responsibility*.

An anecdote helps explain the term "appropriately". A choreographer urged that her dancers needed a few more steps (or a few more seconds to make an exit): should the composer writing the score provide this extra time in the form of extra music? For the story, imagine that this musician was typically *extremely* precious about changes to his works: he typically defended both the importance and sufficiency of every quaver he had written — all were fundamental, and no more were needed! But, recognising the justice of the choreographer's cause in this case, he composed the additional passages — although his work *was* sacrosanct in this example, it was only *appropriately* sacrosanct. So he willing granted small changes once offered a good (local) reason. And, given my general position on practical cases, a particular case should typically involve a debate for choreographers, musicians, maybe dancers, and such like — for what I call "The Republic of Dance" (see Diffey, 1992; UD pp. 71-74; 80-86; AJ pp. 147-173). So that the expression "appropriately sacrosanct" is a kind of place-holder partly because different cases will be filled-in differentially.

Once the general importance of *authorship*[10] to art is granted, our question, "When do dances acquire *authors?*" must be understood as reflecting the nature of authorship: hence must be understood in terms of the kinds of authorship (or even authority) where that person's work was *appropriately sacrosanct.* Of course, in practice this might vary widely. In one way, that emphasis on authorship explained as one's work being *appropriately sacrosanct* is our conclusion here. But this issue was raised simply because it might seem that, say, the ballet *Swan Lake* lacks an author in just this sense. In effect, this argument draws on the historical situation in which the dances were set: that the dance-objects themselves lacked precisely the kinds of importance that would have rendered them appropriately sacrosanct. That is why, as Mackrell (1997 p. 7: quoted above) puts it, "... the choreography is now danced differently." So would it be misleading, for this reason, to see Ivanov and Petipa as choreographers of the *Swan Lake* that has come down to us? Is authorship in this sense *really* not discernible, even in principle? (This line is taken with some Baroque ballets.) The point is not just that many hands were at work in making the ballet, but rather that the resultant ballet was not regarded as *appropriately sacrosanct,* when concluded (one cannot really say "choreographed"). If true, my widespread use of *Swan Lake* as an example throughout this work is rendered problematic — however transparent the phenomenon exemplified would be in other cases.

Again, there is a terminological difficulty here: I talk of *this work,* of *Swan Lake,* of *this choreography,* and so on. Yet, viewed one way, precisely these locutions are at issue: is there one work here? No sophisticated answer can be offered. But custom-and-practice speaks in favour of treating the various performances, versions, and such like, as all *Swan Lake,* all the same work, at least until offered a specific good reason to do otherwise. With Sharpe (1983: Preface), we might think that "...where there is an unreflective distinction made by a consensus it is likely to have a rationale." Clearly custom-and-practice cannot be conclusive: on my own account, for instance, the Mats Ek work turns out not to be *Swan Lake* in this sense; but, rather, a different dance — a token of another type (see Chapter Two). Still, the Ivanov and Petipa *Swan Lake* offers a body of uncontentious cases here. That is certainly how typical stagers regard it. Moreover, one should not rush to prejudgement. So *at least* the locutions should be retained until the enquiry progresses. Then, as we will see, our original resolution has some justice.

Now, in stressing the specifics of Ivanov's contribution to *Swan Lake*, Mackrell (1997 p. 30) suggests that Ivanov and Petipa's work there would count as appropriately sacrosanct. But *if* it were demonstrated that this 'choreography' in *Swan Lake* was not, in this way, regarded as appropriately sacrosanct, that *would* count against its status as art-type dance. Were this demonstrably true of *Swan Lake*, I should cease using it as an example, redrafting my claims at 'its' previous appearances. Of course, no argument for this conclusion has been laid-out *in detail*; but clearly these considerations might have tended in these directions. (*Swan Lake* might still be rescued, of course, by returning to those cases of proto-art!)

Second, one does *not* show that the choreography of *Swan Lake* is not appropriately sacrosanct merely by showing either that it builds-in *opportunities* for variety (for instance, through the insertion of suites of new national dances, as these become fashionable in society) or that there is variety *within* what is performed as instantiating that choreography. In both cases, that is just what one would expect from dance compositions of the time. Although these aspects are complex, the *mere* fact of variety here cannot decide the matter. The possibility of a dance open to performance on a number of occasions (that is, as a work of *performing* art) requires precisely the possibility that 'modifications' deal with new situations, such as the size of the performance area, or the size (or proficiency) of the company, all the while preserving 'same-work' continuity, at least in principle — for otherwise the company would not be delivering the work it promised! Thus, this topic too requires *detailed* debate, rather than glib resolution. And choreographers were certainly given some esteem (and were sought after) by the time Petipa was making dances. Thus, it was recognised that "... the movement vocabulary ... [Petipa] and Ivanov developed was capable of registering vivid states of emotion and subtleties of character" (Mackrell, 1997 p. 31). Further, Sally Banes (1998 p. 15) comments, of *La Sylphide*, "[i]t is Bournonville's version that I will analyze here, because I believe that, although it has been altered in obvious ways over the years, it is still the closest we can come to the original Taglioni version" — the implication being that there is such an original to return to, at least in principle; and that this 'original' could be understood in terms of its choreographer. My defence of *Swan Lake* as an example would begin from here, if I felt such a defence was really needed!

A further issue arises, though, for I am assuming that one broad kind of account should be given of the identity-conditions of danceworks, or in explaining authentic performances of them — that, say, dances from the past do not require a treatment *different in kind* from that of dances of today. For otherwise *Swan Lake* might not be a suitable example. Of course there are differences; and some will be important. But the default position (defended in Chapter Eleven) is that even so-called "postmodern dances" are described and explained in broadly the same ways as those of the past.

§10. Examples C: The disappearance of dances

The giving of examples here is typically more problematic for danceworks in ways germane to the topic of the text as a whole: the example must be familiar to the audience. And this may be fragile. Of course, whenever any artwork is used as an example, the reader may not know, or may be unfamiliar with, that particular work. But, for dance, even diligent readers may be unable to remedy this 'deficiency' in their knowledge of examples. For instance, I am a huge fan of certain dances of Christopher Bruce that I saw in the UK (especially in London) — in particular, *Black Angels* (1976) and *Ghost Dances* (1981); and regularly mention them as examples. Both these dances seem no longer to be in the repertoire. So I cannot depend on my readers taking them as examples in the ways I would. Even when there are *recordings* of these works (DVDs, videos — as there are for *Ghost Dances*), seeing the recordings is not *really* seeing the works themselves — although they may be the best we can get (a bit like a slide in a lecture to exemplify a painting): one does not get the artwork, but one gets either a useful aide-memoire for those who have seen the dance, or a *beginning* for those who have not (in fact, presently the best beginning he/she can have).

Consider three personal examples: first, when writing UD I preferred discussion of works I had seen (even if I hadn't seen *that* performance), although I used video to remind me. Yet I also used revealing critical commentary on danceworks, especially from the writings of Marcia Siegel. To facilitate this, I permitted myself a couple of cases of just using a recording of the dance. In a world where my primary use concerned dance-critical writings, finding revealing criticism was the priority, although not my preferred solution. So when Marcia Siegel offered interesting criticism of a work or performance *and* there was a reliable recording of a performance, I felt a writer on dance-aesthetics could rest content. For these were just *examples*: readers of my work would have the critical commentary, and could pursue the recordings if they chose. Or, if they saw my point, could substitute their own examples.

Second, having danceworks that made sense to me was (and is) crucial: I did not want to be taking someone else's word for them. But how reliable were my philosophical points if the dances themselves (as examples) had disappeared from the repertoire? The danger is that *my* recollection becomes *too* important. Then the access of those who read my work to a recording of the dancework at least offers readers *something*, from which a number of features of the dance could typically be extracted, some of which features might (in line with my description) be key features of the dance. So such a situation might be preferable to one for a dance — equally suitable — of which no recording existed; but only when there are other good descriptive resources for that dancework. A classic case here would be the book *Birth of a Ballet* (Austin, 1976) which provides a permanent resource for discussing the Bruce's *Black Angels* (used extensively in UD Chapter Eleven). Yet even these resources are limited for those having no conception of what the dance looked like. Again, memory is a poor base here, for those wishing to *discuss* these danceworks, for what seem like substantial disagreements can reflect nothing but differential remembering!

Third, suppose that points that I would want to make were well-exemplified by some dances I admired (a couple of dances seen on a trip to Canada in 1978 might be key examples). Although these examples were key for *my* grasp on dance, *you* have not seen them; and (now) will not. For these are works that have totally disappeared. They are part of the history of dance only; they exist (*ex hypothesi*) only in memory. Thus, they cannot provide useful examples for our philosophical discussion.

In summary, then, in the category of 'work of the past' we have (a) works with an extant critical literature and at least some access to the dancework itself, but also a slightly indirect access (say, through video recording); (b) danceworks where there is both some critical discussion and some indirect access, yet with little or no first-person access; and (c) danceworks where my account or experience offers the best access. And this three-fold picture reflects the 'evanescent' status of most danceworks. Thus, danceworks will lack persuasive power to the degree that readers (or listeners) are not familiar with them — although the last category (if we could 'document' or exemplify it) might provide powerful examples for our arguments in philosophy: it is precisely in this sense that dance "... exists at a perpetual vanishing point" (Siegel, 1972 p. 1: UD p. 89). For discussions are facilitated by examples familiar to both sides. And, often, the precise properties of danceworks can only be found when the work itself is made concrete, through a performance. Moreover, John Wisdom (1965 p. 102) is right about the central place of examples in the persuasive structure of philosophy: "at the bar of reason, always the final appeal is to cases". So a failure to recognise an example (that is, one of these "cases") will count against its force for that reader or listener.

Were I a choreographer, I would hope for a posterity for my work (which requires it being both performable and discussible in the future); and that the continued interest in my dances not depend solely on memory. As illustrated above, key works can be lost precisely because they depend solely on memory. So, I assume that — as for the other arts — the creators or authors of danceworks (basically, the choreographers, although nothing hangs on this identification) wish their creations *to have a posterity*: to be available to other generations of audience for dance. Of course, this might be disputed: perhaps there are reasons to embrace a ephemeral quality for danceworks, while not doing so for works in other performing arts, such as music. But, as this comparison with musical works makes plain, embracing ephemerality cannot be the default condition for artworks, even other multiple artworks, such as musical works. So some special arguments are needed here, if one wishes to make-out such a case for dance. In particular, stressing the *practical* problem (that much dance is ephemeral because it is never recorded, and then forgotten) cannot provide such reasons. For such practical ephemerality *should* be a cause for sadness if danceworks followed the model of, say, musical works in seeking relative permanence. Here, then, such a search for permanence can be assumed at least until specific arguments in another direction are addressed (see Chapter Four §4).

Thus the *posterity* of dances is a requirement for their functioning productively in philosophical discussions of, say, the nature of dance; further, with no *direct* access to a dancework, its use as an example may be problematic — others may not share it with us. Moreover, any kind of *indirect* access (say, through a video recording) is useful in supplementation of direct experience of the work. Additionally, that may be the best on offer — but, of course, it is not direct access to the dancework itself. These are points this work will expand. Seen in these ways, then, this discussion is clearly of the philosophical aesthetics of dance.

§11. Conclusion

The argument of this text is directed at the specifics of a concern with the authenticity of dance performances. In general, the chapters pose some issues in the philosophical aesthetics of dance, considering some theses advanced in respect of them, before offering a preferred thesis, and reflecting

on the consequences of this outcome. Finally, each chapter includes in its body references that interested scholars might be followed-up. Then, read 'straight through', this work offers a set of arguments that interested persons could understand; but that it also rewards reading by someone with a more sustained or more scholarly interest. Thus, through references and endnotes, I endeavour to provide places where elaboration may be sought, as well as elucidations of my own. For I hope the reader will be drawn into larger debates in the field as well as those specific to dance. While my preferred framework for philosophical aesthetics — and for philosophy more generally — permeates this text, only rarely is its fine detail drawn on explicitly. The Preface sketched that framework[11], with Appendix in effect a long note on a set of technical issues in respect of one position here.

As far as possible, the chapters are as 'free-standing' as is consistent with this being a single book (or a single, linked investigation). This should make it easier to grasp one key idea without having to grasp them all (which might help students and their beleaguered teachers). This policy has generated some repetition: but, equally, there are cross-references too, so that inter-connections can be followed-up.

Of course, not all chapters are equally thrilling, especially on first reading. Thus, a relative beginner wishing to gauge the interest of the philosophical aesthetics of dance might productively next read Chapter Three, since it more clearly identifies the sort of problem which might appeal to a neophyte in the area (Chapter Two elaborating a necessary but not very compelling set of contrasts), and then move to Chapter Five which, although addressing a general issue, focuses on a topic of central interest in the elaboration of the concept *art*. There are many reliable ways of unfolding the view of the nature of dance — and hence of the philosophical aesthetics of dance — elaborated here; but, of course, the logic of the argument is perhaps best reflected in the ordering of the chapters here.

Part One: Dances as Performables

Chapter Two

Making sense of multiples

§1. Introduction

In summary, danceworks are typically performing artworks, physical artworks, and also multiple artworks. But what exactly does this mean? First, recognising dance as a performing art is recognising typical danceworks are *performables*, in the sense that the *very same dance* can be re-performed on another occasion (despite the differences between such performances: a point to which we return repeatedly); but, second, performances also depend on the specific physicality of dancers. So dance is a physical art. This differentiates dance from music, the performing art that typically it most closely resembles. Musicians, who *produce* the sound that comprises the music, fit exactly Urmson's account: they bring about "... just those things of which the witnessable consists" (Urmson, 1976 p. 243: quoted Chapter One). That is, they *make* or *cause* the sounds that instantiate the artwork. Yet here dance differs crucially from music. For dancers do not *cause* the dance; rather, they *are* the dance — their movements instantiate it. And nothing else could. As Merce Cunningham (1984 p. 27) recognises:

> [y]ou can't describe a dance without talking about the dancer. You can't describe a dance that hasn't been seen, and the way of seeing it has everything to do with the dancers ....

In effect, Cunningham grants that one cannot really encounter the dance itself without seeing it in performance.

Stressing the *bodily* or *corporeal* nature of dance can be a valuable counter-balance to undue emphasis (in the writing of some aestheticians) on insufficiently physical virtues of artworks. But this point can be over-stressed, or poorly understood, or poorly explained. For instance, explaining the importance of the body for dance, Judith Hanna (1988 p. 13) writes that "... the instrument of dance and of sexuality is one — the human body." Her thought is clearly that some of the value of the sexual would *thereby* accrue to dance. But that same body is 'used' for many activities, some meaning-bearing, others not: this fact alone takes us nowhere.

However, it returns us to the transformation of 'ordinary' movements into dance where, for example (Chapter One), the graceful sweeping movement of a road-sweeper might be incorporated into a dance, with a literal choreographer even retaining the broom (UD p. 51; CDE p. 106). That sequence of movement is then no longer mere sweeping (however much it resembles it): it has become *dance*. Following Danto (1981 p. 208), this should be called "the transfiguration of the 'ordinary' activity" into dance. In such cases, what is transfigured is (typically) *already* action, rather than mere movement (Carr, 1987 p. 352). So, to *insist* that dance is 'just movement' is a polemical answer (for a parallel with music, see Cavell, 1969 p. 221). Moreover, after the transfiguration, one has not just action that makes sense as *intended* (Best, 1978 pp. 138-141; UD pp. 243-244), but a dancework — it has become more strongly meaning-bearing: as intentionally *art*, with whatever character follows from that.

Further, dance (again like music) is typically a multiple-art: the same dance can be performed both on different occasions in the same place and on the same occasion in different places. So *Swan Lake* could be simultaneously in London and in New York. Moreover, London *Swan Lake* and New York *Swan Lake* will typically differ, having different casts, and being performed on stages of different sizes. In London, the producer may emphasise certain of *Swan Lake*'s characteristics, perhaps to suit the dancers in the cast. For similar reasons, different aspects may be stressed when that dance is staged in New York. Of course, the limits on such examples of 'the same work' are a topic for discussion, to which we will return.

But there is just one dancework. To see that, one need only reflect that a single rehearsal might serve to prepare the cast for, say, a week's performances: the rehearsal cannot be identified as, for instance, the rehearsal for Monday's performance only. And a typical rehearsal differs quite substantially from any of the performances.

Moreover, with dance, as with music, there are at least two 'objects of appreciation': the work itself and tonight's performance of it. These might be treated differently for critical purposes: thus, the dance seen last night might have been a wonderful performance of a mediocre dancework or (more likely) the opposite. Its status as a multiple-art prompts discussion of the *ontological status* of dances: exactly how should one explain what dances *are*? Clearly, there is a sense in which the dancework itself (say, *Swan Lake*) is an abstract object, only made concrete through a performance (when made physical, or instantiated). Yet if one begins from a comparison with musical works, and from the typical *practice* here of dancers and musicians, there is no need to plunge deeply into ontology (see Appendix). For what is wanted from philosophical investigation is an explanation at least broadly replicating the practices of the professionals; and which can typically be tested against such practice.

§2. Danceworks as interpretations

A particular performance of a dancework is rightly described, with some justice, as a "performer's interpretation", to be contrasted firmly with a *critic's* interpretation. Such critic's interpretations are a feature of all arts, amounting roughly to strings of words said about artworks. By contrast, the performer's interpretation is just a distinctiveness of *how* this dancer performs the dance/role in question, and is constituted simply by his/her performing in that way (even if the dancer also chooses to talk about it) — the performer's interpretation brings the artwork (the performance) into being: at least, into public being.

Such *performer's* interpretation is unique to the performing arts: but, given that it is constituted by actions, stressing its role as *interpretation* can mislead — for *of what* exactly is it an interpretation? Rather, one performer's interpretation should be distinguished from another: that is our contrast — this performer's interpretation differs from that one, yet both count as the very same dancework. That is why the idea was introduced: it sustains our talking of each as an *interpretation*, without positing something uninterpreted.

But the very idea of a *performer's interpretation* highlights two fundamental features of performing arts. First, the artwork is only encountered when one encounters a *performance* of it. This recognises the concreteness or specificity of dance. (One might quibble about the status of, say, video recordings, but the moral is straightforward: if watching the video recording counts as watching the dance, it is a *performance*, albeit an indirect or recorded one. If, by contrast, watching the video recording does not count as watching the dance, it becomes slightly less than a performance [Sparshott, 1995 pp. 448-451].)

Second, many abstract objects share a relevant property: under-determination. Thus, any toy kangaroo must be of a certain size and colour. But if you *imagine* a toy kangaroo (one way to approximate an abstract object), the imagined kangaroo can be indeterminate as to size and shape. In roughly this way, the dancework itself (the abstract object) *under-determines* performances, since each performance makes concrete in particular ways features of the dance which might have been concretised in other ways — indeed, which may have been made concrete in those other ways in another performance of that dance, even one by the same company. This feature of dances is also reflected in dance notation (see later). For the dancers making concrete the dance, instantiating it, might be conceptualised as giving substance to the notation. In doing so, the dancers implicitly emphasise some features of the dance, at the expense of others. This, of course, produces a performer's interpretation.

§3.   Reprising the issue of work-identity

Attending a performance of a particular dancework (for simplicity, think of it as a solo) is always seeing the actions of some particular dancer (and hence typically some performer's interpretation). So when has one seen the *very same* dance — given that two performances typically differ? Asking this raises a numerical identity question for the dancework; and, in doing so, highlights the importance of *numerical identity* for investigations of the distinctive nature of particular dances[1].

The concept of *numerical identity* is a technical one within philosophy, in contrast to the sameness of properties (sometimes called *qualitative identity*[2]). What are the features of *numerical identity*, applied to objects such as cars, watches, and of course people? At its heart, numerical identity identifies *the very same thing* ("the same one") over time. Then arriving at a "yes" answer is concluding that only *one* watch, or car, or person is actually in the story[3]. Thus, "Is the watch that the watch-repairer returned *the very same watch* as the one I gave in? Or has he returned a fake and kept my Rolex?" "Is the car I sent to the spray-shop (then red) *the very same car* as the one I collected (now blue)?" "Is the person who just got the Nobel Prize for Peace the very same person as the kid who bullied me at school? Because, if he is, I can pass on the inheritance from his grandfather." In each case, justice requires the possibility of numerical-identity solutions: the watch he returned should be *my* watch[4]; the car in which I drive off should be *my* car; the inheritance is only *his* if we were at school together. So it would be odd to reject the concept of *numerical identity* — and even odder to attempt to replace it with a notion permitting no change in properties. In all the cases above, the properties of the object at the later time uncontentiously *differ* from those at the earlier time, even when the numerical-identity question is answered "yes". Thus, a repaired watch typically has, say, new parts included; the properties of my re-sprayed car will differ but it is still *my* car; and, for the person, the passage of time usually alters not just the physical properties (he was tall 'for his age', but is now short; he was hairy but is now bald) but also the psychological properties — his views have changed on a host of topics; not least the value of pacifism! So property-differences are *expected* (with justice) even in cases of numerical identity — indeed, some numerical-identity claims would be disallowed were there *no* property changes (say, if the Peace Prize winner still *looked like* the schoolboy).

Of course, numerical identity judgements are not always important. We do not, in general, care whether the chair on which we are presently sitting is the one on which we sat yesterday — at least, if they are the same 'make-and-model', the chances are both are equally (un-)comfortable. Nevertheless, the chair I am presently sitting on is (in fact) the *very same chair* that I was sitting on yesterday: that is (in the jargon), there is *numerical identity* here. Even were this chair not the one I sat on yesterday, there is an identity solution — for then *some other chair* would be that one (unless it had been destroyed). So numerical-identity judgements make clear sense for *objects* — chairs, cars, watches.

Turning to artworks, there are at least two kinds of cases to consider. In that sense, some artworks are clearly *objects*, such as paintings or cut sculptures: these are sometimes called "particular object artworks" (Wollheim, 1973 p. 256; Wollheim, 1980 §§9-10). Their identity-conditions would parallel those of other objects: the watches, cars, and chairs. Of course, these identity-conditions can be very complex, especially in practice; but need not concern us here. They can be set aside by noting that such objects too may be seen on two occasions, where the question of re-identification could arise: is this *that* painting? Because if not, it might be a forgery — and certainly (at best) a different artwork. Moreover, suppose a painting is then painted-over: is this Picasso the very same painting (or even the same canvas) as that Douanier Rousseau? Various cases can be imagined here: say, when the first painting on the canvas was merely *covered* by the second, in contrast to those where, in the second use of the canvas, the first painting was destroyed. So numerical identity questions arise for objects; and (perhaps nuanced) for *artworks* that are objects.

Typical danceworks are not like that. Rather, they are *multiples*, such that *the very same dance* can typically be performed on two different occasions (say, yesterday as well as today) and in two different places at the same time (say, in London and Los Angeles). How should such multiples be described so as to capture the relationship between the work itself (for example, *Swan Lake*) and its performances in London and Los Angeles, both yesterday and today? For all of these are performances of *Swan Lake*: that is, a single artwork is involved.

Since the dancework itself (the abstract object) is only confronted through confronting a performance, we are asking, "Is performance A a performance of the very same artwork as performance B?" And numerical identity conclusions do not turn on sameness of properties: we are not enquiring whether or not the two performance differ — for we grant that they may differ substantially while still both being *Swan Lake*. Nor are we asking whether each performance has the same artistic value. For here too the answer can clearly be "no": think how the performance of *The Nutcracker* by the local dance school in the village hall might contrast with that by the Royal Ballet in the Royal Opera House. Both are *The Nutcracker*, despite their differences. And part of our argument here, recall, draws on the fact that the same rehearsal can be preparation for a number of performances: hence these are performances of the same work, despite differences among those performances. (This is a topic for later elaboration: but this must be our initial, or default, position.)

Returning to personal identity, three features of that case are striking: first, even when thinking strictly about numerical identity, there is a sharp contrast between the practical or epistemological difficulties and the theoretical or ontological ones — the person who staggers out of the jungle either is or is not the (genuine) Tichbourne Claimant although we may never know for sure. But the requirement in typical cases — roughly, of a spatio-temporal 'pathway' from his birth — is still perfectly straightforward, despite these epistemological difficulties. Second, one might ask whether numerical identity is really what is important; or, granting that it *presently* is (through its connection to inheritance and to responsibility), imagine a time when those notions operated differently. And, third, the relative unimportance, in such cases, of shared properties is very obvious — indeed, change of properties should be expected in most cases of numerical identity over time.

By contrast, the identity-conditions for danceworks certain differ on the first two points: if it is impossible to determine for dance cases which identity-judgement is sound, then no identity-judgement can be sustained. As with most 'social objects' which admit of numerical identity, their ontological questions are mingled with the epistemological ones — that is part of what Quinton (1982 p. 98) means in talking of "fruits of human contrivance". So that, for danceworks, we could not distinguish the purely ontological — as we could in the case of persons. Of course, the case of danceworks is complicated because the procedures for determining whether there are such determinables will often be one of discussion and debate — but, again, this is not where we stand on the ontological question for (say) personal identity.

Further, identity judgements will be of paramount importance in any case where we rightly insist that this is a performing art — an art form composed of *performables*: that is, works that can be re-performed on another occasion. For the ontology of the performable imports precisely that idea of numerical identity (of the *same thing* viewed on two occasions).

Moreover, while two performances of the very same dance (that is, two *numerically identical* performances) can differ substantially in their properties (perhaps even as much as two 'people' identified at different times who are in fact the same person despite all these differences), there is something to be said about what is shared here. So, again, the personal identity case seems different. There, no non-genetic properties need be in common between the person identified at this time and the one identified at that: the shared biology is enough. For two dance performances, there seems nothing corresponding to this; and some shared perceptual properties would surely be expected in any particular case — even if *which* properties were only resolved case-by-case. For, of course, these are not like (for instance) two headaches. Asking if, say, the headache I have today is *the very same one* (numerically identical) as the headache I had yesterday makes no sense (Malcolm, 1977 pp. 115-122): how would the *very same headache* be contrasted with an *exactly similar* headache — one of the same intensity, and such like? Here it makes sense *only* to ask about whether *the properties* (the intensity, and such like) are shared. And, as we have seen, such concerns with shared properties are not central to numerical identity. So, it makes no sense to ask if these are the same headache or different ones. By contrast, we recognise that, say, two dances might have the same title and (largely) the same music and yet be different dances — in my example, the Mats Ek *Swan Lake* would be contrasted with the Petipa and Ivanov *Swan Lake*. The *issue* here certainly *seems* one of numerical identity (although, in that case, we arrive at a "no" answer).

To repeat, we asked how such multiples should be described so as to capture the relationship between the work itself (say, *Swan Lake*) and its performances in London and Los Angeles, both yesterday and today. For all are performances of *Swan Lake*: that is, a single artwork is involved. Does our view of the multiple-artworks offer an account in terms of *numerical identity*, since such answers do not arise in all cases? So what about multiple *works of art*, such as danceworks? Are they suitable for a 'numerical identity' analysis?

§4. Simple type-token account

To provide a conceptual structure for discussion of such multiples, some writers (Wollheim, 1980 §§35-36; UD pp. 90-94) employ a type-token framework, such that dance performances are *tokens* of an (abstract) *type*. Although sometimes presented as simply a 'way of talking' about multiples (Redfern, 1983 p. 19), it is more than that.

To understand this *type-token* contrast, consider national flags. Here, one recognises both the *type* (for example, the Union Jack) and *tokens of that type* (a large Union Jack flying on Eastbourne town hall, small flags waved for the Queen on state visits). Thus, if ten people were each given a national flag, there might be ten token-flags but three type-flags (Union Jack, Stars and Stripes, French Tricolour), or ten token-flags and only one type-flag (all the Union Jack), and so on. Also, destroying all the big and little pieces of cloth, paper and plastic would not destroy the Union Jack *itself*. The flag itself (the *type*) is an abstract object, to be differentiated from any of its instantiations (the *tokens*). And all (genuine) tokens are *equally* tokens — none is privileged.

The type-token contrast offers a way to treat multiple objects (like flags):

the concrete object (the token) is contrasted with the abstract object (the type). Then dance performances might be treated as tokens of a dance-type: Tuesday's performance as one token of *Swan Lake*, Wednesday's as another. *Swan Lake*, as a type, is thereby an abstract object (as above). And, as an abstract object, it is encountered only through encountering tokens: and more than one token might be available at any particular time. Moreover, all the various performances are equally *Swan Lake*, despite their differences. To this extent, the type-token contrast captures this aspect of danceworks as multiples.

However, the type-token distinction cannot, of itself, decide what is to count as a token of what. For example, are some of Nureyev's productions re-choreographed or merely re-staged? Noting the difficult borderline (see §10 below) between re-staging a dance and re-choreographing to produce a different (although similar) dance simply recognises a problem in *deciding* whether a particular performance is or is not a token of a particular type. For recognising re-choreography as the production of a different work of art is a way of saying that its performances are tokens of a different *type*.

Does this account permit a numerical identity view of danceworks? At least typically, seeing two performances of *Swan Lake* (even when they differ quite radically) involves seeing the same artwork; similarly, the same artwork is heard when listening to two performances of Schönberg's opus 19. For both *Swan Lake* and Schönberg's opus 19 are 'performables', capable of being re-performed on another occasion. Moreover, this point is recognised when that artwork itself is considered — often in terms of its name ("*Swan Lake*") or its author, as "So-and-so's symphony" — rather than discussing this or that performance.

Some multiple art-objects, like cast sculptures, allow us to ask the numerical identity question about a particular token, "Is this the sculpture I handled yesterday?" And to reply, "No, but it is one from the same casting" — so it is the very same *artwork*, but not the very same lump of bronze. As this case exemplifies, a numerical identity question can also arises for *tokens*: we can ask, "Was it the same piece of bronze?" or "Was it the same collection of pages?" (for a novel). But its being that *artwork* depends on its being, say, that *statue* only (that is, on its being a token of that type), both because another piece of bronze could *be* ("instantiate") that artwork — say, another from the same casting — and because that piece of bronze might be re-cast into something else. So, for such works, there is a numerical identity question for tokens (especially when, as in this example, they are *objects* in a fairly straightforward way). But the most important case of numerical identity will concern the *abstract* object, the type.

A revealing comparison for the issue here is with the idea of a *recipe*

(Urmson, 1976 p. 246): for, if the recipe for a dundee cake is followed accurately, then one will end up with a dundee cake. Further, one explanation that one has indeed a dundee cake involves pointing out that this recipe was accurately followed, the recipe for a dundee cake. But, in the dance case, one does not simply end up with a *kind* of dance (as one ends up with a *kind* of cake, a dundee cake). Instead, one ends up with a particular dance — say, *Swan Lake*. In this sense, our concern here is with *numerical identity conditions* for dances.

So discussing *numerical identity* makes sense, even for those abstract objects that are multiple artworks (like novels, cast sculptures, musical works, dances). And, to repeat, the idea of *one* dance (one artwork) performed on numerous occasions just *is* central to the idea of a *performing art*.

In this form, the account seems vulnerable to two lines of objection. First, is this account adequate to deal with the basic data? It might seem not. For there seem more than two 'objects of analysis' here (although the type-token contrast only has, as it were, two 'slots'): a *performer's interpretation* of a role or a dance is contrasted with the particular (his performance *tonight* of that work/interpretation) or with the general (the dance itself). So type-token accounts of this sort may need modification or clarification (Sharpe, 1979; McFee, 1994; Meskin, 1999 pp. 46-47). This objection might be dealt with by elaborating the role of the dancer. For *dancers*, through their actions, instantiate the *type* in producing a *token* — the differential manner in which this occurs is the 'performer's interpretation. So perhaps no further 'entity' is required, between dancework and performance. (In effect, this option is elaborated in Chapter Seven below.)

Second, the feature from which we began fits at best awkwardly with the type-token treatment: namely, that each performance is *the very same artwork*, not merely one of the same kind — that there is numerical identity here. For in examples typically used to illustrate the type-token contrast (say, national flags or words) *numerical* identity of types, in contrast to qualitative identity, makes no sense. For example, the five-word sentence "My cat ate your cat" employs five *token*-words and only four *type*-words, because the word "cat" occurs twice. If we imagine someone *speaking* this sentence (utterance) or *writing* it (inscription), there are accordingly either two utterances or two inscriptions of the word "cat". But it seems odd to puzzle further if there are one or two *words*, since we know that both utterances/inscriptions of "cat" are tokens of the type-word. It makes no sense to ask if the first and second occurrences of the word "cat" are occurrences of *numerically identical* or *numerically distinct* words, although they are clearly different utterances or inscriptions. Yet just this contrast must make sense for dance performances: if there is only one dance work (say, *Swan Lake*) 'in the offing', its status as *the artwork* guarantees that any performances of it instantiate *that very* artwork, despite differences between performances (see later). But the type-token language — well-suited to the discussion of words and flags — has no obvious way to accommodate this.

Given its complexities, perhaps the type-token contrast should be given up. I prefer to retain it since, from my perspective, it is useful in three related ways. First, it stresses appropriately the idea of a *dancework*, a (single) performable typically realised at many times and places (although doing so requires finding a place for numerical identity). Second, it gives a way to describe the relation of performances to that dancework (as tokens of that dance-type). Third, it suggests that the work itself somehow *constrains* those performances that are indeed tokens of the type. But, since the type is an abstract object, in practice it directs our attention to the concrete places where the dancework can be encountered: to performances, to rehearsals, and to the notated score (where there is one) — or, more exactly, to the possibility of notationality.

On balance, then, the simple type-token account offers some insights here, but leaves a number of key questions unanswered or issues unaddressed. Later, attempts to meet these omissions by augmentation will be considered (see §§9-10 below). But first it is worth considering a quite different account.

§5. Goodman on autographic-allographic

The writings of Nelson Goodman suggest an alternative way of talking about multiple artworks such as danceworks. In his *Languages of Art*, Goodman famously distinguished *autographic* arts from *allographic* arts, promising this as a more profound, or (anyway) more useful, distinction. Instead of recognising danceworks as multiples, as instances of performing arts, and as amenable notation, their fundamental characteristic should be seen as being *allographic* — and hence the fundamental distinction being the contrast with *autographic* artworks (and, by extension, autographic art forms), a distinction reflecting the style of identity-conditions of each.

The distinction is introduced through discussion of forgery, to highlight "... that in music, unlike painting, there is no such thing as the forgery of a known work" (LA p. 112/PP p. 94[5]). Then Goodman explains the terms as follows:

> Let us speak of a work of art as *autographic* if and only if the distinction between original and forgery of it is significant; or, better, if and only if even the most exact duplication of it does not thereby count as genuine. (LA p. 113/PP p. 95)

Thus the term "autographic" is explicitly introduced in the context of discussing forgery, and explained by reference to the notion of forgery. The corresponding introduction of the term "allographic" is very brief: Goodman writes that "... painting is autographic, music nonautographic, or *allographic*" (LA p. 113/PP p. 95). Here, the term "allographic" simply means *nonautographic*. If the significance of distinguishing an original from its forgery explains "autographic", this seems to imply that, for the allographic, this distinction would *not* be significant.

How can Goodman explain "... the fact that some arts but not others are autographic" (LA p. 113/PP p. 95)? He urges that, for a painting like Rembrandt's *Lucretia*, "[t]he only way of ascertaining that the *Lucretia* before us is genuine ... is to establish the historical fact that it is the actual object made by Rembrandt" (LA p. 116/ PP p. 97). Thus:

> ... physical identification of the product of the artist's hand, and consequently the conception of forgery of a particular work, assume a significance in painting [an autographic art] that they do not have in literature [an allographic art]. (LA p. 116/PP. p. 97)

The thought here is familiar: to ascertain that I am presently sitting on the very same chair that I was sitting on yesterday, today's chair must have been made in exactly the same time and place, and by the same person, as the one I sat on yesterday — only then might there be only one chair in the story ("numerical identity"). Finding that today's chair was made in Seville and yesterday's in China would preclude there being just one chair. This kind of 'establishing historical facts about authorship' is termed, by Goodman, "history of production". Similarly, to produce a work in a typical autographic art, a painter must end up with a painting (must "... finish the painting", Goodman says: LA p. 114/PP p. 95). Then, like the chair, the painting's identity-conditions invoke that 'history of production'.

But for music, "... the composer's work is done when he has written the score" (LA p. 114/PP p. 95). And he *could* do this, even if he chooses another compositional method. Moreover, in writing the score one does not actually end up with the artwork itself, but something closer to a *recipe* for the work (compare Urmson, 1976 p. 246). The music must still be played in order to confront the artwork. Yet that work is nevertheless *made* in making the score. So for works in allographic arts (like novels, poems, dances, and musical works), identity questions do not turn on 'history of production', since (as the music case shows) there *is* such-and-such a piece of music — the score has been written — even though no one has heard it: it hasn't yet been played. Thus identifying the artwork in allographic arts (like music) does not require that one confront that artwork at that time. Hence there need be no direct connection to 'the artist's hand': the artist need have no direct connection to that performance or that inscription. Then perhaps the work itself can be identified without reference to history of production.

So, for Goodman (LA p. 115/PP p. 97), the artwork in an allographic art like literature is identified in terms of the words used: so one needs "... exact correspondence as sequences of letters, spaces and punctuation marks". Now reproducing those words *seems* to be simply repeating the poem or novel; producing another token of the same type. Were this correct, it would follow, first, that works of literature would be impossible to forge; and, second, that identification of works of literature would not depend, in this way, on 'history of production' or on "the artist's hand" (LA p. 116/PP p. 97). In fact, for Goodman, the point became definitional: in order that an art form be allographic, "[w]hat is *necessary* is that identification of the ... instance of a work be independent of the history of production" (Goodman, 1978 p. 49/1984 p. 139). After all, if the poem just is 'those words in that order', how they come to be there is irrelevant.

Now Goodman (LA p. 122/PP p. 101) tells us, plausibly, that "[a] forgery of work of art is an object falsely purporting to have the history of production requisite for the (or an) original of the work." Then the 'history of production' issues come together with the 'forgery' issues: forgeries seem possible only when history of production has roughly the importance, in respect of work-identity, that it has for paintings. But will this be true across the arts? Goodman (LA p. 122/PP p. 101) tells us that:

> [w]here there is a theoretically decisive test for determining that an object has all the constitutive properties of the work in question without determining how or by whom the object was produced, there is no requisite history of production and hence no forgery of any given work.

If I produced a *score* of an extant work of music or dance, this *deviant* 'history of production' would not make a performance from my score a forgery — rather, it is just another way to direct the pianist to play, say, Schönberg's opus 19. So (on Goodman's picture) history of production is fundamental for those forgeable works, the autographic works. By contrast, history of production will lack this importance for those works not in this way forgeable, the allographic works — such works might become "... fully freed from history of production" (LA p. 122/PP p. 101).

Clearly, the terms "autographic" and "allographic" are Goodman's coinages — they mean what he says they mean. The new terms' introduction (quoted above) certainly reads like an explanation of the term "autographic"; and the expression "if and only if" makes this *sound* like a definition. So forge-ability certainly seems to define the term "autographic".

But, in later writings, the autographic/allographic contrast is "... not *defined* in terms of those arts where there can be forgeries and those where there cannot" (Goodman, 1984 p. 139). Instead:

> [w]hat distinguishes an allographic work is that identification of an object or event as an instance of the work depends not at all upon how or when or by whom that object was produced. (Goodman, 1984 p. 140)

Now the possibility of forgery no longer plays any role in our account of the autographic/allographic contrast. Only the 'history of production' considerations genuinely *define* the allographic — despite Goodman's earlier introduction of it! As we saw, for Goodman (1984 p. 139), for an art form be allographic, "[w]hat is *necessary* is that identification of the ... instance of a work be independent of the history of production." Thus, for instance, "... a notation as much codifies as creates [such] an independent criterion" (Goodman, 1984 p. 139): that is, notationality allows us to recognise the artwork as existing prior to any performance — and hence independent of, say, a particular moment of composition.

Goodman's position — applied to dance — draws on the possibilities of a movement notation applicable to dance (Goodman evidenced Labanotation: see §7 below). Since, with allographic works, "... identification of the ... instance of a work ... [is] independent of the history of production" (Goodman, 1978 p. 49/1984 p. 139), such works could be understood as a series of words, or movements, or sounds, in a particular order. At its heart, Goodman's picture here is that a novel or poem, say, can be identified (and hence have identity-conditions) depending only on 'the right words in the right order', or something similar. That is why, for a poem, one needs "... exact correspondence as sequences of letters, spaces and punctuation marks" (LA p. 115/PP p. 97). And a notated score would fulfill a similar role. So Goodman was keen to stress the potential for notationality in dance. Hence, by Goodman's principle, two dance performances both satisfying a particular notation are performances of the same work; and performances failing to instantiate that notated score are not of the same work (subject to qualifications about the adequacy of the notation system) — with the greater weight given to the negative judgement. But dance uses more than one notation system, in ways there is not for music; moreover, to date, dance notation lacks the prominence within the dance world that musical notation has in its world. Musicians will typically understand notation — indeed, in some spheres, only someone who could read musical scores would be taken seriously as a musician (for jazz, this is not a strict requirement). The parallel requirement that dancers or choreographers understand scores is nothing like as strong — even a choreographer who was master of one notation-system could not reliably read or perform another. Thus the conclusion(s) above about dance-identity make the particular notation used important (when, if ever, are two scores equivalent?). And, as Goodman (LA pp. 129-154; 211-218) notes, the potential usefulness for dance of notated scores, for purposes both of authenticity and preservation, requires notations both readable and reliable (see Chapter Four §2).

§6. Elaborating the place of 'history of production'

Goodman's account answers questions about work-identity for allographic artworks, like typical dances, by reference to the *score*: a work comprising exactly that sequence of movements (as specified by the score) will be such-and-such a dance — say, *Swan Lake*. But, first, will this account genuinely resolve questions about work-identity? Second, is its conceptual base in the autographic/allographic distinction sound? Or, to put that differently, can dances be identified independently of 'history of production'?

On the first question, Goodman's view is complex. He had thought that all works were either one or the other: the autographic/allographic contrast 'divides the field' because, after all, the term "allographic" was introduced simply as "nonallographic" (LA p. 113/PP p. 95, quoted above). On *this* account, what is not autographic is *thereby* allographic. But, later, he urged that "... not every art can be classed as autographic or as allographic" (Goodman, 1978 p. 49/1984 p. 139). Rather:

> [w]here ... a composer provides prescriptions in a non-notational system rather than scores, the classes of performances called for do not constitute either autographic or allographic works. They are not autographic; for their identification does not depend on history of production. They are not allographic; for their identification is not independent of history of production. ... [I]dentity of work (true, transitive identity) is not established in this case. The terms "autographic" and "allographic" are mutually exclusive, and they exhaust all cases where work-identity is established at all. (PP p. 83)

Still, at least artworks "... where work-identity is established at all" will fall under the autographic/allographic distinction.

Goodman was unsure that work-identity could be established for dances (LA p. 213). He demonstrated by examples that "... a notation is *not sufficient* to make an art allographic" (Goodman, 1984 p. 139), although it is *notationality* that was important, rather than the actual notation. Yet he was suspicious of the claims of dance notation to adequacy for his purposes (LA p. 213). For dance "... the ways, and even the possibility, of developing an adequate notation are still matters of controversy" (LA p. 121/PP p. 100) —

at least if "adequacy" requires meeting Goodman's own conditions. For, he urged, notation systems must have "... unambiguity and syntactic and semantic disjointness and differentiation" (LA p. 156); in addition, scores should ideally be easy to 'read' and easily (and clearly) 'written'. (see LA pp. 129-154; 211-218)! Where does this leave the most widely-used movement notation systems? Well, Labanotation is certainly adequate to the recording of *all* movement (and at least the Benesh and the Eshkol-Wachman system are adequate for *some* movement). But Labanotation is not widely readable in ways Goodman required: in fact, no notated score is typically readable with the fluency and accuracy Goodman requires, taking musical notation as his model. (Chapter Four follows up this topic.)

But, putting aside that hesitancy, Goodman's answer concerning identity-conditions for dance parallels that for music: that (ideally) the score *determines* which work is being performed:

> The function of the score is to specify the essential properties a performance must have to belong to a work ... All other variations are permitted; and differences among performances of the same work ... are enormous. (LA p. 212)

Here Goodman accepts the counter-intuitive consequence that a performance differing from the score by one note (or one step that is specified "essential" by the notation) is therefore not a performance of that work at all! But while such a 'total compliance' condition (LA p. 187) seems problematic, Goodman sees it as "... one of those cases where ordinary language gets us quickly into trouble" (LA p. 186). With our commitment to the practices of dancers and musicians, it would be desirable to find a less idealising account. Certainly this must speak against easy acceptance of Goodman's position.

Our second question asked about the place of 'history of production', which Goodman used to define the autographic: as dance was an allographic art, history of production should be irrelevant to identity considerations for dances. Is Goodman's account defensible? The investigation starts from that account's commonalities with Richard Wollheim's views: for such obviously autographic arts as painting, "the artist's hand" (LA p. 116/PP p. 97) has a clear role. Thus Wollheim (1980 pp. 168-169) remarks, "[i]t is common ground to Goodman and myself that, when a work of art is an individual, identity depends on history of production." And the argument here, securing this result for them both, is just that two works otherwise indistinguishable, but differing in history of production, will not be the *same* artwork. Further, two works, otherwise indistinguishable, which require different treatment — say, as understood in terms of different *categories of art* — will be in the same position. And, recall (from Chapter One §7), Danto exploits this insight in his gallery of indiscernibles: thus, "a minimalist exemplar of geometrical art ... [entitled] ... 'Red Square'" is distinguished from "a still-life executed by an embittered disciple of Matisse, called 'Red Table Cloth'" (Danto, 1981 p. 1: both quotations), even though each is comprised of a canvas with a painted square of red pigment. For, in each case, that work has a place within the history of art in that form typically different for that of works with different histories of production. So, putting that argument the other way round, if we fail to correctly identify the work, we will typically misperceive it. For two works cannot be both qualitatively and artistically indistinguishable: that would make 'them' instead *one* work. Rather, qualitative indistinguishability might combine with categorial difference — as in Danto's gallery of indiscernibles or 'confusable counterparts' — to produce different works. Here, the work is misperceived if it is mistaken for its counterpart. At the base of this argument is the issue of *responsibility* for the work: clearly, *I* cannot be responsible for *your* work.

But misperception of the same sort occurs both when a cubist painting is mistaken for one from another category *and* when a Graham-based dance for a Romantic Ballet: as it were, inappropriate concepts are brought to bear in one's experience. In effect, the work is misidentified; treating it *as if* it were a different work. So the work will be misidentified if its history of production or *category*-ascription is other than we have assumed. Then the problem with this proposed account of the autographic is that, on it, *all* artworks *seem* to be autographic because, for all of them, one must recognise how to appropriately understand the work — and hence how misperception is to be avoided. For this, one must correctly identify the artwork — at least as far as its *genre*, and such like. But correctly recognising what artwork this is (or even what kind of artwork) often requires making a connection to its author or period, since only then can its *genre* (say) be identified. Identifying the object as (say) Donne's "Valediction: Forbidding Mourning" is recognising it as a poem, in seventeenth-century English, and in the 'metaphysical' genre. These features supply some categorial constraints for its appreciation. Such points apply as clearly to, say, literary works as to paintings. And to recognise that, say, the poem is not ironic may lead the reader directly back to Donne's authorship.

So is that history of production *always* relevant? Certainly this feature is typically invoked in distinguishing *this* poem from *that* one — hence, in identifying poems. And, as Goodman (1984 p. 140) grants, "... determination of authorship ... [is an aspect] of history of production". Recognising that point, we must concede that history of production is crucial for all such works. Of course, our object might not be an artwork at all. But when two objects are both artworks, they must either be different artworks or multiples from that artwork (say, tokens of the same type). Also, this account clarifies some of what the expression "history of production" means in this context. For example, two cast sculptures might have the same history of production if (roughly) they are from the same casting, and both are sanctioned by the artist, or some such. Similarly, with a dancework, 'same history of production' would trace *this* performance back to the work's composition — the difference between performances might well be irrelevant when this could be done.

Goodman's point is that the poem we confront might have been transcribed in many different ways: "[a]n inscription of a poem ..., however produced, need only be spelled correctly" (Goodman, 1984 p. 140). When the issue is between hand-written and typed inscriptions, this is right. But that only applies where that string of words is recognised as just this poem: say, Donne's "Valediction: Forbidding Mourning". So, as Goodman (1984 p. 141) grants, cases such as Borges' story entitled "Pierre Menard, author of *Don Quixote*" (Borges, 1962) put pressure on his conclusion. Imagine Borges' story were factual: a young Frenchman (Menard) has written a word-perfect version of Cervantes' masterpiece (assume him to have finished it). Then Borges (1962 p. 49) urges, "[t]he text of Cervantes and that of Menard are verbally identical, but the second is almost infinitely richer". To illustrate, he then quotes a passage from Cervantes and one from Menard, commenting on the different import of the two passages, what they convey, and so on. (Remember, these are identical strings of words.) He continues:

> Equally vivid is the contrast in styles. The archaic style of Menard — in the last analysis a foreigner — suffers from a certain affectation. Not so that of his precursor, who handles easily the Spanish of his time. (Borges, 1962 pp. 49-50)

But what has changed here? Not the words, of course. Rather, the meaning of the Menard differs from that of the Cervantes: comments accurately made of the Menard could not be truly said of the Cervantes — different reasons for judgements become open to readers. So different things are true of each even though they amount to 'the same words in the same order'.

Hence this case raises exactly the issue that Goodman dismisses as of dubious relevance. For, as Borges describes the case, the work of literature — that is, a work one expects to be allographic — *would not* be identifiable solely on the basis of 'those words in that order'. Rather, recognising a work *by Menard* here involves considerations in the 'history of production'. And therefore so does recognising the other as by Cervantes.

Does this case just parallel that of a skillful but explicit copyist — in which, once again, the artwork itself is not at issue? Suppose someone practiced calligraphy by writing the words in a foreign language: when he uses sixteenth-century Spanish (which he does not understand), it *turns out* that his efforts have produced another *Don-Quixote*-token. (Even here we might begin with reservations, except that he is *copying* just such a token!) This is certainly not how Borges invites us to think of the case.

Goodman's own reaction here is revealing— he simply denies that the case as Borges presents it makes sense:

> To deny that I read *Don Quixote* if my copy, although correctly spelled in all details, happens to be accidentally produced by a mad printer in 1500, or by a mad computer in 1976, seems to me utterly untenable. (Goodman, 1978 p. 50)

But this passage assumes the answer to the most important question: namely, whether what he held was indeed (a copy of) *Don Quixote*. If we were sure that this text's origin was a *mad* printer or a *mad* computer, we would be happy — I imagine — to deny that this 'text' was of a *different* artwork, because we would doubt (or deny) that it was an artwork *at all*. My computer has just *thrown out* a text orthographically indistinguishable with Cervantes's masterpiece: once I *know* for sure that this is just an accidental result of some glitch, the resultant object is — in a clear sense — *naturally occurring* (it simply results from the working-out of causal forces, devoid of intention). My computer's *glitch* has resulted in a text orthographically indistinguishable from the Cervantes — has my computer produced another *copy* of Cervantes's masterpiece (as Goodman seems to assume)? Well, the cracks in my wall could not *produce* a particular sonnet, no matter how much the cracks looked like that poem. For the poem is a meaning-bearing object; and that is not within the scope of the cracks in the wall, as the mere working-out of causal forces. Putting aside the size of the coincidence, we should say the same thing of the computer-driven Cervantes. So one could well deny that the computer produced a copy of Cervantes, a token of that type. The same thing could be said of the 'text' produced, instead, by the *madness* of (say) my mad-printer ancestor in 1500: he did not *intend* to make a novel; and certainly not a novel in sixteenth-century Spanish (which he did not speak). For, as I imagine this, it too was merely the working out of causal forces (devoid of intention), although now forces in my ancestor's brain: it is also a (kind of) *naturally-occurring* event — at least, no one is responsible for it. So these cases could be 'recognised heads of exception' to the ascription of *any* meaning here.

Yet Goodman and Elgin (1988 pp. 62-63) contend "... that the two supposed works are actually one. ... What Menard wrote is simply another inscription of the text." So blanket rejection of this sort seems exactly

Goodman's preferred position here. The difficulty lies in *arguing* for this straight-out rejection. If the position is (a) that the allographic/autographic contrast is fundamental — which Goodman had not previously asserted — and (b) that it is explained through a differential relation to history of production, it *follows* that the 'works' of Menard and of Cervantes, being 'works' in an allographic art form, must be different transcriptions of the same work. Yet that simply reiterates the original distinction in the face of the (apparent) counter-case: these *seem* like different artworks; and for roughly the same reasons as those in Danto's gallery (quoted earlier) — namely, that different artistic judgements can (truly) be offered of each.

Re-working the idea behind this story from Borges, Wollheim (1978 p. 34/ 1980 p. 170) imagines a short lyric poem written by an Elizabethan poet, and an orthographically indistinguishable one composed by a Georgian poet. Of course, that second poet operates as poets always do; in particular, he operates "... in complete ignorance of his predecessor" (Wollheim, 1978 p. 34/1980 p. 170) — or at least in relative ignorance of that predecessor, such that we are content to call him an *author* in this respect. So the second is not merely transcribing the work of the other. Then Borges' preferred solution — two works with different properties, despite being orthographically indistinguishable — seems most appealing: each wrote *his* poem by *his* methods or means.

Suppose, instead, that there is only *one* poem in this case: its identification returns us to 'history of production'. For one *still* needs to pay attention to history of production even to conclude "... that the Tudor poet wrote it ... and the Georgian poet merely wrote it out (Wollheim, 1980 p. 170). If *that* line were rejected:

> ... we could stick at the fact that two poets wrote down the same lines in the same spelling and refuse to countenance the further question, Whose poem is it?" (Wollheim, 1980 p. 170[6])

Were this position right, "... poems would not have a history of production: they would be more found than made" (Wollheim, 1980 p. 171). Objects meeting Goodman's condition here would *lack* a history of production, since (for Goodman) appeal to that history cannot resolve either interpretative-questions or identity-questions. But, again, there seems no *argument* here differentiating one class of art forms from the other in this respect; and we notice an unwanted consequence of keeping the distinction in our armoury. Hence the contrast between autographic and allographic should be rejected.

Consider, too, a *parody* of a *specific* work in an allographic art form, such as those executed by Les Ballets Trockadero de Monte Carlo[7]. Thus, do the Trocs really dance *Swan Lake*? To some degree, the answer must be "yes": in some ways, this just is *Swan Lake*. Clarifying that insight requires recognising that the starting point for this work is the Ivanov and Petipa *Swan Lake*; it is not merely, say, inspired by *Swan Lake*. But the person having seen only the Trocs version should be hesitant about claiming to have seen *Swan Lake*. At the least, this dance has a *connection* to the Ivanov and Petipa *Swan Lake* — that is what makes it funny. Recognising the distinctiveness of the Trocs version is precisely a matter of comparing and contrasting it with the Ivanov and Petipa dancework: that is, with taking into consideration the differential 'history of production' of each.

Where does this leave the autographic/allographic contrast[8]? Perhaps "autographic" and "allographic" seem to offer nothing not better captured by just talking about *particular object* artworks and *multiple* artworks, with 'history of production' relevant to the identity-conditions for both. But the stress on 'history of production' which this discussion brings to the fore is important here. For that, after all, is another way to emphasise *authorship*.

§7. Intermezzo: The variety of dance notation

Given our comparison (above) with recipes, something brief about dance notation may be helpful. For a notated score for a dance resembles just such a recipe, at least in principle. In the past, numerous attempts were made to construct a system of graphic recording which recorded all that dancers and choreographers required. For instance, Thoinot Arbeau included notated scores for dances in his *Orchesography* ([1589]1967), by combining pictures and descriptions of steps with a kind of musical notation. And a score in a style based around foot- and leg-movements, a Stepanov score, was produced for *Swan Lake* in 1901 (of which more later). All were ultimately failures, discarded as inadequate to their purposes, that inadequacy resulting in part from the felt need to notate all aspects of the dance, including those that made it the dancework it was.

Today, what is standardly called *dance notation* is essentially movement notation, designed to record accurately movements of the human body, or of humans moving together. Hence, at best, it can be used to accurately record movements of the body (and, by combination, of more than one body). Three well-developed notation systems (Labanotation, Benesh, Eshkol Wachman) are in use for dance. Anthropologists studying movement more generally also use them; in the case of Eshkol Wachman, also predicting the motion of 'space walkers'. Although all are movement notations, some notation systems lend themselves to the characteristics of dance styles: for instance, the 'flatness' and assumed position of the viewer makes Benesh notation especially suitable for classical ballet, performed in a proscenium arch. But nothing in the movements themselves *guarantees* that a dance is recorded —

although the (un)-likelihood of a line of people on pointe being anything other than dance might overcome this constraint in practice. Still, the theoretical point is that movement-scores cannot guarantee that the movement sequence notated is dance (and not some other activity). Yet, for (say) anthropologists interested in movement patterns, this is a strength of such notated scores — whether or not such-and-such is *dance* is beside the point for them: the movement patterns employed exhaust their interest.

So, recognising that such-and-such is dance is already a kind of *interpretation* of it. As Suzanne Youngerman (1984 p. 101) puts it:

> Notation systems are more than tools for documentation; they are systems of analysis that can be used to illuminate many aspects of the phenomenon of movement. Notation scores embody perceptions of movement.

Thus, especially having built-in the assumption that this is dance, notation systems of this sort instantiate methods of analysis or conceptualisation, rather than neutrally describing movements which might *then* be analysed. In part, this follows from conceptualising four-dimensional human activity in the two dimensions of a notated score, with different notation systems finding different resolutions. That a notator divides the movement up in this way, rather than that, follows from using (say) Labanotation — where the temporal dimension is one of those on the page — rather than Benesh notation, which treats time symbolically. Further, notations are interpretative in embodying choices: to notate the movement of a person's arm, one could inscribe the motion-pattern of hand, forearm, elbow, upper-arm, and so on. Given the connections ("the forearm-bone connected to the elbow bone"), notating the movement of the elbow may be sufficient. But another notator might make this decision differently.

Suppose that the notation were used as a 'marker' of authenticity: that a dance conforming to this notation is indeed such-and-such a dance (say, *Swan Lake*). Then someone wishing to stage that dance should pay attention to precisely what is notated (and, by implication, less attention to what is not): so, to the elbow movements in the case above. In this sense, the notator must recognise what is central, what peripheral, to this movement sequence.

Then recording a particular dance in two different notation systems imposes two different sets of constraints for the dancer. Thus each might be satisfied by a (slightly) different sequence of movements. So a performance satisfying a notated score for *Swan Lake* in Labanotation might fail to satisfy a score in Benesh, and *vice versa*. All that can be urged is that only reputable notation systems count here: that the knowledgeable about that art form decide what is and what is not reputable.

Further, talk of 'the knowledgeable about a particular art form' is a way to record that, in the end, whether something is or is not an instance of a particular dancework is a dance-critical matter. Suppose Nureyev's changes mean that his production no longer satisfies a particular notated score for *Swan Lake*: as we saw, one alternative would take this to count against that production. But one could also doubt the appropriateness of that score.

Judgement might be required in other ways too. The renowned notator Ann Hutchinson-Guest reported being asked to notate a segment of a dance which the choreographer (Kurt Jooss) demonstrated by shuffling across the stage. The dancers, reflecting years of ballet training, could not bring themselves to shuffle: so they actually performed a sequence of classic ballet steps (*chassé, chassé, pas de bourrée*). Now, should Guest notate what this group of dancers (and, predictably, future generations of ballet dancers) *did* perform, or what they *should* perform (to 'obey' the choreographer)? In such a case, no answer avoids dependence on the informed *judgement* of the notator.

Equally, faced with a score in dance notation he/she understands, what characteristics will a dancer take as central, such that movements (and so on) failing to satisfy them preclude having instantiated that dance? Or what notated features might reflect *typical* if inessential aspects of the dance? 100% compliance with any score cannot be expected as a dancer's goal, much less as a realistic expectation of typical performances. (Although Goodman [LA p. 187] does expect this "full compliance": indeed, *he* urges that a musical performance where one note played is not reflected in the score fails as a performance of that work.) But a poor performance of a work is still a performance of that work — perhaps, until it gets just too bad (when whether it is a performance of such-and-such a work will be a matter for dispute, with the answer not obvious); and not all performances of less than full compliance are poor. For example, the pianist Glenn Gould produced powerful, expressive performances of Schönberg's piano music (some of which are 'captured' in recordings) — but his performances are often further from the score than less powerful renditions.

Looking back, these thoughts about notation fill in some detail Goodman envisaged when seeking to characterise the identity of danceworks (in principle) entirely in terms of their scores. He recognised, of course, that not all dances would *in fact* have scores; but, equally, that all *could* — that dance was notational. Yet he would have lacked this confidence in dance notation had he not considered in detail such a notation system: in his case, Labanotation. But a contrary point must be recorded. While I, too, often envisage Labanotation when discussing a score for a dancework, this simply reflects my hope that — having spent so long learning Labanotation — that time should not be wasted. In reality, a formal account of a score for a dancework (and hence for the *adequacy* of a score: see Chapter Three) should be offered. This grants that any recipe which, if followed with understanding, produces a performance of the dancework in question counts as a score for that dancework. Indeed, if a set of rules of the kind used for Elaine Summers' chance-based dance *Instant Choice* (Banes, 1993 pp. 47-49) functioned as a normative recipe which, if followed in an appropriate context, produces a performance authentically *of the dancework* at issue, that set of rules would count as an adequate score in context — on the supposition that performance in accordance with them in this context results in a performance of that work, where the work itself is a dance.

§8. Play-scripts are not like dance scores

As we have noted, the features or details of performances are *complete*, in the sense of making concrete all the places where the dancework itself under-determines its performances. That many features of this performance of Bruce's *Ghost Dances* (1981) might have been different is clear from other performances. But these would still be performances of *the very same dancework*. That is the fact about *performables* to be accommodated. So what constrains what *should* be done, so as to perform such-and-such a dance (say, *Ghost Dances*)? How is the normativity of this *should* to be understood?

In this context, Paul Ziff (1984 pp. 87-88) discusses seeing the same play:

> Whether or not you are seeing the same play is fairly easy to determine ... one can be fairly precise about this and say, "yes, this is the same play", no doubt not being performed in exactly the same way; it's a different sort of rendition but it's still the same play. How does one show this? ... The script will show it. ... So we can identify the play on the basis of the script and identify different interpretations of it.

For, Ziff (1984 pp. 87-88) thinks, with a play, "... you can see *Julius Caesar* in modern dress. It's the same play though a radically different interpretation."

With Jim Hamilton (2007 pp. 23-40), I am less confident that one "... can identify the play on the basis of the script" (Ziff, 1984 p. 88); and hence that the play-case is therefore easier than the dance-case, as Ziff claims. As Hamilton urges, the relation of the script — often seen as a literary artwork in its own right — to the work's performances is not clear. So that, in comparing dance-scores with play-scripts, accounts such as Ziff's fail to give the right account of *plays*, as well as failing to grasp their specific difference from dances. Yet a play-script is rightly seen as providing just such normativity in respect of (some) theatre productions.

Of course, Ziff did not imagine a dance being uniquely identified from its score either. Further, he was unfamiliar with developed dance-notation forms, such as Labanotation: he refers to "... notes by the choreographer" (Ziff, 1984 p. 88) as though these provided the best on offer. And he suggests that if "... some splendid notation ... [were] devised which will govern everything ... then this problem could be alleviated" (Ziff, 1984 p. 88). His optimism here correctly highlights three features. First, present movement notation systems (such as Labanotation) are immensely powerful, although they do not determine that one is seeing *dances* — the scores are just movement notations. Second, there still seems no guarantee here that scores alone could "govern everything", providing an exceptionless guarantee of which dancework we are presently watching. A typical score alone may not distinguish between two tokens of the same type (for example, distinguish the Ivanov and Petipa *Swan Lake* from Nureyev's version) nor distinguish them from tokens of a different type (say, Mats Ek's *Swan Lake*). Third, there are at least three different movement notation systems: so what seems *determined* by a score in one notation system, as a crucial feature of this dancework, might seem contingent in a score deploying another.

Still, like the play-script, the notated score functions *normatively* in respect of a dancework, except that selecting a notation-*system* still remains an issue. For the score's virtue is precisely its capacity to generate that fundamental normativity. The attraction of this strategy is that, for (most) dances, performances make the danceworks *concrete*, resolving all those places where *the dance itself* is under-determined. In a typical case, that such-and-such a gesture is or is not included may be neither required nor prohibited. Certainly not *all* the features of that particular performance are crucial to its being the dancework it is — a performance differing (suitably) in respect of some of the under-determined features would still be that dance (though note "suitably" here: not any resolution needs to count). And, as before, 'crucial' features might just be those whose absence was a source of criticism of a performance. So the constraints from the type cannot be generated just from a performance. But that normativity will be found in any score regarded as adequate — what it prescribed would be crucial, while what it proscribed would be prohibited, and other movements would be permissible.

§9.   Type-token artworks
Can something better be done by returning, with these thoughts about the possibilities of notation systems, to the type-token contrast, but reviving a question posed earlier: could a type-token analysis still permit recognition of *numerical identity* here? Doing so involves identifying two performances as the very same dancework in virtue of their being tokens of the same type.

But, since types are abstract objects, that seems problematic both as a theoretical enterprise, and as a way to offer something to the activities of dancers. This second, fundamental issue, turning on the practicalities of extracting constraints from the abstract object that is the type, can be put aside until the next chapter. Can something more be said on the theoretical issue?

Sometimes, asking about numerical identity concerns the relation between different occasions of identifying a token: are there *two* tokens in the story, or just *one*? Are there two watches, or two flags, or only one? In typical cases, *of course*, this is a different token-word from that. Hence they are different words, but are also the same (type-)word — Peirce invented the type-token contrast to characterise just this case. The identity-question seems trivial applied to this case, where the tokens are, say, *inscriptions* because it is usually uncontentious that there are two inscriptions — hence different tokens. The same would be true of, say, dances treated as performances. That the viewer is in a different place or at a different time *guarantees* (for typical cases) that a different performance is being viewed — so any residual numerical identity question relates to the dance itself, the type. And, as with the word-case, we might be unsure in some *contrived* cases whether this is a different part of the same token or a part of a different token. Still, such cases can be put aside as contrived.

Of course, some classic type-token objects (such as *The Red Flag*) admit of identity questions relating to tokens: Is this the *Red Flag* I was waving yesterday? Since the flag itself, the one waved, is an *object*, the question of whether the token identified at this time is the same token as that identified at another time (that is, numerical identity of tokens) can be addressed. Because such re-identification issues for tokens can occur, a 'pair' of tokens might be identified at different times or in different ways: might they in fact be the same token approached in different ways? And typically they would not be. Unfortunately, the type-token language lends itself to other occasions also. Asked whether one was sitting in the same chair as yesterday, the response, "Well, a token of the same type" — albeit slightly unlikely, and a little pedantic — is both direct and informative. Then simply ruling out such a response by fiat might seem arbitrary, especially given the insights that the account promises (see §4 above).

But, here, Kivy (1993 pp. 35-36) voices a pertinent reservation. Having listed "... such candidates for Platonic Realism as universals, kinds, and types", he comments parenthetically, "... assuming one wants to construe types Platonistically at all." And do we want to? In part, the problem is that the type-token contrast has not been fully elaborated; that leaves open the possibility of a number of different elaborations (see, for example, Appendix).

Treating *the type* differently from other abstract notions must be productive here, since the type-token contrast is itself technical. And when there is no issue of re-identification of tokens (or performances), there seems no basis for concern about numerical identity beyond what is implicit in recognising tokens as of the same type (when they are).

Yet how do we decide which accounts of the type-token contrast are plausible? This question partly concerns what features are taken to be clear. Thus, suppose it were thought *obvious* that, say, multiple-artworks permitted numerical identity conclusions, and had a beginning in time. Then an analysis treating the type-token contrast as *not* permitting numerical identity, and types as *not* having a beginning in time, could be regarded in one of two ways. Granting these properties to multiple-artworks would require contesting that analysis of type-token, in order to maintain a type-token analysis for such artworks. Or, beginning from that account of the type-token contrast, and insisting on the properties of the multiple artworks, would require denying that such artworks were, in fact, type-token objects.

So one way forward involves taking Kivy's (implied) advice to not treat types Platonistically[9]. Then, if other abstract notions were treated Platonistically, type-token relations would *contrast* with explanations of other abstract notions. In *The Red Flag* or the term "cat", we have types of which the various instantiations are tokens. For words and flags, and also for poems and cast sculptures, it makes sense to re-identify the token. But it also makes sense to re-identify the type — these really are the *same* word, or the *same* flag, even though different instantiations. That will not hold for other general notions sometimes given a type-token treatment. *Kinds* of chair (say, the Bauhaus chair) or *kinds* of dog should simply be treated in that different way: as kinds, or species, or some such — but, importantly, *not* on a type-token model. That is probably the strategy most true to Peirce and most likely to respect important distinctions in most contexts. What are the constraints in our central cases?

The fundamental cases here, of course, require *numerical identity* — taking two performances as the same artwork, the same dance. And, since the dancework itself (the abstract object) is only confronted through confronting a performance, one is asking "Is performance A a performance of the very same artwork as performance B?" Now imagine scrutiny of three performances, each entitled *Swan Lake*: the 'standard' *Swan Lake*, choreographed by Ivanov and Petipa; the Matthew Bourne 'version' with its male swans; and the Mats Ek *Swan Lake*. Of course, one cannot expect to resolve here these questions of how (if at all) these performances are related. But one moves forward by, first, clarifying the question; and, second, providing a framework for future answers.

The central question, then, is whether or not the performance at issue really is a token of the relevant type[10]; in this case, a token of the type *Swan Lake*. That certainly sounds like a query concerning numerical identity, in this respect paralleling our response to similar queries for another *multiple* art form (namely, cast sculpture) where numerical identity judgements make sense.

The particular problem for artworks that are multiples arises because numerical-identity worries of this sort cannot standardly arise for abstract objects. Thus, is the second occurrence of the word "cat" in the sentence, "My cat ate your cat", the *same* word or a different word than the first occurrence? As this case shows, *real* numerical-identity questions do not arise for *words* (Peirce's favourite example[11]): these are tokens of the same type (hence, *same* word) but they are different tokens (hence, *different* word), where this is a trivial consequence of having two inscriptions.

Contrasting the letter "a" with an "a" in italics shows clearly what question is being asked when one enquires whether these are the same letter; an answer could reflect that fact — that both are the letter "a". Unfortunately, one letter also instantiates another abstract object, 'italic "a"'. That, too, is obvious. But, although *both* are the letter "a", the italic has an 'abstract property'[12] that the other lacks. Then a particular italic "a" counts as instantiating *two* abstract objects — it seems a token both of the type letter "a" *and* of the type letter italic "a" (compare Meskin, 1999 p. 47). So can such-and-such be a token of two different (although related) types?

Such an analysis creates confusion, if offered (say) to characterise the Ivanov and Petipa *Swan Lake* in relation to Matthew Bourne's *Swan Lake*: both were *Swan Lake*, but Matthew Bourne's was somehow a different although related type (as it were, a kind of italic "a"), rather than a new type. Such an outcome is unsatisfactory for danceworks since it proliferates abstract objects; and parsimoniousness (or Occam's Razor) speaks against such proliferation, when we can do without it.

Indeed, should some form of type-token account be adopted, the problem set out above may become a nettle to grasp. Suppose the model reflected the case of inscriptions of the letter "a" and the letter "a" italic, where both seem tokens of a particular type (letter "a"); but "a" italic also seems to instantiate another abstract object (another letter that could be repeatedly inscribed). Then *Swan Lake*, say, might be seen as one repeatable abstract object (that is, one type) and Drigo's interpretation of *Swan Lake* as another repeatable abstract object (and hence perhaps another type?). And, after all, a score might also be written for Drigo's interpretation[13].

Now suppose that the type-token account can only have two 'places' (type or token?). Then that account cannot characterise the relation of Drigo's interpretation to *Swan Lake* itself. For Tuesday's performance is the token, and *Swan Lake* is the type: those 'places' are used-up. Yet Drigo's interpretation — or, above, even Matthew Bourne's — is still *Swan Lake*: even in its creator's eyes, the connection to the past of *Swan Lake* is recognised. (That may not be true of all *Swan Lakes*: in particular, later I would urge that it is not true of the Mats Ek *Swan Lake* (1987). And this involves urging that it is a different artwork.) But all the interpretations which *are* to be treated as the very same artwork here implicitly assign some responsibility to the original authors (say, to Ivanov and Petipa). Hence one way forward (duly grasping the nettle) emphasises that responsibility: that, in the musical case, Pollini recognises that *his* interpretation is still an interpretation of Schönberg's pianowork — his role brings that artwork (for which *Schönberg* is responsible) into *concrete* existence. Similarly, the performer's interpretation of the dancework is (of course) the performer's responsibility. But our discussions should differentiate it from the author's responsibility. Thus performers' interpretations do not generate abstract objects in their own right, but rather reflect the *manner* in which the other abstract object was generated — as though there were numerous roads from A to B, and taking a particular road was a repeatable (and differed from taking a different road) without itself being a terminus (UD pp. 106-107). So these would be thought 'routes to the type' but not themselves types[14].

At the least, this preserves a distinctive feature of the type-token contrast as it applies in the case of multiple artworks. Then each token is the very same thing (say, *The Red Flag*) as any other: as I put it elsewhere (UD p. 91):

> Each token is equally a token ... If we are not prepared to regard the work this way, we cannot use the type-token contrast to characterise it.

So one can simply concede that danceworks are amenable to numerical identity considerations, setting the alternative aside by *fiat* — danceworks will count as tokens of one type only (contrast Meskin, 1999 p. 47). In this way, worries concerning this kind of 'multi-membership' by tokens of particular types can be put aside.

Is there a reason to make this move? Our justification for that stipulation lies in the *bite* the notion of numerical identity has for type-token objects: that recognising *numerical identity* is sometimes *important* for these type-token objects. Clearly, numerical identity is not *always* important: a numerical identity-solution is possible to the question, "Is this the glass from which I was drinking yesterday?" but typically we have no interest in that answer. The same cannot be said of numerical identity for multiple artworks. Numerical identity has an impact, noted above, when the tokens are particular *objects*, such as sculptures. But, for artworks such as dances (and musical works), the *object* is the abstract object; and one confronts the dancework itself only through confronting a performance. So finding just that dancework (or musical work) is a matter of identifying the performance one is confronting as a performance of that (abstract) work: that is, a matter of identifying the tokens of that type. This provides the standard ontology of *the performable* — the artwork that can be performed on more than one occasion. For dances, we regularly want to identify the type, contrasting it with similar but different types — in my example, the 'standard' (Ivanov and Petipa) *Swan Lake* with Mats Ek's *Swan Lake*. So the emphasis is clearly on *artwork-types*: hence discovering that two danceworks were tokens of the same type is discovering that they are *the very same artwork*. This is important precisely because identifying artworks typically draws a connection to their creators — to their 'history of production' — and therefore to the creators responsibility for the works, in both senses of the term "responsibility". That is, I both (a) *made* the dance (I am responsible for its existence), and (b) deserve any *praise* or blame that accrues to it.

Further, for dance (as for other art forms), the types are typically *normative* — they must admit of both well-formed and poorly-formed tokens. In this sense, they are, or resemble, "norm-kinds" (Wolterstorff, 1980 pp. 54-58). The impact of our contextualism should also be recognised: that sometimes what is required, in that context, is (say) satisfied by a one-eyed but fierce lion (UD pp. 108-109), although on other occasions the full complement of eyes will be required. Similarly, on some occasions, the 'cragginess' of the playing of a musical work or the angularity of a particular dance performance may be just what is required. On another occasion, or for another purpose, a quite different performance best exemplifies that artwork.

If correct, this offers a basis for the *different* treatment of the type-token contrast: it would not simply be *just* another one on the list of abstract/concrete contrasts: universal/particular, and so on. Instead, a specific weight would attach to *this* contrast that would not attach to the others: it would permit us to draw *numerical-identity* conclusions.

Of course, the distinction drawn above between works (as types) and performers' interpretations (as 'routes') might be less important in practice that I am making it. For given the centrality of *notationality* here (see below, and in Chapter Three), the constraints from the type can be found in an adequate notated score. But Drigo's interpretation too could be represented by a notated score. Then, in practical terms, the type (discovered from the *adequate* score: see Chapter Three §6) and the performer's interpretations might resemble one another in this respect, even if — when turning to philosophy — they are distinguished.

Does that help meet objections previously raised to a type-token analysis?

That performance A and performance B are performances of the same dancework (say, *Swan Lake*) only when they are tokens of the same type says nothing new. Since the type is also *Swan Lake*, that answer seems uninformative. Yet, looked at more practically, our problem lies in finding constraints under which performance A will be a token of the same type-F as performance B. Can a substantial answer be found to the question, "How does one recognise the constraints from the type, so as to produce same-work continuity? (Or, more simply, so as to perform the work you are aiming at?)"

Although dances are chiefly made by constructing a 'first performance' (that is, by getting dancers to do this and that), most dances could indeed *in principle* be constructed by writing a score (as most musical works are). Hence such a score could be offered a role *in principle*. In UD, I stressed that, in most cases, an adequate *notated score* for a dancework offered a way to identify constraints on the movement patterns from the *abstract object* that was the dance (the *type*). I urged "... a relationship between the type and the notated score" (UD p. 97), so that — once actualised in performance — the work so constrained would be (say) *Swan Lake*. That is, the relation between performances here reflected, at least roughly, *numerical identity*, despite differences among the performances.

Then, a notated *score* might provide the required constraints. So a *Thesis of Notationality* might be expressed roughly as follows:

> *Performance A and performance B are performances of the same work of art (in any performing art) just in case both satisfy or instantiate some particular 'text' in a notation agreed by the knowledgeable in the art form to an adequate notation for that form.*

Such a Thesis makes the notated score important, just because it allows the description (even if only in principle) of whether the object in question is a token of a particular type. However, this *formulation* clearly requires too much, both in seeming to apply univocally to *all* performing arts (they can scarcely be expected to be exactly on a par, such that — for dance — only *one* notation system was used for all works) and, relatedly, in appearing to require (say) *every dance* to meet the same formal conditions: there seems good reason to suppose a more accurate formulation would apply notationality to particular artworks.

Of course, consonant with my general principles, this Thesis does not offer conditions individually necessary and jointly sufficient for same-work continuity: that is, it is not (part of) a *definition* of "same dancework". Rather, at best, it operates defeasibly (AJ pp. 33-34).

Moreover, this Thesis represents an idealisation since many danceworks are not, or were not, notated at all. The Thesis of Notationality will be of practical help only for those danceworks with an authoritative score: only then can one determine in practice whether two performances do or do not conform to the score. But the *insight* lies in treating dances as type-token objects (in Peirce's sense) and, then, seeing the notated score as offering the constraints from the type — that is, as making public and accessible what is, in principle, unavailable to us *directly*; namely, the abstract object. So that Thesis aims to make explicit (in a practical way) the constraints from the type. Then authentic performances should be seen as constrained in line with it even when there are no actual scores. (That is one reason the thesis operates only "in principle" and why the exposition of it is rough.)

If there was no established system of notation, and hence no scores recognised as authoritative by those knowledgeable about dance, should one conclude that, in the absence of authoritative scores, adherence to the Thesis of Notationality would preclude the re-performance of danceworks? Such a conclusion is unwarranted, for three reasons. First, the Thesis of Notationality addresses the question of whether two performances are of the same dancework, and answers in terms of their relation to a score. That is, the idea of notationality is only used to determine (given a score for a particular work) whether two performances are of that work. Where there is no score, applying the Thesis of Notationality gives no result in practice: there is no 'text' to which the performances did or did not conform. The objection, therefore, takes the scope of the Thesis of Notationality to be greater than it is. Second, an emphasis on notationality brings out an underlying characteristic of a performing art such as dance, deriving from the possibilities of the creation of dances. And those possibilities remain even without appropriate notation systems: as we might say, dance is *notational*. Finally, the Thesis of Notationality should be seen in its specificity: it is being advanced today, when such notation systems are in place and any dancework is notatable in principle. Therefore, although slight, the impact of Notationality advances our appreciation of the way the dance-type constrains its tokens.

Further, this idea draws on the possibility of notating what is *important* for that dance. Thus, suppose a particular movement of a dancer's arm is notated by specifying the position and pathway of the elbow. This typically determines the gesture, since the movement of the (rest of) the arm will follow from that elbow's movement; and, using a powerful notation system (such as Labanotation), far more could be specified, were it wanted. Hence, the score could specify what *should* be done, highlighting its *normativity* here. Moreover, the movements of *the dancework itself* always, in principle, under-determine the movements of a particular performance, such that other (slightly different) movements would also instantiate that dance. So one must choose which movements, or which features of a particular movement, to stress — in our example, to stress in the notation, although exactly the same point could apply to the teaching of the dance (say, to a new soloist).

But now the (necessary) under-determination of any performance of the dancework by the work itself is relevant to the issue of what dance is being performed on a particular occasion: the features stressed are the dancework's *crucial features*, those that the performance *must* involve — at least, if that performance is not to be criticised in this respect — while the other features remain 'open'. And, of course, dances in different styles might be specified to different degrees, either typically or in a particular case.

Moreover, in performance, one can certainly then deviate from that score — just as one can *deviate* from a musical score, while still playing it. Then the possibility of criticism of a particular performance for failing to do justice to some *crucial feature*[15] of the dance highlights again our contextualism: that this particular performance was defective in this one respect is compatible with its being uncontentiously a performance of that work (*pace* Goodman: LA p. 187); but — in a different example — a similar failure might *rule it out* as such-and-such a dance.

This Thesis of Notationality offers, at best, a (defeasible) necessary condition for dance identity, when there is a notated score. The lack of such scores is often one reason why the Thesis of Notationality cannot offer practical help. In such cases, one might hope for a (future) score, or see such a score as an idealisation — catching the constraints of the type. Further, the Thesis of Notationality places a certain weight on the particular notation system in question. As we saw, different notation systems might take as crucial different features of the dance; so that movements satisfying a Benesh score might not satisfy a Labanotation score, and vice versa. In response, we can only urge that reputable notation systems alone count here: that those who are knowledgeable about the art form decide what is and what is not reputable. Moreover, anyone rejecting the Thesis of Notationality must still recognise some constraints on possible performance preserve 'same-work' continuity. For it cannot in general be an open question whether or not performance A is the very same dance as performance B. It may be that there is no *one* answer here, applicable in all cases: it may be a case-by-case, dance-critical matter. Yet this cannot become a matter for individual decision, or a subjective matter, for that robs dance of all importance. No doubt there are borderline and problem cases here. But it must be possible for relevant considerations to be articulated, even if one cannot always arrive at a satisfactory conclusion. The Thesis of Notationality accommodates these difficulties, since the notation under-determines the performance, yet still constrains it. This is exactly what is required to avoid subjectivism, and to deliver some of the insights promised (see §4 above) — although some nettles must still be grasped.

§10. Providing a framework for debate?

But, clearly, the type-token distinction does not of itself decide what is to count as a token of what. The borderline between re-staging a dance and re-choreographing it to produce a different dance is difficult to draw exactly. In practice, then, it may be problematic to distinguish two cases. In the first, the threat is of *re-choreography*. For example, in Nureyev's staging of nineteenthth-century works such as *Swan Lake*, he "... has been at pains to reassert the place of the male dancer in these ballerina-vehicles" (Brinson & Crisp, 1980 p. 244): has he simply re-staged (giving the same work) or re-choreographed (making a new one)? Consider, say, the fate of the Bluebird *pas de deux* in Nureyev's versions of *Sleeping Beauty* from the 1970s. Although this role had brought Nureyev to prominence (or perhaps because of that), these versions always reduce the Bluebird, sometimes to the point of disappearing. In a practical case, it may be difficult to determine whether a particular performance is or is not a performance of a particular type. Re-choreography leads to a different work of art — its tokens are tokens of a different type. But to what degree can an example of re-choreography be recognised in practice? The Thesis of Notationality cannot help us here. That Nureyev made certain changes may well mean that, say, his work no longer satisfies a particular notated score for *Swan Lake* — in his version from the 1970s, for example (and predictably), the Prince's part got bigger. Perhaps this is indeed a piece of re-choreography. The other alternative would be to doubt the appropriateness of that score. And nothing said here allows us to decide between these alternatives[16]. But our point is to recognise them as the alternatives.

A slightly different issue arises with a work such as Mats Ek's *Swan Lake* (1987). In presenting this ballet (in the series "Dancemakers", BBC2, 1990), Judith Mackrell spoke of this as "a version of *Swan Lake*", as "updating", and as a "new interpretation" which "retold" the story. Although presented as a *new interpretation*, this is clearly some distance from standard performance of Swan Lake. In fact, this is most certainly a different artwork: not merely is the choreography different, and also differences in the story line and in the music. (For example, some music was specially written for the suite of national dances.) But, the 'world-view' of Ek's ballet is very different — in particular, much less romantic (see below). Given these differences, one might wonder why this work has anything to do with *Swan Lake* (in the Petipa and Ivanov version). Is it really to be described, as Ek himself said, as simply the use of "a new dramatic 'language'"?

In fact, the possibility of our making sense of Ek's innovations in this ballet will involve relating it to previous work — there will be connections to Ek's other work, and to the tradition in which he choreographs, as well as a relation to a *romantic ballet* tradition, with whose conventions he is certainly playing (for example, in his 'dumpy' swans, some of whom are male). For any interpretative understanding of any dance depends on the tradition within which the work was created and has been understood — even when in rebellion against such traditions — where this tradition should be seen, first, as integral to any satisfactory 'making sense' of the dance and, second, as operating both as a 'wider' tradition within which the work is created and as a 'narrower' tradition formed (roughly) by the artist's other works. So identifying a different dancework — as in this case — does not preclude comparisons, even comparisons to (in this case) other *Swan Lakes*.

This case is also revealing in allowing comment on the difference(s) between different 'tellings' of the same tale: that works of art with the same story may still be radically different works of art. The absurdity of supposing something different is brought out by Betty Redfern (1979 p. 18). If one thought otherwise, she notes:

> There would be no need to see, for example, Martha Graham's *Night Journey*, since we could get the same experience by listening to Stravinsky's *Oedipus Rex*, and neither of them need really have bothered since Sophocles already 'said' it all in *Oedipus Tyrannus* centuries before.

So it is important to recognise the diversity which is possible within a background set, in this case, by elements of music and story. One basic story should not be equated with one artwork.

This discussion suggests a productive framework for debates here. As a starting place, dance critic Jann Parry (2002 p. 14) commented that:

> [w]hat you want from your first *Swan Lake* is a production that doesn't mess with the music, the story or the flock of identical swan-maidens in white tutus. Once you know the conventions, the madder caprices of directors and designers can be indulged or deplored to your heart's content.

Her point is that one's understanding of *Swan Lake* (that is, *Swan Lake* the ballet) will be facilitated in this way, indicating the *logical* status of the 'no frills' *Swan Lake*. It provides a background against which later innovations can take place, while still being *Swan Lake*: hence, in contrast to the two standard categories of debate above (see CDE pp. 229-230). So the framework would be:

- 'central' *Swan Lake*, typified by our 'no frills, but plenty of tutus' Ivanov and Petipa version.

- '*Re-staging*', as a way to say "yes" to the question, "Is this the same dance as one I saw last night?" *despite* radical differences.

- '*New choreography*' as a way of saying "no": and here I instanced Mats Ek's superb *Swan Lake* (1987). (On balance, the Nureyev was *not* new choreography!)

Then resolving the identity-questions for a putative performance of *Swan Lake* amounts to locating it on this 'map'.

Thus, the Matthew Bourne *Swan Lake* is not especially radical: despite its "radical gender twist ... [in which] Odette becomes a male swan and Odile a louche freebooter" (Mackrell, 1997 p. 32), conceptually it seems a fairly plain re-telling. To dispute such a conclusion is at least to engage in that debate, with the outcome placing it in any of the camps just mentioned. Those seem critical considerations, to be resolved within the Republic of Dance (see especially Chapter Eleven §§4-6) — and all such resolutions need not be once-and-for-all.

It may help to see this framework in action. For, in contrasting Mats Ek both with Matthew Bourne and with our 'central' *Swan Lake*, my points might seem to concern (say) the differences in narrative structure of these danceworks. Yet they actually concern the *expressiveness* or the *meaning* of each dancework — what is embodied in (among other things) that narrative. Now, at its conclusion, our 'central' *Swan Lake* (say, Ivanov and Petipa) *almost* has a happy ending. As one might put it, in this world a happy ending is *possible* but, regrettably, does not occur. So it is no *accident* that this is sometimes called "Romantic Ballet" — this is a romantic conception of the human psyche: a romantic world-view where, but for a minor mishap, there would be a 'happy ever after' ending. As a parallel here, consider *Romeo and Juliet*: if Juliet had woken up a few seconds earlier, before Romeo killed himself, they would have lived *happily ever after*. Of course, this is not the outcome in this case; but this possibility is crucial to the world-view of the play (and of the ballet). Then Mats Ek's *Swan Lake* takes place in a quite different world, embodying a quite different world-view. At the end of Ek's *Swan Lake*, the Prince marries the Swan-princess (which might *seem* to promise a happy ending) but, at the end of her train, is the Black Swan-princess — he has married them both! This is why, in this world, "... even with swans, everything is not black or white" (CDE p. 80). For we might reasonably expect that the Prince is in for the usual mixture of highs and lows of emotion from his marriage, rather than 'happily every after'.

Does this show, conclusively, that this is a *different* artwork from the Ivanov and Petipa one, rather than just a 're-choreographed' version of the original? Well, my point is just to stress the differences here; and, fundamentally, the differences in the picture of the world each develops. For this might form the basis for an argument in the Republic of Dance.

At this point, my rejection (as a *new* work) of the Matthew Bourne *Swan Lake* should seem principled; for, just as Mats Ek's choreography inhabits a world-view fundamentally different from that of our standard case (the Ivanov and Petipa), the Matthew Bourne *Swan Lake* seems to me — and hence is arguably — cast in the original world-view: of course, what constitutes 'happy ever after' may be different, but its *possibility* is still central to the unfolding of the tragedy.

In summary, on this view, dance's notationality remains important despite some dances presently lacking notated scores: some just *are* not notated, some (perhaps) could not be. But notationality still suggests a conceptualisation of a relationship between the dancework and its performances, exploiting the possibilities of creating dances by creating notated scores. In emphasising notationality, one emphasises the connection between the nature of dances and the character of scores. When there were no established system of notation, and hence no 'texts' recognised as authoritative by those knowledgeable about dance, danceworks were still in principle notatable: they were (still) abstract objects. Having appropriate notation systems, danceworks today are not only notatable *in principle*, but actually amenable to notation.

§11. Conclusion

This Chapter has presented some issues involved in accurately characterising the relation of the dance itself (*Swan Lake*) to particular performances of it. A type-token analysis was suggested, as roughly reflecting — while potentially clarifying — the practice of discussing danceworks. At its heart, it recognised that danceworks, as performables, can be instantiated by very different performances, performances still of the *very same* dancework. Although they all instantiate, say, *Swan Lake*, such performances will not be indistinguishable; and certainly not artistically indistinguishable. In elaboration, an abstract Thesis of Notationality was proposed, since a notated score offered something towards the normativity of a recipe for such-and-such a dance (say, *Swan Lake*). The original version of that account was misleading both in seeming to *define* 'same dancework' and in failing to be specific to dances. Recognising its defeasibility (there, if not sufficiently stressed, in the original formulation) allows its subtle modification in the current reading.

However, the modified 'Thesis of Notationality' account may still be criticised, first, for placing too much weight on notation, and hence underplaying the role of the choreographer; and, second, for misunderstanding the nature of notation partly by a failure to recognise that, for today's dance, danceworks are notated (if at all), not by choreographers in the course of *making* the dances, but by notators after the fact. These topics will be taken up in the next Chapter.

Chapter Three

Authenticity in performance, work-identity and practice

"I was watching a ballet at City Centre ... they were doing the *Dying Swan*, and there was a rumour that some bookmakers had drifted into town from upstate New York ... Apparently there's a lot of money bet on the Swan to live." [from the Woody Allen stand-up routine "Love Story"[1]]

§1. Same-work continuity and the Thesis of Notationality?

A central issue identified throughout this text as vexing the philosophy of dance concerns the *identity* of danceworks; or, if this is different, the *authenticity* of performances as a particular dancework — say, *Swan Lake*[2]. For we all grant that performances can differ from one another while still being uncontentiously *Swan Lake*. Indeed, this possibility is built into the idea of a *performable* — a work performable on more than one occasion — and manifest in the way that one rehearsal can 'apply' to a whole week's performances (UD p. 93). Chapter Two considered some ways to describe these facts: can we say more? Since our topic here is the *same-work continuity* of such *performables*, a major constraint on our account here will be that (numerical) identity be retained despite significant differences among particular performances. (And we might equally have asked about the credentials of a *Dying Swan* where the Swan lives!)

But how does one *create* such a *performable*? Since performables are *abstract objects*, there are, in effect, two strategies (see Wollheim, 1973 pp. 357-358): one makes the dancework (in our case) either (a) by making a recipe, which here is a score or some such, such that if one conforms to the recipe one makes the dance — of course, defeasibly. Or, (b) by creating a performance-token — it might be called a 'first performance', with the scare-quotes precisely to prevent anyone thinking that it had to be a first *public* performance. But producing a performance-token (perhaps only in the rehearsal room, and perhaps only in segments) allows the production of other performance-tokens — we know it does, because that is what happens most of the time.

One strategy recognises that — although dances were chiefly made by constructing a 'first performance' — they could indeed *in principle* be constructed (as most musical works are) by writing a score. So ask oneself for a substantial answer to the question, "How does one recognise the constraints from the type, so as to produce same-work continuity? (Or, more simply, so as to perform the work you are aiming at?)". In reply, I had urged "... a relationship between the type and the notated score" (UD p. 97): that, at least in most cases, an adequate *notated score* for a dancework offered a way to identify constraints on the movement patterns from the *abstract object* that was the dance (the *type*) — treating dances as type-token objects. So that the work so constrained would — once actualised in performance — be (say) *Swan Lake*. That is, the relation between performances here was, at least roughly, one of *numerical identity* — these were the very same work, *Swan Lake*, despite differences among the performances. This combination of type-token (or multiple) with numerical identity was distinctive: it became the Thesis of Notationality, discussed in Chapter Two.

Writing in the late 1980s, I predicted — on the basis of what seemed good evidence — that dance notation would become ubiquitous, rather on the model of musical notation: all makers and performers understand it; and most works are composed by using it (that is, by writing a score). There were three or four competing notations for dance: but *any* of them could be accorded a significant place in the life of choreographers and dancers.

Yet the world has not fitted in with my predictions: almost no dances *are* made by writing scores; if there is a score for a dance, it is usually written by a notator, puzzled by whether to inscribe what the choreographer *says* to do or what the dancers *actually* do, given that these often diverge. Moreover, since some dances were not notated, one cannot *in fact* extract, in every case, the constraints of the type from the score.

This lack of scores shows that dance can indeed get by without scores: and that is fundamental to how my earlier remark about the relationship between the type and the notated score are read. For it can only mean that, when we have the score, we have access through it to the type — and then the complexity of such a relationship needs a great deal more commentary (begun here). For instance, it seems only contingently true both that the dancework did or did not have a notated score and that it *was* created by writing that score (assuming it was). Of course, this truth is contingent, since the work might have been created in another way — through what was called, above, a 'first performance'. But *notationality* (the possibility of notation) should be emphasised here, rather than any extant notated score. In the case imagined, it is not merely contingently true that our choreographer, in creating that recipe (in the form of a score), created a *performable*, a work performable on more than one occasion; and an abstract object. Yet, equally, a performable could also have been generated in the other manner — by creating the 'first performance'. Since most dances *get by* without a score, what should be said in connection with the authenticity of performances?

Further, two specific criticisms of the original 'Thesis of Notationality' account were forthcoming: first, that it placed too much weight on notation, and hence failed to do justice to the role of the choreographer: second, that it misunderstood the nature of notation partly by failing to recognise that, for today's dance, danceworks are notated (if at all), not by choreographers in the course of *making* the dances, but by notators after the fact. Yet a number of other matters must be considered, to explore the issue, before these criticisms can be approached.

§2. Dance is instantiated only through performance

The differences among performances, differences compatible with those performance being of the very same dancework (say, *Swan Lake*), have been acknowledged. But that generates part of the problem. For how is such identity-in-difference to be explained? How is it accommodated?

As we saw (Chapter Two §2), the dancework itself (the abstract object) *under-determines* performances. So the performance one sees is under-determined by, say, the score alone (whoever complete the score) since only the instantiation of that score, on the bodies of dancers, counts as seeing the dance. As with the linguistic parallel, the *statement* I make in saying so-and-so (or uttering such-and-such words) is an abstract object in just this sense: "... the statement itself is a 'logical construction' out of the making of statements" (Austin, 1975 p. 1 note).

Clearly, many differences between performances are planned: they reflect the way *this* company stages the dance, in contrast to the way *that* company does it. Or they reflect different performers' interpretations of particular roles or sections of the dance. But a more fundamental difference here more or less guarantees that there will be differences between performances: namely, the different performers. Then one always sees some dancer or other in each role. So every performance reflects, in some way or other, features of the dancer(s) involved — not only of the dancers, of course: but centrally of them. For differences between performances also reflect the impact of different performance spaces, of different companies (with differing technical prowess) — and even just of a different *night*. Any of these may have an impact on what movements, and such like, get performed to instantiate (say) Christopher Bruce's *Ghost Dances* (1981): for instance, differences on Sunday might reflect performers tired from Saturday night's performance.

For this reason, a famous dance critic, asked to list his favourite dances, replied by listing performances of particular works, rather than the works themselves. One motivation for such a response is easily discerned: the features of, for instance, the London Contemporary Dance Theatre performance on, say, 15th May 1991 of Christopher Bruce's *Ghost Dances* (1981) at Sadler's Wells Theatre in London are accessible in a way that those for *Ghost Dances* (itself) are not. For the danceworks under-determine performances simply because those danceworks themselves are abstract objects. The question, "What are the properties of the dancework?" cannot be answered for most purposes except by reference to occurrences in *this* performance or *that* one — and, where both are permissible, only by tolerating either. No doubt some features of the dancework can be granted independently of any performance of it ("No *Hamlet* without the Prince of Denmark"), but most are transparent only through some performance. So the dance itself admits of various property-ascriptions: it had this many dancers on Tuesday, but a different number on Wednesday. And so on for more important features. Hence, in any place where performances may differ, while still uncontentiously of that dancework, features of the work that differ between performances are typically those left 'transparent' by that abstract object. (Or they may involve errors in performance.) And the *degree* of difference consistent with same-work continuity varies from genre to genre and from work to work. The colours of costumes or the number in the *corps de ballet*, for example, is typically under-determined in precisely this sense. The dance critic above was rebelling against *that* fact. For in a particular performance the features or details are complete, in the sense that all the places where the work itself under-determines its performances have been made concrete — as they will in typical performances. Further, the possibility of these different 'concretisations' of the dancework is among the ways of explaining differences between performances of the very same dancework.

Of course, one might quibble here: like the musician, the dancer confronts *something* by engaging with the score — if he/she can read (say) Labanotation; and hence can confront the work seemingly 'un-concretised'. But, equally, the person who sees only the musical score has not really encountered the work; and the same might well be said for dance! Moreover — just to be clear — the idea of *difference among performances* is central to the conception of a performing art as composed of *performables*; works that can be re-performed on another occasion. So one cannot in general refuse to grant that such differences are consistent with same-dancework continuity; although one can (of course) argue about the *degree* of difference that is permissible, given that we end-up with a performance of *the very same* dancework.

A revealing complication follows: for one must consider what the dancers *should* do, not just what the dancers actually do. That is, our discussion of the authenticity of a particular performance requires a *normative* dimension. For which of the features of the performance we *see* — danced by this company on that occasion — are (crucial) features of the dance, such that a performance which failed to include them might be criticised? Which are the contingencies of *this* performance? Suppose that compliance with our notated score will generate the dancework. Now suppose that a performance uncontentiously of that work fails to comply with our score — clearly the score includes some constraints not *crucial* for the work. Then dance-performances using this score will reflect some features crucial to the dance (perhaps) but also some other features. Nor is this case a mere philosopher's fantasy: it is precisely the situation with the Stepanov score for *Swan Lake*! Although performances which instantiate that score will be *Swan Lake*, some uncontentious performances of *Swan Lake* will fail to instantiate it. In my language, this is not an adequate score for *Swan Lake* just because it does not identify *solely* the constraints from the dancework itself, but only for some performances of that work.

This in turn suggests that our concerns with authenticity of performances cannot be answered simply by an account of what movements dancers in the past used in performing that dancework (or even by a score which did this). Rather, something *normative* over performances is needed — as a slogan, this might seem a search for a *recipe* (or something like it).

§3.   The powers of specific dancers are relevant

Now another complication can be introduced: for much dance today, in being made on the bodies of particular dancers, reflect closely the powers and capacities of those dancers. Then what might — for other works — be mere contingencies of performance seem here *crucial* features (in my sense) of these works (that is, features whose absence from a performance would justify criticism). Yet one must go carefully, to avoid urging that, as a matter of logic, *only* dancer X can perform this work — even if that were the contingent truth at a certain time. Thus, Petipa is widely claimed to have put the thirty-two fouettés in Act III of *Swan Lake* (1895) because he had a dancer, Pierina Legnani, who could do this, at a time when few could (compare Mackrell, 1997 p. 7). Suppose that, at that time, *only* Legnani could perform this segment of the dance: still, the requirement is only for a dancer *able* to do so. If there were only one, that would just be a practical matter. And any other requirements here should be regarded similarly. Thus, Christopher Bruce choreographed a role in *Black Angels* for Lucy Burge taking her as "a dancer of the earth", to utilise her "... richer, more sensual way of movement" (in contrast to the "dancer of the air", Catherine Becque: see Austin, 1976 p. 115). So, for that role one would need — or certainly hope for — another "dancer of the earth". That may be a hard criterion to put on the job advertisement! For it requires a *quality* of dance that may be (fairly) easy to recognise in performers — and especially in those lacking it — but much harder to describe.

This fundamental idea is most easily characterised *roughly* in terms of, say, performances for the piano. How does a merely *technical* performance of, for instance, Schönberg's opus 19 differ from an expressive one? To recognise one of the performances as "technical" is to grant ... well, what exactly? As a first thought, one grants that the performer sounded the right notes in the right order. But both did this! Then the difference between this performance and the expressive one *seems* not to reside in what tones are sounded, but simply in what each performer *feels*. Yet what the performer feels is beside the point *if* it does not make him or her *do* something different — if it is not reflected in, say, the pressure on the piano keys. But when it *is* reflected in differences in what the performer *did* (say, in differential pressure on the keys of the piano), we are responding to *that* difference in contrasting these two performances. So, contrary to our first thought, the performances were *not* of the same notes played in the same manner; rather, there were differences in the performance — and these differences were acknowledged in taking *this* performance to be expressive, *that* one to be merely technical.

This case is complicated, of course, because one cannot always describe the differences here in any more detail than that, contrasting the technical with the expressive. Sometimes this is called an *imperceptible* difference: that description is revealing only because it is completely wrong — for we perceived the difference well enough; our problem resided in *describing* it more exactly. For, here, a general account of expressive performance is not possible: what is needed in *this* case can differ from what is needed in *that* one. An anecdote from Tolstoi's *What is Art?* ([1895] 1930 p. 199; quoted Beardsmore, 1971 p. 12) captures the point: in it, a painter makes some small changes, and "... the poor dead study [of his student] immediately became animated. 'Why you only touched it a *wee* bit and it is quite another thing', said one of the pupils." The painter replies, "Art begins where the *wee* bit begins" — and that "wee bit" could be exemplified, not described.

In practice, then, the *normativity* required to explain authentic performances of a dancework — which a notated score might have provided — must also accommodate any *crucial* contribution from dancers, beyond their simply instantiating the dancework. And such contributions might be very difficult (or even impossible) to describe.

§4.   Some limitations of video recordings

Attention to notated scores, as urged here, might seem unnecessary. Some theorists imagine that, say, a video recording might provide an alternative to a score; for instance, in preserving that dancework. This might seem a neat technological solution to the problem of dancework-authenticity.

Here, we can remind ourselves that a recipe can be used to generate the object for which it *is* a recipe (say, the dundee cake) but also to explain why what one has *is* a dundee cake; namely, that this is the recipe one followed. Similarly, a choreographer might use video (or a similar visual recording) as a kind of notes for what went on in a rehearsal room; say, to remind the choreographer of what has been decided. This would have no bearing on our question about authenticity.

Now consider a video *recording* of a dance — the sort of thing that might be made 'after the fact', effectively capturing a particular performance. Which features of the dancework as videoed are *crucial*, such that one would teach them to the next generation of dancers wanting to master this dance? And which are simply the contingencies of *this* performance? At best, the video preserves all and only the features of *this* performance. To concentrate on it is to lose the importance of the actual *performing*. In this sense Arlene Croce (1982 p. 103) urges that "[m]agnetic tape is making us indifferent to the actual moment of an event; it's destroying 'the art of the moment'". To clarify, imagine videos of the powerful, expressive performances of Glenn Gould playing the pianoworks of Schönberg. Despite the power of the playing, such videos could not simply be offered without comment to the next generation of Schönberg interpreters. First, Gould 'misses' a large number of the notes as reflected in the score (say, compared with Pollini); second, we do not want future interpreters to hum through the performance, as Gould did. So we must be in a position to explain to those succeeding us what are the *key* features of the work, as reflected in Gould's performance, and what are the irrelevancies of *this* performance — the sort of thing a young performer might profitably reflect on, but not *just* emulate. This situation recurs with respect to all videoing of artworks: at best, recordings offer a way to preserve features of a *particular* performance of, say, a dance. (A sophisticated set-up, with cameras from more than one direction, and others concentrating on close-up, might be needed, even to achieve that.) But even our most sophisticated video still records the *whole* performance! So it alone cannot discriminate the *dancework's* features from those merely contingently features of *this* performance.

Peter Brook's *The Tragedy of Carmen* well-exemplifies the problem of extracting *the work itself* from performances: Brook deployed three different leading ladies and the same number of leading men: but, "[w]hen after a triumphal international tour Brook came to film the production he insisted on filming all three" (Kustow, 2005 pp. 255-256). For each contained important elements not shared with the others, so that watching only one omitted something central.

Suppose, then, our dancer-in-training is offered a number of such videos, to move her understanding forward by comparing them. Although clearly better than relying on one such video, this procedure generates at least two problems. First, any of the performances may have left out something important. Hence our dancer — looking just for commonalities — may be misled. Second, features not *crucial* to the work may be shared by *these* performers or companies. (Recall that 'crucial' features are those whose absence was a source of criticism of a performance.) Our dancer-in-training has no method for sorting out either of such cases. So the recording of a performance, while certainly better than nothing, cannot alone offer us the required insight into the abstract object that is the dance itself — into the *type*, as I have put it. What the recording lacks is, of course, precisely the *normativity* of a typical score. Thus the discussion here is, in a sense, a defence of notationality as the best way to capture the normativity of the type.

Perhaps I am being too dogmatic: perhaps, *in context*, these constraints on work-identity might be generated from a performance, by those who knew enough about, for instance, performance traditions to 'extract' those constraints — as Wagner[3] extracted the *whole* work from just the first-violin part for Beethoven's later quartets. That is, someone who knew enough might be able to move from what he/she was *told* to do as dancer *to* what was needed for a performance to count as of the same work. But such collateral knowledge cannot just be *assumed*. Further, the claim to achieve this must itself be tested: *would* the outcome be a performance of that same dance (say, *Swan Lake*) or not? Better, *when* would it be *Swan Lake*, when not? What would the *compliance-conditions* here be? Our first answer lies in the constraints from the work itself, the *type*. Yet, having no direct access to the compliance conditions it provides, where else might one look? In particular, does one have to comply with a score? If so, one returns to the centrality of the score. If not, one must explain from where to discern, in the performance before us, knowledge of the compliance conditions for the work.

Of course, in the case above, Gould's humming while he played is not an important part of his performance. But from where does this insight arise? Not from that performance of course. And comparing Gould's performance with others only shows the humming present in one and lacking in others. Rather, the insight draws on collateral knowledge — say, about what is usual for Schönberg; and then we would need some reason to take the artist as not behaving *unusually* here!

Now a choreographer might begin from such images and, using a computerised editing suite, produce a video of what he/she hoped to achieve in the future, to then function like our recipe (compare Tharp, 2009 p. 65): to perform such-and-such a dance, follow accurately the movement patterns from video — as we might say, the movement patterns those images prescribe. Then that fact would explain why this was indeed dancework such-and-such. Yet this procedure, too, inherits the problems of videoing the work: it does not specify the appropriate normativity here, since one does not know *why* features of the movements videoed are crucial.

§5.   Normativity, performance, and compliance with a score

Since scores are, of course, not causally compelling, some performances might comply rather badly. There is clearly also a lot to be said about *what it is* to comply with a notation. Thus, following Wolterstorff, (1980 pp. 54-58), one might invoke the idea of a *norm-kind*, applied to the *types* — the abstract objects, we are taking danceworks to be — in an attempt to show that one can comply with such types (or kinds) more or less well. Hence, a token (a performance) conforming less well than some other would still count as a *token* of that *type*. And, as is widely recognised, the constraint Goodman (1968 p. 187) suggested — total compliance — leads to unacceptable conclusions. But, of course, only this condition can be specified at all exactly. While one can at least *identify* total compliance (and offer *some* rationale for it, as Goodman does), one cannot begin to justify, say, 65% compliance *as opposed to* 66%. So there seems the potential for a slippery slope in this respect, if one aims at anything more precise by way of specification of compliance conditions.

Still, two or three related concerns here apply to dance. First, any solution should conform (at least roughly) to what the dancers do in practice. So it should not be unduly abstract, if that can be avoided. For the *reason* to consider conditions of compliance is just that, in most cases, dance companies manage this difficulty with minimal effort — hence performances *are* typically authentic, even if we cannot readily say how this is achieved. Second, any claim here, ascribing *this* dance-identity (say, as *Swan Lake*) to this performance, is *defeasible*: one says what would *usually* apply, with the built-in proviso that the satisfaction of 'recognised heads of exception' would defeat the ascription. Third, any conclusion will be occasion-sensitive: in *this* context, such-and-such will count as *adequate* compliance with the score; in another context, it might not. (So, roughly, one point is to ask *why* one wants the compliance: see UD pp. 108-109.) To give the (easier?) music example, in my class of trainee-pianists, Glenn Gould's performance of Schönberg's opus 19 would not count as compliant: it involves too many 'missed notes' — and my aim in this class is showing the trainee which *notes* to sound (which tones to produce). But, when training my emergent concert pianist (or when I want to listen to an expressive performance of Schönberg's opus 19), the Glenn Gould might be exactly what I wanted: and then I count it as (sufficiently) *compliant* with the score — or I would not be treating it as that work!

Looking across to dance, one sees that no abstract specification of compliance conditions could be satisfactory. For one must recognise (as for music) the occasion-specific, defeasible practices of those in the danceworld. So we will not be able to *write down*, or articulate, such compliance-conditions. Each case, and each context, may suggest different requirements of the compliance conditions for same-work continuity. Hence there can be no *general* account. Still, we are committed to there *being* compliance conditions in any case we chose — that is, in any case specified closely enough. This obligation is partly theoretical: that the work can be *re-*performed on another occasion (on the basis of this score) means that there must be *some* ways to rule out competitors which do not, in this context, count as such a *re-performance*; this would (then) be explained as a failure of compliance with the score. Moreover, requiring that other occasions be understood partly in terms of *this* one — which has adequate compliance — is recognising that the constraints are *local* in ways previously articulated. Equally, there is a practical element here: when I show up in the rehearsal room to begin to teach this dance to a new cohort of dancers, there must be *some things* I am holding on to, in this context — so that we end up with *Ghost Dances* and not *Swan Lake*! And to say that the dancers' movements must cohere, in some way, with those "some things" is just another way of talking about compliance conditions here for, say, *Ghost Dances* — where this means "*Ghost Dances* in this (sort of) context".

Notice the variety among what counts as a score, for our purposes, so as to avoid taking too *narrow* a view of it. As we recognised (Chapter Two §7), I tend to write primarily in terms of scores in systems of movement notation such as Labanotation, no doubt partly because I hope the long time spent mastering that system was not wasted! But these are by no means the only styles of score that could count here. The idea of a *recipe* for a performance of that work nicely captures all that is required — and, in particular, the normativity that implies. Thus, if certain rules (such as those discussed in Chapter Four for Elaine Summers' chance-based dancework *Instant Choice*: see Banes, 1993 pp. 47-49) operate normatively, so that movement sequences following those rules constitute a performance of that very dancework, then those rules would count (for me) as a score for that work.

To repeat, some performances may comply rather badly with a particular score. But *if* such-and-such is indeed a score for the work at issue, it cannot be *optional* whether or not, in performing that work, one complies with it. Suppose one asks what the *crucial* (as opposed to non-crucial or inessential) features of the work are. If the notation specifies non-crucial features (without showing them to be optional), then it is poor notation, for that reason (see below: §6). So that, if one imagines the question of notation-adequacy being raised on a particular occasion, *one* answer seems to me a necessary truth (if an unrevealing one): if work-token X differs from work-token Y, then either the differences are within the 'tolerance' of same-work continuity or they are not. If they are not, these are different works (because not tokens of the same type). And the Thesis of Notationality offers one — defeasible — way to determine whether or not they do differ in this way.

Further, finding that a notated score fits one work-token and not another, where both are indeed the work at issue (say, *Swan Lake*), just shows that *this* score isn't suitable to characterise the work. Your performance could fail to fulfill the score without being a different work ... which is a reason to criticise that score.

Any *adequate* score is bound to preserve the key features of the dance — that is a theoretical consequence of its adequacy, seen in terms of its relation to the creation of abstract objects. If this is granted, an adequate score would contain key features (if I knew how to look for them). Then, in practice, a score treated as *adequate* could be interrogated for such features.

Roughly, then, the adequacy, or otherwise, of a notated score is determined by that score's *usefulness* — will it offer us the constraints *from the type?* That is, does it specify the minimum movement content for a satisfactory performance of, say, *Swan Lake?* If so, any performance purporting to be of that work but failing to comply with this score can be criticised for that failure; or, in the extreme case, dismissed as not being that dancework (although, to repeat, all such 'moves' are understood *defeasibly*). This will be our *adequate score*. So the conditions for adequacy of scores cannot be articulated *independently* of the use to which the score might be put. In particular, we will not progress by looking across to the *nature* of the notation system (see Chapter Four); or to the *degree* to which the movements of the piece are made determinate by the score — as long as the movements are specified as closely as they *need* to be, for same-work continuity. And this may obviously differ for different danceworks.

§6.   An adequate score?
In this context, the adequacy of scores can *appear* to receive a stipulative definition — that any score not adequate for *my* purposes is dismissed as an inadequate score. But, in fact, the debate is a real one. Thus, is the Stepanov

score *adequate* for *Swan Lake*? It is agreed on all sides [a] that performing in line with it will generate *Swan Lake*, and [b] that performances which do not follow it — or go against it — also generate *Swan Lake*. So clearly this score does not uniquely identify *Swan Lake*; in my jargon, it does not mirror the constraints from the type[4].

To elaborate this case: first (explaining [a] above), performances which follow the Stepanov score are performances of *Swan Lake*. Someone might deny this, mentioning other reasons for finding that score limited. But those aspects of the score play no part in this discussion. So such reservations for those reasons are beside the point. Perhaps it would be clearer to say that, for the elements the Stepanov score covers, the performance conforms to it. But then that caveat would have to be repeated in the other case, where again reference is just to those aspects covered by the Stepanov score, not to other aspects of the dance. This fact seems incontrovertible, given that this score was developed from a performance of *Swan Lake*. Then, second (explaining [b] above), performances of *Swan Lake* often (indeed, regularly) deviate from the Stepanov score in respect of those aspects it covers. For example all performances of the Ivanov and Petipa 'version' of 1895 exemplify this point: they deviate from the Stepanov score in the relevant respects.

In practice these two options can be consistent. Suppose that the score requires using seven swan-maidens, and we use eight: that counts as the same dancework (in some favoured example), but goes against the score. Yet a performance following the score (and only using seven swan-maidens) would also be of that work. This small difference shows how the sorts of difference between performances uncontentiously of the same dancework allows that one performance conforms to a particular score, while another (still that work) does not. And, after all, any score *determinate* on such a point will be susceptible to this kind of deviation. Moreover, this case suggests an explanation of this (namely, that the score is for an *interpretation*, not for the work itself).

When one looks clearly at this case, its conclusions seem right: that score is for the *Stepanov-score interpretation* (perhaps Drigo's interpretation) of *Swan Lake*, rather than for *Swan Lake* itself. So the constraints it typically invokes go beyond just those of the type. Moreover, a parallel is suggested: a score just for *Pollini's interpretation* of Schönberg's opus 19. Yes, it is a score for opus 19, *but* ... both more (and less) than just that.

Now, an adequate notated score would provide an important basis for deciding what to do in order to stage, say, *Swan Lake*. By definition, such a score includes what was *crucial* to the work (the crucial features from the type, as one might put it). Practitioners who thought of it this way might pay a different attention to the dance when they learn it (for dancers) or set it (for choreographers). On that supposition, when the work itself was set but not notated in the process there would be less room for debate as to what is or what is not crucial. And, recall, "crucial" here may just mean that its absence would be a reason to criticise a performance.

But a poor performance of a dancework is still a performance of that work — perhaps, until it gets just too bad. (Whether this is a performance of such-and-such a work is a matter for dispute, with the answer not obvious.) And not all performances with less than full compliance are poor: pianist Glenn Gould's powerful, expressive performances of Schönberg's piano music (some of which are 'captured' in recordings) are often further from the score than less powerful renditions.

Relatedly, there also *appears* to be the issue of one's *attitude* to the score: thus, even a very experienced notator (such as Ann Hutchinson-Guest) might regard the score she has — perhaps even the score she has written — in a more relaxed way. That is, she might happily set aside aspects of that score when she was 'setting' the dance: but this just amounts to treating the particular score as not, after all, *authoritative* — or, in my language, as not after all an *adequate* score. So that the constraints of the type alone are not to be found from this score. And that is what (say) Ann Hutchinson-Guest implicitly acknowledges in setting it aside in this way. Hence her behaviour here implicitly grants my view of the *possibility* of (some) scores, by not finding that possibility *actualised* in this one.

Moreover, there has always been flexibility in what counts as the same dance — and hence, for abstract purposes, as *same-work* continuity. Thus:

> In ... [*Swan Lake*] Petipa ... gave a lot of dancing to a minor character, the Prince's friend Benno, since Pavel Gerdt, who was the Prince in the first performances, was getting too stiff and short-winded to partner his ballerina and to dance all the steps himself. With today's Olympic-standard male dancers, the Prince dances every step he can get hold of, and Benno may not even get a mention in the cast list, his role is so reduced. (Mackrell, 1997 p. 7[5])

But Benno's eclipse does not typically result in a different dancework.

Further, the adequacy or otherwise of a score might itself be debated: in some contexts, quite ordinary scores might count as adequate, seen in this light. That would be a judgement of the Republic of Dance (or some sub-set of it). For, if we can do all we need with a particular score, such that all performances that satisfy it are *Swan Lake*, and any that fail to satisfy it are not, so that there is no dispute here (and no misunderstanding), we have all that could possibly be needed.

Of course, later stagers might become dissatisfied with that score. Then they might see it as just a score for one interpretation, rather than for the dancework itself. Or they might feel that it left open too many features of the dance. They might then offer a scholarly argument against our chosen score, and in favour of some competitor. My points here are only (a) that such a debate is quite possible, so the 'adequacy' of scores is not fixed; and (b) that other claims to revise the 'official' version (or to reconstruct a dance with no 'official version') draw on the same resources.

How else might a performance of a work from the past be authoritative? Recent reconstructions of works by Siobhan Davies were justified to me in two ways: first, that Davies sanctions them; second, that the restaging process was managed by two of her company dancers[6]. But these are two worthless conditions! As general rules, one should never rely on memory if it one can be avoided; and the claims of authorities should be always disputed. And never more than in examples like this. First, one central character is the person who, in remembering the dance, remembers it from his/her perspective — this typically differs from the choreographer's! Then the two conditions just raised *clash*: choreographer and cast-member may differ. (If there were a reason for *always* preferring one over the other, both need never have been mentioned.)

The priority of the choreographer (as dance-maker) may seem automatic here. A second consideration shows that is not correct. For the choreographer, looking at the 'new' performance, may like what he/she sees — while still remaining within same-work limits as guaranteed by under-determination by the type. So one something *different* might yet have some credentials. The project, after all, is not just reconstruction, but the staging of *that very* dance. For she might respond as Ann Hutchinson-Guest reported for Jerome Robbins:

> ... asking to see a section he had choreographed the day before and finding it unsatisfactory, he would be far more likely to say, 'What *are* you doing? I never gave you that' than 'Was that what I did yesterday? I don't like it. I want to change it'. (Jowitt, 2004 p. 117)

In any case, the constraint here is the dancework's features, rather than those the choreographer ascribes. Then the making of a new dance must be ruled-out (see below): that cannot be left to the *choreographer's* judgement. Yet neither can one *automatically* trust a score: as Ann Hutchinson-Guest elaborated (see Chapter Two §7), one's conundrum may be whether to follow the choreographer's demonstration or what (predictably) generations of ballet-trained dancers *would* do. In this climate, both stager and dancer have roles in turning score into performance, and in arguing (implicitly or explicitly) that *this* performance is indeed of *that* dancework; that it meets the normativity-constraints — which it might in satisfying a particular notated score sufficiently closely. Lacking such a score cannot make the job *easier*! For the score offers insight into *normative* constraints on work-continuity.

§7.   Some issues for the 'Thesis of Notationality' account

Many of the comments thus far in this Chapter reflect two related criticisms of my earlier account of dance-identity (noted above): first, that the place of notation was overrated, thereby underrating the role of the choreographer's intentions. For my emphasis on the virtues of the score seemed to leave no obvious role for the choreographer. Then, second, that I misunderstood the nature of notation partly by failing to recognise that, for today's dance, danceworks are notated (if at all), not by choreographers in the course of *making* the dances, but by notators after the fact.

Now, I certainly *intended* that the choreographer's role be given due weight for the dancework's meaning[7], since (as it were) the presence of the *choreographer's intelligence* within the work is fundamental. That was visible (for me) since the movement notated must still be recognised *as dance* (and as *that* dance). So the choreographer's role was acknowledged explicitly both in speaking of "... any *dance* which conforms to that score — and *which is seen as dance* ..." (UD p. 86: my new emphasis), since "... notationality does not, as it stands, guarantee that the object ... is indeed a dance" (UD p. 98), *and* when the place of "... the traditions and conventions of that art form" (UD p. 87) is stressed — "traditions and conventions" within which the choreographer works (including rebelling against them). For danceworks, although *abstract* objects, are nonetheless *constructed* or *made* abstract objects — at least, one should begin from this commonsense view, on which (say) Mozart composed his works; therefore they would not exist without him, and could not, say, pre-date him (compare Appendix).

Still, notationality was certainly *stressed* when facing questions about dance-identity; and more might have been said more clearly on an important role that this leaves for the choreographer in respect of how the work should be made sense of. After all, UD devoted a chapter (Chapter 11) to giving the choreographer's intentions due weight. And that book, as here (see Chapter Five), deployed an argument from Wollheim to make out this point. (In some cases at least, confusions about my position arose through aligning my views too closely with Goodman's. For *he* seems give a much smaller role to the artist in so-called "allographic arts" (Goodman, 1968 p. 113: see Chapter Two), of which dance would be one. But this picture should be rejected, along with [that version of] the autographic/allographic distinction. Indeed, Wollheim's argument mentioned above [see UD p. 234] occurs in his principled rejection of these very points from Goodman.)

No doubt, my younger self sometimes left points in UD[8] not well-expressed: but the importance of the artist is *there*. A more robust defence, though, would stress the occasion-sensitivity of my discussion of notationality — imagining certain issues being raised, I therefore took myself to be responding to them. Had I been responding to a different set of *issues*, I would have responded differently. And responding to *those* issues, today as then, would stress the potential role of the notated score in making public the constraints from the type: that is, as making plain some constraints on the movements of which that dancework must be composed — or, better, at least to rule out certain options. Indeed, as I put it there, this was an elaboration of a basic (though inadequate) thought "that performance A and performance B were performances of the same work if they contained the same series of movements" (UD p. 110). For notationality permits us to retain the idea *behind* such a stipulation, while giving up the stipulation itself.

That said, there *seems* to be a fundamental disanalogy between typical dance-scores, made after the fact by notators, and typical musical-scores or play-scripts, made by the artist in making the work[9]. The impact of this disanalogy is not entirely absorbed by claiming, first, that dances *could* be made in this way (that writing a score legitimately generates the abstract object, for danceworks) and, second, that this possibility is informative "... concerning the nature of dance" (UD p. 97). The boring fact is that most — indeed, almost all — dances are *not* made in this way.

Now, *one* strategy acknowledges that dance-composition typically takes place in the studio, but dismisses that as simply a *sociological* (or historical) fact about dance — the kind of causal story for dances irrelevant to the nature of dance as a performable. But, first, this sort of origin for danceworks is regularly stressed as *characteristic* of dance — at least by dancers and choreographers. So I will retain this feature as genuinely a set of facts true *of the dance*. Second, given my institutionalism (my commitment to a logical role for the Republic of Dance: UD pp. 71-86, and elsewhere), I cannot take this line. So what can I say about this fact? In the context of my institutionalism, does it refute my position on dance-identity?

§8. Connecting the issues

The objection, recall, was that — insofar as dances were notated at all —the scores were not made (as I had both hoped and predicted [compare UD p. 99]) in the context of *composing* dances. Rather, when there was a score, it was typically produced by a professional notator, after the fact, on the basis of the work as choreographed. So it differed both from typical musical scores and from typical play-scripts in this respect. In the other performing arts, the score more plausibly functions as a *recipe* to be followed; in dance the score seemed more like a *recording*. Further, such dance scores did not typically identify the constraints from the type — as I had both argued and confidently predicted they would — since performances *clearly* performance of that work (say, *Swan Lake*) can be identified although they do not fit (or conform to) such-and-such a score: our example was the Stepanov score for *Swan Lake*. Hence that score cannot embody the constraints from the *type* (if *Swan Lake* is indeed a type-token object).

Further, these objections — although intensified when (like me) one gives *conceptual* weight to the activities of dancers and choreographers — depend on granting philosophical importance to the practices of dancers and dance-makers, rather than on institutionalism as such. And that importance has already been stressed here.

In fact, this discussion of the Stepanov score for *Swan Lake* both clarifies the correct line of response and exemplifies it in action. That score too should be seen as a *recipe*; that is, normatively. But the Stepanov score for *Swan Lake* does not to reflect the constraints from the type (performances uncontentiously of *Swan Lake* failed to satisfy it). Rather, on a parallel with (say) a pianist's version or 'interpretation' of a particular piano work, that score identified the constraints from a *performance-interpretation* (pp. UD 103-104). The parallel was to a score for (say) *Pollini's interpretation* of Schönberg opus 19, rather than for that work itself. Moreover, the constraints from such a score (now seen in the *dance* case) are inevitably more restrictive than those of a score for the dancework itself (at least in typical cases). The performer's interpretation makes concrete features left under-determined by the work itself — and hence by any score for it. So a performance following that narrower score instantiates that *interpretation* of (say) *Swan Lake* or Schönberg's opus 19, rather than just being a performance of the work *tout court*. (There would be ways of failing to conform to *this* score while still instantiating the work.) So this case shows why a score of *this* kind fails to embody just the constraints from the type. Rather, it is yet more constrained: it is too prescriptive *precisely* in virtue of being a score for that interpretation of *Swan Lake* (say, Drigo's), rather than for *Swan Lake* itself. At least, the constraints would be different, for some actions required by Drigo's interpretation of *Swan Lake* would be 'open' in a score for the dancework itself — as a score accurately reflecting Glenn Gould's performance-practice (with its 'missed notes') would offer variability of something otherwise taken as fixed. But the overall point — that the constraints were different — still holds. So (as I said) such a score should be expected to make explicit features of the work left under-determined by a score for the work itself: that is, a score which embodied *only* the constraints from the type. Hence, thinking in *this* way of a score with which one is presented generates precisely the kinds of response from which we began: that (say) a performance conforming to the Stepanov score is *Swan Lake* all right, but so are performances which 'contradict' that score. Yet reflection on the nature of the score (as of an interpretation) explains that fact: it shows why *this* score does not adequately reflect the type, or what this score lacks. And it was in *this* sense that my conception of an *adequate score* could (or should) be understood.

My conception of an adequate score is very loose. First, discussion of the score's happiness or otherwise should be in the gift of 'experts', such as choreographers and critics (and hence debatable amongst them) — this is a matter for the Republic of Dance[10]. Second, questions of the *adequacy* of the score are often *occasion-sensitive* (and certainly might be on some occasions), such that a score correctly judged adequate on *this* occasion might not be adequate in *those* circumstances, or on *that* occasion. In a simple case here, the preferred interpretation of a group wishing to perform *Swan Lake* might coincide with that embodied in the Stepanov score: that score could then be adequate for discussion of this group's decisions of the dancework, but not necessarily outside them. As this case illustrates, there need be no exceptionless answer to questions about the *adequacy* of score.

§9.   Writing authoritative scores

Does this discussion aid understanding of the logical role of the *established practice* of dances being notated only after the fact, by notators (and hence with the potentials for difficult decisions and confusions reflected in my story of Ann Hutchinson-Guest notating for Kurt Jooss [above: §6])? For this issue must press on those, like me, wishing to recognise a logical force to the institutional practices of (in this case) dance-makers. Indeed, it might seem an indictment that my account conflicted with such a basic fact of choreographic practice — which is a way some readers take UD! But no conflict here is genuine. For the previous discussion explains why a typical notated score of *this* kind for a dance cannot be an *adequate score* (in my terms) if our concern is with the dance itself. Such a score (even when well-notated) cannot reflect *only* the constraints from the type. Rather, in being written from working with dancers, such a score typically reflects features of the performance these dancers give: that is what the notator sees — hence what gets recorded. For that reason, what results is a score for a *performance-interpretation* of the work, rather than for the work itself. Again, this is both to be expected in this situation and just what one finds in consulting typical scores. Then those who complain that most dance scores do not meet my criteria for adequacy have a point. For scores composed in this sort of situation are quite *likely* to reflect an *interpretation* of the dancework rather than the work itself.

Is this outcome inevitable? Or could something else be done, if choreographers chose? The activities of a minuting secretary at a meeting suggest a revealing parallel here: the chair *directs* that certain things be included in the minutes, that others not be minuted, and (perhaps) leaves the secretary to make choices in places where no instruction is given. Then he/she *reviews* the minutes prior to their circulation. So the chair has confidence that the minutes are accurate — accurately reflecting what the *chair* takes to be of importance. In a similar way, a choreographer might give the notator *direction*. On this parallel, the choreographer indicates that such-and-such is crucial — and perhaps even which elements of (say) a movement sequence were its fundamental components; other aspects might be recorded simply as an *aide-memoire* for the choreographer; still others could be excluded entirely — they are not even crucial for the performance of *this* interpretation. Then such a score would reflect the constraints of the type, at least as the choreographer viewed them.

A dissimilarity here: the rest of the committee ratifies minutes. But the difference stresses — positively to my mind — the role of the choreographer as *author*; further, the choreographer could institute a kind of 'checking' with the dancers (while the choreographer retained the last word). Even if the choreographer's view does not *decide* the matter, at least it provides a sound starting place (a topic to which we can return: Chapter Five).

Still, there are key differences here in practice. Many choreographers (and most dancers) could not understand the score written. Hence the idea of checking its *accuracy to the author's intention* seems problematic. However, the general idea — that a choreographer might indicate which parts of the work as viewed were for the work in general, which for *this* performance — seems both clear and straightforward.

So choreographers *could* do this: but why *should* they? The answer is, first, that such a score facilitates the preservation of danceworks and their accurate re-creation (or, better, re-performing at a later date). Thus, choreographers wanting the *best* from later performances of their dances have a vested interest in an authoritative score (even were this only one resource among many). Of course, this requires that choreographers know enough about notationality to make this decision — or that they trust their notators, in the light of informed discussion. Then, second, identifying the key elements of a dance sequence (as opposed to peripheral ones) — and ensuring these were notated — may be clarifying of one's own thoughts. In both these ways, this would be one's chance to *specify* the constraints from the type. Then fewer debates would occur about what so-and-so *intended* in such-and-such a dance, where this referred to its *movement-content* — or, more generally, its embodiment — as opposed to its meaning. In this way, the notation becomes a way to enhance and clarify the choreographer's contribution to the *posterity* of the dance.

Yet are these *good enough* reasons, especially as the process of such notation would be time-consuming (and would be facilitated by the choreographer learning notation — another time-consuming activity)? I think so. And many dance-makers might respond well to this idea of the preserving of works. For example, as Easton (1996/2000 p. 431) notes, Agnes de Mille regretted having to rely on "... dancers whose 'muscle-memory' made them the involuntary archivists of her work". Further, de Mille worried at the loss of performances of her works — and especially her own performances in them (compare Easton, 1996/2000 pp. 368-369). Of course, it must be demonstrated that notation offered the best, or perhaps the only, way to preserve the detail of the dances reliably (see Chapter Four): that returns us to logical points about the normativity of notation in respect of performance (see UD pp. 94-97). But, if accomplished, that might encourage choreographers to *participate* in the production of scores adequate to *those* purposes. Or so I hope.

§10. Defeasibility and 'history of production'

Key to my analysis was a certain logical notion of *defeasibility*; in part, a way to insist that the issue here concerned the 'necessary' (rather then the 'contingent') end of any consideration. (This is a way to insist on this discussion's place as philosophy — concerned with conceptual connections — rather than merely history or sociology.)

The defeasibility of the whole topic is picked up when one recognises that a basis for an exception might be found in a case where other things went well. A defeasible notion, such as (legal) *contract*, has a set of satisfaction conditions: it must be drawn up in this way, signed, witnessed and such like. When those conditions are met, there is a contract between us. Yet the claim to such a contract can be defeated if an objector raises one of a number of *recognised heads of exception*[11]. So granting defeasibility here is conceding such "recognised heads of exception" — which would these be? Well, when can one conclusively *deny* that such-and-such a performance instantiates the same dancework as so-and-so other performance, despite one resembling the other[12]?

Commonsense, and a comparison with other arts, suggests one reason based on the claim of the dance-maker as *author* of the *abstract object* that is the dance — and hence as responsible for it, in both senses of that term. (And this might also reflect our emphasis on 'history of production' in Chapter

Two.) Despite postmodernist wailing about 'the death of the author', this issue is live in practice. For instance in December 2005, Pilobolus Dance Theatre had fired Alison Chase, a founding member and the choreographer of many of the major works in the company's repertoire. As reported (see Pasles, 2006 p. E35), Chase urges, "... they don't have clear title to my work" — if this was indeed *her* work, she is (presumably) right; and I am not (presently) taking seriously the metaphysically ripe suggestion that abstract objects are only discovered.

So, one defeating condition would be 'wrong history of production'. Of course, most discussions will not pursue this condition. Indeed, it does not typically need checking, if one *begins* from (a) a context of wanting to stage that dancework (say, *Swan Lake*); and (b) a work, performed in that context, that satisfied the score. For these facts suggest a context of appropriate 'history of production'. Yet, of course, that is just where the burden of proof lies, with defeasible concepts: one need not check for this, if ... where the "if" will be cashed out partly in terms of the score. But the question *can* be raised when someone had reason so to do — and then one recognises this as a defeating condition.

Thus compliance with the notated score could be one satisfaction condition (on our parallel with *legal* contract): one would ascertain that it had been fulfilled (although this might be done implicitly). My emphasis (in UD) on *notationality* stressed *that* point. For one might well appeal to such a score — if an adequate one existed — in what happens in the rehearsal room or studio: one aimed to perform *Black Angels* (1978), and one's movements conformed to its score (say). There is no need to check on 'recognised heads of exception': in particular, there would be no need to consider 'history of production'. Indeed, if challenged on this point, our confidence might be high just where our score ascribed the dance to, say, Christopher Bruce (as choreographer). Yet that issue might still be raised — perhaps even by stressing that the score was notated *far* after the fact, in conditions very different from this idealised above. So one might worry about its *adequacy* as a score for *Black Angels*. That might be one way to problematise the work's connection to its author. If the ensuing arguments in the Republic of Dance concluded that our performances fails that 'history of production' condition, those performances would not, after all, count as *Black Angels*: a 'recognised head of exception' was successfully raised.

Here, disputing the example must be distinguished from disputing the point. In the framework from Chapter Two, it was urged that the Nureyev *Swan Lake* was the very same work as the Ivanov and Petipa *Swan Lake* (that they were tokens of the same time), while a performance of the Mats Ek *Swan Lake* was a token of a different type. Further, that the Matthew Bourne *Swan*

Lake generates more tokens of the *same* type as the Ivanov and Petipa *Swan Lake*. Here, danceworks from the 'same work' category are 'same work *despite* the differences', while those from the 'different work' category are 'different work *despite* the similarities'. And each of these "despites"can ground sustained debate within the Republic of Dance. For neither the *similarities* among different danceworks nor the *differences* among instantiations of the same work should be denied.

But, on any version of such categories, a principled account must distinguish the *limits* of same-work continuity (where one has a token of the same type, although as different as possible from those with which one is familiar or from our standard case) from that of a very similar dancework — for the *Swan Lake* case, this may be largely one using the same music[13] — which is nevertheless a different artwork: a token of a different type. Further, in some cases, doing so might treat the authorial role as a "recognised head of exception" to the claims to dance-identity of a work fulfilling a notated score adequate for that dance.

Here one readily falls into disputing the example, not the point. *Of course*, I regard the Mats Ek and Matthew Bourne *Swan Lake*s as instantiating different categories — hence, for me, one is and the other is not the very same dancework as the Ivanov and Petipa *Swan Lake*. But as long as the *categories* are granted, along with some of the bases for distinguishing them (that the difference should concern expressiveness, for instance), these *examples* really need no defence: they make the points *for me*. If other examples make the points for others, imagine those examples inserted here! This goes, too, for those with reservations about my seeming concern with *Swan Lake* — it is just an example, although its familiarity outside the world of dance practice, and the numerous versions and the score (such as it is), make it a useful example, to my way of thinking.

So the basic categorisation consists of our central case of *Swan Lake* (say, the Ivanov and Petipa version), plus two other cases: that *at* the boundary of same-work continuity (here typified by Nureyev's *Swan Lake*) and that just *over* the boundary — and hence a different artwork (a token of a different type), typified by the Mats Ek *Swan Lake*. A fuller map also includes those cases — mentioned earlier — where, although one succeeds in dancing *Swan Lake*, the success is marginal: it is a very poor *Swan Lake*. A performance such as this (as one might say, one complying rather badly with our adequate score) is perfectly possible, since one can deviate from a score while still complying with it (to some degree). So, here, the *most* dreadful version of *Swan Lake* might be idealised — so bad that, having requested that my company perform *Swan Lake*, you are tempted to 'ask for your money back', as it were. But the debate might conclude that, after all, this *is* a performance of *Swan Lake*, however bad. Then our map can be further augmented by adding a worse-yet putative performance of *Swan Lake*: this is so bad that it fails even to be a performance of *Swan Lake*. (After all, the previous case was [idealised as] as bad as a performance of *Swan Lake* can get, while still being *Swan Lake*!) Yet even these cases are not especially worrying, since other arts familiarly offer both: for instance, those works by Sunday painters that are art, but very poor art indeed; and those that are not (even) art. Our categorisation readily accommodates such cases. Further, these all represent options for debate faced with a particular case, rather than positions to be instantiated.

§11. Artistically-relevant differences?

Throughout, our picture of danceworks has stressed their transfiguration from 'real thing' movement into art: they have artistically-relevant properties. Further, our picture of the dancework as a *performable* (re-performable on another occasion) more or less guarantees that *this* performance differs from *that* one, even though both are performances of the same work. Some such differences might be expected to be *artistically-relevant* in some (if not all) cases. Hence there can be artistically-relevant differences between performances of the same dance work (as opposed to merely aesthetic differences). What should one make of that fact?

Two clear examples suggest themselves: the first concerns difference of interpretation. For we distinguished different *interpretations* of (say) *Swan Lake* — for instance, that in accord with the Stepanov score, as opposed to Nureyev's — our model being, roughly, that between performer's interpretations of piano pieces. The Pollini interpretation of Schönberg's opus 19 can be contrasted with the Gould interpretation — even when other performers play them! Further, such interpretations might even be notated, as the Stepanov score for *Swan Lake* perhaps reflects Drigo's interpretation. Now, clearly these interpretations are not *neutral* with respect to artistic value: at the least, some might be thought *better* than others; more neutrally, one might be preferred to another on a particular occasion, or for a particular purpose, or at a certain phase of one's life. Here, patterns to one's preferences might be expected: given my broad general preference for minimalism in art, in general I prefer more minimalist performance-interpretations of a dancework. And, of course, I might explain why. At the least, such differences would, in a sense, represent *regular* differences between performances of the same dancework, such that corresponding responses to those performances might reasonably be expected. If at one time I consistently favour minimal over less minimal danceworks, one might expect that — during that period at least — I would consistently prefer minimal performance-interpretations of *Swan Lake* over less minimal ones; and that my explanation of this preference would make mention of the performances' minimal character. At the least, there should be a pattern to both my preferences vis-à-vis such performance-interpretations and my explanations of those preferences.

By contrast, and secondly, there are differences *within* an interpretation — the sort of thing a change of cast or venue readily brings about. Here too, on some occasion, one performance might be preferred to another, for artistically-relevant considerations. Further, that preference would typically be explicable: that this role is better suited to that performer. For instance; or, as I found in two performances of William Louther's wonderful *Vesalii Icones* (1969), that the performance 'in the round' was less intimate than that in the proscenium arch.

Of course, one's preferences here need not remain static. Thus, one may come to notice different features — what had at first seemed a desirable fluidity in the movement of such-and-such a dancer may begin to look tensionless. Or one may reflect on the *value* of the feature noted: what seemed intimate can now seem claustrophobic. And such claims might be debated. For all the judgements at issue here are *arguable*: one's learning to see and learning to value this dance means that, if pressed, one can produce a commentary in justification of one's preferences (or find it in a dance critic); and that one's commentary may change over time.

For those who approach dance (or the arts more generally) with a conception of one correct — and complete — interpretation (if only it can be found), this might be worrying. Which of these cases is *the* dance? Which of these is *the* response to *the* dance? Our reply, of course, rejects that picture of determinacy. For the mere fact that these performances instantiate the very same dancework cannot *guarantee* that the very same comments are possible of each, if one set of comments refer to the dance itself (the type) while another relate to the performances (the tokens). In a parallel way, differences between this performance and that one are quite compatible with both being performances of the very same dancework.

Once one sees that there can be a commentary on the *type* and a commentary on the *token*, and variety in each, there is no remaining problem. And the first of those features should be familiar from our paradigm type/token objects, flags. For remarks can clearly be offered on *this* flag (for example, that it is being flown upside down) which are not comments on *the* flag (the type). Equally, our comments can distinguish *this* token (the small plastic flag on a stick) from *that* one — which is large, cloth, and on a flag pole. To repeat, the idea that different remarks might be made here should be familiar, carrying over to our discussion of danceworks. All our case adds is the possibility of different reasons offered (explanatory of the work possessing such-and-such an artistic property) where these reasons reflect differences in the danceworld: or, as I have put it, in the Republic of Dance.

§12. Conclusion

As a summary, let us consider ask whether, on the view developed here, there can be (Danto-esque) "confusable counterparts" (Danto, 1981 p. 138[14]) of a dance; that is, could there be two performances that *we* cannot tell apart (hence where both comply with some notated score), but where one is — and the other is not — a dancework (say, *Swan Lake*)? I offer four comments, in no particular order. First, a *score* here need not be a full movement score of the sort Labanotation would provide. Instead, it is simply a normative recipe which, if followed in an appropriate context, produces a performance authentically of the dancework at issue. Our earlier example was a set of rules of the kind used for Elaine Summers' chance-based dance *Instant Choice* (Banes, 1993 pp. 47-49) — on the supposition that performance in accordance with them in this context results in a performance of that work, these could count as an *adequate score* in context.

Yet, second, what is performed must be a *dance*: there can certainly be 'confusable *movement* counterparts' — movement sequences which could be mistaken for such-and-such a dance but are not that work; indeed, which do not comprise a dancework at all. And, third, other conditions are granted here, in typical cases: for example, concerning the music or costume. Merely complying with the score alone may well not be enough. And, of course, these conditions operate *defeasibly*. Then, fourth, one important defeating condition for the movement sequence (or performance) being either *a* dance or *that particular* dance was its failure to meet the 'history of production' or 'authorship' condition just discussed — the presupposition that this is, say, *Black Angels* (1976) can be defeated by showing that, after all, it lacks the requisite relation to Christopher Bruce as choreographer. Moreover, there is usually no need to check up on particular defeating conditions, if one has no specific reason to raise them in this case. So notationality still plays a key role; but it must be understood in the context of the realisation of dances.

In fact, one might need to consider here both 'performances' which — while complying with a score — were not actually performances of such-and-such a dancework *and* performances non-compliant (with a particular score) which were uncontentiously of that particular dancework. Imagine a very simple dancework, the score of which can be satisfied by (say) a bunch of people leaving the theatre[15]. The score for such a piece could be satisfied by behaviour not a dancework at all: but, of course, *that* a particular event compliant with the score was *not* a dancework could not be discerned from the score alone — the score identifies only the movement patterns, say. So other (contextual?) features must be recognised to rule out *this* occasion of the occurrence of that set of movements as being our dance (call this work of mine *Unsatisfyin Lover*). And clearly the lack of an authorial relation (or 'history of production') would be crucial.

As a second case, suppose that — having depended for some time on a score for *Unsatisfyin Lover* — one now comes to a performance which is (agreed to be) of *Unsatisfyin Lover*, but where the movement patterns do not comply with our score. (Imagine the performance sanctified by the choreographer, if that helps.) Perhaps there is even some larger reason here: for instance, that most of the performers are one-legged (as Paxton had intended to perform *Satisfyin Lover* in 1970 with only the red-haired: see Banes, 1987 p. 60), where this precluded their following some aspect of the score. This case shows that what was *taken* for an adequate score for *Unsatisfyin Lover* — one reflecting only the constraints from the type — was actually not (as is shown by the acceptability of this performance as of the work). Or one could conclude that this performance represented the Republic of Dance *revising* its view of the adequacy of that score for *Unsatisfyin Lover*. If one were writing the history of this dancework, these might be importantly different: the first would indicate a score taken as adequate when it was not, the second the conclusion of an *argument* (however brief) to revise what counted as an adequate score: that is, to revise the work. But, in practical terms, these come to the same thing: from now on, a performance compliant with the *new* score (and made in the appropriate context) would — *defeasibly* — be that work.

This picture, then, mirrors constraints appropriate to *same-work* continuity, permitting due theoretical weight for the dance-maker. But what does the philosophy add? Isn't my answer, roughly, that dancers and (especially) choreographers and dance critics were doing all right all along? — their debate, in the Republic of Dance, was (rightly) what settled the issues. So is the philosophy productive?

Of course, I think it is: and my strategy here (as elsewhere) revolves around the mistakes we *don't* go on to make — and (as I stressed in UD, CDE and elsewhere) I especially want others to avoid the dismissive subjectivism that bedevils so much discussion in respect of artworks. So my point was to show that the Republic of Dance was entitled to its comments; that they were well founded and, in favoured cases, even true! Hence no apology for them was necessary.

Chapter Four

Preservation, recording and dance performance

§1. Introduction

It is a commonplace that dance performances are, in some sense, ephemeral: that they are only available to us as we watch them. Marcia Siegel (1972 p. 1) captured this sense in her slogan that danceworks "... exist at a perpetual vanishing point". But is this limitation merely practical? Is it a *limitation* at all? Perhaps, instead, the ephemerality of dances should be celebrated.

But surely danceworks must have a kind of enduring history. For typical danceworks are *performables*: they can be re-performed on another occasion. Hence they can 'appear' again, even if we lack access to them in the interim. And this suggests something concerning the posterity at least of dances one values. Given the parallel with other art forms (and especially music, which seems comparably ephemeral in performance), the default position here should involve, at the least, the desire to preserve dances so that later generations can see them (should they want to). And, throughout, this desire has been attributed (speculatively) to choreographers since, after all, it seems likely that artists would hope for the widest of audiences for their works. Of course, one worry here might be precisely whether a work re-performed at some later date is indeed the very same work.

For analytic purposes at least, two occasions for this sort of concern should be distinguished. In the first, imagine that the work passed out of the repertoire some time ago, so dancers, stagers, and choreographers of today have comparatively little on which to base a performance of that past work — to be called the *reconstruction of the dance* in question. For the other case, imagine a choreographer who hopes that his or her work will be viewed by posterity; or an audience that hopes the work will be available to later generations. Here, then, the concern is with the *preservation of danceworks*. It might seem that danceworks cannot be preserved, at least beyond the memories of those involved in creating and performing them. Minimally, their preservation seems hampered when relying simply on the memories of dancers, choreographers, and those involved. Both positions — *reconstruction* and *preservation* — have been urged for danceworks. The concern here is with preservation; Chapter Nine will address reconstruction. As with music, a notated score for a work might offer just such a way to preserve that work, although *notationality* (rather than an extant notated score) must be stressed. Or a complex video recording might offer another route to preservation. Exploring that topic requires considering precisely what such recordings of the work might offer. In particular, more must be said about the *logic of notationality* for performing arts. This will involve positive accounts of the value of notated scores for danceworks (were they to be got), as well as the rejection of apparent contenders for a similar role in securing the authenticity of dance performance.

The comparison with music suggests beginning from the score: that is our strategy here. A key distinction (from Chapter Three §8) contrasts the score *as a record* of a particular performance — which seems to follow from its being notated 'after the fact', perhaps by a notator — with the score *as a recipe*, such that following the score in a suitable manner results in a performance of that very dancework; and hence the score can be used (as instantiating constraints from the type?) to differentiate appropriate from inappropriate performances, and good and less good ones too! That is, the score (as recipe) can function *normatively* (in line with Wolterstorff's thought that it reflects a *norm-kind*). Of course, the second of these — score as recipe — draws on the fact that (in principle) one can make dances by writing the score; but it also recognises how the score can be used, however it was generated[1].

So why is the notated score (of whatever form) for a dance *important?* As we have seen (see CDE p. 13), notation systems such as Labanotation are essentially movement notations: they can be used to record bodily movements in lots of contexts (for instance, by anthropologists with a concern with ritual: see Williams, 1991 pp. 259-260; Williams, 2004 pp. 197-198). As Blacking (1985 p. 66) accurately writes, like films and videos:

> ... various notations such as Laban and Benesh are ... useful tools for referring to the object of study [of the anthropologist], but they cannot describe or explain what is happening as human experience ...

For these notations, and so on, record *movement*, not (human) action. And this is a strength of such notation systems, since (by recording movement) they allow comparison of movement patterns across different actions: thus, the dance can be compared with the ritual or with the exercise routine. But (to repeat) if scores in a notation system are used to provide the *constraints* from the *type* (see Chapter Two), those scores are treated as *normative* — as saying what one *should* do in order that one's movement instantiate the particular dancework. That, in turn, means that the score is treated *as a recipe* — even when one actually arrives at the score by notating what was done: that is, as a recording of a particular performance.

Moreover, having a score of this kind enables works to remain in the repertoire just as long as there were performance traditions among dancers which permitted the following of that 'recipe'. So there is a connection here with the posterity of dances; or, what may come to the same thing, with the place of the history of dance in our understanding of danceworks of the present; or even works that are in the repertoire. This discussion also allows consideration of the preservation or permanence of dances. For the fragility of this connection for dances has already been noted.

§2. Goodman's practical concerns for notation systems

Of those philosophers who have seen dance notation (not a very large number), most saw it first in Goodman's work. In that context, the thought was (roughly) that a notated score might uniquely and completely determine the movement patterns required to instantiate a particular dancework. Of course, this is an idealisation: in practice, movement notation "... has never become so precise" (Sharpe, 2004 p. 63) as Goodman required. But, when considering the issue of authenticity of a performance as of a particular dancework, reliance on a notated score alone seems to generate major problems. As in Chapter Three, the problem can be posed by asking: Could there be (Danto-esque) "confusable counterparts" (Danto, 1981 p. 138) here? That is, could two dance-performances be performances of *different* danceworks (or one movement-sequence not be a dancework at all) even though no spectator could tell them apart? And, for *our* context, could each performance comply with the notated score for dancework X (say, *Black Angels*), but only one of them *be* dancework X?

This 'possibility' raises a number of key issues, bearing on the use to which notated scores might be put. Some of our replies have already been noted (see above; and Chapters Two and Three): that one must ensure that both movement sequences are indeed dances; and (perhaps) identifying *that* dance might involve constraints of music, or costume, or some such. Further, stressing that ascriptions here are *defeasible* reiterates an important 'head of exception'; namely, the failure of the 'history of production', or authorship, condition. These all operate within the context of the production of *danceworks* (perhaps, danceworks of certain kinds). Yet that returns us to one central feature of danceworks: their movement content. Many appeals to notation seek to address this movement content, in principle (as *notationality*) if not in practice. But the amenability of movement notations to *all* movement (which is really a strength of such notations) means they cannot themselves distinguish dance from non-dance (effectively, a limitation of them). This discussion, then, helps to clarify the *scope* of our concern with notationality, by highlighting what it cannot (seek to) achieve.

Yet, once in the context is of *this* dance, where do we stand? Notated scores might seem to locate the movement content of a particular dance. And an *adequate score* (see Chapter Three) might seem to preclude just the possibility of 'confusable counterparts', by showing differences in movement patterns. Yet that could only be correct if the *only* way to rule out 'confusable counterparts' was by reference to movement content: this suggestion has already been rejected. Nevertheless, *some* movement content is typically required for particular dances. Hence differences in movement content *can* indicate different works. And this function could be performed by a score in a movement notation.

Certainly, for Goodman, a score must make *clear* what it prescribes and what it precludes. As Goodman (1968= LA pp. 129-154; 211-218) notes, a relevant consideration will be practicality: ideally, scores should be easily 'read' and easily (and clearly) 'written'. So that asking "Who can read what?" is partly a conceptual matter, partly a practical one. The potential usefulness for dance of notated scores, for both authenticity and preservation, requires notations both readable and reliable. (And, of course, dancers trained to instantiate those scores: Challis, 1999 pp. 148-150.) Further, the scores produced must be *complete*, at least in the sense of not leaving out anything crucial. Goodman concludes that "... the properties required of a notational system are unambiguity and syntactic and semantic disjointness and differentiation" (LA p. 156). And his text to elaborates these five ideas. Thus:

> The first semantic requirement upon notational systems is that they be *unambiguous*; for obviously the basic purpose of a notational system can only be served if the compliance relationship is invariant. Any ambiguous *inscription* must be excluded since it will give conflicting decisions concerning whether some object complies with it. (LA p. 148)

The other conditions point in the same direction: that there must be "... [r]equisite separation among characters" (LA p. 132). Then:

> ... anyone designing a notation will try to minimise the probability of errors. But this is a technological concern, differing sharply from the theoretical concern with disjointness. (LA p. 134)

Disjointness is needed precisely because, without it (both for the syntactic and the semantic), one cannot guarantee that "... marks correctly judged to be joint members of a character will always be true copies of one another" (LA p. 134). Further, for a notational system "... *the compliance-classes must be disjoint*" (LA p. 150). In the same way, one must strive towards "... the determination of membership of mark" (LA p. 135). In practice, this may "... depend upon the acuteness of our perceptions and the sensitivity of the instruments we can devise" (LA p. 135). But it will be a flaw in the symbol system if this is not possible in principle.

So the requirements for differentiation (both syntactic and semantic) amount to requiring that any inscription not recognised as shared will be ascribable to only one class: that is, one would like "... a scheme where all inscriptions are conspicuously different" (LA p. 137). Further, for Goodman:

> [t]hese are in no sense merely recommendations for a good and useful notation system but are features which distinguish notation systems — good or bad — from non-notational systems. (LA p. 156)

But this last point need not be accepted — for failing *to some degree* to meet the five requirements Goodman lays down might still leave one with a notational system; or, at least, with something best *called* that, given other obvious alternatives.

These points relate, of course, to Goodman's own reservations about how to balance his preferred *theoretical* constraints with those of practical usefulness. Thus Goodman concedes that:

> ... Labanotation passes the theoretical tests very well — about as well as does ordinary musical notation, and perhaps as well as is compatible with practicality. (LA p. 217)

But he also recognises that this is not his central topic; that, in respect of dance notation, "[p]ractical feasibility is ... not directly the question here" (LA p. 213). He feels that there are abstract constraints on notation systems as such. Yet, first, although Goodman puts aside such questions of "practical feasibility" (LA p. 213), he still regards it as important to set down criteria here. These are, in effect, ways of elaborating features of a logically perfect notation system — although treated as practical constraints. Second, a much looser conception of a notated score is deployed than that Goodman imposes: we noted (in Chapter Two) the variety of things that would count, for our purposes, as a score. Thus, if following the rules for Elaine Summers' chance-based dancework *Instant Choice* (see also Banes, 1993 pp. 47-49) ensures that one's movement sequence constitutes a performance of that very dancework: then those rules are a score for that work. For our conception of scores draws *only* on our picture of an adequate score (from Chapter Three). But Goodman would reject such a view. For him, this is too loose to identify a performance as *this* work rather than that one (even in principle); which he requires of satisfactory notation — as we saw. Then, third, Goodman's emphasis is of a piece with his more general philosophical commitments. At least when he wrote *Languages of Art*, Goodman believed that philosophical questions generated a single set of exceptionless answers, as long as the analysis was carried out correctly, and the concept in question was either not vague to begin with or could be stripped of its vagueness, for instance by disambiguation (see EKT pp. 183-187; AJ pp. 34-36).

This conception of philosophy, as aiming at an exceptionless analysis of a 'logical skeleton' that was concealed from us before the analysis, should be rejected. Instead, with Wittgenstein's insights, we should urge that:

- "... nothing is hidden" [PI §435: also "... what is hidden, for example, is of no interest to us": PI §126]: the kinds of 'conception' identified above would be available to us as spectators, at least defeasibly;

- "... Look and see" (PI §66) — which is the right advice only if what is needed is before our eyes (and certainly not requiring *analysis* to be uncovered to us).

More specifically, we should reject the claims of a single standard by which notationality may be judged. Our point, as contextualists, is that there may be reasons to prefer one notation system to another for this purpose, or in this context, but to prefer the other for a different purpose or in a different context. Nor needs these reflect features entirely extraneous to the notations themselves.

As one brief example, note that, since notated scores are two dimensional, while dance performances are four-dimensional (as well as incorporating relationships between dancers), a fundamental question must enquire which of the four dimensions of the movement are directly recorded on the page (that is, for which there is a direct analogue of some kind) and which are depicted in some other way. For instance, the Benesh system uses the up-down and side-to-side of the paper to record the corresponding movements: this lends itself to a view of the dance from the front, and stresses its side-to-side qualities — just the sorts of features normally of importance for ballet performed within a proscenium arch. But not all dance is like this. One virtue of Labanotation is its decision to record the temporal dimension directly onto the page: that treats a key dimension of dance (time) in an analogical way, but requires that other treatments be given for most other dimension. This does not seem like a virtue in all cases; one need only recognise it as a virtue in some!

§3. Discussing dances from scores

It is a commonplace that typical musicians can discuss typical musical works while looking at the scores for those works; and, while the two uses of the term "typical" make this a truism, it is not far from being true anyway. As I said (in Chapter Three §1), I had expected this situation to be replicated (with corresponding differences) for dance. That has not come about. Still, once the practical issues are put aside, are there any further reasons — any logical reasons, as one might say — for excluding that possibility?

It might be objected here that seeing the notated scores is not encountering the artworks, the dances; but, of course, the same is true for music. Equally, it might be suggested that seeing the video is not seeing the dance (for most purposes). Certainly, faced with the blanket request, "In watching the video, were you seeing the dance?" one should deny that in seeing the video one encounters the artwork, whatever is said in some contexts (see §6 below). But a better response to such a question — because a more contextualist one — would ask, "Why do you want to know?" For identifying in this way the *issue* being raised may make clearer how to respond to it. Then finding a good way through the issue may clarify the role of notation.

Of course, suppose I spend the afternoon watching a video of *Swan Lake*. Then — if asked — in most circumstances I must grant that my time was spent watching *Swan Lake* as opposed to ... say, watching other dances, or engaging in other activities. So that *if* I was watching dance, it would certainly be *Swan Lake* I was watching; and I *was* watching dance, if the choices are that, instead, I was playing bridge or filling-in my income tax return. But, while talk of 'watching dance' may be the best we can say of this case, by way of a one-liner, we can also be more accurate: that we saw a *video* of *Swan Lake*, say. So that, contextually, the question, "What were you watching on the video?" is rightly answered, "*Swan Lake*" — this must be correct. But it is compatible with, "I have never (really) seen *Swan Lake*". For to see, say, the Beatles only on video is precisely not to have seen them. This negative reply concerning *Swan Lake* should be chosen when the context suggested that the reasons offered for actually seeing the dance ("in person") should be *contrasted* with those for seeing it on video. For one might happily grant that, although the best that could be managed from the living-room, watching the video was a poor substitute for actually seeing the dance. In this respect, our comment might parallel Wollheim's criticism of art historians; namely, that

> ... art historians have tended to identify the object of their inquiry with those properties of a painting which a good slide preserves. (Wollheim, 1987 p. 11)

The dancework itself, like the painting, typically has many artistically-relevant properties that the video does not preserve.

Another case makes these points more clearly. When comparing the claims of (say) a CD to record a musical work — and hence the playing of that CD to permit hearing that musical work — with the (parallel?) claims of video to record dance, one is immediately struck by three features. First, one need not grant that experiencing *either* amounts to experiencing the artwork itself — a point to return to. For the standard case of musical performance is surely that where the performers generate the performance *in situ*, as it were: where one joins them in the performance space. And the same is true of dance. This, of course, permits a number of different points of view on the typical dancework — at least, all those from 'good seats'. So no course of action seems *obvious* or *required* for the recorded case, given its difference from this 'standard' case. Then, second, the dance case seems importantly different from the music case just because, whatever we think of the claim that hearing the music *just is* hearing a sound-structure ("tonal sonicism" as the identity-conditions associated with an account of musical ontology: see Appendix), there is no dance-related equivalent: encountering the dance is not simply encountering bodies in motion (even granting these are human bodies) — dances typically involve music, costume, and such like. And the actions must be understood as dance, and not (say) some ritual: the images alone cannot do this. So this may seem a reason to deny that watching the video is watching the dance; and then dance might be differentiated from music in this respect. Or it might make one reconsider 'tonal sonicism' in this light: perhaps features relevant for dance bear on music too (see Chapter Seven; CDE pp. 264-269). Then, third, the 'difference' in the dance case is compounded by the need, in fully recording a typical dance, to present a number of perspectives. For the spatial relations within the dance may not be clear if the view of it as though through a proscenium arch were the only one available.

Of course, on this last point, it might be urged that a spectator to any performance only sees the work from one perspective; but the work itself can be seen from many perspectives — not least those of the different spectators in each audience. So a video hoping to capture *all*, or *most*, of the dance will need to offer a comparable variety. That point will be further strengthened where the video functions as part of a permanent record of that dance.

It may well be that — as a matter of fact — the video is the only record one has of a particular dance. In that sense, it may be the best one can do, if dances are "at a perpetual vanishing point" (Siegel, 1972 p. 1). The same might be said for a notated score. But, at least in the favoured case of "an adequate score" (see Chapter Three), the score actually puts us in a better position: for the score can function normatively — *as a recipe* for the dance (as above: §1). This, in turn, means that the occasion of drafting a score could be used — by a choreographer knowledgeable in that notation system — to ensure that the score does reflect the emphases he/she wants for the work (what I typically call *the constraints from the type*). So the score can clarify for later performers or stagers what the choreographer wanted to stress; it might (in favoured circumstances) even allow him/her to think clearly about the relative importance of *this* feature of the dancework as presently performed, as opposed to *that* feature — one but not the other might be 'crucial', in the sense that its absence would be a topic for criticism of the performance. And answering this question might clarify the choreographer's intention *to himself/herself*.

This in effect identifies at least two roles for a notated score — it can have:

- a role in clarification of the artwork's features, highlighting which are the works 'crucial' features (in this weak sense of "crucial", where absence would be a basis for criticising a performance);

- a role in preservation: that masterworks of dance (from its past) will be irretrievably lost if not preserved; and a notated score might be one method of preservation.

Still, why should the score be a preferred method of preservation? Goodman suggests that:

> [a]menability to notation depends upon a precedent practice that develops only if works of the art in question are commonly either ephemeral or not producible by one person. ... The dance ... qualifies on both scores. (LA pp. 121-122)

Only if one wishes either to avoid returning again to something ephemeral as 'the dancework' or to discuss that work's detail with another person does one need (something like) a notated score. We learned (in Chapter Three §4) that a score was preferable to, say, a video in virtue of its normativity: it could describe what *should* happen to instantiate that dance, rather than what did happen in a past performance or performances. In fact, this point is much more powerful; for only a *recipe* for the dance can have this normative force; and preserving the dance for later performance requires precisely this sort of normativity. Such normativity cannot be generated by even the best video recording (or similar): that simple preserves the features of a past performance, without offering us resources to criticise that performance for either errors (inclusions) or exclusions. Further, the dancers are potentially in the same position: they may know what to do to generate another performance like the one in which they were involved previously. But the best their memory can offer is just another 'recording' of the dance, containing (at best) all the features of a past performance. Even the choreographer's position is peculiar, if we insist that she reprise that dancework, and not create a new (if similar) one. If course, one can imagine the choreographer saying, as the dance was made, that this and not that was crucial to the dance — in my sense of "crucial", where its absence is a source of criticism. Or writing it down. This is just the verbal specification of *the constraints from the type*. These might well be specified in that way, but (if so) they would simply be a score by another name! And most of those involved would have reservations about the extent to which the spoken (or written) word can capture the movement — at least, once one moves beyond the clearly named steps and gestures of classical ballet. But it is agreed on all sides that a notated score can, in principle, capture all the details here, if needed. Then the notated score is not just the *best* way to ensure the normativity required for re-performing a work no longer in the repertoire, it amounts to the only way, since the only alternative is the written or spoken version of the constraints from the abstract object that is the dancework. And these are a kind of score!

So the score both gives the required permanence and, in functioning normatively ("as a recipe"), clarifies the boundary between acceptable and unacceptable performance. Hence it locates future discussion of that work.

§4. Dances as not suitable for preservation?

The argument so far has spoken, implicitly, in favour of a posterity for danceworks. The next thought to consider suggests that danceworks *should* exist "at a perpetual vanishing point" (Siegel, 1972 p. 1), such that they actually do vanish 'when they have had their day'. Of course, this must mean more than just that a particular work has failed the test of time (we would expect that in all art forms). Rather, the perspective of (some?) choreographers — and certainly some of those opposed to dance reconstruction, in one of the uses of that expression (see Chapter Nine) — is that dances *should not* be preserved. But why, exactly? Thus Goodman considers (and finds wanting):

> ... the argument that dance, as a visual and mobile art involving the infinitely subtle and varied expressions and theoretical motions of one or more highly complex organisms, is far too complicated to be captured by any notation. (LA p. 212)

For, as Goodman recognises, this is a confusion: first, this view misconceives the fluidity and flexibility of what is available to the notation system; then, second, it mistakes the whole direction of notation. For, as Goodman notes:

> [t]he function of a score is to specify the essential properties a performance must have to belong to the work ... (LA p. 212: NB Goodman's sense of "essential" is *not* my "crucial")

And this comment should be read in the light of remarks on defeasibility and exceptionlessness (in Chapter Three).

As Renee Conroy (2007 p. 2[a]) makes plain, Mark Franko is a major voice here, seeing a place only for 'radical re-invention', which "... involves actively rethinking dance history's uses as well as its meanings now" (Franko, 1989 p. 58). In his rejection of a posterity for dance, Franko (1989 p. 73) challenges "the old myth of repeatability", since — as he stresses — we clearly cannot realistically hope to bring to the stage a performance visually indistinguishable from, say, that encountered by the original audience at a Ruth St. Denis concert. That is surely correct. But, insofar as our interest is the artistic one broadly identified earlier (Chapter One §7), why should we want to, anyway? That is not typically a goal when staging a dance that our own company performed last season: why should it become one in this case? And here any reference to a feeling of 'pastness' lacking from works recently in the repertoire is a red herring since, logically, what is past is past: that point applies as much to one's own recent performances as to works from the history of dance. Then, talk of the "old myth of repeatability" hides a profound confusion on Franko's part: if one can re-perform *any* dancework (and that *must* be possible, if danceworks counts as *performables*), then a particular work can be *repeated*. Commonsense tells us that the 'repeat' is quite likely *not* to be qualitatively indistinguishable from the previous performance — but any serious thinking about performing arts must *begin* from the fact that performances with significantly different properties can nevertheless be performances of the very same work of art.

Suppose that our 'reconstruction' aims at the preservation of dances in which — in their heyday — an artistic interest was appropriately taken. That will set 'criteria' for success, at least in broad terms. Perhaps some productions designed to make primarily *historical* points will need a different kind of explanation — although even they will deploy the fact that particular performances of a dancework are typically under-determined by the work itself, such that the performance makes concrete what is indeterminate in the dancework itself. If the aim were simply to illustrate *for students* some features of dances of the past, our goal might be set nearer to (say) the movement-styles of the past. But, to that degree, our concern with the artistic is tempered: for our aim is not the artistic aim (only). And one might also ask how much of a particular dancework students need to encounter to grasp the point here: often, it will be less than the complete work. Hence a further rationale may be needed if the whole of the historical dancework is to be performed. But, in any case, there is a *dancework* to be performed (if only in principle).

Franko might also deny the *reality* of danceworks in this sense, for his commitment to an ontology whereby the dance exists *only* at the moment of performance, drawing on parallels in literary theory, might suggest that "[t]here is no original work to which subsequent instantiations ... must necessarily conform" (as Sarah Rubidge, 2000 p. 207 notes). Now, there is something odd about this view of *existence*. As Drid Williams (1991 p. 79/ 2004 p. 72) points out:

> It is as though we are being asked, '*where* is, e.g. *Swan Lake*, when no one is performing it?' Otherwise sensible, rational people who would hoot at the question, 'where is spoken language when it is not being spoken?' ... do not hesitate to ask this question about dancing.

As though there were a good answer! Further, even such theorists treat danceworks as performables[2]: they compare this performance *of the work* with another performance (or one by another company); they regard rehearsals as *for* performances, and those performances as of the work at issue; further, that is what the notators are notating. All this reiterates the traditional ontology of *the performable*[3].

Moreover, since a dancework which *remains* in the repertoire is not a set of indistinguishable performances, it asks too much of our historical case to insist that repeating the work requires indistinguishability from some past performance. (Which?) Now imagine that one goal in preserving a work for posterity is simply to keep that work in the repertoire. Then (a) doing so draws on the under-determination of performance by dancework; the continuity of that very dancework allows for difference. And (b) a notated score will be a very suitable way forward for recording that dance itself (and especially what, if anything, is crucial to that dance. For:

- notationality is not just about preservation (especially preservation 'in the long run'); rather, it offers a way to give clearer judgements about the *present* of a dancework, in ways that bear on its future;

- preservation of some kind is required for 're-performables'; that is, for performing arts. Since that applies as much to the performances on Tuesday and Wednesday of this week as to those in some future, the need to make identity-judgements cannot simply put aside here;

- reliance on memory (and especially memory alone) is problematic;

- reliance on recording by, say, video or DVD is problematic (as we have shown in the previous chapter, since it preserves the *whole* of one performance, with no method of sorting the crucial from the contingencies).

Many of these points surfaced earlier (see Chapter Two). The key issue here concerns the second bullet-point: would any choreographers be happy to let their works die with, say, a particular cast, even though that was not necessary — where the continuity of the dancework (its place in posterity) was not the sterile one sometimes associated with reconstruction, or preservation, ... or dance history more generally? For the notated score precisely offers a freedom here; exactly as much freedom as one wants ... and certainly freedom in line with the standard treatment of 'classics' from the past, which can be kept vivid in performance. So, when we turn to *authenticity*, this indicates the *potential* of the notated score.

§5. Finding the dance from interpretations: another place for scores?

However, a consequence of some remarks on notation in Chapter Three is that, very often, the score that *is* made for some dance — assuming *any* is made — will be a score for some *performance-interpretation* of the dance, rather than for the dance itself (that is, the abstract object, or the type). This will result from the notator being unclear whether certain features of the performance he/she is recording are crucial to its being the dancework it is — whether they represents constraints from the type, as we have put it, rather than contingent features of *this* performance. Of course, we recognised that this could be corrected by the intervention of the choreographer: say, by his/her making plain which were the constraints from the type. And it would be facilitated by choreographers becoming *masters* of the notation (as most musical composers are, for musical notation); but, now, this seemed unlikely to occur.

It follows, of course, that — viewed strictly — these notated scores do not count as (my) *adequate scores* for the dance in question, since they do not circumscribe that dance as such. Instead, compliance with such score guarantees that one performs such-and-such a performance-interpretation of the dance. But another performance, incompatible with this score, might still count as a performance of the dancework in question. This possibility was instanced by recognising that, while a performance complying with the Stepanov score would count as *Swan Lake* (let this be granted), a performance might fail to comply with this score and yet be uncontentiously *Swan Lake*. This was explained that by noting that the performance complying with the Stepanov score was a performance of (say) Drigo's interpretation of *Swan Lake*. But other performance-interpretations were possible.

What should be made of a world replete with dance scores, but where none imported only the constraints from the abstract object that was the dance itself, the type? In particular, where does this leave the *Thesis of*

Notationality? As our arguments have shown, these scores are not worthless in the hunt for constraints from the type. In some cases the dance itself can be considered by looking at the score, if one understands the notation system well enough, and if the score itself is a very full one — to that extent, the situation parallels that for music. But one's access to the type could be yet more indirect: that score may be for an interpretation of the work (such as Drigo's interpretation). As such, it would include the constraints from the type, but (typically) yet further constraints. These would provide a basis for (critical?) argument as to what was *required* by the type, what simply the requirements of this interpretation. Of course, one cannot expect a single answer here (accepted by all) nor that one resolution — if found — would last for ever.

The upshot is that there is no one source of access to the dance. And, as comparison with music suggests (and rightly), *access* to the artwork via the score is not the same as actually confronting the artwork — one does not actually experience the artwork if one merely confronts the score. This follows from the *embodied* character of artistic meaning and artistic value: as urged previously (Chapter One §7), in typical artworks, (artistic) meaning is embodied in this or that particular way (movement, sound, and so on). Hence 'what is meant' cannot ultimately be divorced from this embodiment — in contrast to, say, the report of a traffic accident, where the same meaning might occur expressed differently. Further, this explains why similar or related artworks differ: their meaning, in being differently embodied, is a different meaning (see AJ Chapter Two). By contrast, a typical score lacks artistic embodiment: hence, seeing it is not really seeing the dancework. At best, the score presents the work 'unembodied'. It might seem, though, that one possible 'access' here — that through a recording of the dance — might be useful in preserving the work and yet give the audience-member experience of the artwork itself. This topic is complex: Chapter Ten discusses a key part (via a comparison with recording for music). But we can come to it here by a slightly indirect route, interesting in its own right.

§6. Watching recordings

Having put aside the recording of dance on film or DVD as a realistic alternative to notation, since (as Chapter Three shows) notationality is potentially a stronger guide to the features of the work itself, one can look across at danceworks (or dance-like works) which centrally employ this recording technology, as part of what that artwork is. As it stands, this seems a perfectly accepted hybrid art form, even from the perspective of those who reject seeing dance on film or video as a legitimate way of encountering 'traditional' danceworks. Part of our interest in such cases is that a fuller discussion of them returns us (eventually) to the vexing question of whether watching a recording of a dance *counts* as watching the dance.

Then the thesis under consideration would be that "... dance created or reinterpreted for film or video camera is the only legitimate dance on DVD" (Segal, 2008 p. F9). This thesis might seem to accurately reflect the treatment of some concrete cases:

> Mikhail Baryshnikov dancing excerpts from *Giselle* in the "Turning Point" and "Dancers" can be acceptable because they are feature films. But not Mikhail Baryshnikov dancing the complete *Giselle* as taped by PBS for the "Live from the Lincoln Center" TV series and subsequently issued on home video ... (Segal, 2008 p. F9)

So it might seem that the artistic *rendering* of the dancework (in a film) counts as art, while just *recording* the work as performed does not.

A number of contrasts must be drawn to understand this complicated set of cases. It helps to formulate the initial thesis more carefully: thus, the point is really that dances designed to be recorded and *then* seen are ... well, one might even say (as above) that they were not dances at all, but a new, hybrid art form. Then these are dance-like objects where the fact of their being recorded is not mere accident: one can only encounter that artwork by seeing such a 'recording' — hence it is not really a recording of the dance at all, but rather the film here is the art form! (This means, of course, that — while dances "... created ... for film or video camera" might count as works in this new, hybrid form — dances "... reinterpreted for film or video camera" will not.) And that would be contrasted with simply filming an extant performance of a dancework. Indeed, a useful comparison here might be with the discussion of whether films can actually *do philosophy*; that is, *do philosophy* where this is contrasted both with recording the doing of philosophy (say, by recording a philosophy lecture, or by having the text of a philosophical work scrolling up the screen) and with reporting the conclusions of philosophy, like some introductory texts. There is nothing *filmic* or *cinematic* in these cases where a dance performance is (merely) filmed: the impact of its being *film* is negligible. This is the real point about dance on film: something new is seen when works (say, in our new hybrid art form) are designed to incorporate the filmic aspect. If this is lacking, one gets at best a recording of a performance of the dance, and one that inevitably misses much of the actual performance of that dance[4].

Now, the Baryshnikov performances cited were of two kinds, but neither amounted to watching the dancework (or even a performance of it). The complete *Giselle* would be a recording of a performance of the artwork — we have already broached some questions about its status. The case of the feature film raises interesting issues. Clearly *The Turning Point* (1977) is an acceptable artwork for these purposes just because it was a *film* — designed, planned, executed, and so on, as a *film*. No doubt some of its interest for some viewers came from its portrayal of the dance sequences; but, within the film, that was not Baryshnikov dancing, but instead his character (Yuri Kopeikine).

Certainly, the performance should not be treated as uncontentiously Baryshnikov. For instance, an interesting question would ask: is Yuri a better or worse dancer than Mikhail? In typical cases at least, Yuri cannot be a better dancer — he cannot demonstrate any leaps, say, that Mikhail cannot perform. But perhaps Yuri can perform a certain virtuoso leap more regularly than Mikhail, as Mario Lanza, an adequate Caruso for film, could not (at least arguably) sustain the rigours of arduous performance of the whole opera. Indeed, skillful shooting might even make Yuri's leaps more spectacular than Mikhail's. Further, one can certainly *imagine*, in a film, the character being unable to master some piece of technique the actor/dancer had mastered: hence Yuri might be a worse dancer than Mikhail. So too many conclusions about seeing *Baryshnikov* dance should not be drawn from watching *The Turning Point*, in which — we now recognise — *Yuri* is dancing!

By contrast, there are recording of dances. As our author urges, the problem here is that the artwork 'in the offing', as it were, is the dance. So the problem with watching a *recording* of a performance is that the *recording as such* is not the artwork: at best, the dance might be. This just raises again the central question: is one seeing the dance in seeing a recording of it? Limitations of recordings as ways of preserving dances (compared to notated scores) have been suggested. And the notated scores were not, themselves, the artworks — one could not encounter the work simply by encountering the score. Perhaps the same could be said of recordings of dances.

Judged from this perspective, then, seeing recordings of performances is not really seeing the work performed at all — at least, I will later argue for this position. But, to clarify the situation, let us grant that position for the moment: seeing the recording of the performance is not seeing the actual work.

Still, seeing the recording may be the nearest one comes to seeing that work. Hence there are at least two reasons to be glad when performances are recorded, and to wish that more would be. Both reasons are mentioned (or implicit) in the article under consideration, but they are obscured by not being clearly enough delineated from the different concerns with 'dance on video' mentioned above. The first of these is just to record the *performers*: one would certainly like to see, say, Nijinsky's own *L'Après-midi d'un faune* — and the recording might be as near as one can get, even granting that it would lack something. This is explicitly recognised when the topic turns to "… those more interested in star dancers than repertory" (Segal, 2008 p. F9). But it is not identified as a different topic. Second, those looking to the future of dance must hope that its past is preserved; that there is a kind of *posterity*. Again, the point is to preserve what is available. Ideally, this involves classic works, one hopes (since otherwise even they may be lost — given how few are currently notated), but also "… works by … major living choreographers" (Segal, 2008 p. F9). Further, there is benefit in enlarging the dance community by preserving "… the true range of international ballet in the 21st century" (Segal, 2008 p. F9): those in Southern California, for instance, would have the opportunity "… to measure … [the] repertory [of other companies] against what we know of such relatively familiar visitors as American Ballet Theatre and New York City Ballet" (Segal, 2008 p. F9). So one sees some benefits of such recordings. Then the possibility of 'bootleg' recording of dances might be beneficial in preserving either the performances or the works (as above). The technology might seem helpful: anyone could, in principle, bring the technology for recording to any performance — although a planned recording might still be preferable to that of "… a balletomane with plenty of guts and a steady hand" (Segal, 2008 p. F9).

§7. Watching the dance?

Now one can return to the issue of whether, when seeing only the recording, one has seen the dance itself. Before approaching this issue directly, though, perhaps we should be clear, initially, (a) that seeing the film or video may be the best one can do, such that one can at least determine some of the features from it — as one can when using a slide to replace a painting; (b) that, while time spent watching the film is best described as exactly that, it is not exactly wrong to say one spent one's time watching the dance — after all, one had been watching *that* film, and not some other; (c) that this discussion does not bear on the hybrid art form hypothesised above. So I could well say (and truthfully) that I had spent the afternoon watching Christopher Bruce's *Ghost Dances* (1981), even though I had only been watching the film. None of these claims is being denied.

In the article under discussion, Segal takes a defence of the kind offered here (that the dancework as only confronted when confronting a performance) as merely highlighting a practical matter — yes, we'd all like to have seen (say) Baryshnikov live! Thus he grants that the recording is second-best. But the choice to see the breadth and depth of ballet, not to mention the virtuoso performers, is not open to most of us. So one must turn to the recording: indeed, "… in Los Angeles, our pleasure in dance and even our dance literacy are compromised by everything that we can't see in the flesh". Hence all that must be overcome are "… the rather simplistic perceptual issues raised to demean DVD dance" (Segal, 2008 p. F9).

This entirely misses my point. Without wishing to "demean" anything, the issues are very far from being "… rather simplistic perceptual issues": instead, they concern *what it is* that one is considering — and hence what its properties are. Finding that what is before is indeed a dancework is finding the movement patterns *transfigured* into art; hence, finding artistic properties truly ascribable to that movement sequence. Then one recognises both that a different artwork would have different things true of it and that what was not an artwork could not be a bearer of these properties at all. That returns us to consideration of the nature of the 'object' before us: is it indeed *the dance* itself? Can one see the dancework by viewing it?

Well, would one be content *only* to watch films or videos (what I shall call "recordings") of dances? It is common ground on all sides here that watching more than one performance of a particular dancework offers the possibility of new insight, first, into the work and, second, into what ever aspects of the human condition that work lays-out for us. So the issue here does not merely concern variety.

One comparison might *seem* to be with musical works: but there is a profound difference. Some theorists take musical works to be simply sonic structures, sound systems (Kivy, 1993; Kivy, 1990; Dodd, 2007). Even when that is not *obviously* right, it complicates our taking the musical case as a parallel for dance. Perhaps a person who has listened to all of Mozart's compositions on DVD has heard all of Mozart's music; but someone who has never seen actual bodies in motion (rather than merely the recording of them) does not, in the same way, even *arguably* seem to have seen all Christopher Bruce's dances; or even *any* of them. Yet, if right, this seems to imply that the person who had seen only those recordings had not seen any *dance* at all. That may seem an extreme view. But, equally, we cannot seriously regard this person as an *expert* in Bruce's dances — although that would surely follow if his attention had really been given to the artworks themselves. At the least, it would be hard to claim connoisseurship for dance if one neither attended dance performances, nor felt any inclination to do so. For (and this seems a good way to put the point) such a person has neither seen nor understood *dance*. And that, of course, is my position.

Here, our author wishes to stress the rather limited perspective on dance available in the Los Angeles area ("the Southland"); and does so with ridicule:

My parrot, Steve, lives in a cage near the TV set and so has seen more

dance than many Southland balletomanes — although he much prefers
car chases, parades, game shows, hurricanes and the Iraq war. (Segal,
2008 p. F9)

Here, four comments are appropriate:

(i) How could the judgement as to which the parrot "prefers" be made out? It
cannot be in terms of his squarks, for instance, since these are as likely to
be pain as pleasure. Yet that seems the only possible basis.

(ii) [more seriously] The parrot has not seen any *dance*: he has perhaps seen
images that were indeed dances, but a parrot cannot recognise them as
dance since he cannot see the movements transfigured into art — he does
not have the conceptual range appropriate for such a judgement.

(iii) Further, all the parrot has seen — on this account — is dance on TV: we
have expressed reservations about whether this could always count as
seeing the dance, at least for all purposes. Certainly a person who had
only seen dance on TV would probably not count, for purposes of
philosophical aesthetics, as a *central* case of a dance appreciator. So one
might with justice dispute that Steve the parrot "... has seen more dance
than many Southland balletomanes".

(iv) If one turns now to *what* the parrot (allegedly) "prefers", it makes sense
for a human to urge that, while she did indeed like car chases, she had
only seen them on television. But it is plausible to doubt that a parrot has
seen (or recognised) them. This just returns us to our original puzzle: for
dance, is watching television *only* enough to allow one to count as an
appreciative spectator of dance?

So the initial question might be put this way: so-and-so claims to be a
connoisseur of dance, but has only seen recordings — could he be right? For
what is required for that claim to be true here is clearly a first-hand, first
person acquaintance with danceworks. Would one be happy to grant the
same kind of knowledge of, say, war to someone who had only seen newsreel
footage of wars? Certainly sports fans want to attend the matches, even
though the view from one's couch to the televised version is more
comfortable. And they rightly regard the two events as different. That
parallel suggests that, in most contexts, we should reject our person's claim
to experience of dance.

§8.   A return to contextualism
Here, two problems for such a conclusion (given my other commitments)

should be noted; and a response given. So, first, should contextualism not suggest that watching the recording is watching the dances? As we said previously, someone who has been watching the recording of this dance has been doing something. Further, that person was not, say, watching other dances ... and he/she will, as a result, know things about those dances that he/she did not know before watching that recording. Of course, these points are not being denied. But when our concern is with the artwork — when our interest is artistic interest — we will hope for a *fuller* engagement with the artwork than the recording can offer: as we saw, the recording necessarily lacks some features that might well be important for artistic judgement of this work. So one can with justice insist on the *primacy* of actually watching the dance over watching the recording of it, without minimising the value (for some purposes) of the latter. Indeed, one might usefully insist that such a person had merely seen *dances-on-video*; or recording of (aspects of) dances.

Then, second, why should there by an exceptionless, all-or-nothing answer here? The argument seemed to suggest that, if one had not seen (at least) bodies in motion, one had not seen dances; but need that be treated exceptionlessly? The short answer, of course, is that whether one agrees that one had seen the dance in a particular case depends on the context: on the question asked. So, no, there need be no *exceptionless* answer here — instead, as above, I may well prefer to say that I *had* seen the dance, but only on video, to saying that I had not seen it; not least because my watching the recording may, for some purposes, allow me to hold up my end of a discussion about the dance!

Throughout this discussion, my having seen the dance (on video) cannot without loss be 'translated' as my having seen the dance. If we are interested in the formal patterns of the dance, perhaps my having studied the video carefully, and on repeated viewing, may be a better basis for comment than actually attending a performance — both because of the singularity of this performance and, often, because of the access afforded by *my* seat. (In a similar way, a combination of looking at the score of Webern's *Symphonie* opus 21 and playing its opening on a piano may be a *better* way to get insight into the *canon* which structures that opening than listening to the work. But doing so is not really listening to the musical work: at best, one's access to this artwork *there* is very, very partial.) Since seeing the dance requires *the dance* passing before one's eyes, there is a clear sense in which nothing else will do: there will be at least some contexts in which, for purposes of artistic interest, seeing the dance requires actually *seeing* it, as opposed to seeing a -ecording.

9.   onclusion

verall, this chapter has considered some modes of 'access' to the dance, uch as the score and the recording, plotting at least some of the usefulness f each in context. In particular, the uses to which notated scores might be ut, and the advantages of so doing, reinforce the prior emphasis on otationality. For the score can function *normatively*, to show what actions *hould* be performed, in order to instantiate a particular dancework. Equally, e have been realistic about the difficulties (both practical and theoretical) f 'full' notation systems, such as Labanotation. In passing, our topic is ecognised as, somehow, a *typical* dancework: there will be works in what as called a *hybrid*, dance-like form for which other comments would be ppropriate. Further, the connection of dance-identity to dance preservation as also been acknowledged (a topic for Chapter Nine also); and the dance-c onnoisseur contrasted with the person with a large collection of recordings! his has reinforced our contextualism by rejecting the requirement for an all-or-nothing' answer to questions about the place (or nature) of the ecording of dance: on some occasions, to watch the recording will be to atch the dance, although artistic interest (with its concern with the detail f the *embodiment* of the artwork) will typically require watching a erformance (also?).

Part Two: Making Artworks

Chapter Five

Thinking about the choreographer

A fundamental place for the choreographer as author of the dancework (and especially of that work's *meaning*) was suggested by Chapter Three, in emphasising how one defeating condition — a "recognised head of exception" — for ascriptions of dance-identity would be 'wrong history of production' (in Goodman's sense: see LA p. 122/PP p. 101). By implication, the actual history of production has a place when such claims remain undefeated: this seems a commitment to a kind of intentionalism, on which the intelligence 'behind' the work bears on which work it is or how it should be understood.

Moreover, choreographers sometimes say (or imply) what their works mean or are about; or how to make sense of those works: as when Deborah Hay (quoted Foster, 1986 p. 78) attempts to capture a quality of movement in her dance by saying, "the dancer's body is arched like a supple bow". (A fuller example was sketched: UD pp. 237-240.) Or critics or other writers may relay this information — for instance, that DV8's *Dead Dreams of Monochrome Men* (1988) evoked:

> ... the story of serial killer Dennis Nilsen ... [in which] the four protagonists explored different aspects of Nilsen's psychosis as well as portraying his victims. (Rowell, 2000 p. 87: see also Mackrell, 1997 pp. 115-116)

The choreographer might be accepted as an authority here, since he/she is responsible (in large part: compare Chapter Seven) for what the audience encounters. And the fact of the intelligent making (and especially the making of art) seems to imply such responsibility for what is to be made sense of, even if that sometimes takes the form of a denial of meaning. Thus, choreographers might aim to reject the *idea* of meaning in general, as Merce Cunningham (quoted Jordan, 1992 p. 27) attempts to avoid such a connection, emphasising instead:

> ... something being exactly what it is in its time and place, and not in its having actual or symbolic reference to other things. A thing is just a thing. We don't ... have to worry ourselves about providing relationships and continuities and order and structure — they cannot be avoided.

Yet, as the final remarks implicitly recognise, he cannot really succeed: he is presenting these "things" to the audience in a dance presentation — that is, as art. And, having selected (or anyway licensed) the presentation of those "things", he retains responsibility here.

Or a more specific meaning may be contested. Thus, Douglas Dunn (1998 p. 183) having noted that "... one of the things I disliked was the frequent modern dance theme of the choreographer as ... choreographer", admits that now "... I'm very involved in it. *Lazy Madge* is about it. It shocks me to death" (Dunn, 1998 p. 183). The shock was to find that his work reflected a theme of which he had previously thought little; and that, of course, concedes both that the work embodies a theme and that it does so *intentionally*, despite his best efforts. Hence it implicitly invites us to see the work that way.

But such ideas seem problematic given a long tradition in aesthetics which denies just such a connection between artworks — in our case, danceworks — and the intentions of those works' creators, primarily because looking at the intentions is seen as, somehow, no longer looking at the artworks themselves.

Here[1], the problem as traditionally conceived is outlined; before sketching the contours of its resolution; and putting aside a line of objection from another tradition. That introduces my preferred account (a version of hypothetical intentionalism), contrasting it with moderate actual intentionalism. Finally, a line of objection to that position is considered. Since this issue is raised for all (or certainly most) art forms, and especially for literature, the examples in this chapter range widely, returning to dance by the end.

§1. The standard stuff: intentionalism vs. anti-intentionalism

Now let us spell out (at high speed) the standard contrast here, giving some reasons each view might seem plausible. For only then can the issue be understood aright. That issue is wider than just intention as such: it concerns the extent to which using information about its *creator* (for example, biographical information) is legitimate when understanding or appreciating his/her artistic creation.

To begin: an *Intentionalist Thesis* about art urges that, when we are uncertain about the interpretation of a work of art, our puzzlement can always (or at least usually) be resolved by discovering the artist's intentions — roughly, it is not a painting of Tower Bridge because he/she did not *intend* it to depict Tower Bridge. So a notion such as *intention* seems crucial to avoiding *misperception* of the artwork (where avoiding misperception is a key idea throughout). Thus, making art involves *intending* to make art: further, intending to make it in such-and-such *category of art*[2] (genre, etc.) — so, *ending-up* with a Cubist painting requires having Cubist intentions in one's painting. And *misperception* will be avoided only if its audience *recognise* the work as in its *category of art*. Here, there are two or three kinds of cases — we can:

- mistake music (say, Messiaen) for birdsong (that is, artwork for non-art);

- mistake birdsong for Messiaen (non-art for art); or

- mistake atonal music for poor music in another genre; equally, mistake a Cubist painting for one in another style (so, bad category ascription).

In each case, the artwork has properties other than those ascribed to it; and our missing these properties results from our failures of recognition (perhaps ultimately of knowledge).

Moreover, reference of this kind to intention (or to biography, and so on) is often useful in practice. Suppose one wonders whether Donne's poem "Nocturnal Upon St. Lucy's Day" is ironic. Well, his life at the time of its composition illustrates that he had reason to be depressed. That speaks against the *ironic* reading being the strongest one — some relevant facts, facts from his life, both speak *against* that reading and *for* another (namely, that the poem is bleak). Of course, nothing in the *text* of the poem need, in principle, help resolve such a case.

Here, two big questions arise. First, does one *always* need intention? Or, without certain kinds of puzzlement, might one say nothing here, resting content that the poem or painting was intentional in the sense of not being accidental, but without considering intentions specifically? So, does one *always* need intention? Then, second, is speaking of "what Shakespeare intended" really asking about what he thought or planned, *prior* to the writing the play? (So, what is the *nature* of the appeal to intention?)

At this point Wimsatt and Beardsley ([1954] 1978) introduced[3] the idea of an *intentional fallacy*, where (roughly) looking at intention is [first] looking away from the work and to the artist, and [second] looking to something at best causally connected to the resultant artwork. So, for an *Anti-intentionalist Thesis*, they say:

> *The artist's intention is neither available nor desirable* ... (see Wimsatt & Beardsley, 1978 p. 293)

Wimsatt and Beardsley actually say "author", but — although their concern (with literature) may have some specific aspects[4] — the points can be taken to apply across the arts *mutatis mutandis*. Thus Beardsley (1958 p. 20) moves seamlessly from considering the author of a literary work to "the painter with his exhibition catalogue ...", and to what "a sculptor tells us ..."; while

Margolis (1978 p. 291) remarks that "... counterpart moves seem possible to the other arts".

Further, Wimsatt and Beardsley next talk of using intention as "a standard for judging", but that reflects their initial context: the explanation given suggests it would be as much a fallacy (if it ever is) for the kind of 'making sense of art' sometimes called "interpretation". As Colin Lyas (1992 p. 132) summarises, for Wimsatt and Beardsley:

> ... artists may be in error about their intentions ... [or] artists may be in error about whether the works they have produced in fact possess the properties they intended them to have.

Hence one cannot with justice begin solely from artists' assertions.

Specific cases support Wimsatt and Beardsley's claim concerning (first) what is not "*available*": there are anonymous works, or cases where one just does not *know* what the artist thinks (where he/she is dead or uncommunicative). Here, one cannot *find out* what the author intended. But one may still understand his/her works.

Similarly, cases where knowing the intention is (or seems) uninformative support Wimsatt and Beardsley's claim about what is not "*desirable*". For artists do not always achieve what they intend. As Stanley Cavell (1969 p. 181) puts it:

> ... it no more counts towards the success or failure of a work of art that the artist intended something other than is there, than it counts, when the referee is counting over a boxer, that the boxer had intended to duck.

Again, criticism should be *of the artwork* (of its features), not of its artist. Thinking otherwise involves committing some 'causal fallacy'. And this kind of appropriate attention is sometimes called (suitably for poetry) *scrutiny* of the work itself.

On the argumentative strategy here, if reference to intention (or something similar) is *ever* required to make sense of an artwork, then it is *always* required. By contrast, if it is *sometimes* not required, then it is never really *required*. Hence, the practice (on both sides, but especially for Wimsatt and Beardsley) involves searching for counter-examples: for *if* one finds cases either where ascription of intention is not required to make sense of an artwork or where one gets by without it in practice, that shows conclusively that it is *never* required (given these assumptions).

Further, as Lyas (1992 p. 132) urged, for Wimsatt and Beardsley "... artists may be in error about their intentions". For these reasons:

> ... statements by artists about their intentions have no special authority over the deliberations of critics and interpreters. (Lyas, 1992 p. 132)

This attitude was therefore classically presented as an attempt to guarantee that criticism focused on *the work itself*: this in turn was sometimes presented *directly* as the thesis that criticism should depend on *scrutiny* of the artworks themselves, such that an artwork is treated as "an object to be criticised ... with its own properties against which interpretations and judgements can be checked" (Beardsley, 1970 p. 16); and sometimes *indirectly* as the thesis that:

> the primary purpose of literary interpretation ... [is] to help readers approach literary works ... with an interest in actualising their (artistic) goodness. (Beardsley, 1970 p. 34)

This claim need not be contentious: but Beardsley (1970 p. 34) explicates it in terms of the "affording [of] aesthetic satisfaction". Now, were this indeed the explanation of critical (or, more generally, appreciative) judgement, it is likely to be irrelevant that its author *intended* such-and-such (Carroll, 2001 p. 171): either the satisfaction *is* gained from the work or it is not.

Beardsley's focus treats the (aesthetic) satisfaction as a response by the observer (the critic or appreciator): for him, the alternative can only be a focus on the *artist* (and hence *away from* the work) since "[i]ntention is design or plan in the author's mind" (Wimsatt & Beardsley, 1978 p. 294). As Wimsatt and Beardsley (1978 p. 298) write,"[t]here is criticism of poetry and there is author psychology" — with the implication that doing the second can never be a way to do the first.

But (genuine) appreciation of an object cannot be separated from the kind of object it is, especially given the *transformative* effect of art-status. Or, as I put it elsewhere (Chapter One §7; AJ Chapter One; McFee, 2005), the object's being an artwork means that certain things are true of it that would not be true otherwise — or would be true only in a different way: that, for instance, the tranquillity of the fine-art painting will be *planned* or *intended* tranquillity, in contrast to the tranquillity of the actual scene depicted. So appreciating the work *as art* essentially requires regarding the object (say, the collection of words on the page) *as a poem* — and as a literary artwork. Hence, any beauty or grace ascribed to it is essentially artistic beauty or artistic grace. And these ascriptions are not made solely on the basis of looking at the words on the page. Instead, one must ask how those words are to be taken; or, in what kind of context of appreciation one finds oneself.

By contrast, Anti-intentionalists put such questions aside. They seem to imagine finding a poem, of indeterminate age, in a house of indeterminate but unhelpful age, written in a manner, and language, which gives no guidance as to age, provenance, or such like (could it be typed? handwritten?); then, having found the poem, simply scrutinising *it*. (Wollheim [1980 p. 188] writes more generally of "scrutiny of the literary text, of the music score, of the painted surface.") And one justification for the Anti-intentionalist approach is that one should 'bring nothing' (or 'nothing external') to one's encounter with the poem — for otherwise one will be (roughly) pre-judging it. That stress on bringing nothing is, in turn, justified as egalitarian: since no technical knowledge is needed, no one is excluded.

But such a model is unconvincing even in this favoured case of finding the poem — which may be why it is rarely made explicit. As a precondition for any scrutiny, first, one must know the language — that may involve its temporal location. For instance, the expression "plastic arm" occurs in Mark Akenside's 1744 poem "Pleasures of the Imagination" — mistaking its date, the term "plastic" would be misread[5]. In a similar vein, the modern reader of Jane Austen's novel[6], who discovers Mr. Elton "... actually making violent love" to Emma in a carriage, will probably misunderstand what has taken place: such a reader is "... likely to imagine advances rather more audacious than those which Jane Austen associated with those very same characters" (Livingstone, 2005 p. 120). Second, the discovered text must be recognised as (say) a *poem*, and of a certain type (in a certain *category of art*) — it is a poem and not a shopping list. Third, *irony*, and such like, must be recognised (say, for a poetic version of Swift's *Modest Proposal*), or one will misunderstand. No doubt there are other requirements too. So quite a bit of knowledge and understanding must be brought to, say, a poem to make anything of it.

One suggestion, in line with Anti-intentionalism, is that one bring nothing 'about *this* poem or painting' — but then, what are the features of, say, *this* poem? The impact of *categories of art* on artistic properties must be recognised: the features of this poem (or painting) are only seen aright in that light. So that *whether* the words are taken to comprise a poem, and (if so) what *kind* of poem, bears on what features or properties one can truly ascribe to it.

The overall line of objection here returns to the claim of scrutiny (as Wollheim, 1993a pp. 139 does: UD p. 137), asking, "scrutiny on the basis of what *cognitive stock*?" For if perception — of which scrutiny is a species — is concept-mediated, one can ask what concepts are implicit. Here they will include the ones raised earlier: knowing the language, and the relevant categories of art, as well as recognising *this* (collection of words before us) as a poem, and knowing enough about it to preclude its being, say, ironic. Again, this is far from *nothing*.

These, then, are sketches of Intentionalist and Anti-intentionalist positions, offering some reasons for each, and raising some issues. How should one proceed?

§2. Resolving the issue?

A strategy to resolve the dispute between these factions in aesthetics is suggested by 'Ramsey's Maxim', on which "… whenever there is a violent and persistent philosophical dispute there is likely to be a false assumption shared by both parties" (Bambrough, 1969 p. 10). So, can some shared assumption or assumptions be denied?

[Before continuing, it is worth noting that deploying Ramsey's Maxim does *not* generate 'a middle way' between these alternatives: rather, it denies something they both accept — so *both* are wrong!]

The first set of assumptions shared by Intentionalist and Anti-intentionalist is methodological: that (logical or necessary) connections of interest to philosophy (like entailment) are all-or-nothing. So they can be explored by looking for counter-examples. Hence intention is either *always* relevant (so one case where it is not would be such a counter-example) or it *never* is: again, one case of its *being* relevant would be a counter-example. On the face of it, each of our competitor-accounts offered plausible-sounding counter-examples to its opponent's thesis. This is one set of assumptions shared. The other set concerns the nature of intention. Both Intentionalist and Anti-intentionalist view intentions as 'in the head' of the artist. Thus Beardsley (1958 p. 17) says that:

> The artist's intention is a series of psychological states or events in his mind: what he wanted to do, how he imagined or projected the work before he began to make it and in the process of making it.

That is, on this view, intention is pieces of prior planning at best causally connected to the outcome (the artwork) — as though the thought "dig the garden" went through one's head, and then one's body went out and started digging.

Giving up the first set of shared assumptions emphasises logical connections which are *not* all-or-nothing, by finding a place for *defeasibility* in one's argumentative framework (UD p. 62); or by considering assumptions about exceptionlessness implicit in, say, our using the universal quantifier to treat the claim that "cheetahs can run faster than men" (see Ziff, 1972 pp. 127-141[7]). Anyway, giving up that assumption of 'all-or-nothing' undermines the kinds of argument beloved of both sides. (And *I* would stress the occasion-sensitivity of requests to understand artworks: that one does not need just *one* pattern of explanation.)

Giving up the second shared assumption, about the nature of intention, does not require denying that "… great art emerged struggling from the deep recesses of the soul" (Jowitt, 2004 p. 144). Instead, one simply reflects initially on patterns of *explaining* intention, beginning with simple cases.

Doing so shows that such ascriptions are not really psychological at all. For what I *do* is (other things being equal) what I *intend* to do: it is intending in this minimal sense. Then, (a) the ascription of intention is public (in principle) — at least defeasibly, that I am digging is 'evidence' that I intended to dig; and so is my complaining that the bad weather stopped me digging, and so on. And, (b) I do not (typically) study my intentions to find out what I will do — the relation is *not* (or, anyway, not *straightforwardly*) causal. Thus saying, "I am putting on my coat, so plainly I intend to go home", is not reporting a discovery of a causal structure. In the opposite direction, my explicitly intending such-and-such does not, by itself, bring that thing about — as we know, since what I explicitly intended may yet not occur. Further (c) the ascription of intention involving a kind of interpretation: making sense of what I do, in terms of my intentions, may require reconsidering my past behaviour. Perhaps my past intentions were not what you thought they were; perhaps they were not what I thought they were. Discovering that my action of pumping water to the town poisoned the inhabitants, one might think I made a mistake; or one may look differently at my attitude to those townspeople (see Anscombe, 1957 p. 37; compare Lyas, 1992 p. 142). In summary, intention-ascription can be revealing about human action, but not (typically) in virtue of revealing what went on 'in the head' of agents.

Were that correct, a similar pattern of explanation should apply to art-making. As Wollheim (1987 p. 37) puts it:

> ... the burden of proof would seem to fall upon those who think that the perspective of the artist, which in effect means seeing the art and the artist's activity in the light of his intentions, is not the proper starting point in any attempt to understand painting [or any other art form]. For it is they who break with the standard pattern of explanation in which understanding is preserved.

So one has a right to expect the artist's intentions to cohere with the understanding of his/her work; the case where it does not will be an exception (and itself open to explanation). Yet this is (presented as) a "starting point"; and at its centre is the idea of not separating artist and work. (Thus, for example, Wollheim, 1980 p. 185: the creative process as "... not stopping short of, but terminating on, the work of art itself".)

Employing Ramsey's Maxim in this case involves giving up both the shared assumptions identified above: the commitment to 'all-or-nothing', and the view of intention as prior planning, 'in the head' of the artist, at best causally connected to the artwork produced. Where does that leave us? Before answering, another view should be briefly put aside.

§3.   The death of the artist (especially, the author)

Some theorists, often calling themselves "postmodernists", have endorsed a view much more radical than those just discussed — under the heading "the death of the author", since their primary concern has been with literature (or perhaps even with writing more generally). They stress, not the author's *death* at all, but the disappearance of the concept *author*, with its implications of *intention*, from discussion of novels and the like. On this view, literary works are merely instances of writing, with the author an abstraction, and meaning determined by the reader. Relatedly, a contrast (sanctioned by literary theory) is drawn between text and work, where the *text* is just "a concatenation of signs subject to multiple interpretations" (Lamarque, 2000 p. 457), but where the *work* is (or may be) constrained by purpose, context, genre. And this *work*-concept, which seems to imply authorship, is also disparaged. As Peter Lamarque (2000 p. 457) puts it, "By assigning priority to texts over works, poststructuralisms in effect sideline altogether the category of literature ...". And more than just *avowed* poststructuralists take this line. For instance, Tony Bennett (1979 p. 11) cites scholars who feel that the concept *literature* "... artificially separates the study of 'literary' texts from adjacent areas of cultural practice"; and is unhelpful for that reason — 'literature is just text'. Yet this denies literary value (and, *mutatis mutandis*, artistic value): surely not a move open to an aesthetician!

Further, there is an additional issue: for, in the case of literature, a theory designed for language is being applied to the linguistic — literary works have *words* as their components, at least in some sense. The application to dance requires an additional step. And notice that this is not a critique of a *kind* of dance (call it "postmodern dance": compare CDE pp. 204-207), but a perfectly general critique of features which — were its advocates right — are common to much dance, even if this regularly escapes notice.

But what postmodernists deny is not what moderate intentionalists assert (as we shall see: compare AJ pp. 85-95). The dispute does not concern the place (for understanding the artwork) of the planning of this or that person: postmodernists rightly recognise that, in itself, *intending does not make it so*. Hence, they aim to look at the object produced, not at the thoughts or plans that produced it: they refuse to begin from the actual thoughts of this or that person. Yet that is already our position, achieved through our deployment of Ramsey's Maxim. And two problems for typical postmodernist accounts of intention arise here. First, in denying the role of the author, the imported theory about linguistic meaning seems to imply that (say, for a poem) the *words alone* ("the text") could carry any weight; and then concludes that these words are somehow ambiguous, or in need of interpretation[8]. This result follows, even for words, only when the context of the production of those words (their 'utterance) is set aside. (The words, "Mary had a little lamb", may seem equivocal between a concern with animal husbandry and a concern with dinner. But, in context, their utterance is typically not misleading.) So this is a poor account of language: nothing is *just* text.

Or, more exactly, one arrives at this conclusion by imagining that — in principle — *words alone* might have provided the meaning: for then one discovers that, alone, they cannot have done so. Were that their legitimate role, the claims just discussed would follow[9]. But if, instead, one thinks (more sensibly) that the words alone cannot have this role, one recognises that words (almost) always come to us in some context or other — as a novel, or an advertisement, or a joke, or a philosophy lecture — and then that context sets, or anyway delimits, the meaning justly ascribable to those words in that precise context. Hence, the meaning cannot in general be open (or ambiguous, or arbitrary), contrary to the claims of our poststructuralists and postmodernists. So, in one way or another, this account of language is flawed.

Moreover, and second, the mistaken picture of linguistic meaning the view of language incorporates will carry over to the understanding of literary artworks; for instance, the poem. For, again, the poem is thereby treated as *nothing but* a string of words: its context is set aside. But artworks — here, our poem — carry with them specific and crucial contexts of art; they must be appreciated *as art*. And our understanding of them returns us to the time and place of their production and/or reception: to what has been called their "history of production".

In ignoring both the facts about language and those about art, our postmodernists miss much that is important in granting intelligibility to artworks. And, of course, since danceworks typically incorporate bodies in motion, there is another significant difference here — its exact impact remains unclear. Further, the postmodernist view runs counter to at least three connections between intention and (genuine) meaning. First, meaning is intentional. Contrast the yawn, at some dull meeting, which just *occurs* with the one where I catch your eye and yawn extravagantly. From both, the observer (my boss!) might learn something. But my deliberately yawning is an attempt to *mean* something; to communicate to you how dull I find the meeting. From the 'natural' yawn, by contrast, my boss just finds out how bored I am — the very last thing I wanted her to know! So, in one case, there is no genuine *communication*, and no message: for it was not intended communication, meant communication. Second, causality alone cannot yield meaning. The cracks in the wall *appear* to spell out a loved-one's name: not only do *not* do so, they *could* not (insofar as they really are just cracks)[10]. Since these cracks just occur naturally, there is nothing that they *mean* (although they might be symptomatic of something: PI §354). Third, and more specific, artworks are not blank 'objects for interpretation'; not Rorschach Tests. So one cannot just make of them whatever one wants — although the key thought here (that artworks can be *misperceived*) only implies *some* constraint, as contrasted with the unconstrained 'anything goes'. Neither are the features of artworks *accidental* (unless someone decides they shall be). Here, Paisley Livingstone (2005 pp. vii-viii) reports the story of a painter trying, without success, to capture in paint the lather at his horse's mouth. Finally, in frustration, he throws his paint-soaked sponge at the canvas — which produces exactly the effect for which he had been striving. Livingstone comments that, "[t]he painter knows he had taken up the challenge of skillfully painting the lather, and he cannot pride himself in achieving the goal." But the painter here could as easily have embraced his good fortune — perhaps even adding this technique to his repertoire! And the least, if he chooses to accept the serendipity, it thereby becomes his achievement. So (roughly) an artist's intelligence must be seen behind the artwork. The objections of many who disagree rest simply on assuming a 'one right answer' version of constraint.

And, of course, the case of danceworks offers another significant difference here: for danceworks typically incorporate bodies in motion. And it remains unclear how these points *could* have a bearing there. (This is one reason why there are fewer dance examples than one might like early in this Chapter.)

Moreover, those who urge publicly that one's 'reading' of artworks lacks *any* constraint do not typically mean what they say: they do regard, say, the words in the poem as constraining *to some degree* and *in some way* what can be made of that poem. First, they do not really think that each of us has a different 'reading' (although that claim is often heard) — such that, say, 200 million Americans might have 200 million different readings. At best, they are just recognising some diversity. Second, they do not really believe that, say, *King Lear* could really be 'read' as a farce, nor that Goya's *Saturn Eating His Children* could be seen as jolly: some cases *offered* just seem too implausible. And that reflects the *features* of the artworks. Moreover, they grant that, say, the organisation of books in a book store has some basis — mysteries here, science fiction there, and romances over there. Perhaps some such decisions are arbitrary. But the majority are not. The alternative view, that *all* interpretations are arbitrary, somehow reflecting their origins in language, is " ... a tissue of mistakes. If *dog* is an arbitrary sign for a dog, it is at any rate a sign for a dog, and that must mean it can refer to a dog: and a dog is a dog, not a word" (Williams, 2002 p. 6). Whatever forces seem to open *words* to the charge of arbitrariness carry less weight applied to objects in the world, such as dogs!

Or consider the impact of *titles* here: for example, Hockney's *Rubber Ring Floating in a Swimming Pool* [1971], where "... the arrangement on the canvas reads two ways, as the depiction of the scene in the title, and as a comment on the work of ... contemporary painters" (Hockney, 1976 p. 20). As Hockney (1976 p. 241) said, "... it's almost copied ... [from a photograph] ... I was so struck by the picture's looking like a Max Ernst abstract painting that I thought, it's marvellous, I could just paint it." Without the title, it might be mistaken for an abstract work. A similar impact to the title sustains Alphonse Allais's joke all-white painting, *Anaemic Young Girls Go to Their First Communion in a Snowstorm*.

These ideas, taken together, show how artworks are best understood via such concepts as "meaning", "intention", "artist": for the first two ideas suggest *meant* or *intentional*; the third suggests a *constrained meaning*[11] . Once such meaning for danceworks (or artworks more generally) is recognised as not dependent on some artist's psychology, we are well on the way to locating the meaning-as-embodied in the dance or poem by acknowledging a set of personal properties here: that is why the sculpture could be expressive, witty, and so on, while such concepts could not apply to the meteorite (see Ground, 1989 pp. 25-26) — even when one could be mistaken for the other, as a pair of Danto-esque "confusable counterparts" (Danto, 1981 p. 138). Moreover, this talk of *meaning* does not become irrelevant when one turns to a broadly non-verbal practice such as dance. For here too the intention is explicit in the project of making *art*. As Charles Weidman (1998 p. 67) commented:

> It is often said of modern dance that it is not easily understood, that its silent language of movement is so intricate as to veil its meaning.

But, as he continues, the dancework's intelligibility is crucial to the idea that what one is making is art. Hence this intention is always fundamental (in typical cases). So, to move forward, one should adopt a kind of intentionalism modified in the light of our discussion of Ramsey's Maxim.

§4. "Intentionalism composed out of anti-intentionalist materials"

To repeat, the need to accommodate a distinctive artistic *meaning* gives a place to an intentional concept: for only what is meant in that way can be meaningful. This is why the cracks in the wall not only *do not* spell out my loved-one's name, they *could not* do so. A naturally occurring process (such as the wall's cracking) lacks the intentional force. Thus, when a perceptible property of an artwork makes it (say) expressive, "the property is due to the intentions of the artist" (Wollheim, 1993a p. 155). Moreover, artworks can be made sense of; and hence have the possibility of an audience. Then our understanding of artworks (for us, danceworks) connects any particular artwork to the history and traditions of art-making and art-appreciating; and therefore grants a cognitivist thrust to artistic properties: for instance, a knowledge required to avoid misperception. Thus Sharpe (2000 p. vii) notes "... that certain general ideas about music and its relation to its times affect our judgement ... [and] ... that our experience of music is infected and deflected by *ideas* about music." (my emphasis). Since the point applies more generally, it could be repeated for dance (making suitable substitutions). Further, what is intentional in this sense need not be what common sense calls "intended": one need not have thought about the matter specifically. My walking is an intentional activity (it is not an accident; I am responsible for any damage I do); but I do not, usually, *think* about walking — one way or the other. Despite using the term "intention" and its cognates, an account understood this way will not lose its focus on the artwork — as Beardsley (1970 p. 33) offers, one should be "... a poem-reader, not a mind-reader"; and so on for other arts. So our view will be intentionalism of a kind that has learned in these ways from the application of Ramsey's Maxim to the original debate.

Clearly, the concept *intention* must be found a place in any plausible analysis of artworks, given the connection between meaning and intention. When discussing a play, speaking of "What Shakespeare intended ..." (say, in this scene) is granting that its features are not accidental; that the work here was intended. But how is intention correctly ascribed? As we have seen, the real problem arises when asking about intention (or about 'what is intended') directs us *away* from the work of art, towards the artist — especially when a mistaken view of intention seems to direct attention 'inside the artist's head'. Here there are two cases. Typically, one needs (roughly) 'the intention embodied in the work' (whether or not it was the artist's): as a slogan for this, one can use "intentionalism constructed out of anti-intentionalist materials" (UD p. 230). One must keep close to the sorts of 'scrutiny of the work' of which our anti-intentionalist approved, but in ways that expose the *meaning* — and therefore the *intentional* structures — embodied in that artwork (at least when that work is a success).

But what about intentions *not* fulfilled? This raises our *other* typical case. So (roughly) one speaks of "intention" only (a) for intentions *embodied* in the work or (b) for *failed* intentions ("I meant to do so-and-so, but ..."), where the former will be consistent with Beardsley's injunction (above) to be "... a poem-reader, not a mind-reader". For our attention will not be distracted from the artwork. Further, talk of a *poem* here brings with it the context of poem-hood as well as the artist's intelligence (it isn't an accident)! Both are important. So, in this context, there is *art*; and poems are recognisable (including making mistakes), and related to *genres*, via a narrative of art-history. Further, the activities do not come about by chance. It may be difficult to put the point exactly. Thus, Livingstone (2005 pp. 11-12) urges that "[g]ood golfers can intentionally make a short putt, but no golfer *intentionally* sinks a sixty footer, even though the stroke was made with the intention of so doing ... [since]... the feat is extremely unlikely." But it cannot realistically be thought an *accident* that the putt was successful. And calling the putt-sinking "intentional" need say no more than that. These points would apply directly to claims about what choreographers *intended*: in some cases, recognising that our choreographer is making dances, intelligible against the background of the narrative of dance history, allows us to put the right gloss on, say, Deborah Hay's claim that, "[e]veryday the whole day from the minute you get up is potentially a dance" (quoted Foster, 1986 p. 6) — that nothing is automatically unavailable to a dance. But that is just an invitation to find what is actually the dance on this or that occasion. And, again, no reference to some *intention* (as distinct from talking about the dance — and hence the intention-as embodied) is needed unless that intention was not realised in the artwork.

A complete *theory* is not needed here, but only materials to meet objections that might arise, or questions that might be asked, about the place of the artist's intention in the understanding of her work. These typically relate to decisions about how best to make sense of that work: or, if this is different, what properties are best ascribed to it. A very complex area with a large literature can be resolved by sketching three ideas. First, this cannot be a robust *actual* intentionalism: our account of *intending* something cannot be reduced to, say, what so-and-so person actually thought. For instance, although I certainly intended to go home this evening, this is the first time I have considered it, one way or another. So ascribing intention is often a matter of making sense of action by seeing it as, say, not accidental. The so-called "framer's intentions" for the US Constitution provide a rough parallel: properly understood, the "framer's intentions" are determined by a mixture of history, (constitutional) integrity and practice (see Dworkin, 1996 p. 10; Dworkin, 1986 pp. 176-224) — precisely the sorts of considerations which apply, *mutatis mutandis*, to artist's intentions! Such an account of the US Constitution, which Ronald Dworkin (1996: see SRV pp. 108-110) calls a *moral* reading, grants that thoughts which did not enter the heads of the actual people are nevertheless rightly regarded as part of the intention of the Constitution: for instance, that ideas of 'equality before the law' introduced in the context of *slavery* might imply rights for (other) minority groups. Determining such legal intentions is a matter of making the best *'fit'*: and, as with determining the appropriate reading of philosophical texts, few considerations are absolutely decisive here. Rather, such-and-such a 'reading' arguably preserves integrity better than its competitors (Dworkin, 1986 p. 217). So the difficulty is not unique to *intention* in respect of artworks; but the issue for art is resolved in roughly the way the legal case here suggests.

Since we are not discussing what so-and-so artist *did* think or consider, our account is not necessarily refuted by evidence that the person *did not* think about such-and-such. For example, Dr. Johnson might correct Goldsmith as to what he intended by the word "slow" in first line of his poem, "The Traveller":

> Goldsmith said it meant 'tardiness of locomotion' until contradicted by Johnson. 'No, sir. You do not mean tardiness of locomotion. You mean that sluggishness of mind that comes upon a man in solitude.' (Cioffi, 1965 pp. 175-176)

Here, Johnson offers a stronger 'reading' of the passage: what is resolved is the *meaning* of that passage. Rather than being about (say) what makers or audience *thought*, reference to "the artist's intention" here, as typically, amounts to commentary on the artworks themselves: hence, is true or false of them[12]. This accords with a general commitment to artistic properties as properties *of the artworks*.

Second, our concern is with intentions *ascribable* to this artist, given the time of construction of the work. In the simplest case, a person from a society lacking the concept *art* could not intend to make art, and hence could not succeed (nor fail) in making art. These conditions are primarily used negatively: *this* 'reading' of a work can be dismissed as conflicting with the artist's intentions. In the strongest case, we *know* that so-and-so could not have *intended* such-and-such, because the concepts were not available at that time. So reference to *intentions* here is also a way to talk about the state of the art world at that time (say, the time of composition).

Third, we begin from simply ascribing meaning to a particular work, and then explaining that meaning. And artworks are intentional: hence, artistic meaning is intended (which is why, concerned about the best 'reading', one can speak about Shakespeare's *intentions*). The discussion does not usually ask about what the artist intended specifically, if that means looking to his diary or his psychology, except to recognise (where appropriate) laudable but failed intentions or to point out that a certain 'reading' of the artwork in inconsistent with what *could have* been intended. For misperception must be avoided; and the context of creation and reception has some bearing on *what* the features of the artwork are — and hence on what it would be to misperceive them. Thus, suppose that the dancer in Liz Aggiss's solo *Grotesque Dancer* (1986), "... shockingly defies the conventional idea of female beauty ... [when she] takes off her wig to reveal a shaved head" (Adair, 1992 p. 215: my order). And, further, that she:

> ... is transformed from an ambivalent character in black bloomers, white socks and top to a frighteningly vulnerable creature with a shaven head in long, black satin gown. She limps off, one shoe in hand leaving the audience to make sense of the issues of power, oppression, female experience and imagery which have been encountered. (Adair, 1992 p. 215)

Although the work "intention" or its cognates is not used in the description, granting its accuracy to the dancework leaves us in no doubt that this work embodies exactly the sorts of meanings described here — and this is clearly not an accident, but flows from the choreographer's decisions. That is what talk of *intention* means here. Of course, one might (for a less successful work) have been asking what was *supposed* to have gone on; but that question would typically arise only when the work itself was not successful. If, as here, the work clearly embodies a meaning reflecting human intelligence in dance, there need be nothing more to ask.

The strategy of art critics, say, rightly consists in looking for the best reading of the work, the one giving maximum weight to the details of its features when 'read' in that way. Some constraints on our reading are found in the features of the work (as with, say, the duck-rabbit) and in the 'lay of the artworld', which may (sometimes) include facts about the artist. Thus, as we said, faced with facts of Donne's life at the time of composition of "Nocturnal upon St. Lucy's Day" (Alvarez, 1971 p. 138), we might decide against an ironic reading of that poem.

In a similar vein, Joan Acocella (1993 p. 110) discusses the ups and (mainly) downs of Mark Morris's life; and then comments:

> These facts do not explain the creation of a work such as *Dido*, but they may help to account for its sure-mindedness, its tragic calm.

That is, she points to facts about the life which — were she right — could help us decide between two 'readings' of Morris's *Dido and Aeneas* (1988), facts which might encourage us to prefer *this* reading to *that* one. Moreover, when Acocella (1993 p. 110) continues, "[s]ince *Dido*, Morris has made several works about love, and they are calmer still", we are invited both to find this as a part of the 'intention-as-embodied' in the works referred to (without needing to interrogate Morris himself on that score) and to draw the connection by reference to that narrative of dance-history (and especially of Morris's work) of which her earlier remark forms a part.

Or consider someone offering an account of Matthew Bourne's *Swan Lake* (1995) with its "radical gender twist ... [in which] ... Odette became a male Swan and Odile a louche freebooter" (Mackrell, 1997 p. 32); and stressing Bourne's use of Freudian ideas. Such an account should not be rejected *simply* because Bourne tells us that he did not think of it nor, even, that he has never read Freud! He might have forgotten, or have picked up Freudian ideas in other ways. But a similar account of the Ivanov and Petipa *Swan Lake* (1895) must be *rejected* (or at least modified extensively — in terms of 'precursors', perhaps). Since Ivanov and Petipa *predate* Freud, they cannot be seen as drawing on his *ideas* — at best, Freudian *themes* might be at work. Roughly, that they could not *intend* to refer to Freud's ideas guarantees that they *do* not. That Bourne did not *explicitly* plan to draw on Freud cannot have the same implication.

Two conditions here mirror more general constraints; (a) *mere* intending is not enough ('wishing cannot make it so'), since one must achieve (to some degree) what is intended, while (b) the *mere* fact that one could *justify* a certain account of an object (by reference to public features claimed for it) does not make that account of the object *true*: one is not thereby *justified* in so understanding it! Moreover, the relation to intention should be treated as defeasible, such that:

> I do not wish to claim that everything we find in a work of art is something we have to be prepared to say that the artist intended to put there. But I am claiming that our not being so prepared must be exceptional. (Cavell, 1969 p. 253)

Hence any other account is "at the same level as intention, a qualification of human action" (Cavell, 1969 p. 235 note). This will be one tool to deal with apparent counter-cases.

§5. Intentionalism, hypothetical and (modest) actual

Given that we are elaborating a kind of intentionalism, the literature offers two broad species (see Lamarque, 2009 pp. 127-129). The first, called *modest actual intentionalism*, "... holds that the preferred interpretation of the work is constrained by what can be known or reasonably conjectured of the actual intention of the creator as long as that intention is supported by the work itself" (Carroll, 2009 pp. 147-148). So any intention-ascription must be answerable to the features of the work — thereby avoiding the difficulty of unfulfilled intentions. But one may have intentions, in the sense that others might with justice ascribe those intentions, without being able to avow them oneself — perhaps one had not thought about it. Given these considerations, so-called *hypothetical intentionalism*, the more concessive version, may achieve all we need. So let us elaborate it first. On it (for a painting), understanding that artwork, or grasping the meaning embodied in it, is conceived in terms of what would be most justifiably ascribed to the artist:

> ... on the basis of the perceptible features of the painting, a complete grasp of its context of production, and a full knowledge of the artist's intentions as to how the work was to be taken, approached, or viewed .... (as Levinson [1996 p. 218] puts it[13])

Accounts for other art forms might be drawn up *mutatis mutandis*. Once *intention* is no longer taken as implying some private, prior planning on the part of the artist, one is no longer claiming to know what such-and-such an artist *thought* about on so-and-so day. Hence our claims cannot be defeated in that way. So, strictly, even if this account is "... ascribed to the artist", it is an account of the artwork, not the person (where these differ). Rather, and more plausibly, we are commenting on how to 'read' the work, given what we know about it (both locally and more generally — to pick up "history, practice and integrity": Dworkin, 1996 p. 11). Meaning or intending of *this* sort has a *history* — what can be *meant* depends both on the history of the art form up to the point of one's so meaning (including being in revolution against such history) and on the 'narrative' appropriately given in explaining what the work *meant*. As Levinson (1996 p. 207) puts the point (for literature), the hypothetical intentionalist sees the meaning of the work as (roughly) "... the best projection of what the author meant from an ideal reader's point of view".

In addition to *actual intentionalism* (where author's intentions constrain how his/her works are to be 'read') and *hypothetical intentionalism* (where interpretations are justified as those most likely intended by a postulated author), the literature also contains value-maximising theory, on which interpretations are preferred as they present works in the most artistically favourable light. But, as Stephen Davies (2006) has argued, the differences between the last option and hypothetical intentionalism are slight: that, under some conditions, "hypothetical intentionalism and the value-maximising theory ... [are] equivalent" (Davies, 2006 p. 243). So we shall simply consider the two options.

Can hypothetical intentionalism deal with, say, the ironic? Is an actual intention not required there? Our answer to the second question is, "no": the facts of the author's life are not precluded from consideration by the hypothetical intentionalist — they too offer a basis for generating readings of works. But, on our view, we are not *obliged* to use such facts; and neither are they (always) decisive.

Indeed, a strength of my version of hypothetical intentionalism is precisely that it does *not* assume that the meaning of the artwork (say, the poem) is exhausted by what the author would *say* if asked, both because the claims of authors cannot be decisive and because authors can be capricious. For instance, faced with his mother's angry request, about *La Saison en Enfer*, "What does it mean?" Rimbaud responded, "It means exactly what it says" (see Durrell, 1952 p. 4). However, my view *does* grant both that the work must be intentional *as art*, and that 'readings' of it cannot justifiably deploy concepts unavailable in principle to the artworld at the time of the work's construction[14]. Moreover, it offers a principled rejection of the claim of any 'reading' to be *complete*, if that implies some finite totality of features of the poem *all* accommodated in this reading. For here, as elsewhere (FW p. 116), there is no such finite totality. Instead, a key idea here concerns *the incomplete*: calling a 'reading' *incomplete* need not presuppose the possibility of the finite totality of an exceptionless (or counter-example-free) *complete* reading. Instead, its completeness (or otherwise) is occasion-sensitive.

As a brief literary illustration, consider the poem "Song: Ask Me No More" by the seventeenth-century courtier poet Thomas Carew (1594-1640), whose last stanza reads[15]:

> Ask me no more if east or west
> The phoenix builds her spicy nest;
> For unto you at last she flies,
> And in your fragrant bosom dies.

Suppose one's extensive critical analysis of this stanza does not mention the fact that, in poems of this period, the term "dies" was regularly used to denote male sexual climax: moreover, that this reading obviously elaborates the interpretation in this case. Now there would be a clear sense in which one's prior interpretation of the poem was *incomplete*: something is not mentioned that *could* reasonably have been — thus one could specify the element that was lacking; namely, the aspect around the term "dies". Hence, the sense in which the analysis or interpretation was incomplete could be specified exactly. It counts as *incomplete* just because the manner of its incompleteness could be specified. Then something to this effect could be incorporated into one's analysis of the poem. That would deal with this particular incompleteness. But, although that analysis of the poem would no longer be incomplete *in this regard*, it could not be judged *complete*: although, now, we lack a basis for regarding it as incomplete, we also have no basis for denying that more might relevantly be said of the poem; and then, once the relevance of this *more* was granted, our interpretation could be recognised as having previously been incomplete in that respect. Because there is no finite totality of features of the poem to be relevantly considered, there is no sense in which *all* aspects of incompleteness were remedied. So that revised reading is not *the last word* here — even if it is the last word *I* care to say! For, in principle, other readings of the poem could always be offered, not conjoinable (FW pp. 118-120) with our original or revised 'reading': our poem is amenable to 'readings' not (previously) thought-of — although (of course) one cannot *now* say what they are!

Theses of the kind espoused here about intention in art might seem susceptible to obvious counter-examples. For instance, composer John Cage and choreographer Merce Cunningham each set out to 'avoid intention' both by using aleatory (chance) compositional procedures, so that each did not *decide* what happened when, *and* by explicitly denying that the works they made had *meanings* (for which intention would be implied). But chance compositional techniques still involve the composer or choreographer in making a *choice* of a kind, although a 'second-order' choice — the choice to use this compositional technique; and to select the elements over which the procedure then operates. (And perhaps, for less scrupulous artists, to have a final 'say' as to additional features.) Moreover, taking seriously both the denial of intention and the denial of meaning grants that these denials operate at the same 'level' as what is denied, occupying the same 'logical space'. Further, such denials are only intelligible as aspirations when taken by *contrast* with what is denied (as we understand the revolutionary by contrast). So these are not ways of *extracting* oneself from the consideration of meaning or intention. Thus neither strategy *could* be successful, as long as Cage and Cunningham were engaged in making art.

So artistic meaning requires a context in which it is possible to *intend* to make art: further, one in which that intention (perhaps viewed hypothetically) can be operative in our appreciation. For *art* is a central interpretive category for the activity here, which cannot be given up *without loss* by artists. This in turn limits what could count as *artistic* intention. Thus one cannot genuinely be indifferent to whether or not one's work is art; moreover, one cannot genuinely be indifferent to whether or not art *as such* is (at least typically) valuable, in a non-monetary way. For such value is typical of *art*. At the least, these indifferences are not open to artists. Of course, artists should not *just* be taken at their word: otherwise one would have to take literally, say, Deborah Hay describing her whole life as dance (see Foster, 1986 p. 6 [quoted above]). Often, the artists' points are argumentative or polemical (Cavell, 1969 p. 221). That at least gives a place to start: that they made the works *as art*. Thus, say, surrealism in painting or poetry, say, might seem like a way to escape intention. In reality the paintings of, for instance, Magritte and Dali, and the poems of David Gascoyne, are works of sophisticated technical virtuosity — clearly giving evidence of intention!

However, this case suggests a different way of making art, one that *might* seem to escape even this kind of intention: perhaps a conceptual art of 'found poems' in fragments of text, where (in effect) the methods of composition separate the *work* part from the *art* part (Wollheim, 1973 pp. 107-108). Of course, those of Duchamp's Readymades where the theory of '*rendez-vous*' was at its purest provide the foremost examples — where Duchamp simply exhibited a found object, without (say) writing on it. That is, where the selection of the sensuous surface of the work was at best *arguably* the artist's. But even here the decision to take *this* (and not *that*) — and perhaps to put one's name to the work — highlight that the resulting objects are intentional.

There are, at first sight, sizeable difficulties here: for how are we to determine what makes sense as an intentional structure for the work? In particular, what of works that fail to find an audience?

This difficulty should not be overstated: art has probably always had an *avant-garde* 'edge', found challenging by the audience for established art of a certain period. Think of the shock (even among his friends) that greeted Picasso's *Les Demoiselles D'Avignon*, or of the critical rejection of the early dances of Martha Graham (they were dismissed as angular — in contrast both to ballet and to the rococo elegance of Orientalist dances of, say, Ruth St. Denis). Yet their makers still *claimed* these works as art: in this way, they *argued* (if only implicitly) that what they had made were artworks. And, of course, this 'argument' was ultimately recognised; the works acquired a centrality for later art-making. So nothing follows from the fact that the contemporary audience (then) *took a time* to acknowledge these works. Hence nothing turns on the *actual* or *extant* audience for art. Indeed, that might be the norm. Thus Roger Fry ([1912] 1996 p. 113) urged that the general public (or the critic) forgets that every new artwork:

> ... is ugly until it becomes beautiful; that we usually apply the word 'beautiful' to those works of art in which familiarity has enabled us to grasp the unity easily ... .

This speaks against 'waiting on posterity', even when we remind ourselves of the transformative force — in *some* cases, or on *some* occasions — of the works themselves: thus, there might be a temptation to take the Waltz of the Snowflakes in Mark Morris's *Hard Nut* (1991) as "... iconoclastic, a comment of ballet ... [given] ... that men don't dance well on pointe and that people look funny in hats shaped like Dairy Queen cones" (Acocella, 1993 p. 204: my order). But, as Acocella (1993 p. 204) continues, this feeling does nor persist: instead, these characters

> ... are not a subversion of an old beauty, or not just that. They are a new beauty, a child's dream of winter — of ice cream and snowballs and things flying around, blinding and beautiful — and all this spun into a gorgeous dance, as frenzied as a snowstorm, as organised as a snowflake. The dance shades from wit into magic.

So, in this case, the 'waiting' need last no time at all (if Acocella is right). Still, in any case, we have shown that these works *may* be made sense of (at that time) *as art* — deploying the *categories of art* then in place: we need only explore whether they *should* be made sense of in this way.

§6. Modest actual intentionalism returns

In that sense, our hypothetical intentionalist aims to *uncover* the author's intentions: but in a world where what the author *says* of his intentions is not always conclusive; and where, since there need be no 'prior planning' on the artist's part, our account cannot aim to match any such planning. As we have seen, Dr. Johnson contradicted Goldsmith when the latter asserted what he had meant (or intended): the target is still what our author actually intended. And, in at least some cases (like this one), all sides concede that asking our author cannot guarantee a way forward. Thus my hypothetical intentionalist seems to choose a certain 'reading' of a work as "... the best interpretation, even if we know the author's actual intention was otherwise (say, through personal communication)" (Carroll, 2001 p. 209). This will be pressed as an objection to hypothetical intentionalism by the modest actual intentionalist. Here, the thought might go, the artist's intention is known in a reliable way (from the "personal communication"). That *decides* which account of 'intention-in-the-work' the modest actual intentionalist adopts (as long as it is consistent with the features of the work so viewed).

Such a case assumes that the author's "personal communication" here is *authoritative*: that it tells us his/her "*actual* intentions" (my emphasis). Yet, at least sometimes, if what the author *claims* to have intended conflicts with how best to 'read' the work, our version should be preferred: 'his intentions were not what he thought they were'. This possibility follows from our account of intention; and might sometimes be justified by appeal to consistency.

Still, the target *is* uncovering what our author intended. So Noël Carroll (2009 p. 144 note) rightly imagines our author protesting, "Don't put words in my mouth". That is, the moral imperative here should be accepted: to ascribe only the intentions (genuinely) embodied in the work. That is, not to 'read in' intentions in respect of the artist's actions. But, of course, our attention should be on the *intentions embodied in the work* — the author may not have avowed these intentions; and may be unable to do so. So there may be literally *nothing* in his mouth (or equally, in his mind — since we have rejected a 'prior planning' model of intention). That does not mean that the author's actions were accidental: hence a story must be told. We aim to *make sense* of our author's doings. That is not so far from looking to an 'intention to be retrieved'. Yet this allusion to an (extreme) actual intentionalism (in Wollheim, 1980[16]) is clarifying here. For we are denying precisely his sort of *realism* about intention.

Then we might agree with Carroll (2001 p. 205) — discussing Levinson — that "[r]eading in accordance with hypothetical intentionalism is simply reading for actual intentions". This does not make one a modest actual intentionalist (as opposed to a hypothetical one) since we reserve the right, in any particular case, to reach an understanding of the work (and hence of the intention it embodies) by using *whatever* materials strike us in that context as (arguably) the appropriate ones — hence, to put aside, say, author's diaries if they are inconsistent with what is otherwise taken as certain. So this sometimes involves rejecting what the author claims, in favour of making better sense of his/her doings, in the context. Some species of actual intentionalist would never do that.

Equally, the claims of the author *can* be crucial in some contexts. Then, one may rule-out ironic readings, say, by reference to the facts of the author's biography: as I did earlier in my reading of Swift's *Modest Proposal* and of Donne's *Nocturnal Upon St. Lucy's Day* (*pace* Carroll, 2001 p. 209).

Here, though, my version of hypothetical intentionalism approaches Carroll's modest actual intentionalism, since the 'hypotheses' of hypothetical intentionalism are "... hypotheses about *actual* intentions" (Carroll, 2001 p. 205: my emphasis). But, while that is true, such *actual intentions* (in this context) must not be treated as ones the author or artist might avow. So in what sense are they *actual*? Our earlier discussion of Beardsley's view clarified this topic, rightly rejecting the picture of intention on which that view was based. So the intentions 'at work' here need not reflect what the artist did say; nor even what he/she would say, if asked; nor yet what he/she could say (given his/her knowledge of, for instance, psychology — and this might even extend, in *some* cases, to the knowledge of psychology current in his/her time). All of these depend on taking intention as the kind of prior planning that might be reported; and then locating the *actual* intention would be (somehow) *matching* that 'prior plan' — an account of intention rightly rejected.

Thus when Carroll (2001 p. 205) says that "... if we come upon the author's actual intention, even if it departs from our best theory of it, then that is what we should prefer", he draws a false contrast. For, if we "come upon" the author's actual intention, it will play a key role in our thinking. There are two main cases. In one, our discovering the intention results from our "best theory of it"; and hence they cannot come apart (in the way Carroll imagines). For if the artist fulfilled his/her intention in this work *and* that intention is relevant to our understanding here (that is, the work embodies that intention), our best account of the relevant intention will be the one 'discovered'. But the main work here is done by the second condition. The artist's avowed intention need not, after all, be relevant in this example: not knowing the avowed intention need make no difference to our understanding of the artwork.

This suggestion becomes our second case, where that author *failed* to embody the intention in the work. As Wollheim (1987 p. 86) rightly notes, the only intentions that interest us are those successfully embodied in the work: the artist's *fulfilled intentions*, in this sense. If the author's intentions are not embodied in the work, then that fact — while potentially revealing about the author — cannot be revealing about the work. To understand the work in such a case, one should look to what *it* means, while granting the force of a human being 'behind' the work: it did not come about by accident.

Of course, the work so understood might be a triumph. Here, the artist's actual (or, better, *avowed*) intention might do no justice to the achievement. Then one might still conclude that, after all, this version reflected the artist's intention, just not one he/she could or would avow: thus, setting aside what, up until now, one took as his/her actual intention. This returns us, indirectly, to the case of Goldsmith and Dr. Johnson (above). In the real case, Goldsmith accepts Johnson's account of his meaning/intention. Then it seems right to conclude that (on mature reflection) Goldsmith's actual intention included those elements Johnson ascribed. But suppose we had discovered ("... come upon") Goldsmith's 'actual' (that is, *avowed*) intention prior to this event (say, as a private communication from Goldsmith to this effect). Still, the later event shows we were wrong. And, notice, intention is invoked precisely because it allows modification of our reading of (in this case) the poem.

On my version, hypothetical intentionalism offers an explanation here just because, on it, the work's embodied intention is simply our best account of what the artist intended — given what we know; but granting possibility of the failure of intention (the failure to embody that intention in the work), even in cases where, sometimes, the resulting work is still regarded highly. In such cases, it will always be possible to urge that the artist's intentions were not what he/she *thought* they were; thus, to treat this as the success of a different intention, rather than as the failure of that first considered.

'Elaborating' this version of *hypothetical intentionalism* (and distinguishing it more formally from Levinson's) augments our earlier point — about Levinson's mistaken assumption of a *complete* account of the artist's position, and such like — with a recognition of the expansiveness of our conception. Levinson (1996 p. 178 note 11) allows the hypothetical intentionalist a more limited range of epistemological resources. For instance, he seems to preclude the use of "... interviews, private correspondence, the author's unpublished journals, diaries, and so on" (Carroll, 2001 pp. 210-211) as not being strictly in 'the public domain'; as lacking "... public contextual factors" (Levinson, 1996 p. 207). For:

> ... one of the ground rules of the game of literary decipherment is that literary works are not supposed to require authors to explain what they mean. (Levinson, 1996 p. 208)

This is, in effect, the inheritor of Beardsley's conception of 'bringing nothing' *external* to the work. Literary works (and other artworks) are supposed to stand on their own feet: to be objects for interpretation, in context, rather than needing the *artist's* explanation. That is why "... we are ... implicitly enjoined from allowing an author's proclamations of meaning from having an evidential role" (Levinson, 1996 p. 208). And *this* explains Levinson's disquiet about the use of diaries or interviews — they are not part of the work.

Now, Levinson's objection here is complex. Initially, he asks what might realistically be required of the reader; and comments that one:

> ... mustn't ... require of the reader 'inside' knowledge ... which may be in the possession of family members, private secretaries or clairvoyants ... . (Levinson, 1996 p. 207)

While Levinson might seem to be setting aside only rather arcane 'sources' (for no one trusts the clairvoyants in such matters), he clearly wishes to limit what 'information' is relevant to our making sense of the literary text, grounding that exclusion in "... the underlying rules of literary communication" (Carroll, 2001 p. 213).

Granting this, though, cases where the diaries (or some such) clarify the *categorial ascription* of the work might still be recognised: where the ironic reading is specifically endorsed, say. So, in this way, a *category of art* (say) might be suggested to a critic; and that *category* permit him/her to make good sense of the artwork thus understood — for instance, by recognising its irony. Why is this (supposed to be) forbidden? Critics do use such material;

and, as contextualists, we cannot invoke some global basis for banning it. Indeed, it can offer a contribution to the context of understanding the artwork. So why consider a global ban? Such general restrictions are not needed: of course, what is appropriate here may always be a matter for debate, in any case: a resolution is needed only *in that case*, rather than more generally. Once the idea of *general* 'underlying rules' here is rejected, no *one* way to make sense of all literary work (or other artworks) seems appropriate; nor one set of obligations as to what could be relevant.

Nor is *some* limitation here out of place. Insofar as Levinson (2006 p. 311) rightly identifies the reader's task as to "... set about to interpret ...[the text] *as literature*" (my emphasis), he recognises it as "... one governed by different ground rules of interpretation than are ordinary utterances" (Levinson, 2006 p. 310) — in the sense, that is, that these begin from our *artistic* interest in the works: that is, our *artistic* rather than, at best, aesthetic interests. Of course, a restriction of that sort will not turn on the kinds of evidence, or 'information', relevant to understanding the artwork.

Now, clearly, the meaning *of the work* is at issue — in line with the slogan from Beardsley (quoted earlier), we are not aiming to be mind-readers. And I am an *hypothetical intentionalist* precisely to recognise what is needed as an idealised spectator's point of view (with the artist one such spectator)[17]. As a result, 'the public domain' of the general context seems the first place to look to understand this or that work: to the relevant categories of art, for instance. For the contrast between the work's meaning and the author's meaning must be maintained (in principle). And that may already licence, say, attention to diary information which might bear on category-ascription. But, when 'the public domain' proves insufficient, or when its insufficiency is raised as a 'recognised head of exception' to our defeasible relations, one can certainly look elsewhere. In at least *some* cases, it may be a criticism of an artwork that our understanding of it requires particular associations or relations to its author: perhaps Eliot's notes on *The Waste Land* attempt to avoid such a criticism; and certainly Pound's *Pisan Cantos* have been criticised as "... not wholly a public poem ... [since] their logic is the drift of his most intimate associations; it is fully available only to Pound himself" (Alvarez, 1958 p. 69). Whatever the justice of such a criticism *in these cases*, the general point has a *critical* weight: the work is flawed precisely in being too personal to permit the reader unfettered access. But, understanding the poem (and understanding that about it), requires consideration of that material concerning the artist — say, access to some of the names in Pound's *Pisan Cantos* as "... presumably soldiers at the camp" (Alvarez, 1958 p. 70). So this ("personal") material would need *consideration*, even if only to make the criticism. It cannot ground the limitation of the resources available to the justified interpreter of literature (or art more generally).

Moreover, this distinction between (roughly) the acceptably and the unacceptably private seems unworkable — especially for contextualists, not looking for a 'once-and-for-all' resolution. As Carroll (2001 p. 212) notes, what is or is not in the public domain seems, in general, quite arbitrary: some artists tell us a lot, doing so in contexts relevant to the *intentions* within which their work is to be understood[18]. Other artists offer nothing — or nothing but mystification. Similarly, facts of the artist's biography can bear on how to understand the work before us — in clarifying his/her place in the history of the art, and (perhaps) his/her conception of the art form (say, in terms of *categories of art*): for instance, the facts of Donne's life, as well as his poem about his marriage (Alvarez, 1971 pp. 137-138). But sometimes nothing is known of the artist's life (or nothing that seems to bear). So there seems no 'all-or-nothing' resolution here.

Thus, suppose Deborah Hay (quoted Foster, 1986 pp. 9-10) were correct in asserting:

> I dance by directing my consciousness to the movement of every cell in my body simultaneously so that I can feel all parts of me from the inside, from the very inside of our moving.

And suppose, further, that *therefore* the resultant dance refers to *her* life in ways that would make it (in practice) unintelligible to others: then she would be claiming that her dance depended on *the personal* in a way similar to Pound (above). In the most extreme case, the fact that the work could have no audience (in practice, though not in theory) will count against its art-status. But, in reality, her dances are not unintelligible; and that suggests that, in this respect, her (imagined) account of them is not correct. And, of course, this conclusion is still within intentionalism. As we saw in the discussion of Goldsmith and Dr. Johnson (above: §4), a hypothetical intentionalist can readily say that, in this scenario, Hay is mistaken about what she has achieved — as we might put it, the intention-as-embodied in her dance is not what she intended (or, perhaps, not what she *thought* she intended). But this result is achieved here by specifying closely both the context and what to make of it. Altering the context might generate a different outcome.

In summary, my claim is simply that all intentional ascription of action follows this pattern — that so-called "hypothetical intentionalism" is just *intentionalism*. It is distinguished from even modest actual intentionalism, first, by its weaker commitment to realism about intentions (to have intended such-and-such is not necessarily a matter of prior planning; and hence not amenable to the retrieval of such planning) and, second, by its being less inclined to take the author (or artist) at his word. Given our contextualism, this weaker version does all that is needed.

§7. Intention and history of production

To see this kind of hypothetical intentionalist account in operation, consider how questions of authorship arise in practice. Thus, we are told of the *Four Quartets*:

> They are kept firmly within the intellectual boundaries of the colouring and emotion *the poet thought* most suited to his subject. (Durrell, 1952 pp. 158-159: my emphasis)

The only evidence that this was as "the poet thought" is the poem itself. Recall (from §4 above) that, on my view (roughly), reference to 'the artist's intention' is either a way to talk about the work itself, or a way to explain failures, by noting that he intended such-and-such, but it didn't happen: it is, "intentionalism composed out of anti-intentionalist materials" (UD p. 230).

As we have seen already, the artist's intentions are circumscribed by (roughly) *the categories of art* through which the work should be understood: that is, in terms of its place in a narrative of art history in this art form (including being in revolution against such history). For the past of art has a connection to the "lay of the artworld" (Carroll, 2001 p. 91) at a particular time, and hence circumscribes artistic intention: what can be done or said differs at different times and places because what is intelligible (that is, can be made sense of) at one time may not be intelligible at another time. Consider, say, how the work of Picasso and Braque changed the landscape of art (at least in Paris) around 1910: certain actions became possible, and certain intentions became intelligible, in ways they previously had not. One key factor involves integrating the *changing* force of what we know (that is, of our cognitive stock) on our artistic judgements. For then the character of artistic properties might *fluctuate*. Fluctuations here, going unnoticed, might be taken as *always* symptomatic when they are only symptomatic *sometimes*, sometimes being indicative of logical relations (Wittgenstein's point: PI §354).

Although perhaps have not emphasised sufficiently, the importance of 'history of production', and its connection to responsibility, should also be stressed here. In distinguishing artworks, one powerful feature will be the distinctive histories of production of each. As we saw in Chapter Two, if the chair I was sitting on yesterday was made in Spain and the one I am sitting on today was made in France, it follows they are different chairs — or if one was made yesterday and the other the day before, or ... Applied to the authorship of artworks, this already plausible idea gains impetus. If what I do or make is genuinely *mine*, I am responsible for it — as I would not be for, say, a copy (where all the 'thinking' were ascribable to the artist I copy): then the difference between *this* work's history of production and others will be relevant just when my claim to authorship is. In this vein, the Walter Matthau character in the film *Kotch* (1971), asked "Do you like *Alice in Wonderland* by Lewis Carroll?" appropriately responds, "I wouldn't like it by anyone else": a book by someone else (therefore with a different history of production) would not be the work he admires. Of course, art objects are *specific* in just this way. When a painting of mine is compared with one of yours (the art-status of both being granted), it *follows* that they must be *different* artworks. Hence, a differentiated history of production is artistically relevant even about two (otherwise indistinguishable) works.

This returns us, as a problem case here, to Borges story "Pierre Menard, Author of *Don Quixote*" (reported in Chapter Two §6). In this tale, a contemporary Frenchman, Pierre Menard, creates a word-for-word perfect version of Cervantes; but without looking at Cervantes' text. Borges (1962 p. 49) *says* that, given their different locations in the history of art, "[t]he text of Cervantes and that of Menard are verbally identical, but the second is almost infinitely richer". For example, writing sixteenth-century Spanish is mannered for Menard (the language is artificial for him), as it could never be for Cervantes; and so on — the words have a different power in Menard's use of them. There is a connection here, through the *choices* made, to who is *responsible* for what: that each work has a different author permits differences in what each is responsible for — because, as Wollheim (1978 p. 37) notes, neither Cervantes nor Menard could be responsible for the words as such: "... evidently no novelist thinks that a word is his, that a phrase is his, that a paragraph is his. All these, he must surely recognise, belong to the language" (Wollheim, 1978 p. 37). At least, no sensible novelist should think these things. Rather, each is responsible for his *novel*, a concept beyond even the "macro-grammatical". For each, identifying his work simply as a collection of words misses the sense of it as a novel. Then Menard and Cervantes have different *responsibilities* here. That justifies us in treating each work differently. But each still has principled claims to art-status.

§8. Hypothetical intentionalism, creation and dance

A role for the choreographer, as *author* of the dance, has already been recognised — this means, especially, as author of the dancework's *meaning*. Does our strategy here, broadly in line with hypothetical intentionalism, make that conception more problematic?

As recognised in Chapter Three, the choreographer's *word* as to the work-identity of a particular performance (or score) was not ultimately decisive, although it was a good starting place. Our considerations here generate precisely this result: the intentionalism is only *hypothetical* intentionalism — the author's claims can, in some cases, be put aside. But such claims are, typically, one resource for any debate, *often* decisive in *that* context (although not necessarily, and not in all contexts).

One potential area of difficulty concerns the range of properties plausibly ascribed to a dance by such hypothetical intentionalism. For when are features intended, when not? Here, consider an attempt to 'escape' from explicit intention, by the use of chance techniques. Sally Banes (1993 p. 49) quotes, from the *New York Times*, a description of Elaine Summers' chance-based dance *Instant Choice*, on which "... the display of the method [of choosing movements] was central to the viewing of the dance" — it reads:

> Six performers appeared to be playing on a beach. They had various objects, including a ball, that they tossed around like dice, and the objects were numbered. The numbers that came up on the objects probably gave the dancers clues as to what they would do next. In any event, there was movement of all kinds going on steadily, and for some reason or other, it was interesting much of the time.

Banes (1993 p. 47) comments, "[w]atching a reconstruction of *Instant Choice*, I was struck by the childlike nature of the dance". What should we make of this claim? In particular, was it something Summers intended to be a feature of that dance? I imagine, from the descriptions, that this "childlike nature" would be a feature of all performances. On this assumption, two chief lines of reply are open: first, that Summers recognised this feature, perhaps through seeing a performance, perhaps at a rehearsal, and was content with it. This is clearly a case of intentional behaviour — although not, of course, of prior planning. Or, second, that Summers did not notice it. But, since (*ex hypothesi*) it is a feature of performances, it seems right to call it a property of the dance itself; and then, if Summers did not endorse it explicitly, she also did not repudiate it. Again, hypothetical intentionalism suggests that this is part of what *was* intended: and that seems the right answer.

Here, if the property is plausibly thought true of the dance — and, perhaps, a 'meaning property' — it turns out to be intentional; or, at least, something the author accepted as serendipity. And discussing it is discussing the dance (as the parallel of "a poem reader, not a mind-reader": Beardsley, 1970 p. 33), discussing what the dancework *embodies*. Further, most dance construction is not characterised by a single 'moment' of creation. First, a single motive is unlikely to deal with a typical dance construction. Asked why she made such-and-such a work, the artist typically offers a variety of explanations, including (no doubt) claims to the necessity, for that artist, of the production, the need for money, the desire to learn or to explore, and so on. But, insofar as the work is *art* (that is, insofar as it is transfigured), it is constructed under the intention to make *art*: that brings with it the implication that the object be (in principle) available to an audience. So the case is not of, say, movements done for some other purpose (say, to learn about ... or to explore ...) on which, as it were, the audience 'eavesdrops'. For then the interest could not legitimately be *artistic* interest but, at best, (mere) aesthetic interest. And if choreographers sometimes claim this interest (compare Rainer on *Room Service* (1963) as "... to make ordinary movement qua movement perceptible": quoted Chapter One §7), those claims should be read as polemical.

Second, and more importantly, much of the creation is done in the rehearsal room. As previously, my account of dance — of the *nature* of dance, if you like (to make plain the *philosophical* concern) — should reflect my experience of dance: for instance, that a lot of time goes into the rehearsal rooms, and a lot goes on there. I have spent much time waiting for dances to finish 'rehearsal' — often this was the *construction* of the piece, rather than dancers ("who by tradition and out of necessity are docile": Jowitt, 2004 p. 116) merely practicing it, although that distinction too is hard to draw abstractly or in every case.

Those with no experience of the performing arts often find this point hard to grasp: that learning to perform the dancework is often learning to perform it as *this* stager wants; and that time set aside for 'rehearsal' is often where the works themselves get constructed — like Turner showing up at 'varnishing days' for exhibitions in order, not merely to *finish* his picture, but almost to *begin* it. For it is crucial to see that the *idea* of a dance is not, yet, a dance: that dances are inherently physical, at least in most cases[19].

For much music, it *may* make sense for one to have written the music by writing the score — such that one could compose the second movement of the piece 'in his head' while *writing out* (as it were, transcribing) the score of movement one (as Mozart reputedly did[20]). That may reflect that one typically knows the limitations of the instruments before beginning the composition. Thus, Michael Finnissy's *Alice* (1976[21]), while fiendishly difficult for double-bass players, is at least within the capabilities of the instrument. The choreographer, by contrast, faces at least two very problematic cases: first, simply not knowing the limitations of the dancers one has — there might be a parallel here with opera: can one's soprano hit such-and-such a high note? Second, perhaps closer to being faced with the limited abilities of one's orchestra (say), is not knowing the strengths (or weaknesses) of one's dancers — if one wants to utilise them. For example, while choreographing *Black Angels* Christopher Bruce spoke of Lucy Burge as "the dancer of the earth" (Austin, 1976 p. 115: UD p. 207) and constructed her part accordingly. Of course, utilising the specific strengths of dancers in this way *seems* (and may *be*) limiting for whom you can be choreographing !

But these are practical constraints on choreography — they do not *dictate* that choreography could *only* be done one way (and in particular, do not preclude its being notated, either after the fact or as part of the creation of the work).

§9. Conclusion

As far as analytic philosophy goes, the history of the problem of the intention of the artist had — one might think — two distinct 'moments' in its development. The first (the moment of Wimsatt and Beardsley) was a moment of anti-intentionalism, which met with an 'intentionalist backlash' (the second moment, the moment of Hirsch[22]). An attempt to extend or deepen the understanding here might produce a third 'moment': roughly, the moment of hypothetical intentionalism.

Does my view here entail that a hypothetical intentionalist can never be wrong? Clearly, this is a crucial question since our rejection of the subjectivist "anything goes" will be based precisely on the capacity of *some* judgements of danceworks to be *wrong* (modelled on, say, the diverse but not open 'readings' of the duck-rabbit design). But here the three conditions Levinson implicitly set out (quoted above: §5) offer guidance. For he rightly urges that appreciative remarks be based on:

* *perceptible features of the dancework* — as with the duck-rabbit, there is *answerability* here; and hence the possibility of being wrong;

* *a grasp of the context of production* — not a *full* grasp, of course, but still enough that (finding one had 'the wrong end of the stick' about a dancework's history of production or reception) one might be led to revise one's view of that dancework;

* *the intention of the artist* as to how the work is to be taken, approached or viewed. The simplest case here is that above concerning the title of a work: approaching the dancework with a mistaken general conception (of the sort a title might provide), one is likely to misperceive or mis-value.

A discussion of Mark Morris's *O Rangasayee* (1984) illustrates these constraints in operation, thereby showing the dependence of the commentary on features of the dancework. It begins by acknowledging the features of that work as the basis for the commentary [in line with the first bullet-point above]:

> ... Morris, dressed only in a loincloth, traveled up and down, up and down, on the diagonal, repeating a sequence of steps, but with each repeat varying the steps — shifting the accent, shortening or lengthening a phrase, just as the music did — and each time descending further and further into some consuming inner state, both grotesque and ecstatic. (Acocella, 1993 p. 52)

As the context of the commentary made it clear, this *tour de force* is related (among other things) to Morris's own previous works, such that it:

> ... seemed to take the element of blackness in Morris's work — the interest in the lonely, the ugly, the shocking — and bind it to some nobler force, so that it became a motor of transcendence. (Acocella, 1993 p. 52)

Thus [in line with the second bullet-point] is context is circumscribed partly in terms of Morris's *oeuvre*. Moreover, the intention-embodied-in-the-work had Morris (as the soloist) being "... some dark and private thing, lost in dance, that was wholly his own but nevertheless based on Indian kathak dance ..." (Acocella, 1993 p. 53). Like the previous recognition, this justifies ascription to Morris (as choreographer) of *intention* here [in line with the third bullet-point]. Hence these appreciative comments are easily defended in terms of the dance-as-experienced. And should these claims about the dancework be rejected (on the basis of seeing the work itself), the critical commentary they sustain would likewise require modification — in an extreme case, that commentary might even be rejected. So, in the specific example, the challenge above is met without difficulty: a 'reading' of the dancework of a kind an hypothetical intentionalist might offer must, in this way, be answerable to the work broadly conceived — or he/she will be wrong.

The problem, of course, is just that there is no *general* or *abstract* way of explaining one's being wrong here: but that hope was given up above (under the influence of Ramsey's Maxim) when we agreed that exceptionless relations were not required.

In the end, then, the (modified) hypothetical intentionalism here requires one to make the best of the interpretative situation, such that one's view offers reasons to prefer it to competitors. But four points are stressed:

(i) there is no obvious or decisive limit on what can be brought to bear on justifying one's account of the meaning of an artwork;

(ii) any account of an artwork must be constrained by the need to offer (roughly) evidence for one's reading, especially in the face of competing 'readings' or interpretations;

(iii) although this is not strictly *evidence* — as seeing a pig in front of you is not *evidence* of a pig's being there (Austin, 1962 p. 115: see also Austin, 1970 pp. 106-107) — accounts of the meaning of an artwork operate in line with standard epistemic constraints: in particular, Carnap's *principle of total evidence*, such that:

> ... [in] a given knowledge situation, the total evidence available must be taken as the basis for determining degrees of confirmation. (Carnap, 1950 p. 211)

This operates theoretically, to identify an "idealisation":

> ... the requirement of total evidence ... [compels] us to construct all applications of inductive logic in a fictitious simplified form. (Carnap, 1950 p. 208)

That is, the 'fiction' that one *has* all the relevant evidence is introduced. Practically, applying this principle permits a defeasible, grounded working practice: the evidence one has *is* the relevant evidence — one does not introduce scepticism simply on the basis of the *possibility* of lacking some relevant information. That permits modification of our response when this assumption turns out not to be true[23];

(iv) any such justification takes place in a context. So that one answers the question asked, rather than meeting some exceptionless demand. Thus if, say, one's concern is with the portrayal of the feminine in three Ashton ballets, the features one rightly ascribes to those ballets may be different from the features rightly ascribed to them from a different erotetic perspective.

Indeed, the whole tenor of my approach is against the presumption of exceptionless accounts of the artworks at issue. For I have argued against any strict limitation (prior to investigation) of what *could be* relevant here, given the particular artwork and the concerns we might have with it. But these concerns are with *artworks* — and that implies the intentionality.

Chapter Six

Improvisation, dance and notation again!

§1. Introduction

As has been recognised throughout, giving due weight to the dancer involves, at least, recognising the place of the dancer in the *instantiation* of the dance; hence, in what one sees (or encounters) when one sees the dance. But first there is a simpler topic to address briefly. For the dancers also have a clear role once a place for improvisation (in *some* dances) is granted. Yet what role? And how can we best investigate it?

One obvious strategy draws comparisons (and contrasts) with the case of music. For a place for improvisation is widely recognised in some forms of music (especially jazz). However, there are clearly cases where, although a work *begins* from improvisation, it is then played (or performed) in the same way on every occasion — at least within the limits of such performance. This can occur even for quite unusual artworks. Thus Morton Feldman's *Piano Piece* (1963[1]), which requires the pianist to choose in which order to play the pages of the score, will often be played in exactly the same order by a particular pianist — this is his favourite order, or the one that makes the most sense to him. Further, a particular composer, using a method similar to this one in more than one work, is likely to repeat similar chords. So, even for such works, there need be no high expectation of the degree of difference from other works or performances. And the same point applies for improvisations.

One case to recognise, then, is what might be called *transcription*: performer X improvises and, at sometime, what performer X does is written down (perhaps by someone else). And now there is something that can be re-performed — even by someone else! Further, *transcription* in this sense does not require literal recording or notation: it is enough if later performers use, as the basis for *their* performances, the 'original' provided by performer X. Such *transcription* is what (typically) happens in the composing of dances, except that there need be no improvising after a certain point — what *should* go next is decided in the rehearsal room (highlighting the normative aspect: see Chapters Two and Three); and then *that* is recorded. Our decisions *set* the dance.

§2. Four cases for contrast

To move forward on the issue of improvisation in relation to the dancer's role, four cases might initially be distinguished here, identified by letters. In the first, (a) improvisation is used in composition: no doubt there are many ways to realise danceworks that centrally involve improvisation of this sort. Whatever the details, these should be viewed in terms of some 'suggestion' by the choreographer: in particular, the idea in the rehearsal room that the dancer improvise to 'suggest' the next segment of the dance. This procedure might not be common for some kinds of music, but in dance it is widespread. Such cases can be put aside since, first, someone (say, the composer or choreographer) implicitly *sanctions* the improvised passage — thereby making it both part of the work, and hence no longer counting as improvised. And, second, that same person determines that the improvisation is finished. Here, the work as a whole is not improvised; even this part is no *longer* improvised. Rather, the work as set incorporates (what was) the improvisation. So, in case (a), no improvisation as such remains.

A second case (b) partially resembles this one: on it, an improvised passage remains in the work, but simply as an instruction to improvise at this point. Thus, in some of Rosemary Butcher's dances, the choreographer:

> ... fixes ... [the dance's] limits and spatial design. But within these limits ... dancers are allowed to improvise during each performance. (Mackrell, 1992 p. 57)

Will the differences between one performance of such a work and its re-performance always be bigger than those where the work is more completely set (but where the differences reflect individual performances 'on the night')? There seems no reason to suppose they *must* be. How could we be sure they were? No doubt the desire was to maintain a "freshness" (Mackrell, 1992 p. 57): but, as a dancer, and having found some movement sequence that 'works' for you, there must be a strong temptation simply to repeat it, with minor modifications. Then a notator of such a work might consider replacing the instruction "Improvise" with an account of what that dancer did. It is revealing that, for Mackrell (1992 p. 58), established partnerships within *this* way of working might become as responsive as partnerships elsewhere:

> Kirsie Simpson and Julyen Hamilton ... were as perfectly matched a partnership as, for instance, Anthony Dowell and Antoinette Sibley of The Royal Ballet.

For that too suggests the degree to which improvisation is responsive, and within shared parameters in a particular context: hence, in which improvisation is not simply the opportunity, on every occasion, to do 'whatever one feels like'.

In this way, then, improvisation should be seen as constrained — by the rest of the work, for instance, or by the performance-styles of the performers. For these must cohere. So that the overall work will have a consistency; or, when it does not, this will typically be a topic for criticism of the resultant dancework.

To clarify the version of improvisation intended here, note that, with music, one might record a performance of the work containing such an improvised passage, and listen to it on other occasions — although there is a sense in which, from the musician's perspective the piece was improvised, from the perspective of the audience it may appear fixed. This case then resembles that in which improvisation contributes to composition (case (a) above): in effect, what the performer chanced to do last night becomes part of the recording. So the (original) improvisation simply becomes the work, for future performances. Nor should this case be seen too negatively. For music, the assumption is that when a recorded version is 'played', it is *aurally* indistinguishable from what *would* happen were the work actually performed — in that version (that is, that performer's interpretation) — by the requisite performer or orchestra. Our experience with taped messages of our voices might make us doubt this assumption. And there is always room for new recordings, given the need for *many* performers' interpretations of a particular work (to show the range of the work's features). One need not think that this case freezes the work. Still, even such 'improvised' works are only improvised from the performer's perspective. Hence such works could be recorded; the performer may play or perform it the same way on another occasion. Indeed, in either dance or music, performers may well settle down into a standard pattern to fill this 'improvise now' passage. Certainly, to repeat, a similar phenomenon occurs when pianists play the Morton Feldman *Piano Piece* (1963): although the pages of the score can be played in any order, performers seem to settle on a preferred order, repeating that night after night.

In this way, real pressure is put on the idea of improvised works of this sort as a special case. Standard musical works (that is, those with a score) also permit differences between performance, within same-work continuity: we have repeatedly recognised the expectation of differences among typical performances of the very same work (reflecting a change of location, or of cast, or even just tiredness). Moreover, these differences are 'within limits' of a kind that the nature of the work determines: the degree of permissible difference typically reflects the kind of musical work. Some works require, of new performances that is to count as *that work*, higher levels of 'similarity' to previous performances than do other works: this might reflect the technicality of the piece, or the closeness with which it was set. As Wittgenstein (PI §71) recognised, sometimes the instruction, "Stand over there", is exactly what one meant; sometimes, accuracy here requires that one hit certain 'marks'. This point applies within the instruction to improvise. So our improvised works seem in the same position. Equally, some performers are more likely than others to do something different tonight (as against yesterday).

The next two cases, though, seem at first blush the most important ones for improvisation as part of a performance (that is, settling aside the role of improvisation in composition[2]). So, in kind (c), a structure is provided (roughly, by the rest of the artwork), and the improvisation is seen as 'within' that structure. Thus, one could, in principle, *fail* in one's improvisation, by going 'outside' the structure provided. While one can imagine such a structure provided in many different ways, they all come broadly to the improvisation's drawing on a range of *material*, or *themes*, or *motifs* (or some such) from the rest of the work. For example, suppose that, in *Story* (1963), Cunningham deployed "... [a] choreographic structure [that] allowed the dancers at certain points to make certain decisions regarding the given movements and in other sections to invent their own movements" (Banes, 1994 pp. 103-104). Then this dance might be seen as of kind (c): as described, Cunningham supplied a framework and a context for the improvisation. But it would only be one example. The requirements here could be met in many ways. Of course, whether a particular improvisation in any real case does or does not meet the constraints supplied by the work will rarely be clear-cut: the improvisation as *proposed* should be seen as within the structure provided by the rest of the artwork; and then (in problematic cases) that proposal being contested — for instance, by critics or performers. Since any performance admits of differences from other performances of the very same work (as any work under-determines its performances), the difference of this case from the un-improvised is not so great. (Indeed, as noted above, this case may just be a variety of case (b) above, if one which stresses the performance-aspect.)

Case (d) represents a more radical alternative, on which the work is improvised from beginning to end: this might be what is suggested by the term "spontaneous choreography" (Banes, 1994 p. 341). Still, the example to imagine will still be a *performable* artwork; hence it should meet the constraints for a work of performing art (as opposed to, say, a *happening* — a one-off work with a performing character [on which, see later: §4]). These include the possibility of just *this* work (the numerically identical work) being performed on another occasion — that is, with the work's re-performance on another occasion: for this work is a *performable*. Here again the improvisation must result in (hence, the performance will be) a particular artwork: that is, that particular artwork (the numerically identical one) must be instantiated in this way. And that means that one might not succeed. So, again, sets of actions could (in principle) *fail* to instantiate this work. This means, once again, that one's improvisation is constrained: hence, that some lines of improvisation should be rejected (at least in principle)[3]. As above, the appropriateness of any improvisation may certainly be disputed: that these would be matters to be resolved, if at all, by debate. So that one need only consider those cases where, as it were, this dispute is resolved favourably. But now the logical structure of the possibility just under discussion requires consideration: for what provides the constraints here? How can there be an improvisation which is the *whole* of the work and so one where, although it is constrained, it is not constrained by the (rest of the) work? (That is a way to ask about the internal coherence of case (d).)

§3. Improvisation and choreography

To address such questions, one should ask, again, whether the wholly improvised artwork — option (d) above — really makes sense: will it simply collapse into a version of case (c), where the work itself provides the constraints on improvisation? For Sparshott (1995 p. 393), there is a fundamental contrast here:

> [c]ompositions that determine what a work will be ... [differ] fundamentally from improvisation, in which there is no set of decisions [as to what should happen next] and, consequently, no determinate work that could be correctly or incorrectly performed.

Were this the whole story, option (d) could readily be dismissed as incoherent: it could not constitute a way of making dance*works*. But, as Sparshott continues, the matter is not straightforward, because it may yet be possible to explain *failure* to perform such-and-such a work, even when it is improvised, (Of course, doing so still grants the difference between cases (c) and (d): perhaps the conditions for work-identity for *performables* only permit the first of these.)

We have tried to imagine a dancework both sufficiently *constrained* to count as the very same work (numerical identity) in two separate performances and yet where the work is *improvised* from beginning to end. One revealing candidate in dance might be some works of William Dunas: for instance, his *I went with her and she came with me* (UD pp. 76-77), in which Dunas "... merely walked around a space" (Siegel, 1977 p. 314) — where whatever movements he performed on *this* occasion (as opposed to *that*) were not specified, but there was an obligation on him to do *something*. A clear way to understand some artworks here is as constrained by what might be called "an authorial instruction" to do such-and-such. This model seems especially suitable once one grants that performing arts come, as it were, with the instruction "and now perform it" (see UD p. 102); this explains the under-determination of each performance by the work itself. So the William Dunas work can be read as involving the instruction to walk[4]. But that 'authorial instruction' does not amount to *just* the instruction to improvise. Instead, the direction of the improvisation is constrained — if rather minimally — by the 'authorial instruction'. For the direction to improvise (as we have imagined it) must involve, say, the instruction to act so that one's improvisation be a dancework. Or, at least, with that intention. Of course, that may provide no constraint at the level of what movements were performed, or what costumes were used, or what music deployed. But that is just to recognise that the constraints lie elsewhere: here, a part lies in the title — and, perhaps, in the *traditions of performance* (Chapter Ten) in the dance tradition within which Dunas's works were choreographed. That too limits what counts as meeting the 'authorial instruction' here. The dance might therefore be expected to have some relation to its title, as well as some relation to other dances in similar traditions — this is one way to make out the case for the movements as constitutive of a dancework.

Consider these points illustrated in simpler contexts, by recognising how (some) titles suggest a direction to our understanding of that work. For example, whatever the impact of Duchamp's putting the moustache on the *Mona Lisa*, there is a huge impact from his title for the resultant work, *L.H.O.O.Q.* which might be translated as "She has a hot ass"[5]. If the resultant object is seen *through* this title, it is typically read in line with (what one might think of as) the 'authorial instruction'[6]. As another example, Joseph Epstein's sculpture in New College Oxford might be misperceived — as a woman being martyred by stifling with tight wrappings — were it not for its title. Faced with the title *The Raising of Lazarus*, and therefore its connection to the story of Lazarus, one sees the figure as male and takes the expression quite differently[7]. Here, then, although the work might be 'read' a certain way, the title gives reasons to prefer another reading.

Then, further, if our movements are to constitute a *dance*, in the context for dance in which those movements occur, that context must be recognised (if implicitly). For what is thereby imported are recognised ways to make *dances* (or perform *dance* movements) — even if just *recently* recognised! So, in context, these patterns of dance-performance must be seen carry a weight of *tradition* here — they have become the traditional way to make dances, even if they strike some as *avant-garde*; as, say, Judson did. But a reputable method of dance-making (or of performing dance movements) has been established — of however short a history or fragile an establishment. Thus, relevantly, Banes (1994 p. 219) remarks here on "... a method ... which combined chance and improvisation", called *spontaneous determination*. As she comments:

> Although improvisation was not, statistically speaking, a common device for Judson choreographers ... [they] seemed symbolically to lay claim to a new alternative method for making and performing dances. (Banes, 1994 p. 221)

That offers both a context for improvisation in line with that tradition and, of course, a context for rebellion against the tradition (and hence is explicable in terms of that tradition).

So, then, the work imagined under option (d) above does not, in fact, *simply* amount to the 'authorial instruction' to *improvise*. For that instruction — if it is supposed to yield works in a performing art — always implies further constraints, provided by the artistic context. An instruction *simply* to improvise (without such an implied context) makes no sense. The philosophy of science suggests a parallel: there, it makes no sense simply to ask students to observe and write down all they observe because — with no erotetic context (that is, no question they were seeking to answer, or issue they needed to address) — one cannot know even what *order* of objects and events to record: should they be talking about persons and actions, or the brick construction of the room, or its molecular composition? With no sense of relevance, one cannot decide. Just so, the blanket instruction "improvise" makes no sense. Even giving some background — that our performance is to be dance, for instance — does not seem to provide enough by way of a basis for deciding what to do. After all, given the variety of dance styles and techniques, many movement sequences would count as dance in some context! Our problem is that we cannot know, in the abstract, about *this* context. But supplying more context is supplying constraints on what counts as improvisation here: hence, seeing the resultant dance as necessarily 'improvisation within a context' rather than some (mythical) *pure* improvisation. And the context is, roughly, what would *count* as dance if performed *here*, and in this manner. For not all sequences of movement would. One might conclude that case (d) — on which the whole work was improvised — involves a conceptual confusion since it implies that the resultant movement-sequence could as (art-type) dance in the given context: that involves granting that it was constrained as (other) art is constrained;

and hence amounts to rejecting the possibility of this very *pure* improvisation, on which just anything could be done.

Perhaps one might be more concessive here, and not dispute *every* case. For, in *many* cases, what might appear as pure 'authorial instruction' to improvise is in fact further constrained by that instruction's location as in dance, in this-or-that field of dance, in this-or-that version of dance technique, and so on. (Here, the use of the expression "and so on" highlights that there is no finite totality of properties; hence, that no list here could be exceptionless.) So there will rarely be cases where the range of improvisation is as open as my initial characterisation of case (d) suggests. Any version which takes the improvisation as constrained by reference to the *context* of that improvisation, and which draws on that *context* to resolve the relevant identity questions for the artwork, might readily be thought a case where *more* than just improvisation is required. Yet there is no need to claim that some version of case (d) is completely impossible, however much its plausibility might be doubted. Instead, our claim need only be that (since there *will* be some constraints even in this case) something can be said in discussion of such a work: one could in principle know where to begin — this follows from its still counting as *art*.

§4.   Improvisation vs. 'happening': a place for notation?

Discussing improvisation has stressed the conditions imposed by recognising that dance is a performing art; hence, that danceworks are re-performable (at least in principle) — where this would involve the instantiation of the *very same* artwork. As noted, a useful contrast here is with so-called "happenings", with the 'defining' feature of happenings being that they are 'one-off' performances. That such-and-such is an artwork on a performing art grants the possibility of that very same work being performed on different occasions (say, in different times, in different places, perhaps on a different stage set-up). This is the sense in which they are performables. And some of these features are necessarily missing from happenings. Further, while not *all* works in a performing art could be inflected in *all* of these ways (some of Alwin Nikolais's works may require specific costumes, for example), typical work in a performing art will be *performables* in this sense. But *happenings* are not *performables*. Hence the example of happenings is revealing here. They are not works in performing arts, although they might be *mistaken* for such works, for they lack some features *essential* to performing arts, in that the 'performances' are not *performables* (not amenable to re-performance). In highlighting these as the typical features of performing arts — highlighting them by their absence, as it were — *happenings* bring to the fore the features on which we can typically depend.

As a slogan, then, the happening case (where the object is granted from the beginning to be a 'one-off') might be contrasted with the case imagined for a performing art, such as dance: with respect to improvisation, the requirement for being a re-performable means that either the specific details of the improvisation are important (such that they could be transcribed for re-performance) or it is only important to improvise in *some* way here, consistent with other aspects of the dance. But, if that is indeed sufficient, no more need be said. (Indeed, this was the upshot of cases (b) and (c).)

In part, the problem here arises from the interlock between practices of composition and those of performance: in both (much) dance and (much) music, the use of skilled — and usually technically-trained — performers gives the relevant artists (choreographers and composers), as a compositional resource, the possibility of asking the performers for suggestions, either implicitly or explicitly. Of course, this is not the way classical composers of music typically work. But when one looks to jazz (and also to 'pop music'), one sees the practice of compositions arising out of 'jam' sessions — or something similar. That is, the work comes about when the artist (who may be the composer, or the whole ensemble) decides that the work is finished — at least for the moment. And that decision incorporates into the work whatever contributions have been made be performers.

This practice is especially widespread — almost ubiquitous — in respect of dance composition. Elsewhere perhaps this is a consequence of the lack of a notation system for dance that is both adequate for composition and agreed to be so by practitioners. So, there is still the diversity within the systems of notations used (when any is used). This claim about the lack of a notation system builds in a number of other points. First, those who know the power of Labanotation readily grant that it *could* be used for adequately notating all dances — and might deny this of the other, competing systems. But Labanotation is a complex system both to learn and to use. So that it has not typically been mastered by choreographers; and is not typically learned by dancers. Further, it is time-consuming to notate dances; or even segments of them. Thus, Labanotation could *in principle* be used for dance composition — and hence choreographers could come to the first rehearsal with a full score for the work, which the dancers had already learned. This is what usually happens with new orchestral works: that musicians come knowing their part; but rehearsals give then a sense of how to play the piece *emsemble*; and of nuances of the conductor's interpretation. So, choreographers and dancers *could* arrive at rehearsals in a similar state: but, given the present state of the danceworld, this will not happen any time soon — indeed, the tendency seems to be *against* the spread of notating skills. Rather, the spread of the use of video *as though* it were an alternative to notation has meant that fewer and fewer dance training establishments require mastery of notation. Or so it seems to me. The right parallel (or disanalogy) here is with the ubiquitousness of standard musical notation: that, as far as western Classical music goes, one would not think of oneself unapologetically as either a musician or a composer unless one had a complete mastery of this system of notation, both (as it were) as reader and as writer. Again, this should not be taken to show too much — not all musical artworks deploy this notation; and even some that do *might* have been composed and/or performed without it. But the balance here is the exact *opposite* of that within dance: *there*, the usual case is that there is no score; that, even if there were, the dancers (and often the choreographer) could not read it; and that the work was certainly not *composed* using the score — that is, the choreographer did not compose the dancework by constructing what, elsewhere (above: Chapter Two §7; Chapter Three §8; and see UD p. 95), was called "a recipe".

This last point is crucial in at least three ways. First, it means that, in our sloganised version, the notation of a dance performance could be a *recipe* for future performance (as well as recording the performance) while that of a happening would only be a *record* of the happening. For performables permit the normativity of the score: it indicates what dancers *should* do. Second, it guarantees a separate skill (or, at least, occupation) in respect of dance — that is, as a notator. And, third, it can involve such notators typically creating the score from the established work. Hence the notator must decide (ideally in conjunction with the choreographer: see Chapter Three §6; §9) exactly which are the key features of the dance: as it were, which features are fundamental, and which are merely contingencies of this or that performance. And these points return us to the earlier account of *transcription* — it may be more problematic than it seemed. The story of Ann Hutchinson-Guest notating for Kurt Jooss (given in Chapter Two §7) illustrates one key issue here: should she notate what the choreographer did, by way of example, or what — given their training — successive generations of ballet dancers were going to do? Whatever the answer, the degree of judgement involved must be recognised.

Further, recognising a role for notation even in the context of improvisation is of a piece with insistence that there is some virtue in looking for constraints here in a form as public (and hence usable) as possible — hence that 'making by recipe' was, theoretically, stronger than 'making by first token'. As Wollheim (1973 p. 257: see UD p. 98) accurately puts it:

> Where such a notation is available, then there is a clear and determinate way of individuating tokens as of a given type, and hence of identifying the work of art with the type.

Moreover, the notation may allow us to *see* which features are the 'accidents' of this or that performance, which more central to work-identity. But this contrast too is one for debate, rather than being clear-cut.

In addition, here as elsewhere, the score need not be the kind of 'full score' of Labanotation often envisaged (especially by me). Instead, the kind of minimal score envisage for, say, some chance works fits the bill just as well: it constrains what conditions must be met to *count* as another performance of such-and-such a work. And that constraint applies even for improvisations, *if* they result in works in a performing art — that is, in re-performables.

§5. Conclusion

So from the need for *constraint* — easily to seen for improvisation within art — one arrives at the *virtues* (for performables) of notation. For the notation can help make those constraints explicit. Also, at least typically, a key claim throughout is that the dancework under consideration (say, this performance) is *exactly the same artwork* (that is, numerically identical) as another performance, again, at least typically — to be more comprehensive, the three-fold contrast should be imported (see Chapter Two §10), such that another performance will be:

(i) a classic version of that work, or

(ii) a version about as far from the classic as one can go but remain that work (a token of the same type); or

(iii) a work very similar but another artwork — a token of another type.

Even with highly improvisatory art forms, such as some jazz (which is still notated some degree), the notion of a *performable* in this sense provides a guiding light; and it does so here. For even danceworks with high level of 'improvised content' still represent an artwork ('the very same work') performable on more than one occasion.

Part Three: The Dancer's Share

Chapter Seven

Are dancers artists?

Or, dancers, performances and physicality

§1. The distinctiveness of dancers

Dance has a distinctive place among the performing arts, as we have noted (see Chapter Two). Typical danceworks are *performables*: that is, the *very same dance* can be re-performed on another occasion, despite the inevitable differences between such performances. But the specific physicality of the dancers is drawn on more concretely: in this sense, *dancers* provide the distinctiveness of the art form. Thus musicians bring about "... those things ... of which the witnessable work consists" (Urmson, 1976 p. 243): they *make* or *cause* the sounds that instantiate the musical work. By contrast, in typical cases dancers *are* the dance — their movements instantiate the artwork, rather than merely *causing* it.

Equally, dance differs, in related ways, from other performing arts, such as theatre and opera, once their commonalities are recognised: there is something to the view that "[o]pera is ... *drama per musica*" (Sharpe, 1983 p. 26), despite the stress Jim Hamilton (2007 pp. 58-59) places on the variety within what, in everyday speech, is called *acting*. Here, the distinctiveness lies in the physicality of artistic meaning for danceworks. Any accurate description of the practitioners in both opera and theatre should stress the place of language, or language-like understanding: both typically involve language, which must have a role in any characterisation of the respective artistic meaning. Moreover, the typical *behaviour* of practitioners in these other arts resembles in certain ways the rest of human life: *words* are involved[1]. Hence the movements of those practitioners can be understood in relation to those words, as with everyday conversations. And if the relationship is not always a complementary one, that too is an everyday experience: people's postures and gestures can conflict with their utterances. For dance, though, that meaning or intending is centrally bodily: that begins to distinguish danceworks from those with *linguistic* meaning — setting aside, of course, any critical commentary they develop.

Of course, danceworks, like other artworks, are made to be meaning-bearing, as I would put it: that, as a whole, they embody (roughly) the intelligence of their creators. Thus:

If we wanted to say something about art that we could be quite certain was true, we might settle for the assertion that art is intentional. And by this we would mean that art is something we do, that works of art are something we make. (Wollheim, 1973 p. 112)

So there is a sense in which the features or characteristics of any artwork derive from its author or authors — sometimes seen easily and directly, sometimes in a much more indirect fashion. Yet, as in typical artworks, (artistic) meaning here is embodied in this or that particular way (movement, sound, and so on). Thus, Karole Armitage's *The Watteau Duets* (1985) is rightly thought "... a concentrated exploration of two important ballet conventions: the pas de deux (or duet form) and pointework" (Banes, 2007 p. 314) with "... a frank carnality that most earlier ballets ... only gestured toward" (Banes, 2007 p. 315); and in which Armitage "... seems ... to move on pointe precariously, like a tightrope walker — not through lack of technique but as a result of the daring, extreme positions of her legs and torso" (Banes, 2007 p. 316). But, even when these seem remarks about artists' thoughts or achievements, they are descriptions of the intention-as-embodied: in that sense, then, descriptions *of the dancework*. Thus, as we saw (Chapter Five §3), recognising artworks as made for meaning locates a set of personal properties here: that is why the sculpture could be expressive, witty, and so on, but that such concepts could never apply to the meteorite (see Ground, 1989 pp. 25-26) — even when one could be mistaken for the other, as a pair of Danto-esque "confusable counterparts" (Danto, 1981 p. 138). But these properties of danceworks should not be taken to indicate the thoughts or feelings of dancers.

So there is a clear sense in which the dance is principally composed of the bodies of dancers in motion. While saying this is not to deny the role of music, costume, and so on, recording that fact is fundamental for typical dances. In this sense, the nature of *dancers* — as dancers — is crucial here, distinguishing dance from other performing arts. For the embodiment of the dance depends on those dancers. Can this thought be expanded?

§2.   Dancers instantiate the dance

Recall here Merce Cunningham (1984 p. 27) saying:

[y]ou can't describe a dance without talking about the dancer. You can't describe a dance that hasn't been seen, and the way of seeing it has everything to do with the dancers ...

Cunningham's first point is just that one only really encounters the dance itself *in performance*. Then Merce is right that, in a sense, "... you can't describe a dance that hasn't been seen": that is, one uninstantiated. Further, only in performance is a particular dancework fully determinate — since the features or details of performances make concrete all the places where the dancework itself under-determines those performances.

This allows recognition of another feature of the dancer's contribution to the dance performance, which in turn leads to a second. For, first, since the dancer's activities (along with others) bring the concrete dance-performance into being, one aspect of the dancer's contribution here will be through the dancer's mastery of the 'craft' of instantiating the dance — from the score, or from the choreographer's instructions, or whatever. And this 'craft mastery' aspect is easily missed.

Mention of *craft* here might confuse: the thought here does not begin from the art/craft distinction as, say, Collingwood (1938 pp. 20-41) deploys it. Rather, first, the *artistic* (judgement of art) is distinguished from the *aesthetic* (see AJ pp. 1-28; McFee, 2005) — *craft* in Collingwood's sense will be one way to make (merely) aesthetic objects, but not the only one.

Second, what I am calling "the craft-mastery of dancers" involves a species of professional knowledge roughly identified by Donald Schön (1983: see Chapter Eight §6; EKT pp. 128-129); and in explicit contrast to the 'know how' of what Schön (1983 pp. 30-69) calls "technical rationality" — which is the epistemology of Collingwood-type craft! Like me, Schön (1987 p. 1) expressly describes such professional knowledge properly understood in terms of *artistry*.

Further, there may be occasions when this 'craft mastery' aspect is sufficiently distinctive in respect of a particular dancer as to give a new nuance to the role or part being danced: to generate a distinctive *performer's interpretation*, as we have put it. But even this is typically within the manner of a particular dance troupe or company of delivering, say, *Swan Lake*. Although one might pick out the more distinctive of these performer's interpretations, perhaps as virtuoso performance (see below), in typical cases they really amount to doing what each dancer *must* do — to making the dance itself concrete, given the powers and capacities of his or her body.

But what more exactly is the dancers' contribution? Some writers have thought that the dancework therefore involves a contribution from the dancer. Thus Peter Kivy (2007 p. 101) writers of the performer as "an artistic collaborator". As it stands, this formulation is unclear until the nature of that contribution is clarified. For example, Collingwood (1938 pp. 320-321) writes that:

> ... the author ... demands of his performers a spirit of constructive and intelligent co-operation ... where performers ... are not only permitted but required to fill in the details.

This seems exactly right if one were trying to capture the role of dancers in making concrete what is under-determined in *the work itself*: what, above, I called the dancers' *craft-mastery*. But more puzzling is Collingwood's own conclusion: "Every performer is co-author of the work he performs" (Collingwood, 1938 p. 321). At best, this seems hyperbole for effect! Were it taken literally, assigning the dancer a role as "co-author", what could that mean? In particular, how would it go beyond what has already been granted?

Of course, some dances depend, wholly or in part, on improvisation on the part of dancers (see Chapter Six). Such cases can be set aside as *special*. Is there any other sense to the expression "performing *artist*" here? In particular, should dancers be rightly seen as "co-authors" (in Collingwood's expression) of danceworks they perform?

§3. Dancers as building blocks

The emphasis here on the importance of the dancer does not identify a role for the dancer as artist in the sense of *author* of that work. Yet the claim here — that dancers are not artists (to put it very bluntly) — needs a lot of clarification, lest it be misunderstood. For it does not deny the role Collingwood (above) initially assigned: "to fill in the details". But, since in this context the term "art" means (fine) art, *artists* are makers of it. That is not the dancer's role. Of course, the term "artist" is used in other ways — and dancers might be artists in those craft-mastering ways ("This surgeon is an artist!"); but we are not considering them here. Nor is this claim merely about words: with Wittgenstein, I urge, "say what you choose" (see PI §79), but worry about what *contrasts* you are drawing.

Moreover, the fact that most dances can be performed with different casts highlights an absurdity in assigning authorial responsibility to dancers in such cases: for then, at worst, each performance would be a different artwork — at least when different dancers were involved. But that is just to reject the idea of a performing art: that is, a kind of art where the artworks are indeed *performables*. For such performables must permit of re-performance: that is, *the very same work* can, in principle, be performed on other occasions, at other times and in other places, with other casts, Hence this attempt to treat the dancer as *author* of the dancework, for typical danceworks, does not capture the dancers' distinctive contribution here.

Commentary on the logic of dance-making must begin from the fact that works in performing arts are *multiples* (given a type-token analysis here). And hence on the making of the abstract object that is the *type*: it can be made either by making a recipe (such as a score) or by creating a ('first') performance. Perhaps only a few dances are composed by writing a score, while most are composed by working in the studio with dancers: making the abstract object that is the artwork by making a token. In either case, the final decisions will be those of the artist. Thus the artist, as author, has a clear role, even for performing arts like dance.

Of course, dancers sometimes *seem* like artists in the sense of *authors*: for instance, when dancers offer movement ideas for some composition; but then the choreographer decides — the responsibility remains with the choreographer. Similarly, improvisation by dancers can itself be put aside: the *order* to improvise operative here is a choreographer's order. And the choreographer typically decides when improvisation is over: when the dancework is finished (for today!). Further, one must recognise the number of 'hats' (roles) in play: dancers may have at best a role in the process *other than as dancers* — thus a choreographer may make solos for himself or herself. But even the solo a choreographer makes for himself is a *performable* (part of a performing art); hence it can in principle be re-performed on another occasion, including (typically) by someone else!

Moreover, dancers — like musicians — achieve something praiseworthy (at least in typical cases); so, in denying that dancers are artists in the sense of *authors*, I am *not* denying that their contributions (and especially their achievements) are laudable. But one must understand both what dancers (and other performers) *do* achieve: hence what *is* laudable (when it is); and what they *do not* — indeed, strictly speaking, *cannot* — achieve.

As noted already, what dancers achieve is (a) instantiating the danceworks — without them, there would be no work to be confronted. And part of the dancers' achievement lies precisely in turning the choreographer's instructions, or demonstrations, or the score, or whatever, into a performance of the dancework. Then, sometimes, (b) doing that by offering a version or interpretation of the work — what I have called "performer's interpretation" (UD p. 103), as we might speak of Pollini's interpretation of Schönberg's opus 19, contrasting that with Glenn Gould's version. Both of these areas of attainment by dancers are laudable; and especially the second. Without the first, there would be no dances to view; while the second often explains part of our interest in particular dance performances. Thus one might attend a particular performance *in order* to see so-and-so's interpretation of such-and-such a role — as one might also for a play or an opera. So that sometimes one wonders how such-and-such a dancer would carry so-and-so role: for my generation, the male dancers for whom this question was raised were Nureyev and, later, Baryshnikov. Not all performances need be taken as seriously — and hence as distinctively — as this: one need not insist on a performer's interpretation in *all* cases. (Or, sometimes, another dancer might be performing Nureyev's interpretation.)

Our musical example reminds us that, since both Pollini and Gould offer 'versions', interpretations, of the same artwork, a trip to the concert-hall to hear *either* interpretation counts as an encounter with Schönberg's opus 19 — the artwork itself. Just the same is true of our typical dances. Thus the performer's contribution, although praiseworthy, stands against another contribution; namely, that of the *author* of the artwork, the *artist*. For typical dancers, like pianists and opera-singers, do not *initiate* the artwork: they are not ultimately responsible for that work (despite bearing a heavy weight in terms of the work's performance). So, again, the artist's role as *author* is crucial, not least because the two roles just ascribed to performers in a performing art only make sense against this background. For (in that context) one can only *perform* a dance when there *is* a dance — when it has been choreographed. Further, the author typically has a role when the audience considers in which category of art that work is appropriately understood.

This returns us to a concern with the authenticity of performances as of such-and-such a work, a concern pervasive throughout this text. Suppose one sees a particular dance, or play, or listens to a piece of music, or an opera on Tuesday evening: each counts as one (and only one) artwork. That fact is acknowledged in granting that, in the same venue on Wednesday, one can encounter that same artwork *again*. This is typically independent of differences between the performances — including being different performer's interpretations: both can be, say, *Swan Lake* despite a wide variety of differences. For being *the very same work* is not a matter of *similarity* here — as numerical identity judgements generally are not. Thus, the short, hairy boy who bullied me at school is the very same person as the tall, bald man getting the Nobel Peace Prize — we grant that in letting him inherit the estate of his (or the boy's) grandfather. Here there is numerical identity despite radical dissimilarity. In fact, the discussion 'same-work' continuity here (see Chapter Two §10; also CDE pp. 229-231) effectively recognises a framework built around three kinds of cases:

(i) the standard token (say, for *Swan Lake*, the Ivanov and Petipa choreography);

(ii) the extreme token — properties very different from standard tokens, but still a token of that same type (say, Matthew Bourne's *Swan Lake*);

(iii) the new, but similar artwork — a token of a different type (say, the Mats Ek *Swan Lake*).

Of course, the examples are not crucial; but the thought here is to illustrate sorting candidate *Swan Lake*s into categories, where the first two preserve work-identity. Then a suitable notated score, for instance, would precisely offer the required freedom here; exactly as much freedom as one wants ... and certainly freedom in line with the standard treatment of 'classics' from the past, which can be kept vivid in performance. And, of course, dancers — and their craft-mastery — will be key for such vividness.

Moreover, the performers or company rehearsing on Monday was (in principle) a rehearsal for *all* of the performances they would make of the work that week, rather than for only one of them (UD p. 93). This in turn speaks clearly for our sense of only one artwork here. For many works would seem to require many distinct rehearsals.

So *one* artwork is recognised here, despite its diversities. And the example of *Swan Lake* will be maintained, in line with the arguments from Chapter One: there are objections to it but, if the points are clear, those worried on *this* issue only can supply their own examples. So, in practice, a pretty wide range of diversity is granted within 'same-work' continuity for *Swan Lake*: diversity of company, staging, costume, and even movement. But all of this counts as *the very same* (numerically identical) artwork. Moreover, *one* artwork implies *one* authorship (not necessarily one *person*, of course; but that point need not concern us here). In our typical dance performances, one recognises only one artwork: hence, at most one *authorship*. Furthermore, *this* is the context in which the dancer (or dancers) *cannot* be artists in the relevant sense, since authorship of the work already exhausts that role. And, to repeat, that authorship is already 'used up'.

In this context, the term "performing artist" is confusing (and ultimately unhelpful) here: it could pick-out those who instantiate works in the performing arts, such as dance, to recognise their artistry (their craft-mastery); or it could refer to those involved in works of one-off performance art, *happenings*. But these are very different: we probably mislead ourselves if we confuse one with the other. Of course, some of the 'practitioners' involved in a happening may just be performers — as typical dancers are: but there might be some who *are* the artists in such a case. Moreover, only those in the happenings might plausibly be thought *artists* (in some cases, not all) in the sense, previously identified, that picks-out the *authors of artworks*. By contrast, that is not the right way to see the activities of (typical) dancers.

A thesis in this Chapter can now be stated strictly although, as often in philosophy, what is urged is neither as grand nor as contentious as its first articulation makes it seem. In line with Austin's dictum[2], there is the place where one says it (seeming to claim far more) and the place where one takes it back. It is that dancers are not artists precisely *because* dance is a performing art, one with a role for *performers*. And that is the role the dancers fill! Were dancers *artists* in that sense, it would, at best, turn dances into 'happenings'.

This conclusion points to a *difference* only: in particular, the activities of artists are *not* being rated more highly (nor less highly) than those of dancers, but merely some differences here recognised. We are valuing each, but differently. Thus, this is not an attempt to downplay the importance of dancers — say, to dis-value the dancer. Rather the plan is to *rightly* value the dancer. In fact, that is the main thrust of this chapter! That means seeing differences between dancer's value and artist's value, without ranking either more highly. In a similar vein, when I remarked (UD p. 104) that the term "creative" amounted to something *different* for dancers than it did for artists, some people thought I meant this to the detriment of the dancers. But this, too, was simply an attempt to recognise important differences.

The stress on *authorship* as explaining what is central to being an artist allows us to put aside a plausible-sounding (and revealing) counter-example in which an inferior dance becomes recognised as an artwork because of the contribution of an outstanding performer in 'delivering' it. In effect, this will be one of two or three possible cases, reflecting the prior status of the 'inferior' dance. Thus, is that dance an artwork? As a first case, suppose one grants that it is, and recognises the dance one is seeing — although revitalised — as the very same dancework as previous performances. Then it is still ascribed to its previous choreographer (or whomever): it is still his/her dance, and any plaudits *for the dance* (or any brickbats) belong to that original author. Here, the revitalised version allowed us to see the dance for what it was; or to see what is in it. But, insofar as the *responsibility* for the dance continues to be ascribed to its original author, there is no temptation to think here of the performer as author.

Yet suppose one imagines that — either wholly or partly — the 'new' dance is a transfiguration of its previous incarnation. The simplest case here might be the transfiguration of a folk dance: so let that be the second case. Here, the 'original' dance was not an artwork; and it is the performer's contribution that now makes it one. So it is a bit like finding inspiration in a tree — the tree is not an artwork, but one's painting is. Or perhaps more like a kind of Readymade: one writes a name ("R. Mutt, 1917") on a urinal, and then it becomes one's own artwork. But now the 'performer' does count as the *author* of the artwork: it has become his or her work. So again there is no confusion.

Then, as our third case, imagine a minor artwork brought to life in performance. Since this is not merely a repeat of our first case, the performer must have contributed *more* than in that example. As this might be expressed, it is not merely his *dancing* — his performance — that is being admired. But then what is? The temptation must be to say that it is *his dance*: but now the performer counts as, at least, a co-author — it is his/her dance that is being praised: as we might say, his/her *dance*, and not just his/her *dancing*. Of course, in this case, the dancer would be an artist in the sense under discussion — that is, to the degree that is indeed his/her dance. So, to the degree that the dancework is recognised as the dancer's (that is, the dancer's responsibility), to that degree we see the dancer as *author* — and hence as artist. But, to that degree, we are no longer regarding that person (or persons) simply as the *dancer*. (Thus, for analytic purposes, the performance-role of the dancer is separated from the authorial role.)

Why is any of this important? In part, the answer lies in trying to get an accurate assessment of the areas of possible attainment of dancers — not to offer them a comparison (with the achievements of artists) which claims too much for their legitimate activities. Rather, these legitimate activities should be celebrated, instead of bewailing a failure to attain what was actually unattainable in principle. So one implies neither too much nor too little about them. Perhaps fewer self-proclaimed artists in the world of performing art may mean a happier regime, because fewer *prima donnas*. (At least, that might be a hope.) But due weighing of the craft-related attainments of dancers is also crucial to an appropriate valuing of those attainments. Here, I would reiterate in particular the complexity of turning abstract choreography into a concrete dance performance, the creativity of the *dancer's* role, and the sense in which (like members of other professions: EKT pp. 128-129) dancers may be called on to resolve new or unfamiliar situations. So that someone might say, with justice and with pride, "No, I'm not an artist — that is because I've spent my time, energy, and creativity on being one *hell* of a dancer!"

§4. The contingencies of instantiating dances

Then, when we *do* see dances, we see the *dancers* (as Merce recognised). So every performance reflects, in some way or other, features of the dancer(s) involved — not only of the dancers, of course; but centrally of them. Even attempts to evade this point ultimately reinforce it. Thus, Alwin Nikolais (1998 p. 116) writes:

I used masks and props — the masks, to have the dancer become something else; and the props, to extend his physical size in space.

But these then *become* the features of the dancer *as we experience them!* Here, we recognise (first) that, in this way, features such as these become properties of the dance — and hence of the dancers; and (second) that the features of the dance *on any occasion* are set by the properties of that particular performance. Thus, as noted in Chapter Three, many factors may have an impact on what movements, and such like, get performed to instantiate (say)

Christopher Bruce's *Ghost Dances* (1981) — the impact of different casts, of different performance spaces, of different companies (with differing technical prowess); and even just of a different *night*. So these will be among explanations of differences between performances of the very same dancework. Moreover — to repeat — this idea of *difference among performances* is central to the conception of a performing art as composed of *performables*; works that can be re-performed on another occasion: at best, we can argue about the *degree* of difference permissible, given that the outcome is a performance of *the very same* dancework.

Yet, now, which features of the performance one *sees* — danced by this company on that occasion — are (*crucial*) features of the dance, such that one might criticise a performance which failed to include them, and which are the contingencies of *this* performance? In illustration, consider in some cases where compliance with a notated score generates the dancework. Then imagine a performance uncontentiously *of that work*, but failing to comply with our score — clearly the score includes some constraints not *crucial* for the work. So, here, dance-performances based on this score will reflect some features crucial to the dance (perhaps) but also some other constraints. Recall that this case is not merely a philosopher's fantasy: the Stepanov score for *Swan Lake* presents precisely this situation! In my language (see Chapter Three), this score is not *adequate* for *Swan Lake* just because it does not identify *solely* the constraints from the dancework itself, but only for some performances of that work.

In this section so far, the key role of the dancer in bringing the dance into a form with which the rest of us can interact has been recognised: as Cunningham reminded us, "you can't describe a dance that hasn't been seen". But we have also recognised that some of the features of this performance may reflect facts about the dancers not themselves crucial features of *the dance*.

A further complication is that much dance today, in being made on the bodies of particular dancers, reflects closely the powers and capacities of those dancers. Then what might — for other works — be mere contingencies of performance here seem crucial features of these works. Yet we must go carefully, for we do not want to say that, as a matter of logic, *only* dancer X can perform this work — even if that were the contingent truth at a certain time. Thus, to repeat the example from Chapter Two, it is widely claimed that Petipa put the thirty-two fouettés in Act III of *Swan Lake* (1895) because at the time he had a dancer, Pierina Legnani, who could perform this, when few could (compare Mackrell, 1997 p. 7). So suppose that, at that time, *only* Legnani could perform this segment of the dance. Still, the requirement is just for a dancer *able* to do so. If there *were* only one, that would just be a practical matter. And that is how any other requirements here should be regarded. Thus, almost exactly this problem was faced by Martha Graham's company, in wishing to continue to perform dances that Graham herself could no longer manage — it was not enough to find someone who knew the steps, say. Instead, what was required was a *quality* of dance that was (fairly) easy to recognise in performers — and especially in those lacking it — but much harder to describe.

As before, the point can be illustrated by contrasting a merely *technical* performance of Schönberg's pianowork opus 19 with an *expressive* one. For that difference *is* reflected in differences in what the performer *did* (say, in differential pressure on the piano keys), rather than just what he/she felt. So the differences were *in the performances*, even when we cannot *describe* the differences here more fully. The mistaken description of the differences here being *imperceptible* highlights the problem: first, the differences were perceived well enough; but, second, there seemed no way to *describe* those differences more exactly.

The moral here — perhaps unsurprisingly — is that we may not always be able to *say* how we do these things; but that need not preclude our doing them successfully. For becoming skilled observers will allow us to give due weight to the contributions of individual performers.

The problem concerning the place of the *dancer* amounts to giving due weight to the importance of the dancer as *instantiating* the dancework; so that, when one sees that work, one *always* sees it by seeing this or that dancer. The features of the dancework *as we confront them* are always composed out of the bodies of this or that troupe of dancers. Then clearly the dancers make some contribution here: recording that contribution is (for me) giving a place to their *distinctiveness*.

Of course, one must only give *due* weight here: it is as easy to over-rate the dancer as to under-rate him or her. Either move can generate subjectivism of the kinds rejected earlier. Further, recognising the dancer's *physicality* must grant that the physicality here is *of a dancer* — stressing only the biology (the anatomy and physiology; or even the neuro-physiology) must be confusing oneself, since those alone do not identify a *dancer*.

Here, our concern with dancers profitably be contrasted with Théophile Gautier's fascination with the legs of ballerinas: say, with the "admirable legs" of Eugénie Fiocre, the "slender legs of Mlle Taglioni" (Gautier, 1986 p. 39), or the "intelligent legs" of Thérèse Elssler (Gautier, 1986 p. 35), whose "beautiful legs [resembled] ... an antique statue worthy of being cast and lovingly inspected" (Gautier, 1986 p. 23). This fascination might be mistaken for a concern with the person. And Gautier sometimes wrote as though his concern was just with the dancers (as persons) and not with dance at all:

that *all* that dance amounts to is "... nothing more than the art of displaying elegant and correctly proportioned bodies in various positions favourable to the development of line" (Gautier, 1986 p. 29). Or, again: "... dancing has no purpose but to display beautiful bodies in graceful poses and develop lines that are pleasing to the eye. ... Dancing is ill-suited for expressing metaphysical ideas ..." (Gautier, 1986 p. 16).

Yet, in reality, Gautier's interest in the legs was as the legs of *dancers*: he was not, for example, someone at the stagedoor who inspects these legs in their 'real life' location. So this is not just a concern with the person whose legs they are — with Eugénie Fiocre or Fanny Elssler — but rather with these people *as dancers*. That is, with the impact of those legs on the experience of *this* dance. So that (even if he sometimes expresses the point differently[3]) Gautier is responding to the dance. For saying that these are always typically the legs of dancers is a way to relate their (observed) properties to those of the artworks they help to instantiate. And that *is* the topic concerning embodiment which has been our primary interest.

Stressing that these must be *dancers* involves the recognition, first, that (at the peripheries at least) what is and what is not dance, and hence a *dancer* (as performer of it), is a matter for debate within a culture — better, within that proper part I call "The Republic of Dance"; and, second, that what is involved in being a dancer for these purposes (and especially the kind of dancer suitable to perform fine art-type dances) is a contextual matter.

§5. 'Live performance'

The fact that a dance is instantiated only in a performance has two further features, worthy of mention here. First, performances are needed to concretise that works' under-determined features — yet how do these differ from recordings? Suppose that a musical work is identified simply in terms of how it sounds, as a sound-sequence (so-called "timbral sonicism"), even as a "default position" (Dodd, 2007 p. 5; Caplan, 2007 p. 445). Now distinguishing performance and recording can becomes a *big* issue for music. For "timbral sonicism" seems to guarantee that one can hear the music independent of any performers of it. But the issue is nothing like so important for dance, because dance has no real equivalent of "timbral sonicism". (Still, we may need to discuss the sense in which seeing the video is, and the sense in which it is not, *seeing the dance* — clearly the dance has lots of features not captured by the video.)

Second, performances are needed because mere knowledge of danceworks, and their history, is not enough — spectators must experience the work, in order that their judgements be answerable to the work's features; and dancers must put their knowledge into their actions. In merely knowing 'stuff', one would be like Vronsky in *Anna Karenina*:

> He understood all schools of painting ... but he did not know that it was possible not to understand a single one and yet find inspiration within one's soul. (Tolstoi, 1939 II p. 29: quoted Beardsmore, 1971 p. 45)

This point might be put in terms of the need for the *mobilising of concepts*: "... the concepts the spectator has and mobilises ..." (Wollheim, 1986 p. 48). The point is that merely having learned, say, a critical vocabulary for dance or for poetry is not enough — one must be about to *mobilise* that understanding when one looks at dances or reads poems. But a better way, in this context, returns us to our earlier remarks (§4 above) about the expressive performance and the merely technical one: that difference may be explicable as, say, the particular dancer's *conceptual* mastery, but its reality will be visible in what she *does*. It is not required, of course, for these concepts to pass through her mind *before* (or, worse, *during*) the performance. For our action (although rationally motivated) was typically explained 'after the fact', in response to a question. So that one should not (and certainly need not) look for a chain of reasoning engaged in prior to the resulting rational judgements, or rational appraisals, of (say) danceworks. And neither should the activities of our dancers be seen as rational *only* when the product of prior planning and ratiocination. We are first-and-foremost *agents*: so there is typically nothing more to explain — as Wittgenstein was fond of quoting, "In the beginning was the deed" (OC §403; CV 31). And explanations can be offered when, say, things go awry. But this also illustrates why, from one perspective, what dancers *feel* is beside the point. If one asks, "Is the feeling of individual corps members at all relevant?" surely the right answer is, "No" — we don't care what they *feel*: if they think they are behaving in ways appropriate to ensemble, we only care if they *are* doing so. For the movement's *feeling* a certain way is not a step to, or a test of, its *being* right — not least because it can only genuinely *feel* right when/if it *is* right. If I want to teach you what it *feels* like to have your arm in such-and-such a position, I can do so only by getting your arm into that position. And then what you *did* is important, not what you felt. The same goes for our dancers — except that, having done this many times, they are less likely to be wrong.

Further, dancers (as people) are rightly distinguished from roles or parts: just as one would not let a 'doctor' from a TV soap opera extract one's appendix, one would not avoid — for fear of being transformed into a swan — the dancer who performs von Rothbart, the enchanter in *Swan Lake* (1895). This reminds us that what the *character* thinks and feels should be distinguished from what the *dancer* thinks and feels. One need to *see* the character's animosity; seeing the dancer's animosity would be at best an irrelevance, at worst an artistic flaw.

§6.   Issue of virtuoso performers

The importance of *performers* in the performing arts has been acknowledged — and seeing them as *persons*, rather than merely robot performers. Still, most performers will be relatively invisible   except as the work demands it: the work will be appropriately instantiated, and no more needs to be said.

But there are other cases, such as *virtuoso performers* and the sorts of occasions — I think mainly of dance-galas — where dance offers, as it were, *virtuoso roles*. The second case is more easily put aside: performing, say, Act III of *Raymonda* (1898[4]) in our gala detaches this movement sequence from whatever ("logical') place it had in the dance as a whole — it is not even offered as *part* of a dance. Instead, the interest of this sequence is reduced to its portrayal of the technical mastery, and perhaps prowess, of the dancers: that is, it is reduced to "... an acrobatic performance — ... [just displaying] what tremendous skill it needs" (Rhees, 1969 p. 139). Really, this is unrelated to the *art form* of dance, except parenthetically. Of course, a standard dance performance can be treated *as though* it were such a gala, if all one attends to in it is, say, how close the dancer's leg is to her ear.

Similarly revealing cases arise (at the other end of the performance spectrum) with choreographic competitions: the judges hope to be able to *see* the choreography *through* the performances: and on no other occasion than through *some* performance could the dancework itself be confronted. But if the dancers' performances are weak, it may be impossible for the judge to distinguish, with any confidence, a flaw in the work from, more simply, a flaw in its 'delivery' by this band of dancers. Just as the virtuoso can lead the spectator's eye *away* from the dance, so too can poor performance — although here it might be more accurate to talk of poor performance as simply muddying the spectator's vision.

By contrast, sometimes virtuoso performers are important in giving us a view of a certain role (or whole dance, for a solo) which is definitive: so that how we understand the role takes, say, Baryshnikov's *Firebird* (1910) as quintessential (at least for a time). Then, first, the powerful performance 'defines' the role (see UD p. 94); and, second, what can we say when that performance is no longer *directly* available to us? Yet this turns on the nature of danceworks as, somehow, *normative*: one is looking to what *should* happen in a *good* performance, not what does happen in a so-so one. Similarly, *some* virtuoso performance — in allowing us to see the work clearly — can revise our judgement of it. Indeed, if we take Petipa's choreography in *Raymonda* as "dazzling", our claims derive ultimately from the work "... as we know it from

Rudolf Nureyev's versions for the Royal Ballet and Australian Ballet" (Brinson & Crisp, 1980 p. 63).

§7. A theory of embodiment?

In summary, then, the role of embodiment encompasses the place of the dancer in typical dances. So perhaps we can recognise why an abstract or theoretical account of embodiment is not needed here. In effect, there are two related considerations. The first concerns the specificity of the embodiment of dances: that this embodiment involves these particular dancers on these particular occasions — speaking more generally would just be to have abstracted from the particular occasions. The same is not true for, say, visual artworks such as typical paintings or sculptures: they are relatively unchanging. So the need to stress embodiment in those cases is primarily to show that the specific *meaning* (or some such) of paintings or sculptures cannot be detached from the artworks themselves — that they are not just means to an otherwise specifiable end! Of course, that point must be urged for dances too. Yet it does not require *special* explanation in the dance case. And so cannot require a distinctive theory of embodiment.

But that leads to the second issue. For the embodiment itself amounts to locating artistic meaning here in the transitory movement of dancers (among other sources). As we saw initially, dancers have a role in performing arts different from that of, say, typical musicians: and that role resides precisely in embodying the dance. So am I suggesting that a theory of embodiment suitable for dances is needed, to replace (say) one from painting? No, because, in effect, the centrality of human agency here leaves nothing unsaid: as Wittgenstein liked to put it, "In the beginning was the deed" (OC §402; CV ; PO p. 395[5]). That is, we are *agents* who can, therefore, perform certain actions. And, while able to do certain things, we cannot always say *how* we do them. Further, those actions have normative possibilities: they can be good or bad (say, as chess moves), and they can embody meanings. The typical case here is genuine meaning, which is intentional: it occurs in 'hand language', such as ASL or Padgett, as well as in speech and writing. And recognising its connection to humans as *agents* contrasts it with behaviour that permits insight into agents but without that intentionality (what David Best, 1978 pp. 138-162) calls "percomm"), a possibility shared with, for instance, some non-human animals.

No doubt the craft-mastery involved in training in dance has a bearing here. But it simply offers a more sophisticated range of *actions*: that just stresses again the role of *action* in the embodiment of artistic meaning for danceworks[6] . As with human action more generally, precisely what action has been performed to constitute a dance depends on the 'description under which' that action was performed: correctly identifying the action requires capturing that description — I *really did* score the goal in football; but it is much less clear that I damaged the goal-netting, although that was a consequence of the goal I scored. And similarly for actions in dances. But such 'descriptions under which' can play no role in causal explanations, since how an event is characterised does not determine whether or not it will *cause* another, strictly speaking — the causal powers of a moving billiard ball are not changed by calling it "the white" or "the cue ball", nor those of (what is in fact) a bullet by describing it differently: say, by giving its chemical composition. And once this point is granted, fewer and fewer events in the human world will be regarded as explicable causally, especially where humans are agents.

At the least, the central interpretative categories are either those of the *art form* of dance or (occasionally) those of human action, with its implicit appeal to the cultural. A theory of embodiment would have no place under the second heading — that was Wittgenstein's point about the priority of action — while, if urged seriously under the first heading, it would simply become a theory of the meaning of *danceworks*; and here their status as performables would have its place.

§8.   Dancers and danceworks

Thus far, I have elaborated places that, with justice, stress the importance of the performers in performing arts. Yet giving the dancers *an* importance does nothing to dispute the idea of a *dancework*. For, in typical cases, our dancers display their 'craft-mastery' as dancers by instantiating a particular dancework. Recognising the sense in which dancers are *not* artists is one way to grant this point about the importance of that dancework (and the dancers' importance in permitting it an audience).

This point can be dealt with fairly quickly: even if — on a parallel with comments on theatre by Hamilton (2007 pp. 23-40) — danceworks are seen as "shared cooperative activities" (Hamilton, 2001 p. 566), we still grant that, in typical cases, one can return to such-and-such a dance, see *it* again: and the argument for a *dancework* is really nothing more than this recognition. Of course, talking about *performables* may not be the most important thing to say about the performing arts — perhaps I *stress* the essential repeatability of danceworks only because I grew up at a time when 'happenings' (that is, one-off performance events) were an issue. But one inevitably returns to repeatability as *among* the features of performing arts. That, in turn, localises an aspect of the dancer's role: however unlikely (for reasons mentioned already), different dancers could *always* perform the roles in typical danceworks.

There is, however, a complex qualification required here, to which we must return (see Chapter Ten §10): it can be introduced by asking about the durability of danceworks. On a commonsense view (and mine), each work certainly has a beginning in time, at least roughly (since its composition my go through a number of phases)[7]; and each could (in principle) have an end in time when it can no longer be performed. And a dancework "can no longer be performed" when the traditions of performance[8] it requires have been lost — that is, when there are no longer dancers able to realise it. In one sense, it might also be lost by being forgotten; but this seems merely a contingent loss (as though all copies of a particular play were thought lost, and then one found in a remote library): if there is material for reconstruction, then the dance is never lost completely. But the other condition limits the possibility of reconstruction, again emphasising the crucial role of the dancers in bringing the dancework before an audience.

§9. Conclusion

Artistic appreciation of danceworks — as with any artworks — involves attention to the features or properties of the work itself. That is, understanding dances involves perceptual engagement with the artwork's themselves, because the properties at issue should not be located in the artist, audience, or performer. Then the place of the dancer can seem unclear. Here, a distinctive contribution for the dancers has been urged: indeed, the role of the dancer — when properly understood — marks out a dimension of distinctiveness of the aesthetics of dance from within philosophical aesthetics. For, unlike typical musical works (where the performers *cause* the sounds that comprise the artwork), in typical dances the dancers *instantiate* the dancework. Thus I have defended the centrality of the *dancer as person* — and hence the dancer's *subjectivity*, in that sense — without seeking to over-rate the dancer's role. To put it bluntly, the dancer is essential: as Merce reminded us, one only sees the dance by seeing the dancers. That means that the dance performance reflects features of those dancers.

For the dancer's task (and achievement) revolves around making concrete the dancework. Since dance is a performing art, typical danceworks are *performables*: they can be performed on different occasions, in different places and spaces, and (crucially) with different casts — most cases where this *seems* false reflect a practical problem only. Of course, different performances, while still instantiating that dancework, differ in ways relevant to expressiveness or appreciation. Further, one explanation of that fact (the particular contribution of dancers) may be impossible to characterise at all exactly, although we may learn to recognise it.

Moreover, paying attention to dancers involves giving them only as much attention as is appropriate to appreciating the dancework *as art*: more attention to dancer-virtuosity will distract from the major task of understanding (as art) the dancework under consideration. But that does not assign *all* roles to the dancer. In particular, there is a key sense of the term "artist" (as *author* of art) which cannot apply to the dancer in a typical dance.

However, one can still grant that dancers are artists as a way either to draw attention to their craft-mastery (as we might say, "That surgeon is an artist", without thinking surgery an art form) or to grant their essential place in the realisation of particular danceworks, at least typically — for they are artists in the sense of being (for the moment of the performance) a *part* of the artwork.

Defending in this way the dancer's role is recognising the dancer as *a person*, as an agent. Recognising the dancer's distinctive role in instantiating the dance — and hence the distinctive contribution of the dancer to the properties of particular performances of the dancework — begins in our human, social world, where what *counts* as dance for these purposes may be a matter for debate (as recent history illustrates). Thus stressing the dancers' craft-mastery highlights (some of) what is wonderful about dancers! It recognises the training, skill, and hard work of dancers; this contribution typically functions partly in rehearsal rooms, under the guidance of choreographers or stagers with skills and insights of their own. That in turn shows why no *additional* theory for the embodiment of dance meaning is required. Moreover, the status of *this* dance as art reflects both the present state of the Republic of Dance and its historical development. For, if the over-arching concept here is *dance*, it will be dance *as art*.

Chapter Eight

Mastering movement:
Kinaesthesis, proprioception, and subjectivity

§1. Art and experience

The destructive power of *subjectivist* conceptions of the arts, and especially of dance, has been urged in various works (for instance, Best, 1992). Since that conception is operative in descriptions of dance both by dancers and by choreographers, and in critics and observers appreciating dance, in UD (p. 21), I emphasised:

> ... the idea of judgements, appraisals, evaluations and the like being made within the domain of art as being *objective* judgements ...

Since some writers understood *the subjective* as 'anything goes', my explicit rejection of that position was explained. Similarly, CDE (pp. 2-5) began with a section entitled "Against subjectivism"; and now includes an attack on explanations of the values of the arts in education that contrast its 'babble and rhapsody' and 'profound acts of liberation' with what science offers in education (CDE p. 209). For this 'other side of the coin' argument moves from the objectivity of the sciences, with its connection to knowledge, to a corresponding denial of knowledge as a goal in arts education: such a move is not warranted. And here I have railed against the dismissive subjectivism that bedevils so much discussion in respect of artworks (in Chapter Three). These comments all attack a view of subjectivity (as 'anything goes') or a self-refuting relativism, seen as a consequence of such subjectivism. Granting the importance of the performers in performing arts (as in Chapter Seven) might with justice be read as an *affirmation* of subjectivity. But stressing the importance of the *performers* cannot conflict with rejecting subjectivist (and relativist) thinking. Indeed, the positive purpose here is once again to delineate roles for the dancer in the explanation of dance appreciation; thereby speaking against over-rating of such roles.

Additionally, there is also a related matter for observers of dance. As I put it elsewhere (CDE p. 262), "... nothing *specific* here about the bodily nature of dance makes the spectator's role more (or less) bodily." Of course, the "less" recognises that spectators are essentially embodied, use their eyes (and so on), and do so from a particular spatial position. But these features do not impinge, since the judgements themselves are public and shareable, in principle (that is, they are objective).

Still, my aim here is *negative*: now I turn to three or four unprofitable avenues, where counter-productive claims are made for special role for dancers, or for a subjective element. In general, this reinforces arguments sketched elsewhere.

§2.   No place for kineasthesis in artistic appreciation

The central idea rejected here is that the dancer has some special 'access' to the dance, an 'access' that permits a special engagement with the dancework's artistic properties. That is, the dancer (through performing the dance) has particular insight into it *viewed as an artwork*. This last qualification is crucial since obviously the dancer knows how to instantiate the dance (or at least her part of it). But does this 'knowledge' bear on artistic appreciation of the dance?

One traditional family of theories here drew on the idea of a kinaesthetic sense (and any similar ideas), by which the dancer was aware of her own activity, and which she alone could deploy. Such a sense seems to yield the kinds of subjectivist account noted above, on which the dancer was the absolute authority on what she did. My reservations about such an idea of kinaesthesis (as well as similar ideas) were clear (UD pp. 264-273) under two headings. First, we do not, in general, have such a sense. Following Elizabeth Anscombe (1981), the key fact here, of knowing where (say) one's leg was positioned in space, is simply not something one *knows* perceptually — once looking in a mirror is excluded! Since no sensory modality was required here, none need be postulated. Then, second, even *were* there a kinaesthetic sense, it could contribute nothing to the artistic appreciation of danceworks since (at least in typical cases) such appreciation must draw on *projective* sensory modalities (sight, hearing) rather than on the contiguous ones (taste, touch); this followed from the need for an *audience* for artworks — the audience should not consist exclusively of those whose limited perspective on the work was that of, say, one of the performers. Those arguments need not be repeated here. Finally, following David Best (1974 p. 142), I recognised the absurdity of urging that *having danced* was a prerequisite for appreciating dances — as though having played in an orchestra were a prerequisite of understanding orchestral music: as Best (1974 p. 142) pointed out, the correct parallel here would require not only playing all the instruments, but playing them more or less simultaneously.

At the centre of that argument is the requirement for an audience for art: that, as Cavell (1969 p. xxvii: quoted UD p. 267) urged:

[i]t is tautological that art has, is made to have, an audience, however

small and special. The ways in which it sometimes hides from its audience, or baffles it, only confirms this.

Cavell recognises that a key issue for understanding art and artistic value is: In whose eyes (or ears) does this artwork have its impact? Since an answer here seems required if the work is indeed to be *art*, the transfiguration of (in this case) the movement pattern into dance must be available for recognition. But Cavell also implicitly recognises both the variety of different (kinds of) cases here, and that no exceptionless account of the audience for artworks is possible.

Elaborating the idea of an audience, four issues should be mentioned, highlighting different kinds of cases:

(a) What *counts* as an audience, for these purposes? There is no easy answer. In Jack Rosenthal's play "Bar Mitzvah Boy"[1], a young man makes the relevant statement, not in the designated place, but in a playground. His sister subsequently argues that, since God is everywhere, God counts as *in the audience* there. Clearly, that kind of answer would be unsuitable here: artworks are human products, requiring the possibility of an appropriate human audience.

(b) The point is not whether the work *is*, as a matter of fact, seen or not. Suppose running through a dance solo with 'performance energy' produced a Danto-esque "confusable counterpart" for the performance of that solo: audience or not, this is *not* performing the work, but rather rehearsing it. And seeing that rehearsal cannot *count* as being an audience for dance.

(c) The requirement here is a *logical* one: the performance where no one in the audience shows up is, for these purposes, a performance. For our concern is with the logical possibility of an audience, not the practical one.

(d) The requirement for an audience is, in effect, a requirement that the artwork be understandable (say, in the current climate in the artworld: compare the discussion of Graham's *Primitive Mysteries* (1931) in Chapter Ten §10).

Of course, this does not show categorically that artworks require an audience. But many concepts associated with artistic value — its meaning, its intentionality, its publicity — point in that direction: that losing an audience in this sense is losing *them*.

Recently, two related views have challenged my position: one urges that *proprioception* does, after all, offer a privileged way of 'understanding' and appreciating dances. The other postulates a mechanism *something like* a kineaesthetic sense, ultimately explicable via the neuro-biological hypothesis of *mirror neurons*. Both invoke empirical data; and both draw on causal explanations of behaviour. I will comment on each tendency.

§3.   Could *proprioception* be a basis for artistic judgement?

If the claim here is towards proprioception as motor perception of some kind, my view remains unchanged: insofar as there is any perception here, the perceptual modality is *visual*[2] — thus, in an experiment sketched later, the subjects *look at* video of movement sequences. So, it must be wrong to say[3] that "... the relevant experience is not a visual one, but a motor one". Instead, only a more generous view is needed about what is open to visual perception — that, say, we *see* the peasants in the Breugel picture *dancing*. That is, although the visual image in the Breugel is compatible with its being an 'imitate-the-statue' competition, we *see* the dance, and hence the movement — although, of course, this ascription may be defeated (as there are cases where I *say* I saw a tomato, but it turns out to be only half a tomato, with the cut side turned away).

Thus such an idea of motor *perception* is unsatisfactory, largely because the perceptual mode here *is* visual: if one blindfolds the audience, they will get none of the effects being talked about. Similarly, at best, dancers might have something like this *in their own cases*, but (if blindfolded) not for other dancers. Sight and hearing are the only candidate *perceptual* modes here[4].

Does anything even suggest that 'proprioception' (granting it some as yet unexplained character and status) offers access to the artistic properties of dances? Barbara Montero (2006a, p. 236a) takes part of her discussion to argue that "... proprioception can allow one to perceive aesthetic qualities of one's own movement and positions", commenting "... this is an aesthetics ... from the point of view of ... the dancer" (Montero, 2006a p. 236a). But how *useful* is such an idea, even granting its truth for a moment? For surely the requirement for publicity, for an *audience* for dance, means that "... the focus on the performer is not appropriate to an art form like dance" (UD p. 273). *If* one had to choose between the perspective of the performer and that of the audience (a choice that stressing proprioceptive 'understanding' might force on us), it would be right to side with the audience — but, in general, one *does not* have to choose because either the two perspectives coincide or, when they do not, even dancers must concede that the final 'say' rests with the observer. Where ever the dancer *thought* her leg-position was, she must grant that she was wrong. Indeed, it would be futile to fill dance studios with mirrors were this not true. And, of course, some of Montero's own examples support this perspective. Thus Montero[5] reports overhearing the director of the Royal Dutch Ballet say, "I can tell that that just doesn't feel right". The right conclusion is that the director saw that it *looked* wrong — and that was all he really cared about (he would have re-set the passage on *that* basis, whatever the dancers said).

Further, the emergent character of the understanding of danceworks should be re-affirmed (from UD p. 269): one understands danceworks (to the degree one does) by seeing them as wholes, with a variety of features. That cannot draw only or primarily on the single dancer's perspective. Yet that is all that, at best, Montero's proprioceptive aesthetic can offer.

All-in-all, there is no real case for a proprioceptive sensory modality. Moreover, this is not just about what to *call* the phenomenon — but about the *nature* of the phenomenon.

Are the arguments here directed at mere straw figures? It might seem so: surely no one would think that there was a *genuine* sensory modality here. But authors say these things (for example, talk of "motor perception"); and the words quoted (and others like them) appear in major philosophical texts, places where authors might reasonably be expected to say what they mean. And, to repeat, this *is* what they say. Further, were the emphasis elsewhere, achieving its *claimed* task in this context requires that this possibility be (fairly) specific to our dancers, not something the rest of us share (so: *not* like 'jumping' when being startled). Seen *that* way — say, like a capacity for empathy, which expresses itself through muscular sensation akin to movement — it still needs demonstration; dancers *report* something here; but what? If the description of motor perception offered here is supposed to capture that content, I doubt it. Moreover, our primary concern is with understanding and perception. So even were the argument against the existence (or the possibility) of something like a sensory modality here set aside, we should still insist (at least) on the second set of claims: that this is not explanatory of our interest in dance. That provides sufficient reason to reject the suggestion of a role for such 'proprioception'.

§4. The place of the *mirror reflex*?

Is a useful intermediate step discussion of the so-called *mirror reflex*, explained as "... an involuntary tendency to mirror automatically the behaviour of our conspecifics" (Carroll & Moore, 2008 p. 424[6])? Certainly it offers another feature apparently explanatory in respect of our appreciation of danceworks. (And more so were mirror neurons used to 'explain' the mirror reflex[7]?) As Carroll (2008 p. 185) writes:

> We have an involuntary tendency to mirror automatically the behaviour, especially the expressive behaviour, of our conspecifics.

So this capacity thereby "... freely avails itself of our biological heritage" (Carroll, 2008 p. 189). No doubt, these are "not fully-fledged emotional states ... [but] gestures and postures are also mimicked ... in order to gain information about what is percolating inside our conspecifics" (Carroll, 2008 pp. 185-186). Certainly, recognising the force of reference to causal explanatory structures of this sort might help. One might think that "[o]ne function of the mirror reflex is to gather information about the inner states of others ... [such that] ...[b]y involuntarily mimicking the facial disposition of our interlocutor ... we gain an inking of what is going on inside him" (Carroll & Moore, 2008 p. 424). Yet, of course, this just the old (and refuted) 'argument from analogy' about other minds, except now even less of an *argument*, since this behaviour is not even voluntary. But the thought that your psychological states can be inferred from your behaviour in this way is highly contentious. For how is the behaviour related to one's psychology — in your case or mine? At best, the move from one to the other is suspect. For my own behaviour may be idiosyncratic. And why should your behaviour reflect my psychology this closely? To make this plausible, what is contentious must be assumed: namely, that we are relevantly like our interlocutor; and have enough direct access to 'what is going on inside him' to build up the requisite correlations[8].

The interest Carroll and Moore (2008 p. 425) take in these 'mirror reflexes' comes out clearly when they urge that "[m]irror reflexes ... afford a critical channel of communication that is undoubtedly adaptive for social animals like us". In one way, this is right; but precisely fails to note the distinction Best (1978 pp. 138-162; UD pp. 243-244) introduced between those cases of communication that embody the intention to communicate (Best called it "lingcomm") and those cases where this was not true — where one learns something about the other all right, but without his intention that one do so (Best called this "percomm"). Mirror reflexes, as something "involuntary", at best involve *percomm*: we could learn about another from his behaviour — in this case, his behaviour as we mirror it. Now, perhaps one might hesitate about claiming as *knowledge* something so subliminal. Still, putting *that* worry aside, this is clearly not a "channel of communication" (much less "a *critical* channel of communication": my emphasis) if such communication is supposed to be intentional[9]. Perhaps it allows us to glean something about some other (or others: as Carroll and Moore [2008 p. 431, note 33] rightly recognise, one can respond to "group movement"). Perhaps, were our concern anthropological, we would find an adaptive advantage in this.

If this account of the mirror reflex were true (and, hence, at best), this is just something people do — or have a tendency to do. Applied to dance, perhaps the possibility of our making sense of dance (that is, making sense of an activity of other moving bodies) is partly dependent on such a human capacity. But the classical problem of 'other minds' above (how can one know the thoughts and feelings of another, given knowledge of her behaviour?) has what force it retains simply because the person's moving *in this way* is no guarantee of what she is thinking or feeling: hence, our coming to move in that way too must be similarly uninformative. So the claim for the mirror reflex does not seem to be true.

Further, this propensity to mimic movement cannot function *normatively* here, such that this manifesting indicates — to that degree — a *good* dance; and vice versa (see Chapter Three). Such a human capacity or disposition (were it real) cannot distinguish our interaction with a *good* dance from our interaction with inferior ones. As Frege ([1918] 1984 p. 351) noted, "[e]rror and superstition have causes just as much as correct cognition": that is, both good works (or responses) and poor ones have causal stories. So such stories cannot reflect the normativity whereby such-and-such is a *good* move in chess, for poor moves too will have causal explanations. Like sweating, or digesting my food, or breathing, the phenomena described by the 'mirror reflex' are typically not things one can do *well* (so as to make one's behaviour *praiseworthy*) as opposed to simply doing them effectively — as pneumonia might cause one to have difficulty breathing. More importantly, this 'mirror reflex' is as likely to occur watching gymnasts (say), or non-art dance. Hence the relation to this putative capacity cannot separate danceworks that *are art* from others.

In fact, the absence of the possibility of a *normative* dimension is fundamental here: a dancework cannot be good (nor bad) in proportion to its activating or utilising this (human) capacity. Nor can one infer that what utilises (or draws on) this capacity more often or more regularly is *therefore* a better (or worse) dance: it is simply a dance which utilises that human 'mirror reflex' capacity. But to *understand* is normative: what can be understood, one can also *fail* to understand; or, perhaps, misunderstand. So the possibility of 'getting it right' imports also the possibility of 'getting it wrong'. Such a contrast cannot be treated solely causally. Much here turns on what is or is not *causal*. If we begin by thinking in terms of what follows from the workings out of the causal ('natural') laws of science, it is clear that causality will be typically exceptionless, and independent of the 'description under which' we characterise our actions.

Perhaps, I am more of a cognitivist on such matters than many writers here: I recognise a cognitive dimension partly by seeing the outcome as rationally explicable, and as thereby incorporating how the event or phenomenon is to be understood (the 'description under which' the action was performed). This thought has implications for our *responses* to (for instance) music or movements. It is tempting to see those responses — because immediate and seemingly non-conceptual — as only causally explicable (and perhaps as suitable for causal explanation). Since such responses to music or movement are widespread, there is a phenomenon to be explained. But what are our explanatory resources?

First, what is rationally explicable, and hence cognitive, may yet be immediate: there need by no 'gap' between seeing an artwork and appreciating it (since the appreciation is perceptual: see also Chapter Ten). But, second, ways in which what is *conceptual* (because cultural) pervade the human world must be stressed. For instance, suppose a biological imperative on humans is granted (as on non-human animals) to eat and to reproduce — among other such imperatives. Such imperatives might be causally explicable. Yet the forms in which these practices manifest themselves is not causal in any *straightforward* way: we do not simply take a bite from the first available food-source that passes, within grabbing range, across our field of vision. If there is a causal basis here, it is well below the surface of typical human actions. Similarly, we do not simply seek to impregnate (or whatever) the first object of sexual attraction within grabbing range (even putting aside cultural dimensions of attraction). Rather, what counts as food here, and how it is prepared and eaten, is heavily cultural. In like fashion, the elaborate 'rituals' involved in courtship among humans are not well reduced even to the sorts of causal imperatives operative within the world of (other) primates. So an account of the (human) resources here must recognise that the object of desire (for food as for sex, or love) is necessarily the object as characterised or understood: in this sense, it *is* conceptual — even if one could not *deploy* the concepts discursively. That is, the cognitive dimension in the human versions of the biological imperatives should be stressed.

This highlights once again what is wrong with appealing to the causal origin of some judgement: as we saw Frege recognise, there will be a causal story for erroneous judgements — hence the causal story alone cannot offer the requisite normativity: that is, it can never distinguish what *ought* to go on or what is *praiseworthy* when it goes on.

§5. What about *mirror neurons?*

Suppose, then, one postulates, as an explanation of an additional human capacity[10] for awareness of movement in others:

> ... a class of neurons ... which are activated when one sees certain types of movement, much as they would be activated if one were to perform the movement oneself. (Montero, 2006a pp. 236b-237a)

That is, as offering the *physiological sub-strate* for the human powers and capacities (even granting their existence). And suppose they were called *mirror neurons*[11]. Notice that the title "mirror reflex" (mentioned above) is justified by the behaviour of humans (and animals) in mirroring the behaviour of others. No such justification exists for the *mirror neurons*: their name derives from the behaviours they are supposed to explain.

But why should reference to that sub-strate here be revealing when our concerns are with artistic matters? Artistic communication — or artistic interaction more generally — is essentially intentional: the artist's intelligence is seen behind it. This, of course, rules out the possibility of its being 'naturally occurring', except where an artist selects such a device. As I have repeated, the cracks in the wall — in so far as they are genuinely cracks — not only *do not* spell-out my loved one's name, they *could not* do so: they lack precisely this intentional structure. The moral from such a case applies here directly: given only the biological (or neuro-biological) sub-strate, one cannot offer anything of genuine interest to any study of artistic communication.

Further, a revealing explanatory note begins[12], "[t]he *conjecture* concerning mirror neurons is based on research with macaque monkeys" (Carroll & Moore, 2008 note 23 p. 425). Why should this be taken seriously here, especially since it is conjectural? *Of course*, the conjecture must have some basis — no doubt at least partly recognising a basis in our neuro-physiology, allowing humans to behave in these ways, to the extent that they do[13]. Perhaps the similarities between our neuro-physiologies and that of monkeys justifies investigating the biological sub-strate of the *human* powers and capacities by considering *first* the case of these monkeys. But the capacity for *dance* (in our sense) is, of course, not one those macaque monkeys share with humans: dance the art form is meaning-bearing in the kinds of *social* ways precisely unavailable to monkeys — even those ethologists with most enthusiasm for the parallel of monkey-behaviour with humans only concentrate on attenuated human behaviour (say, meetings between strangers sharing a path in the park: compare Morris, 1977) rather than, for instance, the elaborate verbal interaction between friends. Too many steps must be taken to connect one to the other to warrant confidence in this as an explanatory structure for a complex human capacity, realisable only within a context — such as the capacity to learn dances (since what counts as *dance* here is a cultural matter).

It has been claimed, of mirror neurons, that "[t]hese neurons explain how it is possible to understand the gestures of others" (Legrenzi & Umiltà, 2011 p. 35). Well, at best they offer the causal sub-strate for the human capacity to understand such gestures. No doubt, without structures of this sort in the brain, humans would be unable to *understand* the gestures of others. But the macaque monkeys did not genuinely *understand* the gestures of other monkeys: at best, these neural structures were integral[14] to the monkeys' recognition of what other monkeys were doing (in so far as that makes sense). But, as audience of a dancework, I do not simply grasp what movements the dancers are doing: instead, I recognise the (artistic) meaning of their steps and gestures in the context of *this* dance. And that is to take an artistic interest in those steps and gestures; and (hence) to see them as part of an artwork.

There is a pattern here: in each case, the emphasis is on the *causal* — in some version — at the expense of the *rational* or *normative*. As a consequence, insufficient attention is paid both to the specific context of the particular dance 'utterance' and to the broad context within which artistic appreciation and understanding takes place.

Moreover, a TV advertisement is discussed, in which "... watching music videos on ... cell-phones ... inspires ... [people] to match the movement" (Carroll & Moore, 2008 p. 426). If the point is that much twentieth century dance "... has been, in one way or another, about the feelings engendered by the music that accompanies it" (Carroll & Moore, 2008 p. 426), ... well, the connection is obscure. *Of course,* music inspires choreographers; *of course,* many works grow from this — but they do not grow just by Jo and Jane Public responding to music, but only by *choreographers* (and sometimes, as a compositional technique, *dancers*) responding to that music. That one counts as a *choreographer* or *dancer* here (or that one's actions count as dance) is, of course, a broadly cultural matter. Not *any* movement pattern counts as *dance*; certainly, at one time, the movements comprising a modern-dance classic, like Graham's *Lamentation* (1930), could not be recognised as dance[15]. And not just any dance-planning counts as *choreography* in the sense under discussion. No doubt *some* biological sub-strate is operative here: but the years of training, the insightfulness of choreographers, the (implicit) reflection on the state of the danceworld, the potential of various dancers — all seem far more fundamental; and much nearer the artistic *surface.*

In particular, the capacity to *learn* to appreciate dances seems far removed from what could be explained by appeal to our biology. No doubt there are biological preconditions for our being able to learn such appreciation. But the explanation for someone who fails to learn it will typically reside in that person's human powers and capacities, rather than as a defect in his/her biology — as when someone cannot see each aspect of a multiple-figure (such as the old-woman/young-woman): we do not typically look for the explanation in that person's biology, but in his/her cognitive capacities.

At this stage, a particular experiment might be invoked[16], reporting Calvo-Merino et al. (2005) as follows:

> ... a team of researchers ... asked dancers from the Royal Ballet, experts in capoeira (a Brazilian martial art), and an inexpert control group to watch videos of ballet and capoeira movements while their [the subjects] brain activity was recorded with fMRI.

So the context has monitoring of the neural activity of three groups:

> The researchers found greater activity in various motor areas involved in preparation and execution of action when experts viewed movements that they had been trained to complete compared to movements they had not, while the control group showed the same pattern of neural activity whether they were watching the ballet or the capoeira video.

Faced with this empirical data, the right slogan is: 'Is there no *other* way to read the results?'. Elaborating related considerations for the aesthetics of film, Carroll (2008 p. 171) gives exposition of two views from contemporary philosophy of mind: *the simulation theory* (on which "... we understand and explain others ... by simulating them. That is, we input their beliefs and desires into our own off-line cognitive-conative system": Carroll, 2008 p. 172) and *the theory-theory* (which is "... the *theory* that we understand what others are about by applying something like a scientific *theory* to their behaviour": Carroll, 2008 p. 171). His critique is partly criticism of these theories. Were such a detour through philosophy of mind crucial, the best alternatives in the philosophy of mind must be selected (can that *really* be these?). But a text such as this cannot hope to resolve that matter.

Moreover, our *certainty* that it is *mental states* that need explaining is unfounded. As Wittgenstein noted, "... [w]e talk of processes and states, and leave their nature undecided, ... [thereby assuming] ... a definite concept of *what it means* to know a process better" (PI §308: my emphasis). That is, we assume that our topic is actually clearly identified, although we have not done that identification; then all that remains is our *ignorance* of the specifics of that topic. Next we think that our ignorance *will be* remedied in some distant future: that "[s]ometime perhaps we *shall* know more about [the 'processes and states']" (PI §308: my emphasis). Our mistake lies in thinking that the ignorance is that *specific*: that it represents some *one*, localised topic. So that, if we know that our answer lies in a causal sub-strate, we must be in the right region, even if the detail is wrong. But how could we know that? Instead, what we should do is "... deny the yet uncomprehended process in the yet unexplored medium" (PI §308).

To return: we have granted that there is differential brain activity in the

Brazilian martial artists, the ballet dancers, and the control groups when faced with images of their own activity (or lack of it). So far, this might be expected — that one responds differently to what is most familiar, and so on. The point seems *stronger* once it is claimed that there was "... greater activity in various motor areas involved in preparation and execution of action" [17]. Well, that is certainly what people *say*. But not enough is known about the brain to give confidence in these claims: this would only be evidence of anything were these indeed brain areas *uniquely* associated with 'motor *preparation*' — and even then we are required to associate 'motor preparation' of this kind with some ability to better perceive movements of others.

Yet, we simply do not know enough about the brain to make such an identification of a unique function to this or that brain area. For instance, there are people with conditions which permit only a small amount of functioning brain, but who manage their lives like the rest of us. So there seems nothing absolutely exceptionless here[18]. But the advocates of such brain-based conceptions of human psychology require just that exceptionlessness. For they urge an exceptionless relation between a brain-state and a 'corresponding' thought or feeling such that, from the first, the second can reliably be inferred.

Not all causal claims operate in this way. Thus, exceptionless causation can be contrasted with stochastic (statistical) causation — as when smoking causes lung cancer; yes, but not in every case. The stochastic case can *seem* simply the other, exceptionless kind, but where the requisite information is lacking. Now, the fact of a single explanation in any particular case could not generate causal laws or generalisations unless cases resemble one another *relevantly* — and that is what I deny occurs generally.

Before addressing an illustrative example, we should set aside the (popular) appeal here to *Chaos Theory*: for so-called Chaos Theory is characterised by relationships described by non-linear equations. But now we have explained that point (as it occurs previously). For then a slight difference in the initial conditions is granted to permit a *large* difference in the outcome (FW pp. 155-157).

So let us enquire what it would *mean* for a brain-state to correlate exceptionlessly with a psychological state, taking a simple example. Recall that the thought is to explain how, in a particular case, my being in a particular brain-state relates exceptionlessly to my being in a particular psychological state. For, of course, the person has thoughts — the thoughts are not in the body: but, nevertheless the having of those thoughts is some kind of physical state (especially of my brain and Central Nervous System). Thoughts provide a simpler example here, as having no obvious location: by contrast, the pain *in my foot* seems ... well, in my foot! Then we may not know how to respond if John Searle (2007b p. 110) insists that, in such a case, " a conscious event ... occurred in my brain", and hence that the pain is really in my brain. After all, the pain was clearly in my foot. That is, it has a location prior to this discussion: but this may prompt the introduction of red-herrings, such a phantom limbs, and the like. The same cannot be obviously said of thought. For this reason, then, thoughts provide a simpler case.

Since I am a physical structure, there is some state of that structure that is, say, my having a particular thought: for instance, my thinking longingly about Nicole Kidman. But nothing follows about my future states. Of course, if I were in *exactly* that same state again, I would again be thinking of Nicole. But that is actually impossible! Changes in me — including the physiological ones — mean that I can never be *exactly* the same again; indeed, this "I" here will always have a different composition in the future. But from my being in *roughly* the same state, nothing follows.

To see that, suppose the thought in question has Nicole wearing a thong; and suppose we grant that my thinking it amounts to my being in a particular physical state (especially a state of my brain and Central Nervous System). Now, how would that state differ if I were thinking of Nicole in different undergarments? And how would it resemble *your* thinking longingly of her in a thong? No doubt there would be sets of similarities here (to explain the similarities of content?); but it seems unlikely that one could move from either knowledge of my brain-state to my exact thought, or from knowing my brain-state to *your* thought. There do not seem to be exceptionless laws here, although that is what the position under consideration requires. Further, as above, the passage of time will mean that my brain at some later time could never be in exactly the state it was when I was first thinking of Nicole and the thong — my brain's composition will have moved on subtlely; for instance, as I learn, or forget, or remember new facts. Again, we will never be able to infer reliably the precise topic of my thought. (Of course, asking me might be a key idea; but, equally, not one open to the position under discussion.)

To apply, we do not know enough to say with such confidence what particular patterns of neural firing show. At best, we might comment on what they usually or typically show — if we had sufficient data to determine an uncontentious trend. (Recall the difficulty in establishing a biological basis *even* for the claim that smoking causes cancer!) Further, the claim as reported is only for *greater* activity. Greater in what respect? Greater by orders of magnitude, or just slightly greater (perhaps not statistically significantly)? In every single case in the study, or just generally? And uniformly? Greater than is typical for that person? All of the above? Thinking these questions through seriously highlights the weakness of the claim.

Even those well-disposed to give credence to the 'findings' of contemporary neuro-physiology must grant that their account requires an exceptionless application, such that every time such-and-such occurs in the brain, so-and-so is happening. How could this be demonstrated? (Insofar as evidence locating human powers in the brain exists, it offers nothing like this degree of clarity.) If someone were to assure me, with his/her hand on whatever is the scientist's equivalent of the Bible (I like it to be Darwin's *Origin of Species*), that this exceptionlessly true of human beings I would withdraw this criticism. But I would want to question how he/she could be so confident, given the nature of available evidence; and I would point out the logic of the situation — that if there is just *one* human being, past, present or future, for whom this was not true, then these scientists are *wrong*. So this requires more than, say, the 'conjecture' (which I grant) that so-and-so cannot see because he lacks eyes — for that is merely causally necessary, while the claims here are to the causally sufficient. And our scientists could not have any warrant for this degree of confidence. Certainly, very many claims made in science are merely stochastic (statistical), showing trends or tendencies.

So its advocates must show not only that a single set of functions is ascribable to particular regions of the brain such that no counter-case could ever be found — and, to repeat, how would this be shown? — but also that there is a dependable relationship between the *degree* of firing, such that one can infer that, say, if such-and-such electrochemical activity indicates *preparation for action* (whatever that is), *more* electrochemical activity indicates *more* preparation. This *clearly* seems a huge stretch.

Then, even granting this claim, its relevance to the dance-appreciation case must still be demonstrated: what exactly could it show us about the appreciation of the *art form dance*, when one segment of its data concerns an *art form*, while another does not? What should be concluded once the artistic/aesthetic contrast is conceded, at least for the normative judgements of art appreciation? Perhaps there cannot be a widely-applicable *general* story here. Instead, each difficulty must be confronted case-by-case, dance-by-dance; and hence, perhaps, best realised in a comprehensive critical biography of this or that dancer or company.

So, in summary, we have identified:

• the gap between the causal sub-strate and the cultural facts where the second (the facts about dance viewed as *dance*) concern us;

• the uncertainties within the *claims* made for the brain research: in particular, with its putative 'close specification' of the brain areas associated with human powers and capacities. Most neurophysiologists would concede both that, at best, this is at the level of voxels, not neurons; and that it is not exceptionless. Then they have at best a promissory note against future research as though they know what its outcome should be;

- (also) the issue of deciding that it is *mental states* that require explanation (or description) here.

Further, the impact of theoretical change in science should be considered: would a claim *currently* thought exceptionless *ever* become treated as a useful generalisation but not true exceptionlessly? Or even false in its full generality? (As Newton's Laws were regarded by those who, nevertheless, calculated using those laws in planning the NASA moon landings.) The *future* of science remains open; and claims will carry over into that future. But more specific claims about brain structures — mirror neurons being one example — just deploy the theoretical tools of one group of scientific researchers, likely to be overthrown by later work.

One aspect of our point here, concerning the explanatory force of the biological sub-strate, is well-put by Searle (2007a p. 40 note[19]):

I am assuming for the sake of this chapter that the right functional level for explaining mental phenomena is the level of neurons. It might turn out to be some other level — microtubules, synapses, neuronal maps, whole clouds of neurons, etc. — but for the purposes of this chapter it does not matter what the right neurobiological explanatory level is, only that there is a neurobiological explanatory level.

For the precise detail of the explanation offered cannot be crucial *for philosophy*. Thinking otherwise confuses the relation of philosophy to the (natural) sciences. Since science is empirical, answering to the state of the world, one cannot *guarantee* that any particular claim of science (especially any detailed claim) is right, especially when looking to the newer reaches of enquiry. But, whenever scientific claims are modified, one must ask what that means for the philosophy. Contrast a very different kind of case: suppose that, at one time, the sorts of causal powers and capacities current associated with the brain were thought to derive from the heart. Of course, this might have a profound impact in some places in one's philosophy. Yet if what was stressed was just a unified material parcel that was the seat of certain causal powers, nothing (much) need have changed — in this sense, that view did not draw on the *mechanics* of personal powers and capacities: the philosophy need not wait for the science. Thus it seems odd to require that our understanding of dance appreciation must wait on getting the *right* account of the neural activity (if any account will be right).

No doubt, some *framework* from science must be granted. For example, for Searle (1992 p. 88), the framework might involve "... elementary notions of atomic theory ... [and] the principles of evolutionary biology": so, at least an atomic conception of matter and an evolutionary account of the 'development' of living things. And the *detail* of the science cannot be crucial. Thus Searle (1992 p. 90) is "... not ... concerned to defend this world view", rightly regarding any putative competitors to these elementary building blocks as not "... serious candidates for truth (Searle, 1992 p. 91). Later scientific investigations typically revise the precise details, but within the framework.

Moreover, however well these cases describe the neural sub-strate of human activity, they fall far short of describing humans thinking and feeling. (One of my own favourite examples, although slightly off the point, is a cod map of a section of the human genome which claims to identify a gene for the belief that all bags are carry-on bags — that is *crazy*; but why? I would say because it confuses the biological sub-strate with the human explanation.) Thus, Montero[20] quoted a comment about "... the brain's response to seeing an action ...": that is *so* dangerous; it means, of course, the brain's response to the *person's* seeing the action ... and even that is not quite right, since the brain is a part of the person, and hence it is the brain changes *when* the person sees (rather than the *brain* responding either to perception directly or to the person's perception). For the brain-changes do not *cause* the psychological changes (in typical cases): rather, they constitute them. A helpful slogan here begins from PI §281:

> ... only of a human being and what resembles (behaves like) a human being can one say: it has sensations; it sees; is blind; hears; is deaf; is conscious or unconscious.

And our reflection should note both that Wittgenstein here just gives *examples* of the relevant powers and capacities — that others could be added to the list; and that a particular individual might not warrant *all* of these.

§6.   A complication: 'muscle memory'?

One revealing complication here is the idea of 'muscle-memory'; an expression that really collapses two related ideas. The first is properly thought of as a kind of memory. For instance, Ryle (1949 p. 259) explained memory as "having learned and not forgotten": the idea here is simply about *how* one learns, about the impact of 'learning through doing'. So that dancers can learn sequences fairly quickly, and fairly accurately (compared to the rest of us) — they probably would not become dancers were this not true. So a kind of biological inheritance might be regularly reinforced and 'flexed' in dance training. And this capacity allows our dancer to retain the work of this rehearsal into the next rehearsal, and then into the performances. Moreover, when we ask our dancer, years later, about the dance, this capacity is drawn on: the dancers remember what to do — although they could not, perhaps, have described it to us. Notice, though, that a dancer in a wheelchair might still be able to mobilise this capacity in recognising when a performance by another deviated from that she had been taught. This capacity seems trained into dancers, but doubtless some predisposition there singled them out as suitable for the training. 'Muscle-memory' in this sense is an uncontentious phenomenon — although it might still need to be (further?) explained!

The second idea seems to explain the first: that dancers do this by their *muscles* somehow remembering. Then this provides the explanation of dancers' capacity both to move from the corrections of the rehearsal room to the final performance and to recall the movement patterns of the dance at some later time. Yet such an 'explanation' seems mysterious — does it really add anything to the first account?

Now, another capacity of persons (at least) resembles this one: there are lots of behaviours which become 'grooved' for humans, so that they can be performed without thinking. For instance, having been trained to drive a stick-shift, I can change gear at the sound of the car's engine beginning to labour, but be unaware of either noting this fact or acting on it. However, such a capacity does not require further explanation: when I say that I have become so practiced that I can perform this activity without thinking, nothing more need be said. Of course, if you wanted to claim that my *muscles* remembered how to do it, that would be unexceptionable thus far. But, notice, this is not even as informative as the previous version: in *that* version, the behaviour was 'brought about' (or 'triggered') by *my hearing* something — but my muscles cannot hear. So there *seems* yet more unexplained if we talk of muscle-memory here. But, of course, nothing remains unexplained, beyond noting this capacity in humans — most, if not all, have it to some degree (or they would never learn to drive), but differentially: it comes more easily to some than to others. The point, though, is that (although the *mechanisms* remain unclear) the human power or capacity is not.

It is the *person* (in our case, the dancer) who remembers: as we might put it, that "... the memory is encoded in the brain and central nervous system" (Syed, 2010 p. 35), not in the muscles *as such*. The reality is that the person was able to perform the motion after some time — although perhaps the trigger for the capacity was in movements consciously or *deliberately* made:

that is, made after (and on the basis of) deliberation. For this is not how typical dancers behave in executing dances they have 'learned and not forgotten'. Indeed, in most such cases, the required movements would not be performed as swiftly as they are (and as the context of the dance requires) had the dancer to deliberate about each movement. Instead, trained dancers place *this* complex situation "... within the context of a rich, detailed and elaborate conceptual scheme derived from years of experience" (Syed, 2010 p. 40). That is just another way to say that they are trained dancers, put into a dance context — and, in particular, into broadly *familiar* dance contexts. Since we are minimally physicalists here, in that we accept that these anatomies and physiologies completely comprise the persons we are, there will be a physical sub-strate of some kind for the dancers' abilities and capacities — even if our discussion of thoughts of Nicole (above) highlight complexities in making out the detail of that sub-strate, so as to uniquely identify thoughts with brain-states. But referring to that neural sub-strate adds nothing explanatory to just noting that dancers can do this.

Of course, granting a predisposition to acquire these physical skills if one practices may be conceding a genetic advantage that dispositions to particular physical types offer — although even Ballanchine's vision of the ideal dancer's body was perhaps less prescriptive than that insisting on height in candidate basketball players in the NBA. Further, this predisposition for typical dancers will be towards finding a place as basic for a genetic endowment as part of that the complex relationship between self-motivating attachment to a particular activity (here, dance), the required hours of practice, and the interventions of suitable teachers. But, insofar as our topic is *human* powers and capacities, or (more specifically) dancerly ones, all this adds little to our comprehension of that understanding manifested by dancers.

Then, were a suitable "object of comparison" (PI §131) wanted for this aspect of the psychology of the dancer, one might (with Syed, 2010 p. 42) turn to expert-systems theory from artificial intelligence, to see the dancers' actions manifesting their *knowledge* of dance (and of *this* dance), in a world where "[t]he most important ingredient of any expert system is knowledge" (Buchanan, et al., 2005 p. 100; also quoted Syed, 2010 p. 42). But, as recognised (in Chapter Seven §2, §3), that knowledge is *professional knowledge*: so, neither the kind of 'knowing that' which might be characterised independently of the activities nor the kinds of closed skills (like riding a bicycle) treated as 'knowing how' to do certain things. Moreover, its analysis clearly cannot detach that knowledge from action, nor treat action-guiding decision here as a kind of 'hand-to-forehead' deliberation prior to action. This is one case where:

... the numbers of variables in many real-life situations ... [as in dance] makes in impossible to sift the evidence before making a decision: *it would take too long.* (Syed, 2010 p. 43: his italics)

Moreover, there is no finite totality of such evidence! Rather, the capacity to recognise the appropriate thing to do is best treated as *recognitional*: that one sees the right thing to do, based on one's knowledge and understanding. Indeed, these are precisely features Donald Schön (1983; 1987) attributes to professional knowledge: they explain why the reflective practitioner does not typically reflect *and then* act — rather, he/she behaves thoughtfully in the context. Thus, a typical form of explanation might be, "I just do that", or "It is natural for me", since the dancer has acquired these are action-patterns. The explanation of the responses exhibited even in unfamiliar situations lies (no doubt) in the values that hold those responses in place. But these would not typically be theorized nor would one typically be aware of them directly when acting. Yet, crucially, the point addresses about what professionals can readily explain or say, not what they know. Rather, the professional who "knows how to go on" in the profession has another kind of knowledge ("knowing-in-action": Schön, 1987: 23): he or she "goes on" with various actions. As Schön urges, saying *that* is not denying that knowledge or understanding is at work here — instead, we recognise "reflection-in-action" (Schön, 1987: 29)[21].

There is not a distinctive kind of thinking or reflecting is operative here — there is just a certain kind of acting; but it is intelligent action, as indicated by the flexibility the practitioner displays when unusual events occur. (In this sense, a reflective practitioner is not really someone who *reflects*.) Then, the connection to practice (and to good practice) is clear: one cannot ask, "How does reflection relate to practice?", since the practice is integral to the reflection from the beginning. Thus action is *not* "... only a kind of implementation" (Schön, 1983 p. 165) of ideas detached from that action.

So Schön's reflective practitioner is not someone who is both *reflective* and a *practitioner*. In the technical language of philosophy, the adjective "reflective" functions *attributively*, rather than *predicatively*. The expression "beautiful dancer" is ambiguous in precisely this respect: in one sense, a beautiful dancer is a person who is beautiful and also a dancer — the predicative use — while (in another) it is someone who dances beautifully. In this second use — the attributive one — the term "beautiful" cannot in this way be pried apart from the term "dancer". So Darcy Bussell (who is both beautiful and dances beautifully) is, as it were, a beautiful, beautiful dancer! Just as the expression "beautiful dancer" (in its attributive use) cannot be split, so the expression "reflective practitioner" (in Schön's use) picks out someone who practices reflectively, rather than some who acts *and* reflects.

Further, this account explores what makes a reflective practitioner: these practitioners *do* "reflection-in-action", rather than simply responding in habit-laden or rote ways. All who have supervised student-teachers will be familiar with crude examples of this point: visiting a well-delivered class one day and then, the next day, finding that student teaching precisely the same material in precisely the same manner with a radically different group of pupils. Of course, this student may grow into reflective practice: on the basis of these lessons, he or she is not there yet. So this is not (attributively) a property of some practitioners, but rather a clarification of what is involved in being a practitioner at all, in some full sense of the word (contrast: "he's not really a teacher anymore, although he still draws the salary: he's just going through the motions"). Thus, in Schön's sense of "reflective", there cannot be *unreflective* teachers. Rather, those who fail (wholly or to some degree) to be reflective practitioners fail (to that degree) to really do the job. And the same might be said for dancers. Schön is characterising what effective professionals do, allowing us to explain why some are not effective, or not fully effective, or not effective in some aspect of their professional lives.

Moreover, Schön's book *Educating the Reflective Practitioner* (1987) describes examples, not of reflective practice, but of acquisition of the craft-knowledge to allow someone — at a later date — to do *reflection-in-action*. This is fundamental to thinking about our own practice: one needs to learn reflection-in-action, not learn to 'reflect at leisure'. In this way, Schön's work is an introductory foray into the epistemology of professional practice[22].

I do not want to insist that any of these claims *must* be accepted *as theses in psychology*: they are used here as "objects of comparison" (PI §133), more revealing of the human (and cultural) powers of dancers than elaboration of the physical (and especially neuro-physiological) sub-strate.

§7. Conclusion

Since understanding dances involves perceptual engagement with the artwork's themselves, the properties at issue should not be located in the artist, audience, or performer. Yet, typical danceworks are *performables* — they can be performed on different occasions, in different places and spaces, and (crucially) with different casts. This seems to assign a distinctive role to dancers. Further, in typical dances the dancers *instantiate* the dancework, unlike typical musical works (where the performers *cause* the sounds that comprise the artwork). Thus, in Chapter Seven, the centrality of the *dancer as person* — and hence the dancer's *subjectivity*, in that sense — was defended, without seeking to over-rate the dancer's role. The discussion here extended that one by recognising ways of discussing *the dancer* which are not philosophically revealing for the aesthetics of dance.

One central misunderstanding of the dancer's role assigns the dancer a special access to the dancework, through the idea of some kinaesthetic sense, or something similar. As we have seen, this idea has recently been re-introduced (perhaps as proprioception) by attention to the causal history, and especially the neurophysiology, of dancers. Milder versions, emphasising mirroring process (such as mirror reflexes), may have some role to play in explaining some (unusual) examples of the structure of dances. But they still simply confuse the causal history with that concerning rational appreciation by humans. This confusion is furthered when the neurophysiology is given greater emphasis; say, in invoking *mirror neurons*. Defending the dancer's role recognised dancers as *persons*, as agents. For even the dancer's distinctive contribution to the properties of particular performances of the dancework begins in our human, social world, amenable to rational explanation as *human action*. So does the audience's appreciation (and understanding) of such performances. That runs counter to locating *special access* to the dance for the dancer: say, in kinaesthetic awareness, or its fancy modern counterparts. Such appeals to the causality of processes cannot be the business of the philosophical aesthetics of dance, not least because such attention to causality either ignores or discounts the rational choices of dancers and choreographers or fails to address philosophical issues about appreciation and performance at all.

So the idea of muscle memory was introduced (towards the end of the chapter) to illustrate that explanation does not necessarily require the laying out of a complex causal history. Instead, this is a human power or capacity — and, at best, one needs to consider the interplay between two factors: does a developed version of this capacity make it more likely that one will succeed as a dancer? Or does dance training develop the capacity? The short answer must be, "both". A longer answer, displaying the phenomenology of particular dancers (and hence their subjectivity) must await an occasion directed more clearly at the philosophy of mind and/or philosophy of action. For the explanation here requires, to repeat, recognising the training, skill, and hard work of dancers: as was said, this contribution typically functions partly in rehearsal rooms, under the guidance of choreographers or stagers with skills and insights of their own. And that is one place to look for elaboration of what is involved in *being a dancer* for these purposes.

Part Four: A Narrative of Dance History

Chapter Nine

Reconstructing dances?

Some conceptual questions

§1. Introduction

In the musical version of the film *The Producers* (2005), the central character Max Bialystock (played by Nathan Lane) is in prison, having 'flashbacks' as to how he arrived in this parlous state. But the most distant 'memories', as we see them, turn out not to be his: as he says, "Somebody else's past is flashing before my eyes". Clearly, this situation must be avoided by those who claim that 'knowing where we came from' is fundamental to a proper understanding of dance: the past we gather in must be *our* past. Furthermore, much in the past of any art form is not worth the effort of 're-finding'. At any time, most of the dances composed and performed — like most of the novels, plays or poems written, or paintings and sculptures produced — are, frankly, *bad*. So a justification must be sought for any project of re-finding.

One thought here, fundamental to much aesthetics, stresses the so-called 'Test of Time': that what has remained in the repertoire has done so for a reason — it was the best. In this sense, history has already offered a kind of 'artistic filter' to produce (roughly) the current repertoire. This idea of a 'Test of Time' — applied in this way — generates at least two relevant problems: the first, wholly general, is that what one *takes* for the best often reflects what is familiarly offered as the best; and this can be the result of entirely arbitrary sets of circumstances. Thus, some Impressionist paintings 'disappeared' into the collections of (especially) American collectors: they were not widely seen, or reproduced in books on art. So, on seeing them, one tends to compare them with the Impressionist works which are most familiar. And, typically, to compare them unfavourably with these 'old friends', which were our examples for 'learning to see' and 'learning to value' Impressionist works (see Chapter Ten); and which provide our 'temporary paradigms' (McFee, 1978 p. 70) of Impressionist value. In one way, these 'old friends' have passed the Test of Time (actually, in two ways, as Impressionism itself has been retained in the narrative of art history). But art-irrelevant contingencies contributed to which works acquired this status.

The second problem with the 'Test of Time' idea applies more specifically to dances: for, to *test* the Test of Time, we should consider which danceworks have disappeared — are they really the worst? But that can be hard to consider, since dances remain available to us only as long as they are performables in practice — they need not be *active* in the repertoire, but their complete loss must be reflected in the narrative of art-history. Thus, if various works of Mozart were lost, the narrative of musical history might be rewritten to place less emphasis on Mozart's achievements. And an evaluation from the perspective of that history will inevitably be negative. But the (re-)discovery of these lost works of Mozart — that is, the rediscovery of the scores — could lead to a second revision of that narrative. And, with it, a reconsideration of the worth of works involved. As things stand, this cannot happen for dance: as we have stressed throughout, the ephemeral nature of dances militates against it.

Indeed, one rationale for reconstructing dances could begin from there: to keep 'in the repertoire' danceworks that would otherwise have disappeared with those who performed them. Thus, as Renee Conroy (2007 p. 2[b][1]) notes:

> ... the reconstructive boom of the 1980s was largely motivated by pragmatic desires to access these transient sources of data [dancers entering 'their twilight years'] before they disappeared than by the desire to recapture some mis-perceived aesthetic splendour of yesteryear.

Three or four key thoughts arise here. First, the so-called 'aesthetic splendour' of the works to be reconstructed was sometimes *not there*, despite being thought to be — it was *misconceived*, rather than misperceived. Indeed, neither the work nor its artistic value could be perceived until the reconstruction had taken place, for only then was that dancework open to perception. Second, recognising that dance is evanescent, that it exists "at a perpetual vanishing point" (Siegel, 1972 p. 1), and that large numbers of dances disappear because they are now forgotten and were never notated (at least in an adequate score), may draw one to preserve *what one can* of the past of dance, even when some *reconstruction* is implied. The reconstructor's task, on this conception, simply involves putting that dancework back into the repertoire: that is, in effect, the *preservation* of the dance (to deploy a contrast from Chapter Four §1). Others — such as companies, stagers, and the like — could then add those dances to their repertoires, should they want to. Here the parallel with plays is fairly exact: not all plays that could be performed at a particular time actually are. For instance, the plays of Jack B. Yeats (W. B's smarter brother) have disappeared from the active repertoire; and this seems a judgement on them, perhaps reflecting a kind of 'test of time' which they failed. Of course, that conclusion may be premature: a new director might find an exciting new way to stage one of them (or what he *took* to be exciting and new). Then that play could return to the repertoire, and its fate — its artistic merit, as then determined — would rest with appreciators. Yet (as the third point) that can only happen when the work is still somehow extant. So a broadly reconstructive process could be justified as preserving works. And, again on a parallel with plays, this form of reconstructive preservation might involve collecting scores, notes, photographs, videos and such like, so that (should anyone *want* to stage that dance) he/she would be able to do so.

Of course, that justification for retaining the works would not, of itself, justify the actual *performance* of works thus preserved. For these are not being offered as *worthwhile* works of the period; but only as *works* of the period. Hence, their interest lies in their being available for performance: and that interest is justified to the extent that these works bear on the history of that danceform. In effect, the dance then resembles a play-script on a shelf: the possibility (but not the actuality) of a performance. That would (or certainly might) be enough to preserve a work in a performing art. Yet, then, the additional thought of some *purpose* to a performance of the dancework is required to justify actually performing it: and that purpose, although requiring clarity, need not always reside the dancework's artistic appreciation. Thus, for visual art, preserving what is *live* in art (in an art gallery) is very roughly contrasted with preserving what is of historical importance (in a museum — that some galleries, such as MOMA, are *called* "museums" confuses this point in practice). Fourth, and relatedly, a concern with the *history* of dance — of the kind dance scholars might embrace — might also speak for the preservation of dances. And there would certainly be a connection to the *possibility* of performing the dancework, given that one can only really encounter the dancework itself (the abstract object) *through* a performance. Then discussion would be needed to justify what, and how much, to actually perform. Doing so, however, still requires considering exactly what dances of the past have to offer; and why the students of the present (and future) should want access to these danceworks. Further, and relatedly, we should reflect on the nature of that access — what will the student of the future need to be able to see and/or to do?

§2. Setting up the issues more clearly
For a clear statement of some key issues, consider Kenneth Archer and Millicent Hodson (2000 p. 4[2]):

> Just as ballets do not make themselves, they do not reconstruct themselves
> — we must intervene. As reconstructors, we place ourselves in the middle
> of a historical process. From the time we start the dossiers and
> choreographic score until the time the ballet is premiered, we function as

artists as much as scholars. We must construct the lost parts and incorporate them with what we have been able to retrieve of the original. We take responsibility for the intervention and never claim that the reconstruction is identical to the original work.

This text raises clearly a number of important questions: let us consider some of this passage in detail.

First, the claim that "[j]ust as ballets do not make themselves, they do not reconstruct themselves — we must intervene". Although of course ballets (or other dances) do not reconstruct themselves, this claim is a little odd: in particular, the "just as" is peculiar. For the explanation of the dances not *making* themselves (roughly, that a governing intelligence is needed to *intend* the movement-sequence as dance) may bear little resemblance to the explanation of the barriers to satisfactorily *reconstructing* a dancework, and how such barriers are overcome. To see this, reflect on, say, a parallel case for music. A performance of *just that* work is required here. And music works do not *perform* themselves either. Yet a score can act as a recipe permitting a performance of *just that* work. And, in some cases, having a score makes the performance of the work relatively straightforward. So the work could be performed if only one had the score (or something similar) — perhaps together with some sense of the performance traditions of the appropriate time. That score sets some parameters for 'reconstruction': that is, for performing *now* a work (thought) lost. For the score would provide roughly what is needed. It seems plausible that, with a full score, one need do *very little* to 'reconstruct' that musical work — certainly nothing even vaguely comparable to the making of that work itself, the creative activity of the relevant artist. Then one need only consider what is required to instantiate such a score; and the constraints that sets. The same points should hold for dance. The possession of a score of this kind might become a goal: its attainment renders the idea of *reconstruction* somewhat redundant — with an adequate score, one has a (normative) 'recipe' for performances of that work. Hence the work need never leave the repertoire. (Or so it seems: but see Chapter Ten §10.)

That is clearly not what is claimed for the case under consideration. In the context of this comment, some *intervention* is required: that is, a context where we *already* have a question or issue; where we *already* recognise that some reconstruction is *needed* in order to retrieve (in this case) the ballet in question. (Perhaps a model here — suggested by other comments — is of having only a partial score; or that much of the putative artwork is forgotten by its previous performers.) Then the thought that "we must intervene" says no more than that, since there *are* these 'gaps' in our putative artwork, they must be filled if a continuous work is to result. That already imports a key assumption about the degree to which the reconstructive project *begins* from something less than adequate.

It might be urged that *reconstruction* of dances will only be required in such cases as this — that is what distinguishes *reconstruction* from mere restaging. Thus there is a crucial distinction here: no *reconstruction* is needed for a work where it could instead, say, simply be performed. (At worse, it might need *preservation*, to extend its future.) Thus, there is no need to reconstruct *Hamlet*. Or, more exactly, the issue of reconstructing *Hamlet* only arises when one has reason to doubt one's text of the play or where some other concern prompts returning to an 'authentic' vision of it — say, the thought that drives a concern with 'historically informed performance' (see later: §4).

Then, "[a]s reconstructors, we place ourselves in the middle of a historical process". Two ideas are crucial here: first, that *what* one can reconstruct depends on where one presently is. Thus, I draw on my grasp of (say) ballet technique current in my company, modifying it perhaps in the light of my (current) view of the technique of, for instance, the Ballets Russes. So not everything will be possible at every time. Then, second, the process of reconstruction is itself understood in a particular way at *that* time (and in *that* context) which perhaps would not make sense — and certainly would not be endorsed — at another time. As often, the (changing) ideas of "historically informed music" (Kivy, 2007 p. 91[3]) offer a parallel. For the goals of such performance-practices might reasonably be thought context-specific: why should *this* performance be historically informed? What *virtues* would such a performance have, and why are they thought *virtues*? The answers to these questions will typically differ at different times and with different concerns or interests. Recognising the historical location of the reconstructions is granting these facts.

The quotation from Archer and Hodson (above) continues by mentioning two techniques for reconstruction fundamental (no doubt) to its project: "dossiers and choreographic scores". This claim can be put aside since the *detail* of reconstruction must be set in a historically specific manner; and will reflect the *purposes* of the reconstruction, in ways to which we will come.

Then one arrives at a central claim: during those reconstructive processes, we are told, the reconstructors "... function as artists as much as scholars". This seems wrong; or, at least, an overstatement. In the context envisaged, the dancework as it stood certainly needs supplementation, and the guidance (from score and dancers) could not supply what is needed. Then one is obliged to insert segments of dance *not* based directly on some previously recognised material. In the favoured case, such material might be a notated score, a set of videos, the recollections of performers ... and these might ultimately count with the "dossiers" mentioned earlier, where the ephemera surrounding the production of that dance might also be collected. Then one sees clearly some of the reconstructors' preliminary activity. The dancework will be reconstructed on this basis (or on these bases).

But such activity is not *equivalent* to that of the artist. In a sense, our artist (as *author* of the work: see Chapter Five; Chapter Seven) begins from a blank canvas, even when drawing of familiar themes, stories and the like — that explains why *this* work is his/hers. In reconstruction, one aims to fill in, as best as one can, parts that are missing or sketchy, where the context grants that at least *some* parts *are* missing! Further, that is the right way to conceptualise two key aspects here. First, the 'gaps' in the dancework: they are missing with respect to the work when it was 'live' in the repertoire — although (like all such dances) that work permitted variety between performances, was under-determined by its score, and so on. And then, second, the *project* — what makes this reconstruction *at all* is (roughly) some relation to a work *previously* in the repertoire. In this respect, the task in dance-reconstruction is akin to that of the stonemason who uses his (craft) skills to produce a gargoyle that, while perhaps not resembling the previous one all that closely, is as true to its character (as Norman stone-work) as he can manage. For he is trying to put right the 'gap' created by, roughly, the ravages of time. Thus his work is constrained by factors *other than* those constraining a typical artist — in an ideal world, the stonemason is trying to reproduce the gargoyle that was there before. This, too, applies to our dance reconstructors: their task is no doubt difficult given what is *not* known. So perhaps it *appears* like the 'blank slate' typically confronting the artist; but it is not. Instead, the reconstructors aim to fill in the passages *as they were before*. And their task would be a complete success if, later, a film or score were found that *confirmed* that they had indeed done just that. But, whether or not they are successful, such an idealisation of 'total success' provides a key element of the nature of their project.

Before continuing, notice three points. First, and methodologically, our reconstructor's task could be seen as answerable to such a *hypothetical* score, or some such. (I shall keep saying "score", but nothing turns on the precise nature of the additional information, as long as it is both authoritative and comprehensive.) Our reconstructors' task can always be understood in terms of a target set by such a (purely hypothetical) *score*, or whatever, yet to be discovered. Then, second, our hypothetical reconstructors' project is idealised — fully understood only in terms of a goal whose realisation could be *known* only when, say, later evidence (if found) showed the success of the reconstruction. No doubt, in most cases, such evidence does not exist — and, even if it does, it will never come to light. But the goal there is explained because at one time precisely the evidence needed (say, in the memory of dancers, choreographers and stagers) was available. Our problem is (only?!) that this evidence is now lost — and probably lost for good. Now, third, and more substantially, no more *specific* goal for the reconstruction has yet been introduced: that is to say, there is no particular way to make concrete the idealisation mentioned above. For instance, there will be room to debate as to whether the aim is that the new performance *look like* (and so on) a particular early performance — where returning to the original costumes and stage sets might also be important — or whether that aim involves making the best, for today's audience, of a work lost. (Although this last would more usually be called a *revival*, it is at one end of a spectrum of cases of reconstruction.)

I omit from discussion of the quotation above consideration of the sentence which says roughly what I have just concluded: "We must construct the lost parts and incorporate them with what we have been able to retrieve of the original." For, insofar as this sentence requires elucidation, it should be clarified precisely in line with my earlier remarks.

Next, we are told, "[w]e take responsibility for the intervention" — well, yes, to the degree that one grants that, for some passages in the final performance, little or no guidance was forthcoming from the extant part of the work. But that does nothing to change our *aim* here. So, when the passage concludes "... and never claim that the reconstruction is identical to the original work", comment at length is warranted. *Of course*, in a case where the material originally available is augmented very substantially — drawing on what was known of period, style, genre, artistic intention and the like — these interventions should be 'flagged up'. And, of course, the reconstructors are (solely) responsible for them — especially for any weaknesses or anomalies thereby introduced. Perhaps, for that reason, one should never be comfortable claiming "that the reconstruction is identical to the original work". But that just acknowledges the (practical) limitations of reconstructors. On the contrary, the goal was precisely to retrieve a *performable* for the repertoire: to generate a performance *identical* (that is *numerically* identical: see §6 below) with the original dancework (or, another token of that dancework-type). For that is what it means to be reconstructing *this dance* — to the degree that one is successful, the outcome is just another performance of that dance. Being 100% successful (*per impossibile*) would result in a performance uncontentiously of that very dancework, just as with performances of danceworks that have not fallen from the repertoire. The idealised goal here offers a way to recognise the possibility of success for this project, at least within the limits of diversity in the performances of other works. For, as we know, numerical identity here (its being *the very same dancework*) is compatible with a large range of differences among properties (that is, qualitative-identity issues). So, suppose one understands the standard cases of same-work continuity across performances (see Chapter Three). Then what constrains what *counts* as a *satisfactory* reconstruction? Those constraints will reflect the particular *reason*, or the particular *purpose*, for which the reconstruction is sought. Peter Kivy raised issues of this kind in his book *Authenticities* (Kivy, 1995; and see Kivy, 2007), addressing parallel artistic questions about musical performance. So, having discussed some broad conceptions of reconstruction (in the next section), we turn (in §4) to what — more specifically — a comparison with Kivy's case can tell us about dance reconstruction.

§3.   What is involved in reconstruction?

What may seem "... vague appeals to the value of having a history" (Conroy, unpub p. 2[4]) might be made more concrete if 'read' as endorsing a version of a *categories of art* thesis (see Chapter Ten §2): that one makes sense of artworks — and even perceives them — as in this or that category of art, which then supplies expectations in the form of properties standard for that category, those non-standard for that category, and those variable for the category. Such categories would often reflect genres or movements; but, of course, one only confronts an art-movement by confronting one or more of the particular works that makes it up. And writing a narrative of dance history certainly involves consideration of what are the appropriate categories to make sense of the place we *presently* occupy in the art form by reference to previous artworks, movements, and traditions.

These general points might be augmented by urging the need "... for dance history to be maintained in *live performance* (rather than by other means) ..." (Conroy, unpub p. 2), since only an attenuated understanding seems offered in merely talking about dances one has never seen — and, as Cunningham was rightly quoted as saying (in Chapter Seven §2), my confronting the dance requires its performance: if *I* am to see the dance, *you* must perform it! Yet that will require *some* kind of reconstruction if that dance has already ceased to be in the repertoire. But any reconstruction must aim at truth to what is being reconstructed.

Ideas Belinda Quirey made concrete in her staging of (say) Baroque Ballet offer a version both more strident and more explicitly tied to dance. She was critical of:

> ... those who considered the practice of dance a steady line from barbarism to accomplishment   ... [who] would necessarily have little time for the revival of dancers of earlier centuries, and thought of it only in familiar terms. (Kenyon, 1986 p. 2)

A more realistic conception of the past of dance — because a less linear one — leaves more still to be understood: that is, more that is *different* in the dance of the past. Then Kenyon (1986 p. 2) offers direct quotation from Quirey:

> "They talk of how Ballet is as old as the Italian Renaissance or the France of Catherine de Medici or Louis XIV, but they visualise the Valois court as the third act of *Swan Lake*, and the Bourbon court as that of *Sleeping Beauty*."

To miss the *specificity* of the past will typically result in treating it as too *obviously* continuous with the present of dance. The problem, then, from this perspective is that:

> [e]arly dance was studied as history, not as practice: it was as if we studied the plots, casts and staging of Handel's opera, "but none of us had heard one bar of his music and, insofar as we thought about it at all, imagined that it sounded like Puccini". (Kenyon, 1986 p. 2 — quoting Quirey)

Clearly, this analysis — if correct — highlights a deficiency in the thinking and understanding of those criticised. And points in an unusual direction by suggesting that having certain works in the repertoire alone does not *preserve* those works, if their performance traditions have been lost (an idea to be pursued in Chapter Ten §10).

Yet exactly of whom is this enhanced understanding required? Is the interest here more than historical? (We return to the project of dance history specifically in §6 below.) Indeed, would one care about the misunderstanding of Handel that Quirey sketches if Handel's works were not regarded as of high quality? If so, then the explanation here is at least partially an artistic one, not merely a historical (or archeological) one.

Some other arguments offered in defence of reconstruction of danceworks are more direct. As Conroy lists some typical ones:

(a) that reconstruction "... helps promote the artistic legitimacy of dance" (Conroy, unpub p. 3); and hence works against a (perceived) marginalisation of dance. Thus, Stephanie Jordan (2000, preface) claims that "[r]econstruction is increasingly seen as a political maneuver to establish a power base for cultural identity as well as for the art itself";

(b) that reconstructions "... help to bring choreographers who have made significant contributions to the art form the status they deserve as creative artists" (Conroy, unpub p. 3); again, reconstruction is needed because, all too frequently, "... the circumstances in which ... [such dancemakers] have laboured have practically ensured that their works would die with them" (Conroy, unpub p. 3);

(c) that reconstructions can be "... educational tools for dancers and future choreographers. ... One cannot break with, or extend, tradition if one does not know it, and, in the case of the performing arts, it would seem one comes to know by doing" (Conroy, unpub p. 4) ;

(d) (relatedly) that "... the way to grasp a dancework, appreciate a dance style, or truly understand a choreographer's creative impulse is to have the chance to discover these things from the inside by dancing historically important works" (Conroy, unpub p. 4) — think of this as more fully a part of dance education than option (c);

(e) that reconstructions offer the opportunity to see historically important works that have disappeared; and that "... dance audiences are robbed of the opportunity to be more rounded viewers, and thus to capacity to more fully understand and appreciate concert dance of all kinds, by not having historical works available to them" (Conroy, unpub p. 4).

Notice immediately that these claims justify very different concerns and practices, reflecting the interests of different people (or, more likely, different roles of which people adopt at least one). Then *your* reconstruction is neither better (a priori) nor worse than *mine* except when both are aimed at the same outcome. And some candidate projects (tasks, aims, intentions) have already been listed, recognising their diversity. For instance, some are directed to benefit the dancer or choreographer (such as (c)), while others, such as (d), are aimed at the dance student (who will usually perform some dance, of course, but is not solely 'the dancer'); and yet others see directed primarily at those seeking to understand dance, such as (e) — although [e] might be read, like (d), as involving reference to "the inside" of the dance.

Moreover, the goal here — the criteria of success — will be different depending on which of these is offered in explanation or justification. For a different project will implicitly set different criteria of success: thus the student or enthusiast (as in (c), (d) and (e)) may want to see historically important danceworks, even if they are not, to our modern eye, very interesting artistically. But those wishing to de-marginalise dance (as in (a)), or to demonstrate the worth of its creative artists (as in (b)), require that the artistic power of the works reconstructed be undimmed.

Certainly, one set of concerns here are historical or even archeological: to present the past of dance to a present audience. But then the criteria of success might have nothing much to do with the potential for artistic success of the danceworks as reconstructed — there need be little attention to the *reception* of the reconstruction, for perhaps no one attends the performances for enjoyment: learning can be a slow and painful business (and even a boring one — although that thought must only be whispered).

The purposes (perhaps from the list above) for which even a particular reconstruction is wanted may enliven what is needed *from* it. But there is a prior question. For offering the "reasons in favour" (listed above) as five reasons to do *one* thing — namely, reconstruction — presupposes the *unitary* character of that project. But in fact, in the worst case, each of these reasons could be seen as a justification for doing something different: then five reasons would offer five different projects, any or all of which might be called "reconstruction".

Then (a) the need to 'legitimate dance' by giving it enduring objects would not move in the direction of much current reconstruction — the right parallel would be with performing Shakespeare (or even Gilbert & Sullivan); a performance of *that work*, where it might be pretty heavily 'modernised' — say, in modern dress.

But (b) if the need were to credit choreographers whose work has disappeared, one *might* want something that looked as their work looked. Yet, since we want the work to be of interest to the audience, there would be some 'visually interesting' (what other might call "aesthetic") consideration dominant here — as with (a) above.

Or (c) if the concern were the historical one — a sense of "knowing where we came from" — the constraints might be aimed towards something like 'true to the visual image' of some earlier performance. Of course, this might have little or no visual interest for today's audience. At best the interest might be *purely* historical. [And, of course, (b) and (c) come together if the choreographer turned out to be of limited interest.] This case also requires comment on how (if at all) such works put one in touch with dance history — in particular (and connecting with Hannah Wiley comments on Brahms: §7 below) whether the benefit relates to styles of movement only got through *doing* the dances, for this in turn requires a further argument.

So there is not *one* project, *reconstruction*, here, but rather a number of different projects all of which could (and sometimes do) go by the name "dance reconstruction". This view will cohere better with our contextualism. So, as a default, let the rationales for the 'reconstruction' be lined-up with the nature of the reconstructed object. Then a revealing question will be: What is the *occasion* of one's concern with such reconstruction?

Different *conceptions* of reconstruction for dances bring with them different 'criteria' for success, as noted previously. At the least, it will be important to recognise the reconstructor's goal, and distinguish it (where necessary) from the appreciator's. As Conroy (2007 p. 2[a]) puts it:

> ... one can produce a very good reconstruction of a very bad dancework, or a very poor reconstruction of an excellent piece of choreography.

A very good reconstruction may, indeed, be *required* to show that such-and-such is, after all and despite all the 'hype' from its past, a very bad dancework. But, again, one way to state the *task* of reconstruction here would be that implied before: to return the dancework to the repertoire. As we have seen (still following Conroy), not all that rightly passes for reconstruction *does* have this aim — as one sees in recognising *other* aims.

The other claim, though, is more interesting: for, on some occasions, poor performance can 'cloud' a choreography — one sees this often at choreographic competitions, where the winners, all too often, could assemble a troupe of professional-grade dancers to perform the choreography, and could give the dancers adequate rehearsal time. By contrast, too often, some teacher in higher education reasons, correctly, that the competition is supposed to be about the choreography *only*, and so uses her students as dancers — thinking that, for this competition, the quality of the performance is irrelevant. In this, he/she is correct as a matter of logic. But one must be able to *discern* the quality of the choreography through that performance; and, often, there may be only one occasion for the judges to see that dancework. Then what is not *clear* in that context about the structure of the dancework may well get missed. Similarly, it may be difficult to *tell*, from "a very poor reconstruction", that the dancework in question is in fact "an excellent piece of choreography".

Conroy (2007 p. 2[a]) talks about the "aesthetic merits of a reconstructed dancework *qua* reconstruction". As the case above suggests, that idea is problematic — the cases considered usually concern the artistic properties of the dancework, as they can be discerned through the reconstruction. This point is not just verbal: our concern with the performance here results from taking the reconstruction *as though* a work of (fine) art. For what the audience goes to see — when the intention of the reconstruction is to return such-and-such dance to the repertoire — is just that (famous) dancework.

Two other cases should be set against this one, by way of contrast. First, a dance-training institution might reconstruct a dancework in order to teach its students something about dance of the past, in a practical way. Such a reconstruction would use the original costumes and sets (if they could be both acquired and afforded), or modern copies, together with the musical instruments originally employed, and such like. For the intention would be that students be exposed, as far as one could, to the *history* of dance. Indeed, the performance space might even be stripped of modern technology. But the *project* here is antiquarian: there is no intention to produce a *live* dancework (although of course that might be an unintended outcome); and the 'audience' might be composed of proud parents whose (justified) pride was in the contribution of little Johnny and little Lizzie *to the reconstruction*. (In that sense, the dancework itself would have no *audience* of its own.) Such a reconstruction would not aim to produce a work of (fine) art, judged by artistic criteria. Instead, its antiquarian aim would set its criteria for success. Such an event counts as a reconstruction of a dancework, but — since the criteria for success were not artistic criteria — the outcomes would scarcely count as a *dancework* at all; and certainly not as a live dancework, competing for space in the repertoire. This project might easily be dismissed as "mere nostalgic return" (Conroy, 2007 p. 2[b]), although such criticism of a purely *educational* project is unjust.

The second case returns us to the "historically informed" idea, urging that the *real* work of art is only encountered under certain preferred conditions. (I have in mind arguments offered for reconstructions both of *The Rite of Spring* by Millicent Hodson [1987], and of *Petrushka* by Richard Alston [1994: see Mackrell, 1997 p. 44].) But these would be very different *projects*, each with its own rationale, even were the outcome for such-and-such a dance indistinguishable from that our earlier education-based example produced, as Danto-esque "confusable counterparts" (Danto, 1981 p. 139).

§4.   A brief digression, drawing the comparison with music?

Kivy (2007) provides a revealing discussion of some aspects of that "historically informed" rationale for artwork reconstruction, applied to music. As with one key case for dance, Kivy's discussion concerns an *artistic* justification of the performance; or with its assessment by artistic 'criteria'. One might begin with the thought that:

> A historically informed performance of Bach's Italian Concerto ... will be a performance by a keyboard player who knows how the work was performed in Bach's time, what Bach's performing intentions were for the work, and so forth. (Kivy, 2007 p. 93)

And *mutatis mutandis* for other music, and for dance. Notice the implicit idealisation: that there is such 'body of knowledge' available, and mastered by this performer — these look like contested topics. Further, by implication, the performer's relevant knowledge is finite, as though the "and so forth" could be filled-in from some list. That assumption is unwarranted[5].

Hence, as Kivy (2007 pp. 93-94) then points out, this account only requires that the *performer* be historically informed — it does not require that this 'informed-ness' distinguish *this* performance from those not regarded as historically informed. Thus, Kivy (2007 p. 94) notes that:

> Charles Rosen is a historically informed performer, if ever there was one. But he performs on a modern Steinway piano, and ... conforms to our idea of what is just the opposite of a 'historical' player: namely, a mainstream one.

So "[m]erely having a historically informed performer is too weak a condition for being a historically informed performance" (Kivy, 2007 p. 94).

Then, that performance A *is*, while performance B is *not*, historically informed should make a difference to the performance itself. Yet this idea too is problematic. Kivy (2007 p. 95) notes that, on one conception, a *genuinely* "historically informed" performance needs to consider the whole performance history of the work: "... not merely performances by the composer and his contemporaries, who presumably had it right, but all the performances since, by performers who got it wrong because *they* were not historically informed" (Kivy, 2007 p. 95). For something can be learned about what not to do. This requires reviewing the intervening history of the work and its performances — not the usual focus of this kind of theoretical tendency! So this conception should be put aside. The idea of *learning from past mistakes*, while attractive, does not sit well with the kinds of reconstruction under consideration. Equally, it seems odd to urge that "... the performances of the composer, and those of his contemporaries who share his culture and performance practice, are the optimal performances" (Kivy, 2007 p. 95).

Then, as Kivy continues, *more* than merely the performer's being informed is required: can one look to a performance "... formed, stamped, impressed, imbued with or by history" (Kivy, 2007 p. 97)? That search seems to reinstate a concern with *authenticity*.

In response, Kivy (2007 p. 97[6],) reminds us of three[7] ways for a musical performance to be *authentic*:

- *authenticity of intention*, understood as "... the historical authenticity of performance one achieves when following as closely as possible the performing intentions of the composer" (Kivy, 2007 p. 98);

- *authenticity of sound*, understood as "... the historical authenticity one achieves in duplicating as closely as possible the way a performance of a work in its own time would have sounded" (Kivy, 2007 p. 98);

- *authenticity of practice*, understood as "... the historical authenticity one achieves in reproducing as closely as possible the performance practice prevailing in the historical period of the composition being performed" (Kivy, 2007 p. 98).

Again, these all involve idealisations, such that a single strand of authenticity could be located; and all assume that "as closely as possible" is close enough. But let these 'local' difficulties with each be put aside.

As Kivy (2007 p. 97) argues, these three are "... the most directly connected to the concept of *historical authenticity*": that is, they represent different versions of taking account what *had* happened (say, in some idealised optimal performance — were such a thing possible: compare Kivy, 2007 pp. 111-134). A 'historically informed performance' could be *informed* precisely in respect of one or other of these dimensions. So let us assume Kivy's contrast, not querying it (at least for now).

As we will see, these three accounts each put differently the *weight* of authenticity (and hence of 'informed-ness'). They may not converge on a single, optimal performance — indeed, one readily sees how, for instance, authenticity of sound is best served in ways inimical to authenticity of intention, given technical advances in instruments — or, *mutatis mutandis*, in the technical and physical resources of today's dancers: "today's Olympic-standard" dancers, as Mackrell (1997 p. 7) put it. And so on. Hence each account stresses a *different* understanding of a performance being historically informed; and, with it, different 'criteria' for success in that project. Importantly, in each, the particular 'version' might represent what someone wanted: hence, each might represent a legitimate *concern* for someone — perhaps, then, a legitimate goal for reconstruction.

Yet each account of authenticity also has its own internal problems (as Kivy, 2007 pp. 98-99 recognises). For instance, identifying and implementing the intentions of any document (or artwork) grants that the situation presently confronted may differ from that of its original '*intender*'. So, confronting the contemporary situation may require rational reconstruction of the claims of that 'intender' to reflect what he/she would have done or desired in the present situation, perhaps ones he/she *did not* (maybe even *could not*) conceive. Then both *your* account of authenticity of intention and mine claim to reconstruct (say) Bach's intentions; but your account stresses the 'new situation' aspects differently from mine. This looks a suitable case for discussion, but not one necessarily sustaining a single view of authenticity. Nor does the productivity of our debate obviously require a single view as outcome: we may still differ. But an account of performance-*authenticity* stressing authenticity of intentions would be confounded if no account of authenticity appeared.

Again, authenticity of sound is problematic once one asks whether the target involves producing the same (say) sonic effects in the atmosphere (what Kivy, 2007 p. 98 calls "perturbations of the air"); or, instead, that the audience *hear* what (for instance) the composer's contemporary audience heard. For example, what one hears will be concept-mediated (that is the *categories of art* thesis); and so reflect what one knows and understands — hence, what one has learned. Then 'what the composer's contemporary audience heard' may be unavailable to today's audience for the work. In part, we may have become very much more *sophisticated* as listeners since the time of, say, Bach (or less sophisticated — being coarsened with a diet of muzak); certainly, we may have become *used* to certain combinations of sounds. So this project generates no clear goal; and may be impossible in practice. As Baker and Hacker (1984a p. 4) put a different example:

> We cannot return the apples from the Tree of the Knowledge of History... Though we know the Impressionists were outrageous revolutionaries in the theory and practice of painting, we can no longer *see* them as outrageous.

For the Impressionists are part of an on-going tradition, where later events shape how *we* can make sense of the past. Similar points might be made for our *hearing* of the works of the past. Hence the *goal* of authenticity of sound is not unified or coherent: to selecting one 'version' of it is effectively to downplay others. And neither is clearly a viable aspiration.

Similarly, there seems no single conception of authenticity of practice: for what range of practices should be considered? And why would a (generally) dominant set of practices — assuming one could be identified — be the right, or best, way to perform *this* work? Perhaps this work is innovative precisely in that respect. And what exactly is the range of performance practices? Perhaps practices that encourage (or at least permit) the continuing performance of musical works might be stressed; so, including the training of musicians of technical prowess sufficient to perform this work, and similar works. Or this set of practices might seem too far from the performance itself. There is no easy way to articulate a unique position here. That suggests that the aspiration here is not yet a clear one.

Moreover, one conception of the project might become especially restrictive, running counter to an *artistic* concern with the reconstructed dance. As Kivy (2007 p. 101) summarises, "... what ... [a historically authentic performance] does ... is to close the gap between score and performance.... It is, in effect, from the performer's point of view, a set of instructions for producing a performance of the work": a similar argument might be made for dance. As Kivy rightly reads such instructions, on this conception, little or no room is left for the activity of the performer[8], for our *historically authentic* performance would be taken (*ex hypothesi*) as optimal. So deviation from it will always be a change for the worse. Here the contrast would be with a *real* score which, in under-determining any particular performance, cedes a role to the performer (as we saw: Chapter Seven).

Understood *this* way, historically authentic performance might "... have associated with it a kind of rigid dogmatism suggesting that there is one and only one correct way, or a small range of correct ways, to perform a piece, and all other ways are either bad or just plain incorrect ..." (Kivy, 2007 pp. 103-104). Rejecting such an implication, writers might then turn away from concern with *authenticity* as such and to discussion of historically *informed* performance. For Kivy, though, the constraints on giving a role to history vis-a-vis *authenticity* remain those deployed (or implied) in giving a role vis-a-vis *informed-ness*. Then aiming that one's performances be *historically informed* is ultimately no advance over aiming to be *historically authentic* — both cases lack a clear guide on what to do and any clear sense in which doing so will be a virtue. The insight that *history* seemed to provide can no more be prised apart from the impact of one's actions (or their outcomes) being *informed* by that history than it could when the concern was with authenticity. That leaves it unclear how being historically informed is a *Good Thing*.

Indeed, why should one accept "... that the historicist way is always the best way" (Kivy, 2007 p. 109)? And here, by the term "historicist", Kivy (1995 p. 201, quoting Hume [1777] 1985 pp. 244-245) means "... that posterity, if left to its own devices, uncorrected by historical self-examination, is likely to 'rashly condemn what seemed admirable in the eyes of those for whom alone the discourse was intended'"; and therefore:

> ... one can ... no more comprehend and appreciate such a [cultural] artifact without knowing ... what place it occupied in its culture than one could comprehend or appreciate a screwdriver without knowing that it flourished in an environment of screws. (Kivy, 1995 p. 202)

But the artworks do not have *uses*, or related causal structures, as the screwdriver has in relation to screws. Rather, our present capacity to make sense of *artworks* (in the case, danceworks or musical works) might be expected to help us here. That case does not exactly mirror the one for, say, words — which may acquire different meanings over time (or however the event should be characterised[9]). Of course, a work must be located in *its* place in the narrative of art history (in the form): that is needed to make sense of the work *as art* — is our historicist really claiming more? At the least, this much might be granted, even if the example supports it less than perfectly.

So Kivy's discussion (reported here) highlights, first, that there is no *agreed* or *transparent* account of the historically authentic — any of the senses he elaborates might find advocates and supporters; second, none of the senses Kivy elaborates is clear — each is riven with internal tensions, such that any one, if selected, itself needs clarification in the context of production of any argument for its adoption as the basis for one's 'criterion' of what is desirable in a performance; third, none of the senses of authenticity that Kivy articulates makes clear how such authenticity is indeed a *virtue* (or an asset) of performances — so why should one look to the historically authentic, or even the historically informed? These three issues render problematic any search for a justified dependence on the historically authentic performance in one's search for a rationale for reconstruction. Finally, any account of historically *informed* performance inherits all these difficulties with authenticity, since all offer models of how to make that 'informedness' concrete in the actual performance. But, of course, each of these models can then be subject to a commentary elaborating points sketched above.

It has not been *demonstrated* that similar arguments might ground rejection of other conceptions of authenticity — and hence, derivatively, of historical informed-ness. But Kivy's arguments give us confidence in this direction.

§5.   Fairness in our appreciation of a reconstruction?

To explore one last area of (potential?) disanalogy here between reconstruction for music and for dance, these key difficulties about what the term "authenticity" means must be put aside. For the musical case, consider a performance that might seem 'historically-informed' (say, one using a harpsichord, instead of a modern piano) and a 'historically-uninformed' one (say, one played on the piano). Issues about the *accuracy* of calling the first "historically-informed" were already raised. But if, say, the composer's wrote the piece for harpsichord, an argument in its favour could at least be launched. Yet the piano performance might sound *right*, bringing out the power of the musical work— at least if there was an established tradition of performing this work on the piano; the other might seem, say, *insubstantial* by comparison. No doubt the counter-argument stresses the need to *train oneself* (or, better, to train one's hearing, or one's 'ears') in the ways of those tones sounded on the harpsichord. Yet one can at least insist of *trying* the 'new' sound, by appeal to the composer's intentions. For most dances, the context of reconstruction offers nothing so simple — even though the musical case, as imagined, was grossly over-simplified. Without even knowing what sequences of movements the dancers performed, one is a lot further from the dancework itself than in this musical case as imagined.

Now suppose that one discovers exactly what the dancers of the past did to instantiate, say, *The Rite of Spring*; let the knowledge be acquired *by magic*, if that makes it seem more certain (my own preference would be for the discovery of a complete Labanotation score, including effort notation). One still needs to draw on the techniques of performance current at the time (and then add in the costumes and sets — not to mention the music!) to arrive at the reconstruction. Let all that be done (*per impossibile* — again magic may have to be invoked!). Now we have arrived at that place where the dance equivalent of 'ear-training' can begin: one must learn to see value in the work performed that way.

If that prescription requires that one comes to regard this version as (artistically) superior to the more familiar version, or even regard it as a genuine artistic competitor, the process is being *defined* as one where this change in our perception can be brought about — as though one would return to training *until* it was achieved. That cannot be right. What was wanted was to give the reconstructed version *due weight*; but how can that be? If one cannot make sense of it at all, if it is too unfamiliar or too divergent from the traditional mode of performance, one clearly cannot be fair to it. But neither can a high regard for the reconstructed work be *guaranteed* by the setting-up of the case.

It will be fundamental, when this is our project in reconstruction of a *dancework*, that the 'criteria' used to consider the resultant work are still artistic 'criteria'. And this can be missed, as this kind of visual interest is not always a priority. But that is what seeing it as an artwork involves. And there are other kinds of 'visual interest'. Thus, when introducing the arguments against reconstruction, mention was made of the 'aesthetically' unappealing aspect urged of *some* reconstruction (Conroy, 2007 p. 1) was noted. Here, the contrast between *artistic* interest and *aesthetic* interest (Chapter One §7; McFee, 2005) must be re-inserted: insofar as our concern is genuinely *aesthetic* only (a concern with line, grace, and such like), it has little to do with the appreciation of dance *viewed as dance* (that is, as an artwork). For instance, I am bored by those ballet galas where — to offer some virtuosity — just Act III of *Raymonda* is performed: yes, people jump, twist, support ... ho hum. But the *aim* of such performances was visual interest only: it was aesthetic *rather than* artistic not least because the fragment alone is not intelligible. Reconstructions which tolerate the 'aesthetically' unappealing cannot be ones under discussion where artistic 'criteria' provide an aim (even though this would not be *all*). After all, many artworks are ugly or disgusting by ordinary standards. But that does not deny their artistic appeal or their artistic value. And, for such works, there would be no need to mention that they were aesthetically unappealing. Such a comment makes no sense for a reconstruction reflecting artistic 'criteria'. Instead, the main aim of a reconstruction where this did make sense would be (something like) 'looking as much like the original' as possible.

§6.   Some other cases to consider

Of course, for a full treatment, a lot of different contexts need to be considered here, emphasising the variety in same-work continuity. For a successful reconstruction must thereby produce something with a strong relation to the historical original. Thus, for some purposes, translations of poems or novels count as the same work, and for others they do not. So it helps to give up the assumption of one fixed relation, holding in every case[10]. Of course, in some *other* cases, the reconstruction is not in fact the original: a reconstruction of a battle most certainly is not, and my Model T Ford from new parts, although a reconstruction, has a very peculiar status among Model Ts. Still, given the nature of dances — as type-token objects where *numerical identity* makes sense (see Chapter Two) — at least *most* successful reconstructions should preserve work-identity: that is, the resultant performance should be of the *very work* under consideration. And, of course, this does *not* require indistinguishability from some previous performance.

So one must consider just a little about the 'ontological status' (ugh) of the kinds of things done: the same *target* cannot be ascribed to all the cases mentioned above. (And a comparison with theatre might help.) With reconstruction for historical purposes, the aim must be that the resultant dancework is a token of the type under consideration (for only then is *that* dance reconstructed) — of course, compared to a work revived, it may differ pretty markedly. But that will be accommodated within at least the three categories from Chapter Two (§10):

• the 'standard version' of *Swan Lake*, typified (in my case) by Ivanov & Petipa (usual),

• the version of the same work, with the biggest differences — as in some of Nureyev's version of *Swan Lake* (re-staged): that is, a token of the same type;

• the version of a different work with the highest degree of similarity — as in Mats Ek's *Swan Lake* (new work): that is, a token of a different type.

Then, for homages to so-and-so, one can make new works — a new work despite the similarities. But reconstruction must aim at 'token of the same type' (or one is not *reconstructing* the work). Still, changes might improve visual interest — as I am sure Nureyev justified his changes: these, then, might be consistent with 'same-work' identity, yet with considerable difference (second category).

At this point, too, there is mileage in looking 'over the fence' from other cases. So let us begin from the easiest case. With respect to music, only very occasionally is playing Schoenberg considered a reconstruction: why? At least the three points might apply for (say) his piano works:

(i) the work is still in the repertoire;

(ii) the same instrument (at least roughly) is used now as then;

(iii) today's performers are part of the same performance tradition as the original performers.

Thus, what is already before us does not need reconstruction. All of these points hint at what, for dance, might count as ways of being — or especially of *not* being — 'in the repertoire'. Clearly, for danceworks too, a performance looking to the past would not count as reconstruction of my dancework if that work had never been lost, or had never disappeared from the repertoire: there might still be a historical interest [kind (c) §2 above] even then in performing it in line with, say, some early performance — a work with a long history in the repertoire might have been changed in such ways. Certainly this explanation has a clear place for music, where so-called historically-informed performance might well take place for works that never left the repertoire in *some* version (as discussed in §3 above).

Then in another case (a bit further down that line), from Chapter Three §6, Siobhan Davies revived works of hers that have gone from the repertoire, but recently. So the first case ('reconstructing' the first performance of one of my works, despite its still being in the repertoire) involves pretty much *pure* historical interest — unless some performances captured the public imagination. But the second case just involves retrieving a 'lost work', with criteria for success almost entirely in terms of the visual interest of the resultant, except that one requires that the interest be *artistic* interest (which already draws on the past of that art form). Yet (as was noted in Chapter Three) the reconstruction here should be contrasted with Siobhan Davies simply making a new dance. So, in some way, reconstruction in this case looks back to Siobhan: to her ideas, at least. Her past achievements *fix* these: yet that does not close-off all avenues, uniquely identifying the dancework itself in terms, say, of some specific movement patterns. (The big difference between these cases resides in the presence, in the first, of the score! But then I *would* say that.) So a performance whose constraints captured the past of a work must be similarly constrained as one newly constructed. However, there must be some difference of 'direction of fit'. It would be as though you are buying things from a shopping-list, and I am writing down what you buy: my list will match yours, but with a different *direction of fit* — your list *determined* what was bought, my list *recorded* it. Similarly, since to choreograph anew is to make concrete one's intentions, Davies's reconstruction is (to some degree) constrained in principle by her first construction — that supplies the criterion for success. Again, how *this* is worked out will be a matter for debate, in practical terms, in the Republic of Dance[11] . Still, the logic of reconstruction can be divorced from that of (first) construction, at least in principle.

§7. The point(s) of dance history

The discussion of *dance reconstruction* thus far has stressed that quite a number of different enterprises, with different 'criteria' of success, might be under that one umbrella. In reality, two are most central here, reflecting two different concerns with dance history. One, stressed throughout, is an artistic concern, reflecting our engagement with *performables*: to preserve works of artistic interest. Clearly, this goal (especially in conjunction with the 'test of time' idea: see Chapter Ten) implies that not all works are worth retrieving. As with music, we might ask: *What has stayed in the repertoire?* We still hear Mozart and Haydn — what about Rameau? If he is not a major figure, we may be unconcerned about his disappearance. (And, of course, nothing turns on my example.) For what have we lost of 'our' history if we lose a minor figure from the narrative of dance history? From the artistic point of view, the answer seems to be "nothing" (although, of course, that history can be 're-written' as a result of the reconsideration of a figure thought minor). Then, if the contribution of history is roughly as described in Chapter Ten (it supplies the *categories of art* for our contemporary narrative of dance history), our concern with reconstruction is limited; and all reconstructions must be justified in terms of the artistic merits of the preserved work. At the least, these are the terms of the debate.

On the other hand, an historical (or perhaps educational) concern might be envisaged: those aiming to take the next step towards the narrative of dance history — either by writing it (roughly, as critics) or by instantiating it, as choreographers — will be ill-served were only one narrative of dance history available in practice: that is, if at least that historical narrative cannot be reviewed, with a view to re-casting or re-crafting that history. To be in that position, one must know (or have access to) works other than those valourised in the 'traditional' narrative. As suggested initially, one parallel might be with the historian of drama who, finding the plays of Jack B. Yates on the library shelf (and perhaps reading Beckett's essay in admiration of him: Beckett, 1984), re-drafts the narrative of drama history to find a more expansive place for Jack B. Yates. Moreover, this possibility has potential both for the person writing that new narrative and, perhaps more importantly, for the one who — through his choreography — instantiates the new version: that is, someone, in the parallel case, who has 'learned lessons' (somehow) from Jack B. Yates. At the conceptual level, the impact of dance 'from the past' on dance of the present (and future) must be recognised. But the works of the past cannot be exclusively the *masterworks* of the past, at least if future practice were flexible in molding the historical narrative of dance. Yet not all is worth reconstructing.

Just what does this argument (even if granted) licence? First, the dancers have a role in dance practice — they too must have the possibility of encountering the 'new' narrative of dance history being postulating, since their actions instantiate those danceworks taken by this revised history as masterworks; and reflect the choreographers newly valourised. But that is only possible if the styles of movement these choreographers embrace is not foreign to the dancers at their disposal. Thus many modern-day dancers 'need' to have some mastery of, say, "... the complex rhythms of Bharata Natyam" (Rowell, 2000 p. 107) in order to perform works by 'fusion' choreographers, such as Shobana Jeyasingh. But, in order to perform appropriately the dances of many contemporary choreographers (the example here was Paul Taylor), the fundamentals of the movement-style that created those works must be understood. So suppose that "[t]he contraction and spiral are fundamental to Taylor's style, and together with a sense of weight and undercurve [these] are the least understood movements in the restaging of his work" (Challis, 1999 p. 149): then, and to that degree, Taylor's works should be difficult to restage. Or, again, suppose that "Ashton's choreography is not amenable to Russian interpretation ... [since it grows from] a different cultural tradition and a different historical context" (Challis, 1999 p. 148): then, too, such reconstructions of it should be unsatisfactory for reasons that could be explained. While the examples may be disputed, surely the point is familiar and correct. So it seems as though one needs to train the dancers, as well as to maintain (or preserve) the works.

Moreover, many who go on to choreography learn its resources as dancers. So, if the possibilities of the past are to be kept alive (so as to be integrated into a future 'new' history of dance) choreographers too must have access to them. Given the embodied nature of dance (see Chapter Seven), that engagement should best served by the performance of the works. For only then does one encounter those danceworks themselves. Here we can remind ourselves of the claim by Hannah Wiley:

A dance history course is useful but it doesn't help you know the work kinesthetically. It's reading about the work. I played the cello in the symphony when I was ... an undergraduate, and we got to play Brahms. We weren't confined to reading about it. (quoted Conroy, unpub p. 4)

Her playing Brahms would not raise questions of authenticity — they were not trying to reconstruct Brahms either in the sense of catching the sound of performance from his time (say, in Karl Wittgenstein's house in Vienna in the late nineteenth century) or of finishing off a new work. But this comment stresses the (perceived) need for practical engagement in a performing art.

It might seem, though, that a good video library would be all one needs, on a parallel with the library which preserves (say) Jack B. Yates's plays in those dark days when no one is performing them. In a way, that is correct. Yet here a key difference between play-score and dance-recording resurfaces. The play-script functions as a *recipe*, under-determining any performance. By contrast, the video (for the dance) simply *records* one performance, without highlighting which are its central features. Was the performance videoed a good performance of that work? One might assume it was, to explain its selection for both recording and (then) preservation. Yet that is no guarantee.

Or, to be more exact, at best one can infer that, at the time of its recording, the performance was regarded as good; but would *we* see it the same way? In particular, would we think well of it from the perspective of changes in the narrative of dance history since the time of that recording? Or, were there no such changes to date, from the perspective of dance history suggested by a difference performance of the work at issue (itself improbable, at least if one considers how small a difference might count as a change here might be)? In an ideal world, works to be preserved would be maintained in the repertoire: where this is not possible, sensitive reconstruction offers the best for which one can hope.

Therefore, faced with the question: *what is the point of dance history?* two broad lines of reply might be sketched. On the first (central to the next chapter), concern with the past is justified by its role in generating the categories of art, and other concepts (such as *genre*) which imply a past, deployed to consider (under artistic interest) the danceworks in the repertoire, in the light of our best contemporary narrative of dance history (in the relevant dance-form). The net effect there will emphasise certain works as masterworks of the canon (or tradition) that narrative constructs. On the second, the flexibility required was identified through recognising that this narrative of dance history might well be re-written in the future which re-writing might also need materials for other, competing narratives; hence our concern with 'the canon' goes beyond the masterworks that the best contemporary narrative takes as *live* for us.

§8.   An omission recorded

One major conception of what is wrong with reconstruction has been left aside: that which treats dances as *texts*, invitations for the creation and experience of dance, rather than as (meaning-bearing) *danceworks* as such; and hence rejects a distinctive past for such-and-such a dance, and so the goal of *reconstruction*. That omission was deliberate. Despite its wide occurrence, such a view should not be taken seriously.

Reiterating succinctly five thoughts (from Chapter Four §4; Chapter Five §3) highlights the mistaken view of meaning presupposed by such a view, and its implications, since this whole idea of "text" as applied here should be rejected. First, meaning is not made arbitrary by the arbitrariness of signs, nor their connection to language — as Bernard Williams (2002 p. 6) notes, if the word "dog" is an arbitrary sign for a dog, it is a sign *for a dog*, not for a word. Second, artworks cannot be Rorschach Tests, inkblots where one can with justice say whatever one likes — rather, what can be said appropriately about a novel or poem is constrained at least by the need to accommodate the fact that this word follows that one. Similarly, for dances, at the least this movement follows that one, or (sometimes) that there is such-and-such narrative. So danceworks too are constrained objects. Third, the constraints are person-made, or intentional: the cracks in the wall not only *did not* spell-out one's loved-one's name, they *could not* do so. Fourth, the constraints at issue here derive from art-status. So the dance has kinds of meaning that depend on the transfiguration of the movements. (Thus, at best, our dance should be more realistically modelled as a poem rather than a *text*: to make us resemble "a poem-reader, not a mind-reader", in line with Beardsley, 1970 p. 33.) Fifth, dances are made at times and in places — and these facts are important concerning how they should be understood or 'interpreted'. So, if they were *just* texts, they would be a pretty peculiar kind of text. In fact, that problem is more general. As noted in Chapter Five §5, the nearest case to someone really 'reading' something *as a text* only perhaps occurs in Derrida's *Limited Inc.* (1988). There, Derrida's reading of elements of John Searle's text treats it simply as a context-free collection of words open to interpretation. In this way, it takes no account of its context of presentation or the constraints the words provide. So that Derrida's sustained discussion both of the copyright notice and Searle's name, from the typescript, seems to treat that piece of Searle's writing as though Derrida failed to recognise it as a text of a particular kind: in this case, as philosophy. So, the convention of sending one's co-symposiast a copy of one's paper is treated as highly problematic; and so is the discussion of "Let's be serious" as a speech act (see Derrida, 1988: pp. 30-31; pp. 34-36). At best, this treatment seems a joke — except sometimes the misreading seems gratuitous. For what Derrida received, in context, was a text in philosophy: his treating it *as text* begins by ignoring that fact. Such a strategy will preclude one's engagement with philosophy. And a parallel strategy, setting aside the context of danceworks, would preclude our making sense of them.

§9. Conclusion

It is important to understand the project of this chapter. It has not characterised *dance reconstruction*, nor justified it: neither of these was its project. Instead, it has begun exploring what is implicit in that concern with the past of dance exploited by version of the project of reconstructing dances. In that way, it has provided material for comment on particular *projects* of reconstruction, and — in doing so — highlighted flaws (following Kivy) in uncontentious advocacy, as uncontentious, of *historically authentic* or *historically informed* performance. This in turn illuminated some of the resources needed for the construction of a narrative of dance history of the kind as central to the making sense of danceworks of the present as those of the past. The flexibility required of an open-ness to future re-drafting of that history surfaces when one sees that the *masterworks* of the past are those the *present* narrative of dance history endorses. Then a concern with *the past* reflects the place of *present* history (in line with the argument of Chapter Ten). But it may also reflect the basis for re-drafting that history. For, at another time, a different set of works might constitute our *masterworks* (or "temporary paradigms": McFee, 1978 p. 70), as noted initially. In such a world, one should re-think the narrative of dance history; and everything that follows from it. And our discussion of dance reconstruction stresses this.

A further benefit, of course, lies in awareness of the past of one's chosen art form — divorced from the practical topics stressed thus far — which resides in its showing that, at other times, things were done differently[12]. In this way, it may immunise us against what taking the *familiar* to be 'natural' or 'inevitable'.

Of course, a basis for rejecting "... Mark Franko's injunction" (Conroy, 2007 p. 2[a]) against reconstructions was developed. Clearly, it would be sad if *all* that happened was reconstruction, especially if understood in terms of our lacking a complete dancework even in, say, in people's memory. For, even though some works from the past (other than masterworks) are needed, equally clearly a future to dance requires both re-performance of masterworks of the past and the choreographing of new works. There seems no reason to fear for *that* situation. Certainly nothing in our argument for some value (or set of values) for dance reconstruction makes this the *only* value here.

Chapter Ten

Dance-understanding and dance history

In effect, the centre of the 'appeal to history' in the arts brings out the connection between the art of the past — in our case, the danceworks of the past — and the understanding of current artworks; by which is meant, roughly, danceworks currently in the repertoire, or perhaps including also those that have recently left it (those still accessible in the memories of dancers). For the past of dance clarifies the *categories of art* within which current danceworks (as well as works of the past) make sense. So our argument begins by revisiting that *categories of art* thesis.

§1. Understanding categories of art

A key role in understanding any artworks — and hence danceworks — is played by what, following Kendall Walton, are called *categories of art*. For they indicate how the artworks should be (appropriately) understood. What are these *categories*? How does one learn to apply them? Neither of these questions admits of a neat, and once-and-for-all, answer. But thinking (again) about the misperception of artworks can bring out their relevance. As we saw, our classic cases of misperception are, say, the birdsong mistaken for music, where an aesthetic object is misperceived as art; and the Messiaen misperceived as birdsong (artwork taken for aesthetic object). Yet a work (recognised as art) may nonetheless be *mis*taken if inappropriate assumptions about it are imported: say, taking the atonal music for discordant tonal music, the cubist painting for a poorly executed one in another style. For dance, a classic of misperception would think ill of a work deploying Graham technique because of its flexed feet, its contractions, and so on. Where are the pointed toes, and the pointe-work? If one begins from Classical ballet, one will be misperceiving that dancework. The concepts employed in one's perception of the artwork must be appropriate: that is to say that artworks must be assigned to the appropriate *category of art*. Thus, in learning about (say) cubist painting, one learns what features are characteristic of such paintings ("standard": Walton, 1978 p. 92 [2008 pp. 198-199]), such that lacking them raises doubts that this is indeed a cubist painting; what features tend to disqualify the work as cubist ("contra-standard": Walton, 1978 p. 92); and what features do neither of these things ("variable": Walton, 1978 p. 92). What is contra-standard for cubism might be either standard or variable for some other category (as here, categories tend to be genres, styles, kinds ...). So, taking such-and-such as standard features, and finding them only poorly exhibited (or not exhibited at all), one tends to think ill of this work — it is not a very *good* cubist painting! Yet, of course, it might not be one at all: then the features taken as standard might be contra-standard for some other category, and vice versa. So that, in the dancework above, the flexed feet are deliberate, the lack of pointed toes no accident! And each may be justified in context. But in learning the sorts of things to say (truly) about current danceworks, one begins from categories learnt from past works. This highlights the importance of categorial ascription: any art form — and hence any artwork in that form — must be understood as part of a complex tradition of art-making and art-understanding, although this may put the matter unduly rationalistically. One need not have learned the category in, say, lessons in art-history, but instead through process of appreciation, for instance.

Further, the object must be seen or recognised as an artwork — such a perceptual *base*, at least, is required: my critical remarks about a dance or painting would be rightly dismissed had I never seen that dance or painting (at best, I am repeating someone else's judgement). In this sense, the judgement here must be perceptual. And that perception must employ an appropriate *cognitive stock* (Wollheim, 1993a p. 134). Then, only an artwork located in its category can be appropriately perceived, and hence stand a chance of being appropriately understood. But taking such an artistic interest in an object already sees it (defeasibly[1]) as having some value, of a kind characteristic of artworks.

Thus reference to *categories of art* brings with it a critical vocabulary appropriate to works in that category (McFee, 2005; AJ pp. 3-4), since that work (and others) can then be considered using the concepts one has acquired. Moreover, in artistic judgement, its appropriate history or tradition informs how that artwork is understood. Then such a history gives substance to the categories of art, and hence to art-criticism deploying those categories. As such, it may be re-worked if later theorists take a different view of art in that form: it is what Noël Carroll (2001 especially pp. 63-75; pp. 83-95) calls a "narrative", since there might be competing ones. So learning to understand art is, in part, learning to locate works in their appropriate narratives of art-history, with any conclusions offered as *debatable* — although not as thereby uncertain.

In illustration, recall (from Chapter One §7) how an explanation of Isadora Duncan's ability "... to solve the problem of the stagnation of theatrical dance ... [involved] repudiating the central features of the dominant ballet and by reimagining an earlier ideal of dance" (Carroll, 2001 p. 91). So that narrative connects the dances of Isadora Duncan to those of the ballet tradition contemporary with her activity, through her *repudiation* of aspects of that tradition. Such a narrative draws heavily on the established feature of past works, represented by that ballet tradition; so it takes for granted both *some* art-status and *some* value to those past works. Against that background, the narrative illuminates the advantages Duncan claimed for this revitalised dance: her pronouncements and her actions constitute an 'argument' for a modification of practices of art-making and art-understanding. The narrative also stresses the values Duncan brought to bear, becoming "... a symbol for free, exalted and sensuous womanhood" (Mackrell, 1997 p. 73). Further, this 'argument' succeeded in changing taste (to some degree). That in turn is informative about the state of the dance-minded community at the time: for we know that Isadora's strategies were appropriate, because they worked! Other strategies might not have met with such success: this is hard to judge, since then Isadora's work would have disappeared from the tradition of art-making and art-understanding; or, at least, acquired a less prominent place. It would feature less strongly in the narrative of dance-history. Thus, the narrative renders intelligible the artist's activities in part by looking at the values challenged, in part by considering what, following Carroll (2001 p. 91), is called "the lay of the artworld".

Someone ignorant of dominant narratives of art history cannot see or judge works as part of those narratives; and hence cannot join in a debate such as that envisaged above. But narratives can be mastered in many different ways, typified by different ways of learning about them; for example, as artist, art historian, theorist of aesthetics (and so on). Perhaps all who know particular narratives can *do* some particular things (or some overlapping set of things sufficient to credit the same knowledge to all) but certainly all cannot be expected to say (or to be able to say) the same things. Having learned the narrative of contemporary portrait painting only as a painter (from a teacher of portraiture, say) might precisely *not* equip one to *articulate* much of that narrative in words — perhaps none of it. Someone who *appeared* to be in this position, but could articulate such a narrative, might well have other sources of knowledge at work.

Nor does this perspective *fix* the impact of particular artists or works, by *fixing* the narrative of art history. As Meyer Schapiro (1995 pp. 26-27) suggests:

> ... Mondrian's [art] would have to be characterised very differently according to one's choice of a particular phase as typical.

So that, when one *writes* (or *thinks through*) Mondrian's place in — and contribution to — the history of art, taking different phases of his art as significant locates him differently, and hence ascribes differentially the importance of *Mondrian*: a different *narrative*, both of art and of Mondrian, becomes available to us — with Schapiro (1995 p. 27) sketching some of the candidates! Equally, a particular art-movement might be re-conceived on this basis. Even were this *case* disputed, the points it makes should be clear.

Of course, this concession poses questions about cases where, having taken one period as typical, one later comes to see another as typical; and, of course, this might happen as the work of an artist (or art movement) unfolded. For now, it is sufficient to recognise both the importance of such narratives *in the background* of our understanding of artworks and movements, and how particular understandings bear on the narratives (hence, might modify them).

§2. Cognitivism in art-understanding?

Thus far, the idea of *categories of art* was explanatory of ways for artworks to be misperceived, emphasising both the crucial role of such categories in artistic judgement and their connection to the history of the particular art form, through mutually sustaining narratives of art-history. And a cognitivist thrust runs through the arguments thus far: danceworks (and other artworks) are objects of understanding. The place of knowledge — that is, of concepts deployed in perception — is granted by our attention to the categories of art appropriate to our appreciation of particular works. Perhaps this cognitivist emphasis in not warranted. So difficulties for such an account should be considered briefly.

At the centre of the cognitivist account here is the fundamental role that one's knowledge — one's cognitive stock — plays in *what* one perceives. The artwork provides the *intentional object*[2] of one's artistic experience. The work's properties, appropriately perceived, are what one's appreciation is *of*. So that this account supports the claim that, say, in virtue of bringing a different cognitive stock to bear in one's perception, one *sees* different things — as Lavoiser *saw* oxygen combining with mercury in combustion, while Priestley (who was committed to the phlogiston theory) saw something being given off by the mercury, although both were witness to the same event. Yet it can seem, therefore, that *more* than mere looking is involved: perhaps Lavoiser and Priestley *saw* the same things but drew different *inferences*. But then their conclusions would not be perceptual (or, certainly, not *just* perceptual).

Then, the cognitive elements of appreciation involve both the *identification* of this work as, say, deploying Graham technique and the *location* of such works in the history of dance (their location within an appropriate *category of art*). For one misperceives the dancework if one fails in category-ascription: thus, the dancer's flexed feet look just ugly when one expects the pointed toes of Classical ballet. Yet that angularity can appear powerful (or tragic) once this work is understood as within modern dances deploying Graham technique. For one's experience is best understood in terms of ways of viewing appropriate to this artwork, based on appropriate ways of viewing artworks appropriately similar. Failing to grant that point leaves open the question of how danceworks (in our example) are misperceived, given that they are! But we began from that fact. For bringing the wrong expectation to a dancework can involve, or lead to, our misperceiving it.

Those critical of our cognitivist position in effect urge both (a) that cognitivism stresses properties that artworks do not have; and (b) that its emphasis on understanding loses the experiential, or affective, or genuinely appreciative (see §8 below). For how can an artwork provide the sort of cognitive content implicit in being the *intentional object* of one's artistic appreciation? At the least, this seems implausible from the perspective of *artistic* (or even aesthetic) judgement. No doubt a narrative — say, from a dance, but equally from a painting or poem — could contain information: say, that a certain poet had a certain mistress, who became degraded (for MacMillan's *Manon* [1974]: see Mackrell, 1997 pp. 64-65; but equally for the story of Manon Lescaut on which MacMillan drew). Yet this factual information could be conveyed either by an interesting and insightful artwork or by a mundane one. So knowledge of this kind might be embodied in the artwork, but cannot be the sort that typically bears on one's appreciation.

By the first objection, then, on our cognitivist picture, observers 'read in' properties that danceworks do not have. So the properties thus ascribed do not follow from just *seeing* the dancework. Instead, these would, at best, be inferences one draws. Hence the movement itself cannot be tragic nor powerful — one is only *inferring* such features; which amounts to reading them into the dancework. Then conflicting inferences might be urged. By the second, what get 'read in' is the expressive or emotional force (mistakenly) attributed to the artwork.

Defending such conclusions can highlight the diversity within what might be urged concerning this artwork. How can these be features of the dances if only some can see them? Moreover, if others claim to find something else in a dance — as they very well may — how can they be gain-said? On one occasion a student of mine received the wrong programme at the dance performance; and so, having read the programme notes, he 'saw' different things in the second work on the programme from those the rest of us saw.

This seems a clear case of such 'reading in' (assuming the student was not unusually perceptive).

The attribution of properties of this sort to dances poses a key question. For surely the distinctive power of any particular dance is fundamental to it. Hence, in failing to recognise these as features of the dance (*its* power, *its* tragic aspect), one is not recognising *this* dance (as opposed to *that* one) — or, indeed, perhaps one is not recognising *dance* at all, in contrast to, say, gymnastics or some other movement activity. This point is especially strong for evaluating the dance. That seems to require that appeal to dance-related reasons for one judgement acquire that status through their deployment in the past of dance.

Consider, again, the bemused student mentioned above: what he knew about dance (quite a lot), and what he thought he knew about *this* dance (from the programme), brought a particular cognitive stock to bear in his watching of the dance. Yet he was mistaken. Some of what he thought true of this dance was false of it — it wasn't evocative of a great desert wind: that was a different dance in the company's repertoire! Yes, he saw the dance differently from the rest of us (which is not to imply that the rest of us saw it only *one* way). Bringing to bear a different battery of concepts, he saw 'the dance' differently, since *what* he saw reflected the battery of concepts, the cognitive stock, that he mobilised in his perception of the dancework. So the movement patterns as he identified them differed from those the rest of us recognised. In the actual case, he found the 'work' deeply confused! But suppose he had found a way it made sense in terms of the programme. Still, in the typical case, once the error was pointed out, he should acknowledge it — things were not as he thought they were. Hence what he took for features of the dance were not. We might almost say that he saw a *different* dance from the rest of us, as Lavoiser saw a different chemical 'event' from Priestley. And, as in that case, one way of looking at the event was misconceived. (As before, the description he read fitted a different work.)

Perhaps, of course, this student discovered a new and interesting way to see that dance: that possibility cannot be ruled out — it is clearly within the scope of our hypothetical intentionalism; and might be a dance-equivalent of Dr. Johnson correcting Goldsmith (see Chapter Five §4), except here weight is given to both 'readings' of the work. But this case is clearly unusual, for typically the coherence of the dance viewed from its category of art will not be shared when it is viewed from another. (Hence the student found the work he 'saw' as *confused*.) When one succeeds here, the dancework in question is still located in its past: the dispute concerns what constitutes *its* past!

These cases illustrate that one *sees* the dance this way, rather than seeing something neutral and then *inferring* that it is dance, ... and *this* dance, with *these* features. The traditional counter-argument here is a variety of the argument from illusion, identifying what (it urges) is genuinely *observable*, by setting a limit to it. One is not merely *observing* such-and-such if, for all ones sees, something else could be there instead. The fact that one might mistake a light close by for a distant star means that there is *something in common*, that one really sees on both occasions[3]. Then one infers one's actual judgement from seeing this *something in common*. So, as above, one arrives at the dancework's properties, through an *inference* drawn from the perception or observation.

But that is surely false to the phenomenology of perception: I simply *see* the dancing peasants in the Breugel painting — I do not infer that, say, they are not engaged in an 'imitate-the-statue' competition. Nor could I do so. And even if I 'get it wrong' as to what I see, I am not typically being "taken in" (Austin, 1962 p. 26). Of course, one *learns* to see the events as dance, and as dance of a particular type. But, once one learns to do this, one simply does it: there is typically no further step. Moreover, I could not typically describe what I see as *other than* dance ... at least if I am to avoid leaving out a great deal.

As a parallel, consider here someone viewing a multiple-figure (from psychology), such as the old woman/young woman. First, one can typically *explain* to others what they might see; and, in this way, teach them to see it ("this, which you took for the old woman's mouth, is a choker around the young woman's neck"). As this illustrates, one's accounts of the design depend on that design's features: the lines and patches that compose it. Second, typically some people cannot see one of these two aspects, despite strenuous efforts at explanation. But the problem is not with, say, patterns of light and shade falling on the retina. It does not depend on his/her perceptual mechanism — the state of the eyeball, the rods and cones, and such like, nor with what he/she *infers*. Yet it affects what that person sees — or can see. At issue here is the person's ability to mobilise his/her concepts in experiencing that object or event (see below). For someone may know certain things (in that way, correctly be said to have mastered those concepts) and yet be unable to mobilise the concepts in one's experience. This perfectly general phenomenon is of special importance for understanding art. For, in effect, it reiterates that — in order to properly judge or appreciate a dancework — one must manage to bring one's art-historical knowledge to bear on one's perception of that dancework.

§3. Criticism as applying the rules?
Since the appreciation of danceworks is found in dance criticism,

considering such critics may help our understanding of this appreciation. It is common knowledge that art critics (and dance critics among them) typically perform more than one function[4]. Still, two stand out: critics are read to help decide what dances or films to see, what novels to read, and so on — more generally, what artworks to enjoy. As Carroll (2008 p. 192) accurately suggests, this role might be called *consumer reporter*. Again, the critic helps us to see what is in the dance (or other artwork); and, in the process, to see that as valuable, when it is. So the critic is, as it were, acting as a *taste maker*: he or she is aiming "... to shape the taste of their readers" (Carroll, 2008 p. 193). Although such roles are no doubt practiced to the fullest degree by professional critics in newspapers, magazines, and books, both roles are adopted — if less formally — by all of us when discussing danceworks (and other artworks).

How should this critical role be understood? Since there is clearly a knowledge-element here, the simplest account presents the critic as learning *rules* (or "criteria") and then applying them. This might, with justice, be called the *Critical Rules Account*. It notes correctly that, if one judges dance A to be better than dance B, one does so for some reason or reasons. Then the Critical Rules Account sees itself as giving a place to those critical reasons.

Such an account, although widespread, faces at least two challenges: that such rules or criteria cannot readily be identified — in particular, plausible criteria in one case cannot readily be applied across the board; and that, were they identified at a particular time, they would soon become redundant in the face of artistic practice (Carroll, 2009 pp. 26-27; UD pp. 131-132). Let us consider them in that order.

So, first, the explanations typically offered of the merit of particular danceworks do not form a single, unified collection; nor even constitute classes of such collections: hence such rules or criteria cannot readily be identified. Thus, if a work of Martha Graham is praised for its angularity, its "... tense angles and driven falls" (Mackrell, 1997 p. 5), ought one not to praise the same things of other works? Or, at least, other works in similar-ish styles? So how can one also be praising "Merce Cunningham's quizzical gestures and asymmetrical rhythms" (Mackrell, 1997 pp. 5-6), especially once granting that these"... imply very contrasting ideas of what the body can and should be doing" (Mackrell, 1997 p. 6)?

Then a difficulty for the Critical Rules Account is that the same terms (say, "angular") are not used in all, or even most, critical discussion; and, when they are used, they are not *always* terms of praise — nor yet always terms of blame. In practice, doing so-and-so, while a virtue in this work, might be a vice in another. Praising the compression of one work is compatible with complaining about the claustrophobia in another. One might begin with 'rules' for good practice drawn from extant artworks — as perhaps Aristotle arrived at his 'rules' for tragedy by studying the works of the tragedian Sophocles. But one soon recognises that, while generally good advice, such 'rules' cannot be applied exceptionlessly. Indeed, Aristotle recognised the genius of the tragedian Euripides, who did not abide by Sophocles' rules. Any checklist of 'things to look for' may help in some cases, but cannot fit them all. Hence one never arrives at the hoped-for rules or criteria. In part, this reflects a neglected fact about rules: that they can always confront cases with which they were not designed to cope. Hence the apple cart can always be upset (see SRV pp. 44-47).

Of course, workable 'rules of thumb' can be formulated; but they are not exceptionless. Thus, for example, painting-students in art school might be told *always* to cover the whole canvas with pigment, so that no canvas is visible. And this is a good rule of thumb for easel painters; but, since Van Gogh regularly ignored it, it cannot function as a criterion of worth here.

In part, the difficulty here is that the rules offered, like Aristotle's comments on tragedy, typically "... pertain to artists. They belong ..., if at all, to the production side of things" (Carroll, 2009 p. 26). That is problematic because the Critical Rules Account was supposed to explain what Carroll (2009 p. 26) aptly calls "the reception side": the process of evaluating the artworks, not that of creating them. So it cannot address the problem it was suppose to answer.

This stress on exceptionless rules is also problematic because artists, faced with such rules, are implicitly invited to bend or break them. This generates the second, related challenge. For it might seem that there *cannot* be exceptionless rules for art: that this would, for example, impede artistic creativity. Such points can be over-stressed. But they certainly count against the project of listing the relevant criteria or 'rules', as though they were currently extant. For avant-gardist artists can always create new forms or genres. They might even do so *in the face* of such an extensionally-adequate account of extant artworks. Perhaps some of the most general terms of critical praise (say, "unity") would be applied to such new works by their defenders, even though the rest of us cannot see it — and then, perhaps, we can! In this way critical insight moves forward. For here too reasons must be offered for the evaluations.

So, of course evaluations of danceworks (as of artworks more generally) must be justified in terms of reasons — where the reasons, if not necessary compelling in all cases, are at least debatable in ways the knowledgeable about the art form know how to pursue. But that evaluative process cannot be modelled as the application of extant rules or criteria. Now one moves forward by listening closely to a form of words used to characterise the nature of things: I offer to tell you 'what the thing is like'. That expression, suggesting that one turn to what the object is *like* (or with what it is constructively compared), directs our attention to the comparative nature of evaluation. Yet against what standards can such comparisons be made? The search for abstract standards here is, in effect, the search for criteria of excellence — a search just set aside. Of course, in practice one turns, not to the abstract, but to the concrete: to the embodiment of artistic excellence in established artworks.

There might seem to be an overriding objection to that course of action: for the impossibility of an (exceptionless) account of what dance *is* has repeatedly been granted. And it might seem that dances must be classified before one can evaluate them. In defence of that idea, it might be pointed out that the concept *dance* cannot itself be positively evaluative, since the concept *bad dance* makes perfectly good sense (Dickie, 2000 p. 97).

In fact, this defence is flawed. First, the fact that there is *bad dance* is compatible with an evaluative element to the term "dance": for perhaps this barely makes it into the category of dance — it raises one of the recognised defeating conditions for dance; but at least it is *dance*, however bad. (The next example has not even *that* going for it!) But, second, the connection between classification and evaluation becomes more intuitively plausible when one recognises that *good dance* is actually logically prior to dance. For one begins from cases of *acknowledged* dance, and then asks whether other objects are dance, even though they are not *as* worthwhile as those one started from — just as one begins thinking about reasoning from cases of *sound* reasoning: the rest counts as reasoning *at all* (when it does) to the degree that it approximates sound reasoning (Grice, 2001 p. 35). These points run equally for art in general.

§4. 'Masterworks' in learning to understanding dance

A discussion of dance criticism need not *all* be about evaluation. With Carroll (2008 p. 192), we noted that even critics have more than one role. Further, such discussions need not say *all* one wants about evaluation. Our point here stresses one *specific* aspect: namely, that some of the criteria for (some) critical acclaim can be provided from what might be called "masterworks" (CDE pp. 79-81) — namely, established works in a particular art form. One often learns to appreciate artworks from such masterworks, in combination with a narrative concerning this or that masterwork, perhaps locating it in the history of that art form. At this point, then, the impact such masterworks is recognised. Thus, training in music standardly involves studying compositions of major composers for, say, the piano — perhaps in combination with learning technical virtuosity on the piano. As this case illustrates, the procedure builds-in an assumption about our ability to recognise such "major composers": that is, it imports the idea of a musical canon.

Perhaps the role of masterworks is clearer for multiple, performing arts — that is, *performables* — where, despite the expectation of variety among legitimate performances, one might still fail to perform the work in question. Further, the study of works from the past (including the recent past) highlights the structures at work in the musical examples. In the way, the student learns both to *recognise* such structures and to regard them as *valuable* structures. In doing so, the procedure shows students the kinds of structures that they might adopt (or adapt) in their own composition. This process might be summarised in a two-part slogan: the students both *learn to see* and *learn to value*. But these are really one process — the process of those students becoming *competent judges* in respect of whatever (McFee 2001 pp. 100-108; AJ pp. 45-47). This account connects with one's grasp of that history — which might seem like a detached, academic concern — with one's actual *responses to* (or experience of) the artwork: in our case, one's responses to the dance in question.

Such 'learning to see' is best understood by a comparison with a similar 'problem' facing someone looking for the first time at X-ray photographs (say, of the chest). Differences in *cognitive stock* between radiologist and beginner reflect the mobilisation of *different* concepts in the perception of each of the same patterns of light and shade in the X-ray plate. Radiologists distinguish the condition of the internal organs, when the untrained barely make out the ribs[5]. But one can come to see the X-ray plates in that way for oneself, the process closely paralleling that for the multiple-figure (above) — one is encouraged to view the characteristics of the X-ray plate in a certain fashion. In this way, one learns to see X-ray photographs appropriately: one learns to 'read' them or to understand them, although this is just a matter of *looking* at them.

This situation mirrors one's learning to understand artworks: one learns to see their characteristics (that is, their characteristics once *transfigured* to art) — and certain ways are appropriate to doing so (not only one, but not 'anything goes'). The first slogan ('learning to see') identifies the perceptual base of artistic understanding, recognising the possibility of misperception: that is, of failure of artistic appreciation resulting from inability to perceive an artwork in ways appropriate to it.

Appreciation then takes the form of perceiving the work (looking at the painting, hearing the music, and so on) in the light of such understanding. As Wollheim (1993a p. 142) puts it, "perception of the arts *is* ... the process of understanding the work of art": given suitable conditions and knowledge, people have the capacity for such understanding of art because they have the capacity to perceive artworks. But, of course, this is merely a precondition for such understanding, since neither the requisite *sensitivity* nor the *informedness* is guaranteed.

In line with the second slogan, artistic value is *recognised* in perception. So learning to *see* the artwork in question appropriately is learning *what* to see as *valuable* in it (or how to see it as valuable); and hence learning to value it — although one may rebel against what one has learned! Thus someone claiming merely to understand what a particular group valued in an artwork (without finding it valuable himself/herself) would, for that reason, be failing to view the object as an artwork: failing to make artistic judgements of it. As earlier, this account (if true) would, in typical cases, ground our argument that this person did not understand this particular artwork: after all, this person sees no artistic value in it. So how is it more important or interesting than, say, wallpaper?

At the least, artistic appreciation is appreciation *of that object* (painting, dance, and so on) — and artistic value is value inhering in the artwork: so such appreciation minimally requires perceptual engagement with those works. For appreciation is demeaned if considered as a kind of elaborated daydream stimulated by the artwork. Of course, such daydreaming is entirely possible. Yet the person engaged in it is not really appreciating that artwork, because not engaging with *its* properties — hence, not really doing artistic appreciation (although of course such a perceptual engagement is, at most, just *necessary* for such appreciation, rather than guaranteeing it).

When errors in understanding artworks depend on the *misperception* of those works, failures can be both to *understand* the artwork appropriately and to *appreciate* it appropriately. Treating music by Messiaen *as though* it were genuine birdsong (no doubt pleasing, but meaningless), I misperceive it by applying the wrong *category*; but I also mis-value it — since the *normativity* that follows from recognising it as art (rather than as *merely* aesthetic) is inappropriate to birdsong. Treating it, instead, as though it were *tonal* music imports *a* normativity all right — but my judgements will be inappropriate *to the Messiaen*. And hence my valuing of it will also be inappropriate.

So learning to *see* the value of artworks (and to see certain features of the works as *reasons* for my judgements) is engaging with the narrative of art history in respect of that art form. When my judgement of that artwork is explained or justified to others, reference must be made to the history and development of the art form in question — perhaps referring to a revolution against traditional ways of working in that form. For this connects my claims for *this* work to what is acknowledged as valuable from *other* works — and hence to artistic value!

§5. Masterworks, and an 'ideal observer' for art?

Such *learning to see* and *learning to value* art of the relevant kind sketches the beginnings of the powers and capacities of 'ideal critics'. To elaborate them, Jerry Levinson (2006 pp. 366-385) has developed an attractive *Ideal Observer Account*, drawing on its connection both to the idea of a *canon* (or, as they are called here, *masterworks*) and to the Test of Time. For the appreciation of masterworks is a "... touchstone for identification of the right sort of critic or judge who is a reliable indicator or identifier of artistic value ..." (Levinson, 2006 p. 380). Since the two strands here should be kept apart, both the general discussion of this Ideal Observer Account and its specific issues in this context can be postponed until the next two sections. Broadly following Levinson's account, partly stitching together quotations from his text, should avoid raising too many extraneous issues.

First (and briefly), what is so *good* about art? Why spend one's time on it? With Levinson (2006 pp. 384-385), these topics can be set aside by starting for a group of art-interested persons. Or, if that answer seems lame, by conceding that as a matter of fact many persons value art, while granting that it is typically problematic to identify *the valuable*, once one moves away from utilitarian or financial value. So, someone who asks what friendship is *for* does not understand it — he views it merely prudentially. If you think yourself my friend for some external reason (that I give you trips in my car, say) you are not really my friend, for the same reason. And this provides our model for the ascription of values as not prudential or functional (with friendship our example). Then granting artistic value grants that *something* is good about some artworks. One can move on from there.

Then disputes about artistic value, or even the art-status of some putative 'artwork', can be understood as implicitly appealing to some fixed points of artistic value as manifest in our masterworks. As we have seen, such a canon is a prerequisite for the ascription of artistic value since, without it, we could not offer uncontentious examples from a range of the artistically valuable. But *which* artworks form this canon?

Some broad consensus around judgements follows from our being competent to discuss a certain topic: if your list of composers of classical music does not include *any* of Mozart, Beethoven, Bach, Mahler, Stravinsky, Schönberg ... it will be hard for a conversation on classical music to start — your taste in music is just too eclectic (see Cavell, 1969 p. 193). So this might begin our (open-ended) list for musical works. Doing so acknowledges the canon, while suggesting a version of the 'Test of Time' — one needs to avoid fads, and so on. Then these works are:

> ... notably appreciated across temporal boundaries (that is, their appeal is *durable*) and cultural boundaries (that is, their appeal is *wide*), and are

appreciated at some level by almost all who engage with them (that is, their appeal is *broad*). (Levinson, 2006 p. 380)

Such works then provide a solid place in the world of art; radically divergent claims about *those* works at least can be put aside. Further, these three conditions — a durable, wide and broad appeal — suggest how the 'Test of Time' idea might be expanded. First, these works have passed the test of *being* explained — the explanations offered have proved sufficiently durable, so that no good reason for rejecting the claims of these works has achieved dominance; and, second, that explanation has appropriate connections to the current narratives of art history in that art form. In this way, the reasons given on its behalf still seem good reasons. Therefore they offer insight (primarily in the form of examples) for any new works with which one engages.

But the relation here is complex, since the 'Test of Time' does not operate symmetrically across those works that *pass* the test and those that *fail* it. As Levinson (2006 p. 382[6]) puts it:

... that a work *passes* the test of time is a strong prima facie reason to think it has significant artistic value, but that it *fails* the test of time is only a weak prima facie reason to think it lacks significant artistic value.

So the success implicit in, at least, passing the 'test of time' is recognised. Four notes of caution are needed. First, the status of such-and-such as a masterwork may not be permanent: later generations may revise the list. In this sense, our current masterworks function as *temporary paradigms* only. Second, one learns about art-status (and artistic value) partly by noticing it for these artworks; works having passed the 'test of time'. But this test is not a "... *criterion* of artistic value" (Levinson, 2006 p. 382): works can 'hang around' without being regarded in the positive way sketched above. So mere endurance does not suggest the required appeal as *durable, broad* and *wide*: instead, one must look to the reasons offered. Then, third, our *temporary paradigms* may not offer (for us) *vivid* experience of art: although masterworks, they can still appear stale to us (as, say, Beethoven's fifth symphony may). Perhaps they could be made vivid to the uninitiated. Fourth, for dance, the changing nature of the repertoire implies that works important in the danceworld at one time may disappear from the contemporary scene — companies may no longer be performing them! So the general picture of masterworks as (only) temporary paradigms is compounded when access to the masterworks of the previous generation is not guaranteed.

In summary, these are *masterworks* precisely in being "... works standing the test of time ... [which therefore] constitute the standards of taste in a given art form" (Levinson, 2006 p. 376). But *judgement* is needed to determine the similarity between *this* work and *that* one — and especially if any similarity is relevant to the value of each. Thus some weight must be given to the powers and capacities of those who understand these works sufficiently well to appreciate them. Then one has:

> ... a canon of masterworks passing the test of time, which is in turn used to identify ideal critics, who serve as measuring rods of such value generally ... (Levinson, 2006 p. 377)

Central here is the (recognitional?) ability to make such judgements: one does not learn 'what correct judgements *are*'; rather, one learns to *make* correct judgements (compare PI p. 228 [h]). Still, there remain different explanatory structures, considerations to be met (say, through education) in different ways, usefully characterised (via two slogans mentioned previously: §4 above) as *learning to see* and *learning to value*.

Further, the canon of masterworks in the genre at issue must (in principle) be logically independent of the judgements of those ('ideal') critics, at least in broad terms, to avoid a circularity between these roles. Then *at least* those masterworks offer a beginning for making sense of other works in that genre.

§6. The powers of the 'ideal critic'

In summary:

> Ideal critics are the best suited to judging the potential of such [new] works because their artistic tastes and appreciative habits have been honed on and formed by uncontested masterworks ... (Levinson, 2006 p. 382)

What must such a conception of 'ideal critics' involve? Here, Levinson (2006 p. 368: all five quotations) uses Hume's five "... obstacles to optimal appreciation" to elaborate his Ideal Observer Account by explaining what such a critic might *lack*, or otherwise misapply. Let us consider each in turn, commenting briefly. They are:

- "insufficient fineness of discrimination" — clearly this is a matter of 'learning to see', rather than of the development of ocular powers;

- "insufficient practice with works of a given sort" — this should be resolved by training, and by greater experience (and, perhaps, by not counting as an ideal critic *tout court*, but only one in this or that genre, and so on);

- "insufficient comparative appreciation of works" — as above, this should be resolved primarily by training, but poses yet more sharply the question, "training of what form?": see below;

- "insufficient application of means-ends reasoning in assessing works" — this one is puzzling: is one's appreciative judgement ever of a means-ends character?;

- "*prejudice*, especially such as prevents one from entering into the spirit of a work on its own terms" (my emphasis) — this is not really prejudice (which implies that those judged do not get their 'just deserts'), but the expression of predilections: say, my predilection for the minimal, rather than the florid — I have learned these ... and could justify them.

Of course, the (appreciative) perception of artworks is mutable under changes in what is thought or known: what *concepts* are mobilised in that perception. Changes here might be voluntary, as when I endeavour to expand my *knowledge* of, say, Martha Graham's dance or my sensitivity to it — this last both by watching it and from critical discussion. Equally, (some) artistic judgement is relatively 'fixed': given who *I* am, knowing what I *know*, and so on, I may be extremely unlikely to change my judgement. For instance, my appreciation of Martha Graham's work may be *so* central to my view of dance that revising it substantially would revise my whole 'narrative' of dance history (say), or the range of categories and critical concepts I deploy, thoroughly overturning many of my other judgements of danceworks. While not strictly *impossible*, this is highly improbable. So perception of art is neither as fixed, nor judgement of it as mutable, as might have been thought[7].

On a particular day, one may not see particular works as one normally would: one is tired, or not in the mood for material of this kind. Equally, recent, sustained experiences of a very different art-genre (say, piano music by Schönberg) may alter my perception of a particular artwork (say, piano music by Scriabin): my usual appreciation of the second is affected by that sustained attention to the first — so that, for instance, the Scriabin now sounds inflated rather than rococo. Again, the (relative) *inexorability* of artistic judgement reflects the fact that, in my imagined example, no new *learning* has taken place: I simply mobilised (in my experience of the artworks) concepts I already possessed.

Of course, a work previously seen a certain way can become regarded differently; or an 'insight' of yesterday can seem insubstantial or misconceived today. Here, a difference lies in how the work *taken*: mobilising different concepts in one's appreciation of that work would be explicable to some degree — for example, 'explained' by one acquiring *new* concepts or becoming able to mobilise *different* concepts in one's experience of the work. The first of these might involve *bringing to bear* concepts not previously brought to bear, other narratives one had *found* relevant — perhaps because, say, of the re-hanging of a familiar picture.

Given who I am, and what I know, *that* dance (today) looks such-and-such a way, and have so-and-so valuable features, and so on. And these characteristics might justify my judgement, if challenged. Similarly, *failures* of judgement can readily be explained in terms of *failures* of knowledge or *failures* of sensitivity (this is sometimes cashed-out in terms of a failure to mobilise certain concepts in one's experience of the artwork in question). For instance, difficulties with the dances of Martha Graham might be explained via ones *huge* experience of works in the Classical Ballet repertoire, and ignorance of Modern Dance: now, the flexed feet can look *ugly* — perhaps even suggesting poor technique in the dancers. Where are the pointed toes and the pointe-work? Then one might be taught to recognise the virtues of Modern Dance, a contribution to one's cognitive stock. Or perhaps one knows *a lot* about Modern Dance but cannot *see* the dance that way — as many who (having been taught a critical vocabulary for poetry) cannot 'find' that vocabulary in the appreciation of poems: and then, suddenly, they can! Here, the change is not in cognitive stock but in its now be mobilised in the experience of the poem (McFee 1997 p. 35).

Equally, the contribution from knowledge here need not be *explicit*: the requisite knowledge and understanding can be acquired in many ways, other than through (say) art-history classes — most dancers, for instance, acquire them *en passant*, in training and performing. But they *do* know: and, *if pressed*, might even explain what they knew (although that ability is not required). Still, such dancers perhaps then draw on the knowledge and understanding, maybe as choreographers.

More generally, explanations are required only when some *specific* reason requires them in that case — so, not in the usual or uncomplicated cases ('no modification without aberration': see Cavell 1969 p. 13). A reason to say more is *therefore* a reason for treating cases as non-typical — and vice versa! Thus, if (say) the *formulated* intentions of some artist suggest that a case is non-typical, one therefore has reason to say more. So, if John Cage explicitly asserts his attempt in some musical piece to subvert previous artistic structures — or if Merce Cunningham tells us this (for dance studies) — with the resultant works uncontentiously art, articulating enough of the *narrative* of art history may justify that conclusion: say, by quoting Cage's remark that "the twelve-tone system has no zero in it". Further, explanation of action is typically 'after the fact' — one just does such-and-such, and is then called for (roughly) an explanation by way of justification. Thus, asked to elaborate my understanding of Mats Ek's *Swan Lake*, I then comment on what is striking about it — recognising that these features are not valuable in *all* the works in which they occur, and that confronting a different questioner might require my saying something different.

§7. Problems of idealising

Now five(-ish) objections to the kind of *Ideal Observer Account* developed here can be considered[8]. So:

First: there will be "... disputes about what facts are relevant in the first place" (Sharpe, 2004 p. 133).

If the 'ideal critic' role is someone who "... knows all the relevant facts, experiences the relevant expressive features of the music [or dance] and understands all the possible relevant approaches to the music" (Sharpe, 2004 p. 133), can such a person be identified? Since one does not know *which* features are relevant, there could be no basis for idealising mastery of some of them. Further, there is no finite totality of such features — hence, even if one knew which features to consider, it makes no sense to imagine mastery of them *all*; for there is no *all*! (See AJ pp. 90-91)

Second: there will be disputes unresolvable even in principle:

> ... the existence of many different interpretations, all of which may be defensible but some of which may not be mutually compatible, means that the deliverances of the ideal observer who takes account of all points of view in an impartialist way cannot be coherently characterised. (Sharpe, 2004 p. 133)

Again, there is the problem of *all*; but does one need total compatibility? Or would it be enough that these different views were debatable? As below, the answer to these questions is that our Ideal Observer's judgements must have a rational basis in the work of art itself, cohering with the contemporary narrative of art in that art form (or instituting a new narrative). That condition can be met without some appeal to consensus.

Third: "... the entire and complex relationship that we have with ...music will be affected if we think that the position of the ideal observer is something to which we should strive." (Sharpe, 2004 p. 134)

This seems an issue Levinson (2006 p. 372) pursues: "Why are the works enjoyed and preferred by *ideal* critics ... ones that I should, all things being equal, aesthetically pursue?" In one way, this question has a simple answer:

Aesthetically [artistically] good artworks will ... be works favoured and approved by the sort of person who is capable of appreciating masterworks, who can thus gauge the extent to which the reward of such [artistically good] works compare to those which acknowledged masterpieces can, under the best conditions, afford. (Levinson, 2006 p. 378: my additions)

This gives one reason to listen to what such persons might say! In this way, it explains why, in context, the judgement here might be authoritative.

Fourth: the *Ideal Observer* account "... does not accurately describe how we arrive at artistic judgement about the status of a work." (Sharpe, 2004 p. 135)

Sharpe (2004 p. 136) visualises this picture entailing that one might "... accept the verdict of others" — the judgements would not be *mine*. But, of course, this need not follow. Our Ideal Observer must be able to *mobilise* the relevant concepts in *his own* experience of the work (that is, must be able to see the work that way). This surely grants that these are indeed his judgements.

Fifth: there is also "... the problem ... of irreconcilable divergences of opinion even among the qualified". (Sharpe, 2004 p. 138)

This returns us to the first and second issues above. For it seemed that our ideal critic *approximated* the 'right' judgement. But the thought here is that there is no (single) judgement for our ideal critic to approximate. Now any case investigated requires both that each of these 'irreconcilable' judgements must be genuinely *arguable*, given a plausible 'reading' of the features of the artwork. If this were not so, the implausible or ungrounded judgement could be rejected. And that each judgement must preclude the other; or, at least, be unconjoinable with it (compare FW pp. 119-120). So these genuinely are *arguable* judgements *of the work* in question, taking it as an artwork; and yet irreconcilable. But a rational basis for each conclusion is postulated, such that our idealised critic might happily, and with justice, endorse one such basis (and the conclusion to which it led) on Mondays and Thursdays and the other on Tuesdays and Fridays — having Wednesdays and the weekends off! For each base is agreed to be arguable, and connected to *this* work. Since both judgements have a rational base, our critic cannot in principle be *precluded* from endorsing each. But why should one hope to do so? The aim, in introducing the ideal observer, was simply to give due weight to the features of the artwork: in this case, doing so simply permits this variety of judgement.

Of course, one idealisation lies in imagining someone who has not merely overcome the obstacles (from Hume) sketched in the previous section, but done so to the nth degree — so he has *no* such-and such (for all five obstacles listed). Here, though, there is an asymmetry: our *Ideal Observer* has none of these deficiencies but that does not (yet) explain his powers and capacities. Thus, although the position presents an ideal observer (or ideal critic), he is only ideal *negatively*: he lacks certain deficiencies. In the end, one is not committed to spelling-out precisely what he *can* do; or even to the possibility (in principle) of such spelling-out.

At the heart of the idealisation, and hence of objections to it, is the view of "... [i]deal critics, identified as those capable of appreciating *to the fullest* ... [whatever]" (Levinson, 2006 p. 381: my emphasis). This is, at best, an unfeasible idealisation — as with Carnap's 'Logically Omniscient Jones' (" LOJ" for short) — seemingly at the logical extreme of a practice in which we are presently engaged, if at a lower level. Treating our ideal critic as LOJ would concede that, at least in principle, *all* that is relevant here might be known (say, in the way of narratives of art history, as well as the relevant concepts, and such like). That, in turn, posits a finite totality where, in principle, there could be none. So, on this model, our ideal critic does not actually *know* something or *understand* something which 'we' could not — and certainly he/she is not "... appreciating to the fullest" (Levinson, 2006 p. 381), while we appreciate to a lesser degree. For there is no finite totality here to permit characterising *the fullest* (and then lesser degrees). Rather, as urged (Chapter Five §5; AJ pp. 90-91), a judgement can justifiably be called "incomplete" when a *particular* incompleteness can be specified — and any particular incompleteness can be rectified, without thereby generating a *complete* account; but merely one with no (as yet specified) incompletenesses! Here, an element of idealisation is simply granted, one permitting the concession that what is *debatable* for such-and-such an artwork is *idealised* as having a resolution. Yet, in reality, not every dispute can be resolved *in principle* here, but only those where *we* — as I would say, the Republic of Dance (see UD pp. 71-86) — arrive at resolutions (when we can). So one model of an *ideal* cannot be deployed here.

Contextualism here seems to speak against the idea of an ideal critic (or *Ideal Observer*), by recognising the variety of contexts or questions here: how can one come to an ideal critic? Yet, in reality, the contexts here are relatively localised: this is *artistic* judgement (in line with Chapter One §7; AJ pp. 54-55). So, in one way, our contextualism offers no basis here for rejecting without hesitation an ideal observer (or ideal critic). However, it permits a more flexible 'reading' of the ideal observer than would otherwise be available — in particular, as above, the (apparent) need for a unitary account of the basis-in-understanding of our ideal observer, faced with an especially perplexing artwork, can be rejected.

In these ways, the 'charges' that Sharpe's critique brought against the general idea of an *Ideal Observer* (or ideal critic) can be met. Doing so reinforces the picture of a *competent judge* in respect of artworks of these kinds: a person of requisite understanding, knowledge, experience and sensitivity — granting that in a particular case such a person might still need to be "suitably prompted" (Wollheim, 2001 p. 13).

Then a grasp of the history of the art form — here, dance — in its relevant variety (what was earlier called 'a grasp of the *narrative* of history in the art form') is manifest in the concepts appropriately deployed in making sense of artworks, both works of the past and new works. And that is really what we idealise. So that locating the work in its history is not merely an *historical* project, but also a critical or appreciative one: it bears on one's experience in (appropriately) experiencing that artwork. For our understanding of the experience of the work *as art* is precisely to be made sense of through the powers, capacities and abilities of the (imaginary) ideal observer, even though his/her powers are contextualised to the topics of enquiry[9].

§8.   A distinctiveness to dance experience?

Something important might still seem left out of this appeal to our understanding of dances in terms of the history, and the categories of art: namely, all reference to the *experience* of dance itself. (This was the second objection, raised in §2 above.) For our discussion seemed to emphasise the *concepts* mobilised in that experience, rather than (somehow) the *experience itself*. Our response emphasises, first, that (for philosophical aesthetics) experiential dimensions of artworks provide the contribution of what Danto (1997 p. 195) called "embodiment"; that is, a sensuous quality to the meaning of artworks is recognised. Then, second, the experience of dance should be seen as the recognition of qualities/properties — for example, in speaking of the "brilliant integration of virtuosity, drama and spectacle" (Foster, 1996 p. 253[10]) in *Giselle*, and then identifying how it is achieved or manifested. This 'realism' about artistic features, although not strictly required, fits naturally with our view of artworks: at the least, on this view, the properties in question are clearly 'of the object'. Moreover, third, the study of this experience should investigate the *concepts* mobilised in (appropriate) experience of the works: that is, those mobilised in its artistic appreciation.

Then how might the experience of, say, *this* dance be contrasted with the experience of *that?* This cannot be revealingly done in terms of some distinctive 'feel' here, as is widely recognised (for instance, Kivy, 1990 pp. 95-101). Rather, for philosophical purposes, the difference is located in what is experienced: that is, the difference lies in the *intentional object* of that experience. As one might put it, the experience is of the *intentional object* of that experience (and hence only characterisable via discussion of that *intentional object* — which, here, is the dancework). So that my experience is characterised in terms of what it is an experience *of*: that is, the dancework. Granting this (again) focuses philosophical interest back onto works themselves, rather than onto differential *experiences* of them. For, once our different abilities and conceptual masteries are factored in, the second difference — that between experiences — can only be understood in terms of the first!

Indeed, the difference in the experiences of a cricket match offered by watching, say, a wicket being taken and (re-) watching that wicket as an action-replay make this clear. (Were these not distinguishable, there would be no [sporting] reason to go to matches, nor reason to watch the players rather than the 'big screen' when one was there.) For, while the *experience* is different, in what ways? Answering here returns us to the *intentional objects* of those experiences. For the intentional object of experience *of the dance* must be the dance; not something else — in particular, what is experienced must count as an instantiation of this dance (a performance of it), not a recording of that dance. As we saw in Chapter Three, using video to identify dances ties dance-identity too closely to a particular performance — contrary to the ideas of under-determination of work by *type*. And one feature driving in that direction is the role of *real-time* as one characteristic (among many) distinguishing these experiences as of *performances*. For typically, with genuine performances:

> ... the sounds [for dance, the movements] to which the audience attends are sequenced and co-ordinated by human performers in real-time, in the presence of an audience, for that audience. (Gracyk, 1997 p. 140)

The actions of dancers (in typical dances) are performed in real-time, in just this way. Thus, for dance (if less reliably for music), "... the appreciation of a performance includes evaluation of these actions" (Gracyk, 1997 p. 140).

Modelling the ideal observer (or ideal critic) for dance recognises the conceptual background and the associated powers, capacities and abilities involved in making sense of danceworks; and, in particular, its relation to masterworks of the past. The nature of that evaluation depends on the concepts mobilised in one's experience of the dancework. But doing so considers again the actions (and so on) that comprise the dance.

§9. Recording: An ontological issue?

In this light, then, let us address the application to dance of an argument (about music) that asks whether the hearing of a recording is "a superior mode of access to music" (Gracyk, 1997 p. 148). In considering the tentative "yes" answer, Ted Gracyk deploys two main strategies: first, to imagine the experience of recorded music supplemented by skillfully recorded (video) versions of, say, the pianist's playing — what (of artistic significance) is then missing? The second strategy involves imagining what would be lacking from a world with recordings but no live performances (in particular, from the artistic life of such a world). If the answer is "nothing", or only events of social (rather than artistic) significance, Gracyk could conclude that performances[11] have no artistic role beyond that filled by recordings.

For Gracyk, one issue seems to be (roughly) whether a recording could provide the same *experience* as attending a concert, or an experience equivalent for artistic purposes. Indeed, he explains "aesthetic experience" (by which, in context, he means our *artistic* experience) as "... the rewards of grasping a musical work under a particular interpretation as it unfolds in a series of sounds to which one listens attentively" (Gracyk, 1997 p. 100 note). For listening to musical works is not *just* listening, but ... whatever follows from transfiguration. Consider Collingwood (1938 pp. 140-141), who urged of music that:

> ... what we get out of the concert is ... something which remains for ever inaccessible to a person who cannot or will not make efforts of the right kind, however completely he hears the sounds that fill the room in which he is sitting.

As Collingwood recognises, *merely* hearing the sounds is insufficient to hear the music. For Gracyk, the emphasis is on equivalent *experience*. As we have seen, that is not *our* question: rather, for us, the question concerns *replicating* (or, better, instantiating) the features of the dancework. For, as Gracyk (1997 p. 142) recognises, "... the sounds heard during normal playback offer either a reproduction or a representation of its *performance*." Whatever is said for music, for dance one can note that neither reproductions (say, of painting) nor representations (of those paintings) are artworks; and that what we need here is that our access be to the *works itself* — to *its* properties or features.

Of course, one problem here concerns the 'openness' of the "properties of the work", given the variety of ways those properties might be instantiated in different performances. But that is just a fact about the properties of *performables* such as dances; and need not detain us unduly here.

Since much dance-study today begins from dance on video, the question of recording seems key for dance. (Indeed, in seeing videos, is one is *genuinely* seeing the dances themselves? We have already urged, in Chapter Three, that one is not.) Moreover, one should not be too idealistic here: no doubt my grandson beats me at *chess*, even though I give him a Queen advantage. In *that* context, though not in all, this counts as playing chess. In a similar vein, in some contexts, I *have* been watching *Swan Lake* even though all I have seen is the video. (I certainly have not been watching some *other* dance!) But, for many discussions in philosophical aesthetics, this would *not* count as experiencing the dancework — for, in watching the video, some of the work's crucial artistic features or properties *cannot* be experienced; hence, some elements of the work's *meaning* are *logically* beyond comprehension on that basis — what can be watched on video necessarily lacks them (although viewing this may still be better than nothing!).

So what are the features or properties of a dancework, properly seen (that is, the work's *artistic* features)? An artwork may be studied with attention to something less that the properties of the work itself. As Wollheim (1986 p. 11) notes, tartly:

> Since the days of the great Heinrich Wölfflin, art-historians have tended to identify the objects of their enquiry with those properties of a painting which a good slide preserves.

But these are typically recognised as *second-best*, used for want of access to works themselves. This becomes problematic, were music just organised sound (see Appendix). For then a CD providing access to the relevant organised sound seems to provide access to the artwork. Here, Gracyk (1997 p. 148) concludes, "I am not claiming that recordings are, on balance, a superior mode of access to music." But he is claiming, at least implicitly, that recordings offer one mode of access to the music itself, although he rehearses some reason to doubt this — basically, that it is not a performance (Gracyk, 1997 p. 140): these are claims with ontological implications, if not ontological claims.

This is not the place to debate that musical ontology: at the least, the physicality of (typical) dances makes it far less plausible for dance (compare Chapter Six) — it is easier to identify features that recordings of dances lack. Indeed, the idea of recordings of dance completely replacing live performances is contentious partly because of the difficulty of even imagining the application to dance (*mutatis mutandis*) of the thesis that music is *just* sound-structures. (Those who claim that dance is 'just movement' are making a polemical point: UD p. 253; Cavell 1969 p. 221.)

Of course, such an emphasis on recording minimises the impact of individual virtuosity on the part of performers. But virtuosity as such is not the issue, as Gracyk (1997 pp. 144-145) recognises: and for two reasons, reflecting the different claims of virtuosity. First, there is no *artistic* value to virtuosity for its own sake — what Belinda Quirey (1976 p. 122) dismissed as "circus tricks". Like tongue-twisters, such virtuosity for its own sake is not an artistic virtue. Nevertheless, certain virtuoso performances can become famous; and acquire — for a while — a notoriety as *the* (ideal) way, for instance, to perform a certain role. One hears, in reviews and from friends, about the height of the jumps or the degree of the leg extensions, as though they were crucial features of the dancer's dramatic characterisation (or whatever). (At one time, Sylvie Guillem perhaps fitted this bill.) This kind of gusto undeniably makes dance performances more vivid; more likely to stick in one's memory (see Chapter Six). To the degree that one's attention is captivated by this virtuosity, it is not on central artistic features of that dance performance. The 'interpretative' virtuosity of the performer (seen through this 'performer's interpretation') gives reason to attend to his/her performance as *different* from others — but, of course, that interpretation could be recorded (as Pollini's interpretation of Schönberg's piano music has). So this reason *alone* cannot motivate attention to performances rather than recordings, since it seems capable of appearing in recordings.

Second, this other kind of virtuosity — the one plainly of artistic relevance — is interpretive, making "... greater demands on a performer's understanding than the sorts of skills most often associated with virtuosity" (Thomas Mark, quoted Gracyk, 1997 p. 144). At its heart, such virtuosity must be consistent with the work as a whole (or this will be a basis for criticism). So one difficulty lies in performing the work *as a unity*: as with some music, one such difficulty is apparent in the complexity of performing *ensemble*. As Michael Finnissy[12] explained, with respect to a score of Webern's:

> The score is not "technically" difficult for any individual instrumental parts, although it demands (as with all of Webern's music) extreme refinement and sensitivity in performance. Making two notes "speak" in a way that is going to be meaningful to the listener is much more difficult than playing an entire melody. The problem of performing Webern well is the problem of *ensemble*, for sounding 'together', of making your two tones blend with the two notes of someone else before and after you, and of sublimating individual virtuosity in an essentially unifying approach.

For dance, the problem is fitting together with the other dancers while there is no clear, overarching relation (such as unison or canon) between your movements and theirs. But virtuosity of this sort — unlike the 'circus tricks' variety — will not generate rapturous applause from uninformed audiences. Rather, it involves the thoughtful, intelligent performance of the work. Indeed, this might not even be regarded as virtuosity, although both clearly craft-skill of the highest order and the province of the few among dancers, as elsewhere.

§10. Performance traditions and traditions of performance

What explains the abiding appeal of particular artworks, the sort of thing sometimes (with some justice) enshrined in the idea of a *test of time?* For urging the value of artworks involves urges their enduring value. Yet how should this be explained? One way points to the possibility of continually 'finding something new' in a particular artwork, perhaps in terms of (subtly) different critics' interpretations of those works. Of course, this applies (when it does) across the arts. But performing arts have an additional set of possibilities here. Thus differences *between* performances seem crucial to the abiding appeal of performing arts. And such differences are of two basic sorts: first, differences of 'performer's interpretation', as when Pollini's Schönberg *opus 19* differs from Glenn Gould's; or, second, differences in performances as such, as when Pollini plays *opus 19* with slightly different emphasis today compared with yesterday, although both are *his* performer's interpretation. (Very often, performances differ in both ways — although typical audiences are most aware of one aspect or other.)

The parallel, applied to dance, is more revealing. For dance performances generally offer these differences each time: one may watch the same dancework, in the same performer's interpretation, but with different dancers, and on a performance-area of a different size (or even a wholly different type — as I saw William Louther dance his solo masterpiece *Vesalii Icones* (1970[13]) under a proscenium arch and 'in the round'). Hence work in the performing arts has inexhaustibility of a kind additional to that of the other arts; and dance another over, say, music. But treating all such cases as ones where the audience just spots mistakes, or waits for errors of virtuosity would be mistaken — so these are not of the 'crash and burn' type that Gracyk (1997 pp. 144-145) imagines, but of the *intelligent* (and hence reasoned) re-doing. And, although such 're-doing' is not required by the arts as such, it is a feature of typical performing arts — it follows from the possibility of *performables*: that is, of seeing the very same artwork at different times and in different places. Further, the idea that it is *reasoned* here gives importance guidance. For such reasoning cannot be entirely the province of one dancer or stager. Rather, the thought of 'reason' here indicates two aspects of 'skill', highlighting their importance: what might be called a *performance tradition* and a *tradition of performance*.

Of course, these are really only separable for analytical purposes — by the first (*performance traditions*), I mean that performers require appropriate skills in order to perform particular danceworks; and especially works of the past. Here think first about *dance techniques* (such as Graham technique) which, while they constitute bodily conditioning and the "inculcating [of] certain fairly specific bodily skills" (UD p. 201), also involve the learning (or, at least, acquisition) of a 'vocabulary' of movements appropriate for dances created using those techniques: such that for (say) Graham, "... emotion molded the whole body into a heightened gesture" (Jowitt, 2004 p. 208). This comment applies to the technique, although also the dancer's mastery of it. In this sense, then, Marcia Siegel (1972 p. 107) is right to speak of "technique-as-aesthetic". Those of us who watch performances by dancers in training, and by poorly trained dancers, become adept at noting when this is missing: in the lack of appropriate bodily tension for such-and-such, or the lack of a 'feel' for this choreography — for me, the second most clearly manifest in Nureyev's dancing of Graham dances (see Siegel, 1979 p. 202; Croce, 1978 p. 162; UD p. 203). Moreover, the history of most techniques — arising from the requirements of specific dances for the companies concerned (UD p. 205), and often from their choreographers — reflects this connection between technique and dance-character. And, even if dancers' training is no longer built on specific techniques such as these, with their origins in specific danceworks, that training still involves the dancers learning to perform the patterns of movement appropriate to particular dances. (One fear, at least on the part of old fogies such as me, is that what is learned is inadequate to perform dances of the past — if so, this would be a flaw in training; and criticisable as such!)

On this model, though, dancers undergo a kind of apprenticeship, in which they learn two (or two-and-a-half) crafts: they undergo the bodily training and are inducted into the understanding of the movements (and the dances) that result — and they may in this way gain insight into choreographic processes (although they need not, so this is the "half"). Further, expectations can change: thus Jowitt (2004 p. 45) claims that:

> Today's ballet dancer tries to show straight knees and pointed toes as much of the time as the choreography permits — that is, on descending from a jump, the toes stay pointed until the last second; the standing leg is arrow-straight in pirouettes.

And comments that "Ballet Theatre dancers of the 40s cared less about these issues ... the shape of a phrase seems to matter more than the pictorial beauty of each individual movement" (Jowitt, 2004 p. 45). All of this is within what I am calling a *performance tradition*: dancers learn to perform *dances*, and to understand them in a dancerly way. And, typically at least, both that learning and that understanding took place in the context of a *company* whose members were trained in that manner of delivering the choreography. That tradition, of course, allows the performances of dances of the past in what I earlier called a "reasoned" way: that is, in *new* performers' interpretations (UD pp. 100-101). For any changes can then be explained by reference both to the tradition and to the kinds of deviation that tradition licenced. For the tradition has a *normative* dimension. Without such a tradition, no one would be capable of genuinely performing certain dances; dancers would not understand how such movements *should be* performed. And so, even if the dances were 'preserved' (say, in notated form), they could not be danced. For dancers would not see *how* the danceworks should be performed; or what qualities a performance should respect. Just such *performance traditions* would be threatened if attention to recordings replaced attention to dances. (Interestingly, the substance of Gracyk's position seems to assume the continuation of a performance tradition — part of what he means by a "craft tradition": Gracyk, 1997 p. 144[14].)

Suppose one asks whether the *performance tradition* for, say, the current Royal Ballet dancers overlap sufficiently with those of (say) Paul Taylor or Fredrick Ashton to permit those dancers to perform these choreographers' works; and concludes that it does not (see Challis, 1999). Such cases suggest that the *performance tradition* required for these works either never was part of the training regime for these dancers (Taylor) or has ceased to be (Ashton) — because, say, a British style of ballet performance, with its "emotional depth" has been replaced by a Russian style, with its "formal precision" (quoted Challis, 1999 p. 147, both quotes). At its most extreme, this outcome could render the performances (and hence the danceworks) unintelligible even to a knowledgeable audience (see below): in the less extreme case, this audience would just struggle to understand. For the *performance traditions* would be lacking. Certainly, such a possibility illustrates what it would be for *performance traditions* to cease to be available. Another example familiar to some (and in a similar vein) might be the lack of clarity of works as experienced in, say, some choreographic competitions, where the performance skill of dancers is insufficient (or inappropriate) in ways that make it difficult to see *the dance* (through these performances).

But another aspect of performance needs to be ensured (although, again, contrasted only for analytical purposes): that I call a *tradition of performance*. By this is meant that an audience of 'competent judges' for danceworks (McFee, 2001 pp. 104-108) is required; and such an audience comes to understand these works through experience of them *as performed*, since that is how such audience genuinely confront such works. Similarly Rhees (1969 p. 159) speaks of "... the way in which a piece of music may remain uninteresting until you hear it played by a really good pianist." So these difficulties have a direct bearing on dance experience, for identifying *dance meaning* through such experience remains problematic. Although such *traditions of performance* in the audience amount partly to understanding the narrative of dance history, they also embody contemporary understanding of how these danceworks should (typically) be performed — an understanding that later stagers might contest profitably in making new versions of particular (extant) dances, and one to which choreographers could respond (as Mats Ek does, in his comic traducings of the typical expectations of classical ballet: say, in his *Swan Lake* [1987]). It permits (a) the audience to distinguish interesting and valuable difference from mere mistake, and (b) the impact of 'posterity' to lead to a revision of that judgement. For a 'knowledgeable audience' is just one that can distinguish originality from mere novelty (is Matthew Bourne's *Swan Lake* [1995] really doing anything new at the level of artistic meaning?); and can find the continuity within trivial changes. Here we draw both on the conditions for retaining danceworks one might thought lost and on those for losing works that might be thought retained — both of these turn out to be *dancerly* or *artistic* matters; and therefore (for me) to have priority over the claims of the very abstract metaphysics of abstract objects like types. Here, too, the audience should recognise (at least) when dancers fail to instantiate a particular choreography[15].

All-in-all, such traditions form a background here (part of "the lay of the artworld": Carroll, 2001 p. 91) which permits the choices made to be *reasoned* choices, defensible (in principle) in discussion. Without such a tradition, and the understanding it subtends, "... however small and special" (Cavell, 1969 p. xxvii), choices here could only be arbitrary. And that reinforces our earlier discussion of the 'objectivity' of the canon of masterworks.

Sometimes my enthusiasm to find a role for dance of the past in the creation and performance of dance of today, as well as in its criticism, has been misunderstood. For, as suggested above, a dancework may lose its audience in a manner that has little to do with a "perpetual vanishing point" (Siegel, 1972 p. 1) of performance, with its emphasis on being retained in memory (say), although it does bear in part on dance's condition as a performing art. Consider briefly a kind of case well exemplified in a comment by Arlene Croce (1982 pp. 28-29[16]), who writes:

> I watched Martha Graham's *Primitive Mysteries* (1931) die this season in what seemed, for the most part, scrupulous performances. The twelve girls looked carefully rehearsed. Sophie Maslow, who had supervised the previous revival, in the season of 1964-65, was again in charge. Everybody danced with devotion. Yet a piece that I would have ranked as a landmark in American dance was reduced to a tendentious outline, the power I had remembered was no longer there ... Perhaps there's a statute of limitations on how long a work can be depended upon to force itself through the bodies who dance it.

Of course, the example does not matter: but the phenomenon described here

is all too familiar to those who have been watching dance for a long time —
and, moreover, this description sets aside some of the explanations familiarly
offered. So it is not that the dancers lacked rehearsal, or that those rehearsals
failed to be scrupulously conducted. (After all, a similar pattern of rehearsal
can be imagined to have preceded that "previous revival" referred to here;
and it was a success.) Moreover, as described, the problem was not strictly
one of *memory* of the previously-successful sequence of movements (and so
on), since this unsuccessful version shares at least the 'supervisor' —
someone involved in transmission of the movement-sequences (and so on).
Croce here offers only two hints in explanation: first, perhaps "devotion" is
not the right attitude for performance; second, she refers to some kind of
transition in "the bodies who dance it". Let us consider each in turn.

The first of these (if I read it correctly) *is* a criticism of how the dance was
presented, presumably by those who supervised rehearsal: to present a
dancework of the past in its artistic greatness, one must approach it roughly
as one would a current work — the term "devotion" suggests the wrong
attitude to the possibility of the current performances differing from those of
the past. For devotion surely will attempt to preclude any change at all from
the 'object of devotion' (real or imagined). Since that possibility exists in all
cases where performing arts are at issue, it must be acknowledged here. But
adopting instead a view of the dance which exploits its artistic potential in
the danceworld of today does not mean that one lacks proper regard for the
dancework itself. On the contrary, the work is respected as *in a performing art*
— as a performable — precisely by thinking carefully about how much
deviation from past performances can retain same-work identity. (And, of
course, one asset here might be a notated score, *adequate* in my sense: see
Chapter Three §6.) For works from the past should be treated like any other
work — after all, the works from last year's repertoire are, in one clear sense,
now works from the past: they were not choreographed specially for this
season. And, to repeat, the term "devotion" suggests that the dance
company's attitude to the past of this work was unduly reverential. While
knowing how this can come about, it is clearly something one would hope to
avoid. In that sense, if true, this *is* a criticism of the company's activities.

Croce's second point (as I read it) recognises differences in "the bodies who
dance it". This criticism should separate, for analytical purposes at least, into
two aspects. One is broadly technical. Compared to dancers from the past,
the typical dancer of today has been trained in a number of techniques
(since 'regular' employment requires this), and probably trained to a higher
pitch — thus justifying Judith Mackrell's reference to today's dancers as
"Olympic-standard" (Mackrell, 1997 p. 7[17]): they usually have physical
conditioning beyond what was common in, say, the 1930s (when *Primitive*

Mysteries was choreographed). The powers and capacities of such bodies differ from those on which the choreography was initially composed: these bodies may have greater flexibility; and sometimes their movements reflect their mastery of different dance-styles; say, of Bharata Natyam. The other point, though related, is more directly aesthetic; that, as noted above, *dance techniques* (such as Graham technique) have a connection with the expressiveness of works deploying that technique — as one might say, to "technique-as-aesthetics" (Siegel, 1972 p. 107). And points of this kind were brought together in the demand (above) for relevant *performance traditions* for dancers. Without the preservation, or continuity, of such a background, dances would be unintelligible to performers. But, above, the parallel demand on competent judges was also stressed: *traditions of performance*, as I called them, must also be preserved, or re-constructed, if works are to be understood aright — and, in effect, that makes this a constraint on these works being understood *at all!* With the disappearance from the background of the features required for intelligibility, one would expect exactly the sort of disappearance of danceworks from the realm of *understandability* by audiences that Croce describes as the 'death' of Graham's *Primitive Mysteries* (whatever one makes of the example); as well as its connection to the failure by the rest of the danceworld to grasp such works any longer. So, in this concrete case too, failure to maintain either *performance traditions* (among dancers) or *traditions of performance* (in the audience) generates one kind of failure of a dancework of the past. And this failure might well constitute the disappearance of the dancework in question from the artistic canon, since it will no longer be experienced as expressive. Hence the very tools which, elsewhere, explain the persistence of dance of the past and its centrality for understanding and performing dance today can also explain cases where even established works disappear from the canon.

So, first, this work "dies" because it loses both its audience and those able to instantiate it — in that fashion, its demise results from its losing an audience that responds to it: one can no longer see it as it was seen. But, second, Croce describes an extreme version. For the kinds of response that would have kept the dancework alive need not be *very* positive. As we might say, one kind of 'life-support' simply involves being in the repertoire (or not far out of it, so that the work could be re-staged relatively easily). For such works might continue to be staged, but without an excess of enthusiasm. Works can remain in the canon, even functioning as temporary paradigms, even though they are now regarded as pretty *weak* — they are still clearly works of a certain kind, at least. So they might limp by, without dying but without immense enthusiasm. And, of course, as noted (again!), *most* of the works currently produced in any art form at any time are pretty weak! So the dancework from the past need not suffer by comparison with contemporary choreography.

Thus, the conclusion here is that a 'live' artwork must be both performable, and open to appreciation — these two conditions together sound *just* like a truism. But complexities within each mean that, instead, this just points to the beginning of the discussion. Thus, to be *performable* here as a particular artwork in a multiple art form requires at least meeting the constraints from *the type*; any performance must reflect those constraints to be a candidate for a performance of that work. For instance, the artwork must not be forgotten, or otherwise lost. Hence, in the simplest case, there would be an authoritative score. Further, as the discussion of Graham's *Primitive Mysteries* (1931) above shows, the capacities of the dancers must be appropriate — and these can be lost; and lost, in the contemporary danceworld, partly because today's dancers must typically have some mastery of numerous dance techniques, to become what Susan Leigh Foster (1997 p. 255) has rightly disparaged as the "hired body" with its "... rubbery flexibility coated with impervious glossiness"[18]. In that way, the connection that once existed between the company and the choreographer (and especially her choreographic style as reflected in the technique used) can be broken. Likewise, openness to *appreciation* too has a connection to the dancers as well as the audience. Thus, Croce's discussion seems to highlight simply a collapse on the part of the audience: the work was no longer available to that audience. But, in fact, there was a more total collapse in respect of that work. The work *as performed* lacked something; but that reflected defects in the dancers' ability to *instantiate* that work, given both their training and their understanding. That is, this had become a work that standardly-trained dancers could not perform.

Of course, the requirements for an audience able to appreciate this work applies in other art forms, as well as in dance. So what is the new ephemerality here? How does this case differ from (say) painting? The discussion of Arlene Croce illustrates the additional need to retain traditions of performance and performance traditions: for these are prerequisites for the training and experience of the dancers; and — since those dancers will be performing — of a genuine audience for dance also.

The upshot here: the *experience* of dance has such traditions implicit within it. I do not mean, of course, that all audience members must be able to recite the history, and so on. Rather, these traditions must be part of what the audience knows. Still, the knowledge might well be acquired *other* than as kinds of book-learning (for dancers, it almost always will be); and manifest in action and in intelligent attention.

§11. Conclusion

As we have noted, the capacity to 'see' artistic properties (and hence artistic values) in an artwork depends on various conceptual masteries (that is, on one's cognitive stock) — even though this is not *all* that is involved. Many of the applications of these insights to dance are negative: it does *not* require that one be (or think like, or feel like) a dancer — all these are incoherent requirements. While clearly *something* 'connects' the possibility of dance to the reality of movement for most of us, this insight is a long way from being usable, because art-status is *transfigurational* (Chapter One: Danto, 1981). Hence, what one sees as dances are crucially different from movements encountered elsewhere. For danceworks are intentional or meaning-bearing (see Chapter Five), embodying the intelligence (or the intention) of their creators.

So a philosophical investigation cannot discuss, productively, *how* (or, worse, *if*) dance experience is central to artistic appreciation of dance; nor can it attend to the *nature* of such experience (as though it had *one* nature). First, dances cannot really be appreciated without first-hand *experience*, and without finding them powerful (or otherwise) on the basis of that experience — where the *experience* is centrally that of dance's audience. Second, experiences are not helpfully characterised in terms of their distinctive 'feel' (part of what Wollheim [1984 p. 38; pp. 42-45] calls their "phenomenology") partly because, to *capture* the experience, one must refer to what it is an experience *of*: that is, to the dancework (the 'intentional object'). And, third, if one wishes to be more explicit, that experience is only characterised at all exactly via the *concepts* under which that experience takes place (the concepts *mobilised* in that experience) — exploring these concepts *is* exploring the experience. Fourth, while the experience is not exhausted by this focus on concepts, that part can be readily examined. In particular, discussing "mobilisation-conditions" is really a positive-sounding version of the 'recognised heads of exception' for claims to critical appreciation; hence, it explains our failures to make sense of particular danceworks.

To understand the connection between that understanding of danceworks and the past of dance, we saw how the *categories of art* in terms of which danceworks are recognised and appreciated (and through which such works must be recognised and appreciated so misperception of them can be avoided) inform the *canon* of danceworks — those an Ideal Observer would value, or which pass the Test of Time (as masterworks). For our narratives of dance history are constructed using such categories. And the requirements here come to *learning to see* danceworks as in this or that category and *learning to value* them as in the relevant category. Moreover, as we saw, this cannot be reduced to a *Critical Rules Account*.

These points could apply to the appreciation of any art form. But they apply to dance without significant modification for three related reasons. First, and equally true for all art form, the appropriate perspective here (as above) is that of the audience; second, the audience for dance is as much a visual and/or aural audience as that for painting or for music (respectively) — dance offers nothing special here. In particular, artistic experience of dance does not require one to experience dance other than perceptually (for example, kinaesthesis is not required: UD pp. 264-273; see Chapter Eight). Third, the distinctive experience of dancers is a quite separate topic; and not one expected to be very revealing, given the variety within dancers, within dances, and within the perspectives on a particular dance afforded to each dancer — the solo dancer knows all of the dance 'from the inside' (at least, all of the movement of the dance); which means, of course, just that he/she can perform it, not (necessarily) describe it, nor talk about it. By contrast, one member of a group has that 'inside' perspective only on his/her segment of the dance; that may not be a *useful* perspective from which to take in the dance as a whole! (Certainly, the parallel points should be readily granted for, say, musicians in an orchestra — although [as we saw earlier: Chapter Eight] their relation to the music differs from the dancers' relation to the dance.)

Chapter Eleven
Conclusion: Making sense of dance

§1. Introduction

This text as a whole might seem to have ignored one fundamental question: "But is it dance?" applied to the more bizarre examples. In reply, the irrelevance of the question of definition should be stressed both for philosophy quite generally, and specifically in the case of dance (see §2 below). For it contributes nothing: if our (supposed) *definition* conflicts with our experience of a performance as of dance, following the experience will often be right. Indeed, any 'definition' aims to capture that experience. And we understood *dance* prior to any definition offered, and independent of it — even were it correct! Further, suppose that "[d]ance-driven passages have always been in ... [Pina Bausch's] work, but usually they are subordinate." (Segal, 2007 p. E1): does it matter whether a work of hers is or is not dance as long as one can draw on concepts appropriate to the understanding of that work? Yet that question really just asked that this work be located in the narrative of art-history for dance. Perhaps, in the end, there is no more to being *dance* than that.

Distinguishing dance from non-dance has often been recognised as problematic. Thus Adam Smith ([1795] 1980 p. 210) writes:

> Though the eye of the most ordinary spectator readily distinguishes between what is called a dancing step and any other step, gesture or motion, yet it may not be easy to express what it is that constitutes this distinction.

Were this generally correct (when Smith wrote it), the problem then resides in the exact *articulation* of this distinction, since recognising "the dancing step" means (roughly) recognising *dance* and distinguishing it from what is not dance. But, at least for Smith, that distinction should be visible to "the eye of the most ordinary spectator": that is certainly no longer *obvious* (if it ever was). Instead, the recent history of dance has meant that, in general, a quite sophisticated '*eye*' is required. For some time, most danceworks were not elaborated in terms of characteristic patterns of *movement*. Rather, the tendency has been towards the emancipation of movement-patterns characteristic of activities outside such (traditional) dance as ballet. But, of course, this movement was *transfigured* into dance.

There are three main reasons for the (seeming) 'omission' from this text of the question of when some action is, or is not, dance: first, the question itself is unclear. Beginning (as throughout this work) from a concern with those dances that are art — or from those dance-forms that are art forms — seem to assume a clear boundary; yet that is contentious. There may be no such *distinctive* class of objects, identified independently of one's purposes. For some debates, perhaps some works by Pina Bausch should be treated as *within* the compass of the debate; for others, as outside it. No context-free distinction may be possible here. Then, second, such discussion standardly hopes for a *definition*: but both the possibility and the usefulness of such definitions should be rejected in this case (see below: §2). It is therefore a diversion to offer what *others* might find a definition. Those points are elaborated (still briefly) in the next section. Third, the whole debate here turns on the identification of such-and-such a performance as so-and-so dance: the identification of *this* movement sequence as dance is treated via the thought that this sequence is this or that *specific* dance — say, *Swan Lake*. But such identifications presuppose particular accounts of the *history* of dance-as-art; and particular relations of the works at issue to that history.

§2. Some issues of defining "dance"

In summary, the major reasons for not discussing directly the question of defining *dance* are:

(a) The philosophical problem with the philosophical project of searching for definitions, understood as conditions individually necessary and jointly sufficient (or as a concise yet comprehensive characterisation of whatever, having an 'exact fit'). That project should be rejected on three grounds (McFee, 2003a): (i) as impossible of completion, since there are no definitions of non-technical terms of sufficient complexity to be interesting — all will succumb to counter examples, or to the charge of being circular (UD pp. 16-20); (ii) as unhelpful in philosophy, since one can understand terms without being able to define them (the point best exemplified by *time*); and (iii) as not part of *philosophy's* project, since I understand what, say, *games* are before I have the putative definition offered by some philosopher: for instance, by Bernard Suits (1978[1]). And this grants — what in fact I deny — that the 'definition' Suits offers fits extant cases: that is, is extensionally adequacy (SRV pp. 24-27). So this is a wholly general objection (expanded in UD).

(b) Nothing distinctive of *dance* makes a definition either more likely or (more important) of interest to the *philosophical* aesthetics of dance — for the reasons under (a) above. In particular, the idea that art is *expansive*, in that new artworks might always contest the borders of any 'definition' one had, cannot in fact make the situation any worse; it merely offers another version of a difficulty already recognised. (But, of course, it does not give *extra* plausibility to the search for a definition of "art".)

(c) A more *specific* issue might seem to be raised by the fact that dance had a prominent modernist phase, such that "... the genuine article [of art] ... really does challenge the art of which it is the inheritor and voice" (Cavell, 1969 p. 219). That might suggest that, for dance, the centrality of art of the past has dissolved, with a postmodernist phase, into a kind of eclecticism, with a loss of traditions — and that dissolution might in turn amount to the dissolution of any sense of the relevant art form (here, dance) as evaluable in a safe or shareable fashion. But, again, such arguments are rooted in a misunderstanding (see CDE pp. 204-207): there was no (exceptionless) definition of dance during its modernist phase (for the reasons sketched above); and adding (say) eclecticism or loss of traditions does nothing to change this, or to increase its urgency.

In practice, though, two points are fundamental. First, one can understand concepts without being able to define them. And a great deal of complex discussion of the relevant concept is manifest here in the discussions in dance criticism and dance history, for instance. So one has *examples* of the understanding of dance in action. Indeed, any putative definition of *dance* must roughly match the picture of dance that such discussion manifests: this would be the 'test-bed' for the adequacy of the (putative) definition. Then one's purchase on that discussion offers all the access needed to the concept *dance*.

Now, second, suppose an adequate definition of *dance* were offered (as Suits thought his definition of *games* adequate): it would (by definition!) have an 'exact fit' on the concept *dance* in its key uses. But where did one stand *before* being offered that definition? Clearly, my understanding of dance did not depend on that definition, since I did not *know* it. Yet in general I understood what were dances, and what were not; I could recognise problem cases, and peripheral cases, and such like. The philosophical interest resides in these powers and capacities of mine, which are clearly independent of the definition of *dance* — even if there were one. Then both points might be elaborated and defended, discussing examples.

Taken together, these points explain why hunting for a definition of *dance* has no central place in a philosophical aesthetics of dance: at best, the *hunt* might expose something interesting, but (by the first point) it will not be a definition of dance; and (by the second) even if it were, it could have no philosophical relevance.

§3. Concepts and moments in history

These considerations suggest that, at its heart, nothing has changed here. Still, might recent events in the narrative of dance history seem to create a *bigger* issue for understanding than previously? At the very least, perhaps old 'certainties' have been undermined. Thus it might seem that:

> [t]he result of the recent history of postmodern dance is that while our fundamental ideas of what dance *is* have been shaken, we are left feeling that the lines should be firmly drawn *somewhere* and redefinitions attempted: if *anything* can be dance, what's the point of making distinctions between dance and non dance at all? (Banes, 2007 p. 111)

Of course, the suggestion *here* has never been that "... *anything* can be dance": such subjectivism is rejected here, as elsewhere (UD pp. 21-38; CDE pp. 2-5). Instead, any sequence of movement *might* have (or have had) a place in dance. Deborah Hay makes that point, in saying that "[e]veryday the whole day, from the minute you get up, is potentially a dance" (Foster, 1986 p. 6): namely, that each of her movements *could have* been part of one of her dance compositions. With its emphasis on "potentially", this is of course unexceptional; for it does not say that any of the movement *is* or *was* (part of) such a dance.

Yet what precisely does the expression "postmodern dance" identify? This question has special resonance because the term "post-modern dance" acquired a distinct usage in dance theory or dance criticism, prior to the upsurge of interest in the postmodernism of Jean-Francois Lyotard and his cronies (CDE pp. 215-218). To what does calling a dance "postmodern" commit us (Sally Banes, 1987 p. xv: "post-modernist"; and see also Banes, 1994 pp. 301-310)? In particular, does understanding danceworks urged as postmodern necessarily draw on notions from, say, Lyotard or Jean Baudrillard? That issue is not merely terminological: rather, it concerns what values are embodied in or presupposed by these (different) dances. Perhaps, as above, it merely stresses eclecticism, connecting danceworks to a different narrative of dance history. If so, it too asks about the narratives that accommodate particular danceworks within practices of dancemaking and dance-understanding: hence about what elements must be central to any narrative affirming their art-status or artistic value.

A discussion by Danto, although not focused on dance, explored exactly that issue for modern artworks. The case, from "De Kooning's Three-Seater" (Danto, 1987), is revealing because — at first blush — its conclusions are the opposite of what some might expect from Danto. In the case, de Kooning had decorated the seat of a three-hole 'outdoor' toilet in a style "... reminiscent of the style used by Jackson Pollock" (quoted Danto, 1987 p. 59). If Danto's ideas are understood as offering a broadly institutional account of art (see §4 below), both de Kooning's status as an artist and the variety of objects that have found their way (as artworks) into the contemporary artworld might suggest that Danto's conclusion would endorse the de Kooning three-seater as an artwork. The art-possibility of plumbing fixtures seems licenced, since the Duchamp *Fountain* is a urinal. And Danto even discusses Giacometti sketching and drawing while in the outside water closet in his studio in Paris. Of course, these sketches were artworks (or, at least, *candidate* artworks) "... if Giacometti drawings are works of art at all" (Danto, 1987 p. 60) — which, surely, they are!

Further, the visual effect of the thrown and dripped paint might have seemed controversial in 1947: Danto (1987 p. 59) recalls Jackson Pollock demanding of Lee Krasner to know whether these works of his were indeed *paintings*. But by 1954, when the three-seater was painted, that was no longer an issue; similarly for the techniques Pollock used. So the look of the three-seater perhaps *resembled* that of paintings. Yet this alone is not enough. We might not know what to make of, say, a field mouse painted by Jackson Pollock (especially if the paint were applied accidentally: Danto, 1987 p. 59): luckily, such cases have not been forthcoming.

The primary interest of this discussion lies in what it shows us about the mobilisation of the narratives of art history (in respect of a particular art form). Danto identifies (surely correctly) some central difficulties this case raises. For, as he recognises, the question *But is it art?* "... cannot be asked of isolated objects" (Danto, 1987 p. 60). Rather, there is "... an implicit generalisation in the question" (Danto, 1987 p. 60). For one is really asking whether things *of this kind* are artworks: and, of course, (by now) the Duchamp *Fountain* is easily recognised as a Ready-made, one of the class of "... commonplace objects transfigured into works of art" (Danto, 1987 p. 60). As Danto notes, getting *one* work of a *kind* (such as this) into the artistic canon in effect licences Ready-mades — it licences the production of Ready-mades as a legitimate way to intend to make artworks, although (of course) many will be *unpromising* artworks! So that, even if Duchamp had in fact stopped at one, the *place* has been prepared for (further) Ready-mades. For the beginning of a narrative locating Ready-mades within art-history had been written. As one might put it, the power of the argument-form, "It is art *because* it is a Ready-made" was conceded: the *kinds* of reasons that might be deployed here have been recognised as *candidate* reasons for art-status — whether they were *good* reasons in any particular example could then be explored case-by-case.

But, in fact, this is not the situation for de Kooning's three-seater. True, "[o]bjects similar to it were to become accepted [as art] in the next generation of artists" (Danto, 1987 p. 61). Yet de Kooning did not develop in this direction; nor would such a development make *obvious* sense (especially given how de Kooning's development is presently regarded). Here Danto (1987 p. 61) rightly quotes Wölfflin's slogan: "Not everything is possible at every time". And he disputes that *this* object at *this* time could fit that bill since — although it might fit into a narrative of art — it will find no place in the narrative of de Kooning's *oeuvre*. Or, more bluntly, this was not, then, a way for *de Kooning* to make art! Danto (1987 p. 61) concludes (a) that "... this particular object can be a work of art only if it is a de Kooning"; but (b) "... there is no way it can be that" (Danto, 1987 p. 61). Hence it is not an artwork.

This account (following Danto) needs augmentation in three ways, faced with three (plausible) comments. The first suggests that, after all, de Kooning *might* rightly be seen as a precursor of, say, Jasper Johns; and hence it is *wrong* to state so categorically that this work cannot be *precursive* of Johns; thus a place within de Kooning's *oeuvre* might be found for it, perhaps with some re-writing of the relevant narrative. But Danto explicitly denies this since, as he rightly recognises, "... there is no space in his [de Kooning's] corpus for an object of 1954 like this" (Danto, 1987 p. 61). Substantial re-writing of de Kooning's corpus, and the trajectory of his art, would be required. This may not be *impossible*, but it seems so improbable that, here, it can be put it aside (with Danto).

As a second case, Danto (1987 p. 61) raises in illustration "... a sheet of drawings done for an illiterate servant by Michelangelo, illustrating what he wanted for a meal: two rolls, some fish, etc.". No doubt such a sheet of drawings would be a valuable *artifact* — as the three-seater was. Deploying the artistic/aesthetic contrast here, this drawing doubtless has aesthetic merit. But it would not be an artwork, no matter how skillfully drawn. The broad institutionalism implied is also fundamental to our wider account of art.

Yet, third, the history of art of a particular kind (or, picking up Danto's point, that narrative which brings such a kind 'within the fold' — as Duchamp did for Ready-mades) is not written *once-and-for-all*: that is one moral from my *forward retroactivism* (see McFee, 1992b; AJ pp. 119-145). That thought returns us to the sorts of *huge* changes in the future of art required to bring it about that, in 1954, de Kooning might create something *precursive* of Jasper Johns (or whomsoever): such changes to the dominant narrative of art-history are not *unimaginable* — although we think them unlikely. So our theoretical perspective is robust enough to deal with either outcome.

§4. Dealing with the Republic of Dance

Danto's resolution of this de Kooning case rings true, suggesting revealing answers to parallel questions in respect of dance. It allows putting aside the question of the *first* work of such-and-such a kind of art. The case of Ready-mades shows how acceptance (by the Republic of Art) of *one* example will licence that *kind* as *candidate* artworks, to be confronted case-by-case. Then, we see how the work of a particular choreographer (Pina Bausch) or of a particular group of choreographers (the Judson Church group) might *in practice* answer questions about what *counted* as dance; and do so both through their activities (rather than theoretically) and in ways *in line* with my account of the workings of the dance aspect of the Republic of Art (see also Preface §4).

It helps to sketch the workings of the Republic of Dance, on my account (UD pp. 71-86; McFee, 2008; AJ pp. 147-173). First, then, on theories or accounts of art plausibly called "institutional", what is and is not a work of art is determined by humans and, arguably, for humans (see Quinton, 1982 p. 98); or, art-status is a product of some kind of human consensus. But, for institutional concepts of this sort (like "machine": see Storer, 1962; "science"), not everyone is entitled to pronounce, as 'native speakers' might in respect of language: instead, there is an *authoritative body* (Baker & Hacker, 1984b pp. 272-273)—the artworld, or Republic of Art ... or one of its proper parts!

In the specific case of dance, this "Republic" is composed of choreographers, producers, dance theatre owners and so on: and, in particular (other) dance-critics and dance-theorists. Ours is a two-stage theory: thus, any movement sequence put forward as dance (self-election) and accepted by others (other-acclamation by the Republic) is indeed an artwork, at least defeasibly: in this case, a dancework. If a work put forward as dance does not receive this 'other-acclamation', two courses of action are open to those putting the work forward (apart from simply accepting that the sequence is not (art-) dance after all and letting it sink into obscurity). The first is waiting for the judgement of posterity — assuming that one is right about the art-status (and artistic value) of the work and waiting to be *proved* right, when later dance-theorists, dance-critics, and so on, regard the work as art. That is to say, when the judgement of the Republic changes. And, of course, it is easy to cite examples (such as Van Gogh's work) where this occurred. Still, this is a doubtful path to success, particularly once one reflects on the history of the art form as a whole — not much really changes. A second, more enlightened course of action attempts to *shape taste*, so that one's work is accepted as art; that is, so that it receives the necessary other-acclamation. This can either be done oneself — as T. S. Eliot's criticism created the taste by which his own poetry was admired — or by others; so Clive Bell created a climate of criticism appropriate for the appreciation of Cézanne. My favourite dance example of changes in artistic values (see UD pp. 72-73), and hence in the thinking about dance, is that initiated by the critic XXX through his writing in the *Journal des Debats* from 1828 to 1832 (Chapman, 1984). In contrast to other critics of the time, who emphasised the narrative, literal and dramatic elements of the ballet, XXX enjoyed the dance for its non-literal appeal. So his writing emphasised the expressive quality of the dancing itself. Perhaps these reviews and articles, amounting to a sustained polemic for that view, led to the subsequent shift in critical interest from pantomime-type effects in ballet to a (pure) dance. The outcome of such a shift in taste would be the other-acclamation of works previously not seen as art. What was actually done here was a kind of public relations job. But it involved the *validation* of certain critical concepts: these events changed the vocabulary of criticism and, with it, the sorts of things that counted as *reasons* for artistic judgements. A similar case might be urged more recently:

> ... not all American dance theatre works had to be storytelling, genre or period pieces, but that a purely formal approach could be made to composition in a strictly native vein and still be good. (Jowitt, 2004 p. 103)

For this conclusion too might re-shape contemporary understanding of those danceworks one confronts.

Other dance-examples are often less clear than Chapman paints the earlier one: for instance, writings on ballet by Adrian Stokes offer a related kind of outcome. Thus, one aspect of modernism in ballet involved precisely that "... the action of a modern ballet is expressed in the dancing itself" (Stokes, 1935 p. 105) which, Stokes urged, necessitated the replacement of narrative based on "mimed action". However, as Chapman highlights, the achievements of XXX were on the 'leading edge' of the change in sensibility: Stokes' work (though important) was on the 'trailing edge' of a rejection of the primacy of the representational initiated by Clive Bell and Roger Fry. So, in effect, Stokes argues for the application *to ballet* of changes in sensibility well established for the *avant-garde* in painting.

Moreover, when (say) the action of a roadsweeper is transfigured to become part of my dancework, there is a clear sense in which it *is* changed — a set of properties is acquired — and a sense in which it is *not*: the patterns of muscular movement, say, might be the same. This tells us something about the nature of the new properties: roughly, saying that a movement pattern becomes *transfigured* into a part of a dance involves say that the movement pattern can (and should) now be seen that way — this is what its being different consists in! These changes result from the institutional action.

Further, a 'decision' on the part of the Republic could either down-grade an artist's work (this seems to happen periodically with Sibelius) or simply eject it from the canon of art works. Or, consider the Republic *admitting* (as art) works previously not seen as art. This is reflected in the re-shapings of taste achieved by Ruskin, Bell, and so on. So both *art-status* and *artistic value* are in the gift of the Republic. Hence this account is not merely classificatory, since it bears on artistic value as well as art-status.

The variety of objections offered to broadly institutional accounts of art need not be considered here (see McFee, 2008). For this text requires no explicit attachment to the concept of the Republic of Dance: such institutionalism was never considered directly. But brief comments on five revealing topics can be included. First, this institutionalism aligns naturally with the intentionalism of Chapter Five: that making art requires, roughly, that one *intend* to make art — which in turn requires that the concept *art* be present in that society. Similarly for *recognising* objects as art.

Second, and defeasibly, the fact that such-and-such is an artwork means it is minimally valuable — well, *at least* it is a dancework! For the activities of the Republic of Dance generate *artistic value* as well as *art-status*. Of course, this implication of value can be defeated both in cases where the work is poor but still art, and those where it is no longer art. Critics typically expect to specify independently what counts as an instance (say, of a dancework), and then (here) invoke standards of valuation. They therefore see classification as logically prior to evaluation. But we begin from cases of *acknowledged* art, and then ask whether other objects are art, even though not *as* worthwhile as those from which we started — just as we begin thinking about reasoning from cases of *sound* reasoning: the rest counts as reasoning *at all* (when it does) to the degree that it approximates sound reasoning (Grice, 2001 p. 35). Hence *good art* is actually logically prior to art. So there is no intrinsic difficulty with the position, advocated here — which endorses the possibility of such a priority.

Then, third, the possibility of explaining the 'decisions' of the Republic makes its conclusions rationally explicable, at least at any particular moment. For the 'transfiguration' into artwork is important just in bringing with it a critical vocabulary of the kind appropriate to art. For that work now has a place in a 'narrative' of art history, or in a tradition: a *category of art* now applies. And a different critical discourse follows. The required perspective here is, roughly, that of Feyerabend's *practitioners*, rather than that of philosophers[2] — as practitioners in science might, with justice, regard their predecessor's work as mistaken, while the philosophers of science find the views incommensurable, passing one another by. The practitioners — as members of the Republic of Art — rightly make the judgement from the contemporary viewpoint. So critics can *see* that, for example, Warhol's *Brillo Box* is (now) art.

A fourth 'reason', extending the third, may seem self-evident: that stressing the Republic of Dance in this way is acknowledging that many key decisions are in the gift of dancers, choreographers, stages, and the audience for danceworks — that they decide, for instance, *whether* such-and-such is a dance) if only temporarily), such that it would be an impertinence on the part of philosophy to intervene. Indeed, such cases provide the 'test-bed' of examples to which the arguments of philosophy must be answerable — although there will be room for *some* 'grasping of nettles', and some places where issues of consistency prevail.

Here, a fifth reason for insisting that the concept *art* is institutional (in the relevant sense) is that it implies that such points (concerning the practical workings of the concept) are parts of the *philosophy* of art, not (merely) the sociology of art. For the idea of an institutional concept (in this sense) gives due weight to such factors: if there are institutional concepts in this strong sense — and, in particular, if *art* is one of them — facts of these sorts will be of relevance to the explanation (the 'analysis') of such concepts.

In her perceptive review of Banes (2007), Renee Conroy (2008 p. 314b) urges that Banes's work generally (and her achievement in this book) teaches us that philosophical reflection "... can be productively and revealingly done with two bare feet planted firmly on the rosined floor of the dance studio". Implicitly, she contrasts that position favourably with a commitment to our armchairs and imaginations. Were this criticism aligned with her earlier suggestion of "... a shift of focus away from the abstract notion of 'the institution' (or 'the Republic of Dance') towards the visceral experiences of audience members" (Conroy, 2008 p. 314a), it might seem to bear on the position sketched here. But it does not. For the bare foot in question is a *dancer's* foot; and the audience's reactions are *to danceworks* or *dance performances*. These are facts crucial to what occurs in the cases Conroy mentions; but these are institutional facts.

§5. 'First art':an issue for institutionalism?

However, before addressing such cases directly, what might seem a special problem (concerning the dance equivalent of the Altamira cave-paintings) deserves some attention; one that seems to flow from any institutional account of art. In his book on the philosophy of music, Bob Sharpe (2004 p. 36) identifies, as one of the "... two difficulties ... that are most often aired" in respect of institutionalism, the problem of what he calls "first art" —

although both are introduced as problems for *proceduralism*, which (he says) "... differs little from what was previously called 'institutionalism'." (Sharpe, 2004 p. 36)[3].

Then Sharpe (2004 p. 37) identifies, as *'first art'* "... those artifacts that were created before anybody possessed anything like our concept of art". The expression "our concept of art" here just means *art* or *fine art* — the expression "our concept" is not here doing work; it is not as though the makers of the Altamira cave paintings (Sharpe's example: p. 37) had some *other* concept of art (but see below). Then, of these 'first art' cases, Sharpe (2004 p. 37) comments: "We count these as art ...".

Yet such a point need not simply be *accepted* in every case. For these objects do not suggest ways for a *current* artist to make art (except perhaps as kitsch). Putting aside a misconception of the 'first art' idea helps. It might seem that there *must* be a 'first art', a set of objects initially considered in the way artworks are: but how (on an institutionalist view) could that be? For what *institution* (what artworld or Republic of Art) licences *their* art-status? But that question arises from a misconception, like those involved in looking for language and pre-language, or asking how one can acquire the concepts concerning the external world needed for the experience that those concepts then mediate, if concept-acquisition has an experiential base. This is an example of what Wittgenstein rightly called trying "to go further back" (OC §471) than is possible. So the problem of 'first art' is not the problem of 'art prior to the artworld.'

Thus the 'first art' problem relates to objects arising (so anthropologists tell us) from societies lacking the concept *art*. Where this is the case, there seem two types of examples. For one type, the most common, we should accept that the objects are *not* art, despite their decorative appeal or their similarity to objects otherwise regarded as artworks (such as some frescos and murals). For such works, having no place in the narrative of art history, cannot imply strategies for contemporary art-making. This tough line is surely consistent with the thought (not dependent on institutionalism) that, in order to make art, one must *intend* to make art — although some peripheral cases might warrant reconsideration, such as sketches (not intended as art) but later seen as part of an artist's *oeuvre*. (The guiding thought here is a perfectly general one: that one is responsible for one's actions.) Relatedly, considerations of the *extent* of the object itself are imported: the painting is an artwork — hence that painting constitutes a single, complete 'thing' (not including the wall on which it hangs), as a pair of spectacles are one thing, divorced from the case containing them or the surroundings, despite their internal complexity. For cave paintings, something similar is done because (the thought seems to be) genuine *artworks* are typically circumscribed in roughly this way. So the cave paintings are treated like our art-painting: each is one 'object', but the other wall of cave is another, and so on. Yet such a view is not obviously correct: perhaps the makers of these objects considered the whole cave for their (ritual) purposes; or the whole cave including some of the surrounding area. Then these would delimit 'one thing'. Certainly there need be no reason to think that their makers viewed these objects, and even their limits, as we do. Without knowing what, for their makers, constituted a *unity* here, one cannot know what *the object* is! It makes sense to withhold (or deny) art-status to such cases.

The second type of example from societies lacking the concept *art* concerns objects treated as art *by extension* or *by convention*. These are highly *peculiar* cases of art; for instance, in lacking authors (and not just as when the author is unknown). Rather, since these objects were not made as art, there cannot be any artist as *author* of them. But deciding to treat them as art draws explicitly on (what we know of) the *past* of art: that is, on the institution. So, somehow, reference to the institution, the artworld as it were, is introduced.

It is clear, then, that no difficulties for institutionalism flow from either type of cases — respectively, the objects are either not art *really* (despite the words sometimes used of them) or are art only by extension from the current artworld.

However, we may be *unsure* as to the status of some other candidate 'first art' objects, since their function is not known, nor enough about the societies from which they originate to ensure that these societies do or do not have the concept *art*. What should be made of such cases? This is how Sharpe (2004 p. 37) initially treats 'first art': he says, "there is certainly no reason to suppose that ... [their creators] thought of them as 'works of art'"; but also no reason for confidence they did not. In this situation, anthropologists and historians may help, of course. Still, when that help is exhausted[4], two cases must be considered. If the most plausible 'reading' suggests that the relevant society *lacked* the concept *art*, the objects can be treated in either of the ways outlined previously (when we were *sure* the societies lacked the concept *art*): as *not* art, or as art-by-extension. And these pose no threat to institutionalism. But when that reading suggests there *was*, after all, a conception of *art* in the society, it implicitly acknowledges an artworld: hence it too is poses no threat to institutionalism.

So the 'first art' idea need generate no special problems here, even if one adopts a broadly institutional account of art. And that line of argument could sustain a similar conclusion for the 'first art' equivalent for dance: that is, for art-type dance. In this way, institutionalism concerning dance could be defended against what many think is its most fundamental objection.

Consider again. Suppose (with Sharpe, 2004 p. 37) that the Altamira cave paintings fit the bill of objects made in a society without the concept *art* — they were hunting magic of some kind, expressed in a decorative form, and hence not art; and the society which produced them lacked the concept *art*. (Let anthropologists have determined these facts.) Then, someone who claimed that these painters just lacked *our* concept of art would be mistaken. For that is where comparisons are drawn to find if the society had a concept of art; and our evidence includes the fact that such decorative objects have clear non-art purposes, uses or intentions. Now suppose a similar comment is made about, say, the North Indian dance form, Kathak: although insisting that Kathak is art, its advocates claim that the makers of these dances lacked *our* concept of art. Clearly, this issue is important: the artistic/aesthetic contrast, as we have drawn it (Chapter One §7), is fundamental throughout this text: in particular, in characterising the limits of the concept *art*, or what art is *not*. Could there be some *other* concept of art? To enter the debate here, one must first show that a concept of art was indeed at work in the society that produced Kathak — and a part of this demonstration might involve recognising its differences from its ancestor-form, Bharata Natyam. For Kathak was no longer an act of worship, was performed for an audience, was sharply distinguished from other kinds of physical activities: these would be the first steps in acknowledging Kathak as art. That it was, say, non-purposive, observed and regarded as meaningful would be the beginnings of an argument for its art-status, just because these are features of typical artworks. And the development (at a slightly later date) of a 'for-an-audience' version of Bharata Natyam might also be noted; as if the concept *art* was *then* being taken into this context as well. So this might constitute an argument for the art-status of Kathak. Such an argument might be disputed if, for instance, someone insisted that the meaning-bearing character of Kathak operated differently from meaning-bearing in, say, ballet. Then both the truth and the significance of this 'fact' could be discussed. Does it show that, after all, works in Kathak are not art (perhaps by highlighting a purposiveness)? Or that the range of meaning-bearing within art is greater than was first thought? Again, a contrast with *our* concept of art makes no sense. Debate here is within the concept *art*, exploring its features; and could include kinds of public relations exercises to reshape that concept. But these places for contestation are within a shared framework: in this, they resemble the debates of detail among evolutionary biologists — the framework is not contested.

Of course, my view makes art perhaps less important in human life than it is on some other views; many humanly-valuable activities have nothing to do with art. Thus, suppose I make an anthropological voyage, living with a number of groups of people very different from my Western European background. As a result of my experiences, I return with two objects made as part of my participation in those societies: first, a text written on the basis of some experiences in a kind of sweat lodge — this resembles a short story; and, second, an elaborately decorated penis cover. These objects should just be recognised as having the significance, or value, that each had in the societies from which they originated. I made them both; but neither is an art-object. If I display them on my wall, that might be an appeal to their aesthetic properties — and those aesthetic properties might be fundamental to their proper functioning in those societies. But why should they be called "art"? Or thought of as art even by comparison with, say, my 'Sunday painter' daubs — or my poems — which (on a good day) just sneak into the *fine art* category? I see no basis for disputing the non-art status of these objects, even though these were made by someone who (*ex hypothesi*) understands the concept *art*; or at least comes from a culture having such a concept.

§6. But, still, is it *really* dance?

Still, much turns on the narrative of art-history in the relevant art form (here, dance). Sally Banes (2007 p. 110 — originally 1984) notes that, since:

> ... so many of the rules for doing, watching, and understanding dance were broken — or at least tested — in the 1960s ... to group ... current hybrids as falling outside of dance seems like beating a dead horse.

Of course, the title alone of this interesting piece ("Nearly Sort of Not Dance Maybe": quoted at the beginning of §2 above) makes a point: it may be impossible to resolve the question of whether a work is indeed dance — it may honestly be, as Banes titles the piece, *Nearly Sort of Not Dance Maybe*: as I unpack it, this ends up meaning that the work is *probably* dance (or dance-ish).

Her point is that our *confidence* in what is (definitely) *not* dance cannot be strong in a climate that rejected so much that *had* been taken-for-granted in works in (or, anyway, close to) the mainstream of dance. Thus a favourite ballet of mine, the Mats Ek *Swan Lake* (1987) includes vocal sounds by the dancers — "OK (one can imagine some purist urging), vocal sound but no speech". But immediately counter-cases to these general theses come to mind. Thus *Strange Fish* (1992), by DV8: Physical Theatre, included speech; at the time, that was about as mainstream as one got in dance in the UK. Further, it might be claimed that dances *never* follow slavishly the structure of music — except, of course, that this is exactly what happens in some major works of Mark Morris, such as the second movement of his *L'Allegro, il Penseroso et il Moderato* (1988) to a Handel oratorio of the same name[5]. As Joan Acocella (1993 p. 241) puts it, "When the music runs, plods, skips, sweeps, glides, meanders, so do the dancers". Further, Banes seems to be describing the dancer at a particular moment. Of course, the movement training for highly skilled dancers is no longer regarded in quite the same way[6]: it has come to seem necessarily more *varied*. For a dancer looking for work, the varied training must be an advantage. But then, in one way, more can be demanded of the dancers — say, that they are athletes to "Olympic-standard" (Mackrell, 1997 p. 7). Yet, in another way, the expressiveness and technical aesthetic of, say, Graham technique cannot be demanded: for it would be unrealistic to look for such expressiveness (say) across the board, in all the techniques of which our typical dancer is 'master'. Thus it must be taught 'as one goes along' — but not so as to disadvantage the dancer's getting the *next* job, with its *different* technical requirements.

So at least two of the *traditional* ways of understanding the characteristics of dance are no longer satisfactory: namely, in terms of characteristic movements or characteristic training — the sorts of thing large permanent companies can foster. But we get by quite well without these props to our understanding. Here I offer four thoughts. First, one can become good at recognising the intention of both *dancer* and *choreographer* (which, recall, is *embodied* in the dance) by looking at a lot of dance, discussing it with other concerned parties, or perhaps reading criticism. Hence one can see when those intentions run counter to dance as such — as they might in a gala offering nothing but virtuosity and physical prowess. Second, the niceties here concern us less: if vocal sound, or speaking, *precludes* this work being dance, well ... so much the worse for "... the extremely narrow definition of dance ... [that is] being proposed" (Banes, 2007 p. 112: I prefer "account" to "definition"[7]). Such 'works' are watched as something else! So one is not left at a loss as to how to make sense of the work under consideration: for lots of other works 'break' whatever narrow rule was under consideration.

A third thought insists that, although of course granting art-status to a work — here, dance-status — is minimally evaluative ("At least it is an artwork"), typically nothing *more* than this very minimal sense is suggested. At any time, most of the art produced is bad; and some of it is *so* bad as to be *barely* art — or, even, in some instances beyond that particular pale. Thus, taking this work into our (broad) canon is not granting a lot: in particular, its place is not in our more narrowly evaluative canon of masterworks. And the constitution even of that canon is a moveable feast: the place and importance of works may change over time.

Then, fourth, one cannot begin from a fixed number of art forms: so this *might* be, not dance exactly, but a genuinely new hybrid form (as Chapter Four §6 suggested treating certain primarily moving-image artworks as something other than the kinds of dance being talked about): hence, as something other than (typical) dance. But that was never meant to deny their similarity to dance; nor their art-status; nor, again, their *relation* to dances — and especially perhaps when thinking about the evaluation of such works.

This bridge leads neatly to two ideas from Danto. The first, new here, recognises the *institutional force* of, say, a critic being asked to review a particular exhibition (or performance): that, in a typical case, a large number of people are already involved in the thought that this exhibition (or performance) is not time-wasting for those knowledgeable in the appropriate art form. For reference to both self-election and other-acclamation (see §4 above: AJ pp. 149-150) can mistakenly seem the province of a small number of individuals. In exemplification, I interpolate — with some commentary — a longish passage which reflects the *practice* in the artworld. Primarily wearing his critic's 'hat', Danto describes the situation as he encounters it; thereby highlighting the nature of the Republic of Art as the art critic encounters it.

Initially he reminds us that the art critic's judgement of the quality of a work will be "... based on a lot of data, much of it connected with institutional factors" (Danto, 2005 p. 356). In explanation, he continues:

> One primarily reviews exhibitions, and the fact that an artist's work has been selected for a museum exhibition, for example, is evidence that a number of individuals, who have undergone training and acquired the experience that entitle them to make such decisions, have come to the shared conclusion that the work merits display and that the public will benefit in various ways by seeing the work in this format. (Danto, 2005 p. 356)

Hence the work has been 'other acclaimed' by the Republic of Art. But notice how tentative this is: Danto calls its position in the exhibition "evidence" — the relation here is recognised as defeasible; and therefore *prima facie* a basis for the conclusion, but not any more (nor any less) than that. Further, Danto embraces the minimal evaluative (or normative) force of this 'decision', again defeasibly: it implies that the work will be of benefit to its audience in broadly (some of) the ways artworks are. For all this to be true, as Danto (2005 p. 356) continues:

> The work will have made its way somehow into the consciousness of the art world, and a consensus will have emerged as to where it stands and what it does. The art world is defined by an ongoing conversation — a

dialogue — among its members, who know something about the history of art and the present state of art, and the concept of quality is connected with the work having become part of this conversation.

Although no explicit "consensus" should be looked for here, it makes plain that the work has transferred into the 'collective consciousness' of that artworld. Further, the sense of a conversation here catches exactly what is wrong with the idea of a (hard-and-fast) consensus. But such a conversation is not, or necessarily, *merely* open-ended — we should remind ourselves here of the connection of the idea of *dialogue* with that of *logic*. Then, as Danto (2005 pp. 356-357) continues:

> The latter [that is, this 'conversation'] will convey the reasons people are talking about it, and these in turn give the critic a reason for wanting to see the work and to enter the conversation through writing a review. The reasons vary from artist to artist and time to time.

Here one sees, from a critic's point of view and with the due speed of a real-world practice, what — from philosophy's perspective — makes the introduction of a critical vocabulary an accompaniment to the acquisition of art status. But also see that the 'vocabulary' thereby provided is typically occasion-sensitive, both to the critic's concerns and to the "lay of the artworld" (Carroll, 2001 p. 91): so there is variation in the reasons operative here both between critics and from "time to time".

So that one is a kind of *informal* critic of those art forms (and sub-forms) with which we have any concerted engagement (at least). Hence, one does not come to them completely *cold*. That returns us — as a second point from Danto — to his comments on the de Kooning three-seater (see §3 above): that it *could not* be a de Kooning; and hence *could not* be an artwork. The argument there involved locating the work in its history and tradition, where one could. So these ideas are reinforced. While one should not be *too* prescriptive here, two thoughts from this text should give comfort. The first is the epistemic force of Carnap's *principle of total evidence* (see Chapter Five §9) — so that in favoured cases one must assume that there is no missing 'evidence'[8] for our judgement or appreciation of a work. Thus, for de Kooning, my intuitions agree with Danto's (and with the result of fifty years of art history): the three-seater could *never* be a 1954 de Kooning. But were we wrong about the material that could provide (relevant) 'evidence' for some (revised) judgement, the principle of total evidence sanctions our being wrong — and permits the revision of the judgement in the light of new (and relevant) 'evidence'. It was a defeasible judgement, with a failure of the total-evidence condition as one of the heads of exception. Yet that principle also applies when the case under consideration is *not* one where the kind of certainty postulated initially was possible. Instead, beginning from doubts about the comprehensiveness of our 'evidence', the principle precludes our coming to any *firm* conclusion — we have *grounded* doubt in this very case. While there seems no such basis in the case of the three-seater, our way is clear; but if some basis for doubt appears, that too is accommodated into our position in a straightforward way.

On the other hand (and our second thought: see §3 above), revising much of the history of de Kooning here would revise much of the history of Western art as we presently have it. Quite a lot would be required to make that seem either likely or attractive. But it is not impossible. So the kind of radical revision sketched above might take place. Its doing so would revise lots of the conceptual connections presently taken for granted when one comes to consider, not just de Kooning, but almost *anything* in Western visual art since that time (and both "Western" and "visual" are included as hedges only). Yet, *were* such a revision achieved, conceptual connections would still be drawn here: the past of de Kooning *plus* the innovation initiated by the three-seater would imply a kind of unity.

To apply these thoughts, perhaps the abstract resources here are sufficient to describe the complexity of the case. So that avant-garde works of art would not be the kinds of "... isolated objects" (Danto, 1987 p. 60) where one does not know what to say. Rather, one can imagine making the *argument* that they resemble such-and-such sufficiently that one can make sense of (or, more fundamentally, evaluate) one of them by drawing on (an interpretation of) criteria appropriate to the other.

The upshot, of course, is just that there is no single, abstract and general answer here: to look case-by-case, and share our conclusions (thereby *testing* those conclusions) with the ideas of others is to engage with the institutional debate around the *new* works. So the *art-status* and *artistic value* of such works can be considered, even where (at the most extreme) a radical revision of the narrative of art-history is at issue. Further, most works will not be so radically avant-garde as to pose these problems for us. Still, when they are, this work suggests that intellectual resources suitable to dealing with them are available. And *that* conclusion (suitably modified to context) has been our target throughout much of this text.

§7.   Conclusion

As noted initially, some issues for the philosophical aesthetics of dance are really issues for philosophical aesthetics more generally. Of course, a great many of those issues, although bearing on the aesthetics of dance, are not broached by this work (some of them *are* broached in UD); and a great many places here where a problem or issue is raised and either postponed or simply left as an issue. These cannot typically be completely and conclusively resolved here. (Our contextualism precludes it!) So one should not overrate what this text *attempts* (before coming to what it achieves). But the majority of issues for the aesthetics of dance that are specific to dance are addressed here.

At its heart are commitments to the importance of questions of dance-identity (or 'same-work' continuity); and to the place of the choreographer (and hence of the context) in the resolution of such questions in practice. Moreover, it inherits (from UD) commitments to a potential role for notationality in dance-identity, and to a type-token analysis of the character of danceworks. I hope in these ways to have better explained my earlier account and to have elaborated it. But one constraint on such elaboration was to see its connection back to the practice of dancers, of choreographers, and of the stagers of dances — as well as dance critics. For one part of my concern here is to explain why (by-and-large) the practices of the danceworld are justifiable; and, indeed, justified!

However, these conclusion rest ultimately on a view of the project of philosophy (not fully articulated here) which others may not share. My response has been partly to show the virtues of this conception in practice, offering (as it were) to "... demonstrate a method, by examples" (PI §133); partly to include some methodological comments, especially those in relation to *defeasibility* and to the role of a *principle of total evidence* in our argumentation; and partly to stress my opposition to assumptions (within philosophy) of the need for, or virtues of, exceptionlessness (see also EKT pp. 177-193). Yet, throughout, the aim has been to provide only as much on these topics as one needs to pursue the conclusions in respect of our understanding of the character of danceworks.

§8. And finally

It has been put to me that this text fails to accurately reflect the danceworld in at least one crucial way: that many dancers, choreographers, and dance critics adopt the account of dance (as *text*) that I have rejected out of hand (in Chapter Five §3; Chapter Nine §8). Hence, this is not a case of philosophy leaving "everything as it is " (PI §124), as urged in Chapter One. (This objection has been phrased to me as reflecting badly my commitment to 'analytic philosophy'.)

A full reply would require detailed description of the varieties within the *dance as text* idea: in their most extreme forms, those (characterised in Chapter Five) which begin by denying the category of literature because there is *just* language should be contrasted with those which stress the importance of central human practices, while still denying authorship. (The first group typically take Derrida as hero, the second group typically take Bourdieu.) But neither recognises the radical contextualism imported into the philosophy of language (and of thought and meaning) by acknowledging *occasion-sensitivity* (Travis, 2008; AJ pp. 36-44). And, once that is granted, my reservations about the claims of *dance as text* become clear.

First, I doubt that this view is held as widely as is supposed, at least if *holding* the view requires understanding (and accepting) its ontology, and its methodological under-pinnings. Indeed, I am confident that most of the danceworld accepts the 'default' ontology in which one performs a particular dancework (say, *Swan Lake*) on Tuesday and Wednesday; on which this performance of *Swan Lake* is better than that one (for reasons one might share); and on which a particular rehearsal 'informs' a whole week's performances. At its heart, this is the 'ontology' of *performables* — of a dancework performed on more than one occasion. And all this must be given up if one seriously treats dances as *texts*.

Second, and relatedly, I doubt that most of that danceworld has the slightest interest in the underlying theory. In particular, it is hard to find really clear elaboration of that account of language which undermines the distinctive possibility of literature. So I doubt these are widely read. And, even then, I doubt the palatability to the danceworld of the implication of such a view — the implication that there really is nothing interesting or distinctive about *dances*, in contrast to other movement patterns! At the least, I see no need for the danceworld to be thus engaging itself with theory from philosophy. For Roger Taylor (1981 p. 121):

> ... Yeats was right in thinking that the less academic one's mind, the more easily and fully one could allow oneself to flow into dance activity.

Although this seems quite wrong, I would accept that — for many people — the time and energy taken to be a dancer will predispose one away from some kinds of book-based academic study. Further, that being a dancer or choreographer cannot *require* that one study, say, philosophy in these ways.

Third, and amid these doubts, I am not opposed to some 'rational reconstruction' of the views of others. For instance, I was keen to insist earlier that — whatever she thought she was saying — Deborah Hay did not think that her whole life actually *was* a dance: so any of her words seeming to offer that view require 'rational reconstruction'. And a similar tack might be taken with pronouncements which seem to support the thesis of *dance as text*. But that is legitimate work for philosophy, to un-puzzle those who (hearing what, for instance, Hay said) were rightly puzzled. And this work operates in that spirit.

Appendix

Technical Matters for Type-token Ontology

§1. Introduction: the place for ontology?

Perhaps my head does not lie with ontology, to adapt a comment on Descartes from Hobbes, as reported by John Aubrey (1982 p. 161[1]). At the least, I require that ontological investigations of art forms should have some pay-off by offering insight into those art forms. Thus, for me, an ontological structure which makes most of our claims about such art forms false, useless or radically confusing should be rejected for that reason. If that means that I do not investigate the ontology of dance, ... well, so much the worse for dance ontology (I would say). For Bertrand Russell (1912 pp. 93-94), it came as a surprise that "... hardly anybody except students of philosophy ever realises that there are such entities as universals." But that is precisely to assume the accuracy (indeed, the primacy) of the philosophising. And that is both far from obviously right in *every* case and in need of argument.

That rant is brought to bear when one considers how to characterise the status of dance as a multiple-art or performing-art. Clearly, the dancework itself (say, *Swan Lake*) must be discussed as well as this or that performance of it — and other kinds of comments *may* be needed too. But these at least *seem* to reflect the ontology of dance. So, in Chapter Two, the virtue of a type-token way of speaking is urged, while recording that this way of presenting the matter had consequences not always recognised (UD pp. 91-91). Such moves seem to introduce a Platonist element, "... assuming one wants to construe types Platonistically at all" (Kivy, 1993 pp. 35-36). Of course, I do not want to do that, as my discussion in Chapter Two (§9) illustrates. To expand my rejection, I will comment on a sustained attempts to describe (and explain) the type-token contrast: namely, Julian Dodd's book *Works of Music* — a view that occasioned the rant in the previous paragraph!

As we shall see, the 'half-time score' is that finding Dodd is right about what types *must* be (and, in particular, that they must be property-less and eternal: see below) would be a refutation of my claims that danceworks — indeed, any artworks — could be type-token objects. But the remarks on Dodd's position here use his comments on *musical* ontology as a foil for my investigation of *dance* ontology, leaving aside how (if at all) any of my points could, would, or should be applied to music.

§2. Dodd's theory

What are the constituents of Dodd's theory? Outlining the main features of Platonic Objects on his view, Dodd (2007 p. 80) identifies types as "... abstract, unstructured, unchanging and eternally existent entities". We will focus on two of these, as the most problematic:

- "unstructured" — they are part- or property-less; but dances (and musical works) *seem* to bear properties (to be witty, say) and to have parts.

- "eternal" — they are timeless; but dances (and musical works) *seem* to have been made at a particular time, and hence to exist after that time but not before.

Interestingly, given my preoccupations, Dodd raises the issue of 'understanding' in respect of music. Even though "... we should not assimilate ... understanding [of musical works] to the understanding of a sentence" (Dodd, 2007 p. 136), a connection between meaning and understanding should still be recognised, at least once we recognise (and put aside, as not relevant here) that the term "understand" has other senses (relating to causal structure). For the cracks in the wall not only *do not* spell-out my loved one's name, they *cannot* do so: if they appear to do so, this is an illusion. They do not *mean* anything (except symptomatically): therefore they cannot be understood (nor misunderstood). So my view rules out the idea of 'naturally occurring music' — however attractive, the naturally occurring sounds cannot really be *music*; instead, I take meaning and understanding to be correlative. But this in turn directs us to see the *understandable* object as an intended object.

Against this view, Dodd (2007 p. 137) offers a comparison with found art:

> ... in the case of a work of found art, the mere fact that the artist makes choices in selecting it does not entail that it is created by her. Such things existed already. So it no more follows in the case of music either. The composer's choices lead him to uncover a pre-existent work ...

This passage contains a number of problematic ideas: one is, "[s]uch things existed already". For the point is precisely that, while the driftwood existed already, driftwood *artworks* did not. Second, the argument here appears weak — it amounts to urging that, since *some* artworks (of the 'particular object' kind) can be 'found objects', then *all* artworks of a quite different, multiple kind are too (or, even, might be too). If not plainly a non-sequitur, that is not plainly a sequitur! It stretches too far Dodd's claim that, "... according the Platonist, [works of music] are akin to found art" (Dodd, 2007 p. 137): the kinship does not appear that great. Third, one might think this a weakening of Dodd's case: that musical works are *like* found art in this respect seems odd, since found art is often contentious, towards the boundaries of the concept *art* as we understand it, while music is not — no one would think that all art aspires to the condition of found art!

This case is revealing, but not in the way Dodd hopes. For what distinguishes the art-driftwood from other piece of driftwood on the beach? This is in fact a "confusable counterpart" (Danto, 1981 p. 138); Chapter One 7) for such pieces. Only the art-driftwood is a suitable candidate for the kind of understanding which goes beyond looking to the causal story. If this were correct, of course, the parallel case to music would be that, even if the sound-sequence was eternal (perhaps), the musical work was not. For, on the analogy, the musical work would correspond to the driftwood *once selected*: it would have kinds of properties not shared by its non-art cousins. (Of course, Dodd would reject this version by flourishing the other main thesis of his account, his sonicism [see below]; but this just begs the question if — as Dodd urges initially — both matters are up for debate.)

§3. Two key questions?

As Dodd makes plain, his book in effect develops two key theses, reflecting his answers to two key questions:

- *the categorial question*: the issue of "which ontological category music belongs to" (Dodd, 2007 p. 1); to which Dodd responds with the type-token contrast — music works are types.

- *the individuation question*: requiring "an account of the identity conditions of musical works" (Dodd, 2007 p. 1); to which Dodd's answer is *(timbral) sonicism*.

As Sharpe (2004 p. 63) suggests, "... the motivation [to think that musical works exist eternally] is to do with the notion of music being essentially some sort of pattern of notes, or structure of sounds ...". Thus, given that musical works are sound-structures (given the "sonicism"), it seems to follow those very sound-structures — and hence those musical works (for Dodd) — could occur divorced from the contexts in which, for the rest of us, they regularly occur. Thus, that the sound-sequence that is a particular Mozart symphony could come about from the wind moving through the reeds on the planet Zog two hundred years before Mozart's birth. Were this correct, the ontological status of musical works must be explained fairly carefully, as we will already know they are frankly *weird* objects.

But suppose Dodd's two questions are asked in the reverse order — ask first if musical works really are just sonic structures, and one surely comes to a different result: for surely musical works are composed (that seems, at first blush, a fact about them). And, on this common sense view, Danto-esque "confusable counterparts" (Danto, 1981 p. 139) are readily imaginable: that is, objects (say, sound-structures) we can *mistake* for musical works. The easiest cases involve the wind passing through the trees in 1700 — this *cannot* be so-and-so flute sonata, for two reasons: first, since the work was designed, or intended, any naturally occurring event *cannot* be that work. So, at best, this would *sound like* the sonata. Second, since the sonata was designed, or intended, in 1800, and drew on musical conventions from that time, any "sonic events" prior to that date are not that work — at best (or, maybe, at worst) they merely *sound like* it. These seem the sorts of starting points that would be persuasive if one had no prior ontological axe to grind; and also preclude one taking the route Dodd takes, at least initially. (Surely almost *any* alternative should be explored before one comes to Platonism — although, as we will see, this is not Dodd's view. Rather, he takes Platonism as a "face-value theory": Dodd, 2007 p. 31.)

One feature of the argumentative strategy here is worth highlighting. For, although Dodd (2007 p. 3) grants that " ... neither the ontological nature of types, nor the nature of the relation they bear to tokens, is well understood", he also claims that the type-token contrast is familiar. Why? Because *words* function in this type-token way (Dodd, 2007 p. 43; and see p. 38 for a list a "familiar" type-token kinds): although I *use* the particular token-word on a particular occasion, I must grant both that *the word* pre-existed my use of it (compare Cavell, 1981 p. 64), and that *the word* in this sense is an abstract object — a type. This familiarity explains, for Dodd, why his view should be taken as "the default position" (Dodd, 2007 p. 5; Caplan, 2007 p. 445): that is, "... the account that is *prima facie* correct and must be accepted as long as it is not defeated" (Dodd, 2007 p. 8). This, we are told, is "the face-value theory" (Dodd, 2007 p. 31); and, as we noted, Dodd (2007 p. 204) explicitly takes his other position, sonicism, as "the default position".

One difficulty here is that this case is nothing like so clear: words do not *obviously* have the features Dodd ascribes to types. Thus, Wollheim[2] (see also Dodd, 2007 p. 45; p. 85) is implicitly criticised for saying that types can be brought into being — Wollheim (1973 p. 357-358) actually claims that one can make a type either by making a token or by making a recipe, such as a score for a musical work: in any case, he accepts that types can be made, and hence they have a beginning in time, a 'start-date'! But that is exactly how most of us regard words: we think that the (unlikely) term "supercalifragilisticexpialidocious" [or how ever one spells it] was invented at a particular date. Moreover, study of the history of languages offers a rough date for the beginning of modern English: again, a 'start-date'. So one might think, if one must begin from intuitively plausible accounts of word-meaning, words (as types) can be created; and do seem to have proper parts (namely, letters).

We can return to these ideas once Dodd's own picture is sketched. Recall that Dodd (2007 p. 80) identifies types as "... abstract, unstructured, unchanging and eternally existent entities". We decided to focus on the claims that they were "unstructured" (that is, part/property-less) and "eternally existent" (that is, timeless). Let us comment on each in turn.

With respect to properties, Dodd (2007 p. 45) begins his assault by commenting critically on Wollheim's introduction of this type-token language into philosophical aesthetics, where Wollheim develops the features of the type-token relation (rightly attributed to Peirce[3]) by discussing the relation of the Union Jack to the specific Union Jacks flying over the town hall, on the cricket pavilion, and so on: the first is a *type* while the others are *tokens* of that type[4]. But, as Dodd (2007 p. 45) points out, the *abstract object* that is the type cannot (at first blush, at least) have properties like, say, colour — just as the horse I ask you to imagine need be of no particular colour, although all extant horses are of some colour or combination of them. This suggests that the types cannot *share* their properties with tokens since, taken strictly, the types *have* no such properties. Thus, the claim, "the Polar Bear has four legs" seems obviously true; say, in contrast to the claim that polar bears have one hundred legs. But *the Polar Bear*, the type, must be instantiated in all polar bears — those with three legs, as well as those with four. Moreover, the four-leggedness of the Polar Bear might suggest that, say, one of its legs could constitute a part of it; but it is an *abstract* object, and that seems to mean that it will not have spatial relations, of the kind parts seem to require. Then, as Dodd (2007 p. 47) points out, much that we say about types will be false — especially when we attribute properties to them.

Were this true of the type-token relation, and automatically "... shared by *all* types" (Dodd, 2007 p. 80: his emphasis), that might give us pause, as above, before that relation was used to explain how an artwork of the appropriate multiple kind (say, a dancework or musical work) relates to its performances. Indeed, the case might be even more perplexing for cast sculpture: surely it is not just the *tokens* of Rodin's *Burghers of Calais* that are bronze — surely the work itself is bronze! (A version in plastic, for example, would surely not count as *that work*.)

But on the face of it, our standard examples, used to explain the notion of a type, have proper parts or can be ascribed properties — the colours of flags, the letters comprising words, the movements of musical works. How should one understand the claim, "The Polar Bear has four legs" (Dodd 2007 p. 47)? Certainly not as a claim about all (extant) polar bears — in some way, it is a claim about an *abstract object*; and, moreover, one which functions as a norm-kind (in jargon from Wolterstorff, 1980 pp. 54-58). Still, what we want to say — in saying that the Polar Bear has four legs — is still true. But, as we saw, ascription of legs (or parts more generally) seems to make sense only when understood spatially. Since abstract objects are not in these ways spatial, this claim cannot be ascribing real properties. Or so it seems. So some other way must be found to characterise what is going on. To save the intuitive plausibility of his contention, Dodd distinguishes the way the tokens have properties from the possibility of *predicates* applying to the type: "It is not that types and their tokens can share the same *properties*, but that they can share the same *predicates* ..." (Dodd, 2007 p. 46). For "... our pre-theoretical intuitions are trumped ... by mature philosophical theory" (Dodd, 2007 p. 86). So these cases should be viewed as the sharing of predicates only. And what goes for spatial parts goes for temporal ones also.

But what are *predicates* here, if not ascriptions of properties? A revealing discussion in Goodman (1979 p. 347), begins:

> ... the English language makes ... [objects] white just by applying the term "white" to them; application of the term "white" is not dictated by their being antecedently white, whatever that might mean.

But then they *are* white. In reply, Dodd (2007 p. 46) recognises such uses of terms as 'analogical predication', such that "predicates ... when applied to types, express properties that are *systematically related* to properties expressed by those predicates when applied to their tokens." The difficulty lies in seeing this as a solution here; or, to put it another way, as "... mature philosophical theory". For does it really explain to us what is going on in these cases?

One problem is to read, "The Polar Bear has four legs", so that what it says is true of the abstract object that is the Polar Bear — one did not mean this or that polar bear, nor *all* polar bears, nor *some*[5]. And if it is true (as it is) that the Polar Bear has four legs, then it seems odd to *deny* that the Polar Bear has parts. To deny the very *possibility* here is not something one just comes to. Instead, this is the *imposition* of a philosophical theory (yet to be judged for maturity!). The upshot of the theory involves insisting that the truth of, "The Polar Bear has four legs", is ensured by treating the expression "has four legs" applied to the type *differently* than one would in urging that Peter the polar bear has four legs (although his cousin Janice only has three — as the result of an injury). That may well be alright, although there seems a strong connection here between what one truly says of the type and of its token, Peter; a connection to be explained. Dodd takes the further step of insisting that this means that it is *false* that *the Polar Bear has parts* — when of course, we all agree that the Polar Bear has legs, ears, eyes and such like! So the difference claimed here is nothing like as compelling as Dodd makes it seem. And it does not help to be told that appeal to analogical predication is "... the only way of solving the puzzle" (Dodd, 2007 p. 46): that should just encourage us to look for ways of not embracing such a 'puzzle'!

Further, in general, words have proper parts — letters: but Dodd assures us that *types* cannot have parts. His assurance that "... all predications of structure to tokens and types fall under the doctrine of analogical predication" (Dodd, 2007 p. 51) does little to give one confidence on that point. For the whole idea of 'analogical predication' seems just an *ad hoc* way to solve the 'puzzle' by speaking *as if* abstract objects could have justly applied to them predicates indicative of spatial or temporal relations, while at the same time urging that such predication is not *literal* — that the objects necessarily lack these properties.

The situation seems yet worse if one turns to flags (one of Wollheim's preferred examples of the type-token relation): they seem to have properties, such that the Union Flag is red, white and blue, for example. Now, badly faded flags, and flags damaged by gunfire, for instance, present complications to this case. Still, the temptation must be to say that it is the redness here, the blueness there, and so on, that makes this the Union Flag. And the point would be stronger if we consider, say, the tricolours of France and the Irish Republic. Now ask: how do those flags differ? The answer, from the point of view of common sense, must be that these two flags differ only in their colours. Or so it appears. Now it seems very odd to follow Wolterstorff (1980 pp. 61-62) in taking this to be only quasi-predication (he calls it "analogical predication: see Dodd, 2007 p. 4), since it *seems* to define these as the objects they are. For what was not a tricolour in these colours would not be the French flag.

Of course, Dodd (2007 pp. 31-31) has rightly emphasised that our *types* have a normative force here: they suggest what should happen in order that, say, *Black Angels* be danced — this is the sense in which they are norm-kinds. But, for that reason, Dodd (2007 p. 249 + note 6) denies that claims about the individuation of works entail claims about the essential properties of those works: is this just a problem with *entailment* here? Or with the idea of *essential* properties? Perhaps Dodd would run the thesis even in a weaker version; say, where both issues were treated defeasibly. He only claims that "[q]uestions concerning the individuation of entities are *distinct* from questions concerning their essences ..." (Dodd, 2007 p. 249 note 6: my emphasis — see also Dodd, 2007 p. 31). So perhaps no features of a flag, say, are truly *essential*, such that no counter-case could be imagined (once we see our flag as very badly tattered by gunfire, very badly faded by the sun, and so on). But the type here still constrains its tokens, even if in ways we cannot specify. That is all the term "define" above required. For Dodd (2007 pp. 46-47), formulae such that "is coloured in such-and-such a way" should be 'translated' for analogical predications (roughly) as *being such that its tokens will be coloured in such-and-such a way*. These devices seem merely arbitrary, *ad hoc* introductions to preserve the theory. For what could it be for the type to be such that its tokens should be coloured in such-and-such a way? That thought would certainly be expressible by calling the type "coloured". And it might be strengthened by recalling that at least *some* properties — such as colours — are *sometimes* regarded as powers the objects have. For then the redness of the pillar-box depends in part on the possibility of our response.

§4. Made or discovered?

Let us turn to the second of Dodd's characteristics of types — that they are timeless, or eternal[6]. As Dodd (2007 p. 99) recognises, the big issue will be creation, for the thought seems to be that what is abstract is therefore timeless. Hence, a composer "... did not create the piece: he could only have discovered it" (Dodd, 2007 p. 112).

But can one *create* an abstract object? First, I do not see why not; and, second, if not, where would this leave variants? For commonsense suggests that Beethoven can *change* his work; where this is not the discovery of another work, merely a note or two different. Thus, asked what he has been doing all day, Beethoven can correctly say that he has been *refining* the passages he wrote in the morning; on Dodd's view, if speaking exactly, he should say that he has been discovering new, and slightly different, works all day (at least once the changes are sizeable). So although Beethoven's *Fifth Symphony* 'exists' (at least in some sense), it both replaced (by becoming) the 'work' Beethoven was doing prior to his finishing it (in the sense in which he did); and somehow permits variants, while excluding (as works in their own right) all the possible 'minor differences (of sufficient sizes)' one can imagine. Of course, this formulation is pretty inexact.

With respect to these points about variants, one strategy here would point out how full Dodd's world is — it comprises all the works composers and choreographers will in fact "compose" (as we ordinarily think of it), but also all the ones they might. Moreover, it embraces all the one-note-wrong, or one-step-wrong, versions; and so on. Indeed, we should return to the linguistic case. Since uttered sentences are (for Peirce at least) tokens of a type, Dodd's conclusion means that his linguistic world is replete with all those sentences which Chomsky locates with his talk of *creativity* (Lyons, 1970 p. 86); that is, the ones not yet heard, but good English — and recognisable as such — when or if uttered. Further, were Dodd correct,

(Chomskian) *creativity* would need to be re-characterised — since, on this view, there could be no new sentences, but only new token-sentences[7]. So Chomskian creativity would become simply the ability to recognise as grammatical *new-to-us* sentences. That is before one comes to 'sentences' which fail some grammatical test. But one need not think all sentences (or all statements) are existing prior to any assertion to explain this (human) capacity[8]. Nor need the musical universe be treated as so replete.

Moreover, the difficulty about the constraints on composition is compounded when Dodd disputes a claim (by Kivy, 1993 pp. 70-71) that Archimedes could not have discovered Newton's gravitational laws: that this happen merely requires, for Dodd (2007 p. 125), that "... *the history of science up until the time of his discovery would have to have been different*" (his italics). And that is not impossible: it just means "... that possible worlds in which Archimedes discovers Newton's gravitational laws are *distant* ... But there is no sound reason to suppose that such worlds do not exist" (Dodd, 2007 p. 125: his italics). In what sense of the term "exist" do such worlds exist? As Kripke ([1972] 1980 p. 44) warned, "[a] possible world isn't a distant country we are coming across, or viewing through a telescope. ... 'Possible worlds' are *stipulated*, not *discovered* by powerful telescopes." Now the sense in which musical works are *extant* is unclear: do they exist only as possible worlds exist? Were this correct, then our universe is suddenly full of possible worlds as well as (possible?) musical works.

That returns us to the objection to creating 'eternals'; or, better, to the temporal character of creation. Here Grice (1986 p. 90) offers a related example. He imagines that:

> [m]y next novel will have as its hero one Casper Winebibber, a notorious English highwayman born (or so I shall say) in 1764 and hanged in 1798, thereby ceasing to exist long before sometime next year, when I create (or construct) him.

This might seem puzzling — as though a character created in 1985 died almost two hundred years before. But there is really no puzzle:

> This mind boggling situation will be dissolved if we distinguish between two different occurrences: *first*, Caspar's birth (or death) which is dated to 1764 (or 1798), and *second*, my creation of Caspar, that is to say my making it in 1985 fictionally true that Caspar was born in 1764 and died in 1798. (Grice, 1986 p. 90: original italics)

In this case, his (direct) creation of Casper is consistent with Casper's having temporally-specific properties (such as those relating to his birth and death) in conflict with those we attribute via Grice's act of creation.

So, *when* was it true that Casper was born in 1764? In one way, this was not determinably true until (as we are imagining) Grice wrote the book in 1985. Before that, there were no *facts* about Casper to determine. But once Grice creates the novel (and, with it, the character) things are timelessly true of Casper. So we might even think it true in the fourth century BC that Casper will be born in 1764. And that case only becomes problematic when our time-machine returns us to the fourth century BC. For there seem special problems about truth for future conditionals in fictional cases.

The moral from Grice's case: what is *identified* at a particular time can thereby be identified as timelessly true prior to that time. These are features of the process of creation here — that is, they are among the sorts of things our actions can create. Grice's point can be extended: he creates tensed truths about Casper, but ones which precede Casper's real creation in 1985. Our thought was just that creation at a point in time could also create what was, in effect, timeless; hence would be available in principle prior to its own creation. But this would be a kind of illusion: the act of creation here *creates* a timeless object!

For music, and perhaps for dance, one need only to expand this point: that the music, once created, is timeless turns out not after all incompatible with its being created at a particular time. Is it *eternal*? Once it is created, there are time-free facts about it — such as its structure — which could explain why, hearing about the sound-sequence that occurred on the planet Zog, we might indeed call it "Mozart's symphony". And why we might be right so to do. The fact that this sonic event preceded Mozart's birth by two hundred years would simply not be to the point! We are 'looking back' at the event. Moreover, we have a reason to call the sonic event *Mozart's* symphony, since that identification is post-Mozart.

With respect to the possibility of making abstract objects, then, why not take Wollheim's remarks at face-value? There are two main points here. First, Wollheim (1980 §§35-37) is *explaining* the kinds of abstract objects *types* are — and he does so with a carefully chosen example. That is, he fills the lacuna mentioned above by showing features of types, at least in this case. For a flag which was not at least predominantly red, white and blue would — for that reason — *not* be the Union Jack. Of course, one should consider how faded a Union Jack can become; or a Union Jack shot to pieces in battle. But (a) these are questions about the tokens and their properties; (b) an abstract object was first posited to aid us with cases of these kinds; and (c) any answer given here will be occasion-sensitive[9].

In a second key discussion, Wollheim (1973 pp. 357-358: UD pp. 95-97), addresses two ways of making an artwork — that is, making the type that is the artwork. In doing so, he perspicuously highlights at least two ways of *making* new abstract objects. The easiest to see involves making the abstract object through the creation of a recipe, such as a notated score: that allows the instantiation of an artwork that could not otherwise be instantiated. In this case, the abstract object is created *without* creating a concrete instantiation (which I will keep calling a *token*). So, for some purposes at least, the work dates from its composition as a recipe, rather than its public appearance. This suggests that our commitment to an abstract object here is not a mere *façon de parler*: we are not simply lumping together comments on this or that concrete instantiation — in this sense, the justification for our abstraction and generality goes beyond Berkeley's criticisms of Locke[10]!

On the other method for making artworks, one arrives at a concrete instantiation (a token): one makes the type by (or through) making a token — for instance, in the rehearsal room. This method is almost always used in literature, as well as being most typical of dance composition. Now, I have commented elsewhere (UD pp. 95-97; CDE pp. 226-228) that this method does not readily allow identification of which of the features of this token will be those that the *type* embodies. For, clearly, a typical token has a number of features not required by other (genuine) tokens. By contrast, the recipe (or score) can make explicit which features of this token are fundamental here (either absolutely, or as a norm kind[11]). And this too suggests that the type is not simply an *abstraction* from tokens.

As noted above, part of the problem with Dodd's account is that he runs together the two theses of his book: if musical works are 'just' sound-structures (as his second thesis guarantees), then one can imagine them existing, or occurring, independently of human beings or human agency. Thus, on this assumption, the wind through the vegetation on the planet Zog just might produce a sound-sequence which, if heard, would be sonically indistinguishable from a Mozart symphony, even though (a) humans had never been to Zog; and (b) the event preceded human evolution on Earth. And, moreover, there are no suitable 'hearers' on Zog. But, at best, this conception seems only suitable in the case of music (if there). How could dances and (cast) sculptures pre-exist human activity in this way? That seems difficult to conceptualise. So any plausibility to Dodd's account of the *general* ontological point rests on his specific thesis — and that, in turn, rests on his example[12]. Thus, if our task is to look at the type-token relation across the arts, this seems an inappropriate starting place.

That a certain *theory* is propounded by, say, Einstein offers one reason to think one can *make* abstract objects: what exactly requires us to claim that — since theories are abstract objects — it has always existed? For instance, the concepts deployed in the theory of relativity only make sense in the light of that theory, making no sense in a different (Newtonian) conception of physics. So commonsense suggests that assertions about the theory of relativity make no sense prior to that time: even (SRV pp. 161-162) an assertion about Einstein's birth, if he is centrally described as the inventor (or discoverer) of the theory of relativity. But if the theory — as abstract object — were timeless, this would not be so: it would *in fact* be clear what the expression "theory of relativity" would have meant, even though no one would have been able to understand it[13]!

Kivy (1993 pp. 68-69) suggested a possible intermediate position, urging that *creative achievements* are never wholly creation, nor wholly discovery: "Might we not say ... that Edison *discovered* a practical way of getting light out from electricity?" (Kivy, 1993 p. 69). Clearly, we might: but this is the invention of the electric light bulb (the incandescent bulb, to be a little more exact). Further, Kivy grants that the bulb "... didn't exist before Edison invented it, and did afterwards" (Kivy, 1993 p. 69). So this account does not treat *this* invention as timeless. But surely the light bulb in my hallway is a token of a type (although it might not be, if one took seriously one suggestion above) — so what should one conclude? The issue for Edison bears, perhaps, on the sense we have of the artist as responsible ... which *seems* to imply creation, but need not (see Kivy, 1993 p. 41). For Edison is responsible for the discovery: and that gives a sense to its beginning in time. (For Dodd, I suspect this illustrates Kivy's not following-through on the Platonist insights.)

§5. Eternal 'objects'?

Dodd's response here begins from his characterisation of abstract objects: 'how can abstract objects be property-bearers?', he asks rhetorically; and, 'how can such objects come into being, or cease to exist?'. But that assumes that we know (and accept) Dodd's account of abstract objects. For just what are the properties of abstract objects? Thus Kivy (1993 p. 47) quotes Margolis: "Clearly, sculpture ... and etching can be destroyed ...: hence, they cannot be kinds." This thought, if granted, might appeal to Dodd (who only discusses musical works): for Dodd, what is *not* eternal is not a type. Yet this conclusion is not inevitable. For instance, suppose this showed that cast-sculpture and etchings were not timeless. Since they are standardly treated in type-token terms, that might just be information about the timelessness of types *of this sort*.

This is one alternative to simply taking Dodd's word for the properties of abstract objects: one might incorporate what is known about multiple-type artworks, such as musical works, and — since they are abstract objects — let that inform our understanding of what abstract are like (or must, after all, be like).

To contrast the strategies, consider one worked example, from Dodd (2007

p. 68): Whittle and the Jet Engine. In effect, Dodd's argument here is roughly this:

> The Jet Engine is a type.
>
> If types are such-and-such (eternal, etc.), then one cannot invent the Jet Engine.
>
> And types are such-and such.
>
> Therefore one cannot invent the Jet Engine.
>
> [That is, it operates fundamentally by detaching.]

And, of course, such an argument is valid, as far as it goes. But one is not gifted the truth of its premises. So, faced with the same initial claims as a starting point, one might, by contrast, contrapose:

> The Jet Engine is a type.
>
> If types are such-and-such (eternal, etc.), then one cannot invent the Jet Engine.
>
> But Frank Whittle invented the Jet Engine.
>
> Therefore types are *not* such-and such.

And it is not as though we really have some clear grasp on either the idea of an abstract object or the idea of a *type*, to which appeal can be made *independently* of what to say about central cases of abstract objects — such as musical works!

In this context, Dodd (2007 p. 126) writes cryptically of what is (and is not) "... integral to the work itself", as though this were something transparent — or simply given in perception (and that perception concept-free). Indeed, Dodd seems, later, to embrace a "moderate empiricism ... [on which] ... [t]he limits of musical appreciation ... are what can be heard in the work, or derived from listening to it" (Dodd, 2007 p. 205). Revealingly, Dodd there ascribes this view to Beardsley: but Beardsley's view (reflecting "the ideology of the New Criticism": Wollheim, 1993a p. 133) is defective precisely in failing to recognise "... the interlock between perception and cognition", as Wollheim (1993a p. 134) put it. So the hopes that Dodd's 'moderate empiricism' will provide a useful tool here will be dashed once it is granted that what we can perceive — which, here, means "hear" — will be inflected by our concepts: as we might say, by what one knows, or has learned. For there can be no genuinely "innocent eye"[14]. Then one cannot truly say that "... such facts ... play no role in determining a musical work's aesthetic value" (Dodd, 2007 p. 205).

Of course, for me, the issue of "aesthetic value" for musical works is ambiguous: for a musical work rightly so regarded, this will be what I call "artistic value" (McFee, 2005; AJ pp. 2-10), while treating it simply as pleasing sound will be (merely) "aesthetic" — but treating it that way will also be a species of misperception. But even were I wrong about this, even were the (merely) aesthetic perception the only one available, that perception would still be concept-mediated.

§6.   Found art again?

I have already commented briefly on Dodd's parallel (or kinship) between musical works and found art. On this view, Beethoven's *9th Symphony* is no more *Beethoven's* than Halley's comet is *Halley's*: both were discovered by the persons whose names they bear.

Could he be right? Is Beethoven's *9th Symphony* only Beethoven's in the sense in which Halley's comet is Halley's? The "no" answer seems right for two related reasons. First, the comet was there before Halley identified it, and independently of his identification. Yet the musical structure — as opposed (perhaps) to just the sound-structure — is a fit subject for understanding precisely because (on this view) Beethoven 'identified' it. One might expect Dodd to reject such a picture.

But, second, there is the issue of responsibility. Suppose, in the future, Halley's comet hits a spacecraft (and, to give the example more weight, assume some people die as a result). Of course, a mindless reaction can be imagined which, say, desecrates Halley's grave. But, equally, we recognise that it *is* mindless, since Halley is not responsible for the comet. The term "responsible" has two related uses: to indicate to whom praise or blame accrues ("he is responsible, so he pays the fine") and to indicate authorship or ownership ("he did it/made it, so he is responsible"). Here, denying Halley's responsibility amounts primarily to his not being due any praise or blame that accrues. So, here, any deaths are not his fault. Yet applied to Beethoven, such an idea is philistine: Beethoven is responsible for the symphony, in the sense of getting any praise or blame that accrues. And (for me, as for common sense) this is explicable partly because he is the *author* of the symphony — *responsible* for it in the other sense! And, indeed, this explains his 'responsibility' in the first sense.

Then one comes, as Austin (1962 p. 2[15]) might have predicted, to the bit where Dodd takes it back; where his thesis proves much less radical than it first appeared. Again the notion of *understanding* a musical work is central. As Dodd (2007 p. 137) says, "... understanding a work of music requires us only to view it as *composed* by someone, not as *created* by someone." Were this correct, only all talk of the *creation* of musical works needs be given up, in favour of talk of their *composition*, to arrive at a position Dodd will accept. So when, earlier, Dodd (2007 p. 126) urges the Platonist to "... stick out his chin and grant that *In This House, On this Morning* [actually composed in 1992] might have been composed in the sixteenth century", this simply means that it might have been *discovered* then, since *composition* is not equivalent to *creation.* And there are lots of good contextual reasons why it was unlikely to be 'discovered' then — just the sort of reasons the rest of us would offer to show that it could not have been *composed* then; namely, (roughly) that it would have made no sense offered to the music world of the time; and that its acceptance would have required a rethinking of the whole past of music. Further, Dodd too can call these *reasons* why the work could not (or, any way, would not) be composed then (see Dodd, 2007 p. 126).

On a parallel, doing X at an earlier time would simply not have constituted *dance* (compare the struggles of Duncan, Graham, and so on to get their movement sequences accepted as constituting danceworks). So that X — that is, those movements — do not constitute dance *in the absence of* ... the context[16].

Further, this suggests one way in which my earlier characterisations of Dodd's view is mistaken: I suggested that, for him, the wind through the reeds on the planet Zog might instantiate a Mozart symphony, by being just that sound-event. But perhaps, for Dodd, this sound sequence would not — of course — have been *composed* by Mozart. But that will suffice: now we have two pairs of expressions, at least roughly equivalent. First, the Dodd-pair takes the musical work as occurring on Zog, but grants that this was not Mozart's symphony; instead, we only here *Mozart's* symphony when we encounter the sound-sequence as selected by Mozart; just as Halley's comet becomes *Halley's* at a certain time, although Halley did not create it. Then, the common-sense-pair says that on Zog there are (miraculously) reed-sounds which sound like Mozart, but are not; and, here, we have Mozart's symphony — those sound transfigured into art by Mozart; and created (I would say) as musicians often create the type that is the musical work, by writing a recipe (the score).

§7. 'History of production' again

A further consideration here, connecting this discussion with that of Chapter Two, notes that the identification of, say, a performance as of *this* or *that* artwork (say, *this* or *that* musical work) turns on what Goodman (1968 = LA p. 115/PP p. 97) called 'history of production'. Thus, thinking about type-token, Wollheim wants to see how the type might constrain its tokens: one of his examples (Wollheim, 1973 pp. 101-102) is an imagined attempt at a 'blank-page' poem by Mallarmé. It is crucial to the example that this is indeed a (candidate) poem — and hence, for Wollheim, a type-token object — and that, if I am to make the type, I should do so in ways that at least constrain in *easy* cases what counts as tokens of that type. So, for instance, it may be enough (for these purposes at least: compare Davies, 2003 pp. 11-29) that Cage's infamous *Four Minutes Thirty-three Seconds* is a piece in three movements — so that any piece in four movements is *not* it. Further Wollheim acknowledges that the most usual form of constraint for poems is in terms of the words used, and their ordering: certainly this is not all; and perhaps it is not always enough. But it is a beginning in ways unavailable in the case Wollheim imagines. So (for Wollheim) Mallarmé cannot really succeed in making a poem by this strategy. Wollheim brings that point home by imagining Yevtushenko producing a 'similar' object: is this his poem, or Mallarmé? Or what? No answer could be forthcoming, for such 'poems'.

Certainly, there *may* be considerations suggested by discussion of the "Pierre Menard" case (see Chapter Two §6) that suggest, in a different situation, that the history of production of works be brought to bear. And, of course, that is the line one might take if both Mallarmé and Yevtushenko offered us the blank pages as, say, works of visual art — that is, as works of the particular object sort, a bit like Readymades. For then there would be a basis for contrasting them: for regarding them as "confusable counterparts" (Danto, 1981 p. 139) perhaps. Wollheim's reservation in the original case concerns seeing that what is offered is genuinely a poem, despite lacking the sorts of constraining devises (mentioned above) characteristic of poems That there is no basis for such an ascription makes it plain why, in respect of a poem, in this peculiar case (although not in most) the difference in history of production is not decisive.

But, were the two offerings regarded strictly as visual works, one could, in the more usual way, arrive at 'confusable counterparts': that is (roughly), different works separated not by straightforwardly perceptible properties but by considerations reflecting differences in 'history of production'; and hence differences in responsibility. Or, again, Cage might produce a 'confusable counterpart' of a Stamitz symphony, as "Cage's Symphony No. 1" (Kivy, 1993 p. 62). But, if they are indeed different musical works, as suggested by the different 'histories of production' of each, then musical works cannot have the sorts of existence Dodd predicts. For they would no longer be simply sound-structures. And the case seems even stronger for danceworks. For, again, the particular dance must be performed by these people on this occasion (if it is performed at all); and, anyway, it must have been choreographed either in a studio over such-and-such period or by writing a score. So there is a sense in which it seems dateable. And hence a sense in which its dating might create a 'confusable counterpart' situation through comparison with the dating of the 'history of production' *behind* another performance. So that Dodd's claim for musical works might be conceded (for the sake of the argument only) — somehow treating them as unlike other artworks — while still insisting on the possibility of 'confusable counterpart' dances.

§8. Conclusion

Where have we arrived? And where does this leave *dance*? Five points developed thus far should reduce any anxiety Dodd's pictures may have raised:

- There seems no convincing reason to accept Dodd's position as 'the default' for music (and our interest did not reside with hunting for the right account *of music*).

- Other ways of accommodating the points he rightly stresses suggest themselves, although no attempt has been made here to weld them into a unified 'ontology'.

- Some of the arguments for Dodd's picture of the type-token structure depend (at least for their motivation) on his sonicism: but, whatever the plausibility of sonicism in the philosophy of music, a parallel account for the philosophy of dance seems deeply improbable — indeed, it is hard to conceive what form such an account would take, especially if one accepts that dance is *transfigured* movement. For the movement itself is already a human phenomenon, making no sense apart from humans (and hence no sense on the planet Zog); further, dance is clearly *other than* 'simply movement'.

- Given the importance of authorship, it seems preferable to grasp some nettles to preserve it, if there must be nettle-grasping; and Wollheim's insightful comments offer us a way to make sense of the creation of the type — moreover, one which fits with dance practice (although of course it fits music even more snugly, since musical works are more usually made by the writing of writing scores).

Our summary would leave us hopeful that positions of the sort Dodd raises need not be addressed in detail .

Then setting aside some of the questions that drive Dodd's enquiry might prove helpful. Indeed, a quick way here might reject the whole concern with ontology as just an attempt to make concrete the 'problem of universals'. In such a context, Searle (2007a pp. 24-25) offers a short way forward: to recognise:

... that any meaningful predicate ... immediately allows us to form a corresponding noun phrase, which refers to the property expressed by the original predicate. Hence the existence of the objects named by these noun phrases is automatically guaranteed by the meaningfulness of the predicates.

Thus, given that objects in the world (say, postboxes in the UK) are red, it follows that *redness* exists. But there is no puzzle as to the character of that 'existence'. As Searle (2007a p. 25) continues:

> There is no separate realm of universals, but rather there are alternative ways of talking about the single realm in which we all live, the real world. Universals do indeed exist, in fact their existence is a trivial consequence of the meaningfulness of the corresponding predicates, but their existence introduces no new facts and no new ontological realms. To talk of universals is just an alternative way of speaking.

Moreover, Searle (2007a p. 25) notes that this strategy:

> ... works as much for universals that are not exemplified as for those that are. We can say either, "No one is a saint" or "The property of saintliness is possessed by no one."

But if little remains of the problem of universals, there may be little reason to plot the ontology of abstract objects in the way Dodd assumes.

Further, one need not start from the ontology of types and tokens, as though the relationship could be treated in a fashion wholly detached from its application. If, instead, one begins with an interest in artworks, and what is known of their character, it seems self-evident that *artworks* have authors in the strong sense which, typically, one associates with having *made* the thing (and hence being responsible for it in both senses). Then, even for artworks not the product of one's hand, as Duchamp did not make his snowshovel, one is at least entitled to any praise or blame it warrants — as one would not be for a 'naturally occurring' event, such as the cracks in the wall or the shape of the meteorite. And if the starting point for our discussion is what is *true* of artworks — and, of course, this may leave room to look for differences specifically for musical works — they might be characterised in precisely the terms Dodd wishes to deny (that is, as being made and having properties). But, if so, a *type-token* contrast might still be used. In that case, discussion would begin with types as the kind of abstract object that is makeable: the coining of words seems one clear example (as above), and another would be the giving of *promises* (if, as I assume, *promises* are abstract objects — since "promise" is obviously an abstract noun). So if one begins from aesthetics, rather than some abstracted view of ontology, one's *default position* (Dodd, 2007 p. 5) or *simple view* (Dodd, 2007 p. 1) or *face-value theory* (Dodd, 2007 p. 31) might be more realistic.

Notes

Chapter One

1. Our writer's suggestions involve doing away with the traditional repertoire, a plan with its own dangers. (For comments on loss of masterworks, see Chapter Ten.)

2. See, for example, McFee, 1998a; McFee, 1998b; McFee, 2000a, as well as UD.

3. The philosophy of numerical identity concerns itself with watches disassembled for cleaning; with the serial part replacement of ships (or watches); with sticks broken in two (as opposed to merely broken at the end); with amoebae; and many more. See also Chapter Two.

4. Throughout, standard abbreviations are used for works of Wittgenstein (elaborated in "Preface"). Although this is not a work of Wittgenstein scholarship, his ideas influence my thinking throughout; the version of them I favour is from Baker, 2004.

5. Say, in the manner of Julian Dodd, 2007: see Appendix.

6. On a more extreme version, the concept *art* might seem inevitable bourgeois and elitist; hence to be rejected. Thus, Taylor (1978 p. 155) writes that *art* "... is a value the masses should resist, not just ignore." This version need not be addressed here, since our audience has an interest in *dance* in just this sense (the sort of thing seen in theatres); but see Sharpe, 1983 pp. 2-4.

7. Of course, this is a technical contrast, *not* one reflecting how these terms are used in English: see McFee, 2005 (from which some paragraphs here are adapted).

8. This occasion-sensitive view is elaborated in Travis, 2008: see also AJ pp. 36-44; McFee, 2010a = EKT.

9. This comment was offered in a radio programme in the UK about André (reported Fuller, 1981 p. 115).

10. Here, the "death of the author" idea is put aside without comment: I do so more fully, in Chapter Five.

11. For those interested in expanding on some of these issues, EKT (pp. 177-193) elaborates my remarks about exceptionlessness, while AJ elaborates the framework as a whole.

Chapter Two

1. See Wiggins, 2001 p. xiii:

> To see that the principle of individuation for a buzzard is not the same as the principle for a bat, to see that the principle of individuation for a teapot is not the same as that for a housefly — there is no more to this (and no less) than

there is to seeing what a difference there is between these things *from the practical point of view of singling them out, of keeping track of them and of chronicling what they do.* (original italics)

2. In English, the term "identical" more usually indicates *qualitative identity* judgements: my watch being *identical* to yours usually means that both have a Rolex — hence that there are two watches!

3. See, for instance, Scruton, 1997 p. 101: "When two objects have all their properties in common, they are qualitatively identical; but if they are *two*, they are not numerically identical."

4. Too, the *age* of a watch cannot be reduced to the age of its parts — although sometimes the age of the *parts*, not of the watch, interests us ("This spring is good for another ten years").

5. A key chapter of Goodman, 1968 (cited as "LA") is also reprinted in Goodman, 1972 (cited as "PP") pp. 85-102, with an introduction.

6. Someone who thought poems timeless abstract objects might conclude this.

7. Founded in 1974, this a group of professional male dancers, marked by its love of classical ballet, and its repertoire. Ballet enthusiasts, they present a playful and entertaining, if slightly parody-like, view of the masterworks of classical ballet. The comic aspect of their approach relies largely on the fact that, here, men dance on pointe without falling over. (The spelling of the group's name can vary.)

8. Even when deploying the possibility of forgery, this contrast might not be defensible exceptionlessly. Suppose a musicologist conspires with a composer to 'authenticate' as by Mozart a score the composer had recently written — could a performance from that score be a Mozart forgery (compare Kivy, 2001a pp. 218-222)? Certainly the possibility of forgery of paintings typically (always?) requires *some* provenance being provided for the work.

9. Treating types Platonistically involves urging some real existence to the type: for example, a Platonising account of *numbers* postulates a realm of numbers existing independent of our practices with numerals — that is why the topic is "Platonic Realism" (as Kivy, 1993 p. 35 noted).

10. Contrast here Goodman's rejection of *types*:

> The type is the universal or class of which the marks [Goodman's word for *inscriptions*] are instances or members. Although I speak in the present text of a character as a class of marks, this is for me informal parlance admissible only because it can readily be translated into more acceptable language (LA p. 131 note 3).

For Goodman is a nominalist:

> I prefer ... to dismiss the type altogether and treat the so-called tokens of a type as *replicas* of one another. An inscription need not be an exact duplicate of

another to be a replica, or a true copy, of it; indeed, there is in general no degree of similarity that is necessary or sufficient for replicahood (LA p. 131 note 3).

11. Peirce [1934], 1960. [§537ff; p. 423-424]:

A common mode of estimating the amount of matter in a MS. or printed book is to count the number of words. There will ordinarily be about twenty *the*'s on a page, and of course they count as twenty words. In another sense of the word "word", however, there is but the one word "the" in the English language; and it is impossible that this word should lie visibly on a page or be heard in any voice, for the reason that it is not a Single thing or Single event. It does not exist. It only determines things that do exist. Such a definitely significant Form, I propose to term a *Type*.

As Peirce continues:

A Single event which happens once and whose identity is limited to that one happening or a Single object or thing which is in some single place at any one instant of time, such event or thing being significant only as occurring just when and where it does, such as this or that word on a single line of a single page of a single copy of a book, I will venture to call a *Token*. ... In order that a Type may be used, it has to be embodied in a Token which shall be a sign of the Type, and thereby of the object the Type signifies. I propose to call such a Token of a Type an Instance of the Type. Thus, there may be twenty Instances of the Type "the" on a page.

12. Compare Sharpe, 2004 p. 64 on *abstract particulars*; and see Appendix.

13. Indeed, the Stepanov score is! (See Chapter Three §6, §8.)

14. Then, are they abstract objects? Grasping the nettle here involves setting that question aside: that piece of the 'ontological puzzle' is not needed, since all we need to say can be said without raising it. Answering that question either way just introduces a verbal convention for a particular purpose.

15. Talking of "crucial features" here identifies features whose absence from a performance would be a topic for legitimate criticism of that performance. (Previously, I called them "essential features", although neither expression is entirely happy.)

16. For me, this will be a dance-critical matter, in line with my institutional account of art (UD pp. 67-86; AJ pp. 147-173].

Chapter Three

1. My thanks to Charles Travis for reminding me of this.

2. Recall, from Chapter One, the discussion of our decision to continue using this example.

3. The story is from Ernest Newman's four-volume *The Life of Richard Wagner* (1945), volume one, p. 130.

4. I take this to be the actual situation. If anyone doubts this, he/she can read it as a stipulation of mine.

5. See also Francis Sparshott's description of the case, from Battin et al., 1989 pp. 215-216.

6. Often, scores are not adequate: then there is an appeal to a stager: see, for example, the suggestion (Lidbury, 2000 p. 94) that, for works by Kurt Jooss, "... until recently, ... [Markard] has been the only player in the staging of his works." And compare the suggestion of a justification for Ashley Wheater staging of Ashton's *Cinderella* for Joffrey Ballet: "Having danced for Ashton and Joffrey qualifies Wheater to stage 'Cinderella'" (Levine, 2010 p. E8) [c].

7. For instance, UD p. 110: "We shall see in a later chapter [Chapter 11] how the intentions of the artist may be seen as important."

My thought was against "the mythology about the importance of the artist's intention" (UD p. 110) — where a feature of that mythology concerned the nature of intention (as prior planning, at best causally connected ...). Compare Chapter Five.

8. NB UD p. 110: A misleading passage — one that needs to be read in the context of the whole chapter (plus I may have changed my mind a bit!): "... we do rule out identity if they [the two performances] do not satisfy the same notation" (UD p. 110). For clearly this would only be straightforwardly true once this was acknowledge as an adequate notational score for the work itself: it could be adequate in *this* context (not that), and my stated condition would not hold without qualification.

9. Yet, in UD, I treated n*otationality* as applying (in principle) to all performing arts. Thus (UD p. 97) that Thesis is expressing in terms of "... *any performing art*".

10. See Chapter Eleven; Diffey, 1992; and UD pp. 71-74.

11. For *contract*, these are usually stated as the positive-sounding condition that the contract must be 'true, full and free': compare CDE p. 229.

12. In UD (pp. 92-93) I articulate two conditions here: (a) both A and B need to be dances: 'sameness of movement' is compatible with this not being true. And this includes the relation to authors, and to 'history of production; (b) lack of exactly the same movements as any *particular* performance cannot show that A is not the same dance as B — there is flexibility within the *same-work* identity, to accommodate rehearsals, and so on. This second condition I aimed to model with the Thesis of Notationality.

13. Key here: the way segments of the score (especially the national dances from Act III) were regularly revised (or replaced) even in Tchaikovsky's time.

14. The beauty of the idea of confusability is that — unlike talk of 'imperceptible difference' — it does not require a detailed account: the point

need not be that we cannot tell one from the other, if we cannot reliably identify the artworks (a) from one another, and (b) from the 'real things'.

15. It might resemble Steve Paxton's *Satisfyin Lover* (1967): see Banes, 1987 pp. 60-61; pp. 71-74.

Chapter Four

1. Above everything else, Chapter Three showed how the concern with notationality of (typical) dances readily combined with a regard for the role of the choreographer as author of the dancework. We return to that concern with *authorship* in Chapter Five.

2. For instance, Franko (1989 p. 58) writes of the reconstructors as aiming "... to evoke what no longer is, with the means of what is present": this does not seem to reject, to the same degree, the ontology of danceworks as existent at a particular time.

3. As Renee Conroy (2011, pages forthcoming) pointed out, it is easy, in this way, to locate some major problematic ontological commitments of those who see the choreographer as producing an endlessly open *text*, to function as a catalyst for the dancer's performance, the reaction of the audience, or some combination of them. For this view denies that there is a distinguishable, and relatively persistent, *dancework*. But that is precisely what is involved in being a *performable*.

4. A tricky parallel: *Marat/Sade* — a very literal filming of the stageplay performed.

The persecution and assassination of Jean-Paul Marat, as performed by the inmates of the Asylum of Charenton, under the direction of the Marquis de Sade. (1966)

Chapter Five

1. My thanks to Terry Diffey for helpful comments on earlier drafts of this material. A different version was read, as "The Intention of the Artist", to a seminar on aesthetics at University of Oxford, May, 2007: my thanks both for the invitation (from Sabina Lovibond) and for the contribution of those present. It also benefitted from discussion with graduate students and staff of the Philosophy Department, University of Washington, Seattle: again, I am grateful for their contributions.

Some paragraphs in this chapter are recycled from AJ Chapter Four: having written on them as clearly as I could, it seemed best to repeat them here.

2. See Walton, 1978 p. 89 [2008 p. 196] on "... how far critical questions about works of art can be *separated* from questions about their histories", in a world where art-status is *transfigurational*. See especially Walton, 1978 pp. 90-94 [2008 pp. 197-201]. (This notion is explored further in Chapter Ten.)

3. In fact, of course, their discussion theorised some New Critical practice, current at the time.

4. This may require modification: certainly, there are specific issues concerning literary arts deriving from the role/place of textual meaning.

5. By contrast, for Beardsley (1970 pp. 19-20): "'Plastic arm' has acquired a new meaning in the twentieth century, and this is now its dominant meaning ... Consequently the line in which it occurs has also acquired a new meaning."

6. Jane Austen *Emma* [1816] Harmondsworth: Penguin, 1966 p. 148.

7. Also Russell (1956 p. 41): "... 'a man' denotes not many men, but an ambiguous man" — contrast with EKT pp. 179-183, where I discuss Ziff's example "A cheetah can outrun a man": the key idea is that any 'translation' should mean the same as the pre-translation version (in particular, that it should have the same truth value). And this is not true for, say, remarks about *some* cheetahs — not least because one can ask, "Which?".

8. As Wittgenstein (PI §201) points out, there must be "a way of grasping a rule which is *not* an *interpretation*"; and, for these purposes, expressions resemble rules. For the speaker's own understanding of what he said is not an interpretation.

9. The nearest case to something really being 'read' as pure text in this sense occurs in Derrida's *Limited Inc.*, discussed briefly in Chapter Nine §8 (and Chapter Eleven §8). Derrida seems to read elements of Searle's text without regard to its context (as philosophy) or the constraints the words provide!

10. Thus, artworks are not 'naturally occurring', not accidental (except where someone decides to go with the accidental).

11. NB these points actually go for, say, all writing — only the one below stresses directly the connection to art.

12. A view I. A. Richards (1924 p. 20 note) dismisses as "delusion"!

13. Levinson, 2002 presents and meets central objections to hypothetical intentionalism: for us, it is just a default position.

14. Of course, some concepts can only be *applied* with hindsight; for instance, *precursor of ...* .

15. See Kenner, 1964 p. 352.

16. Wollheim (2001 p. 25) explicitly rejects hypothetical intentionalism (on one reading): for him, "[e]verything depends on what goes on in his [the artist's] head" (Wollheim, 1987 p. 18).

Wollheim's *realism* here is visible in his thought that the reason some art of the past is inaccessible to us is because, although there is a determinate intention, it is not retrievable (Wollheim, 1980 p. 204: see also Wollheim, 1993a p. 179). But — like us — he rejects, as a "... totally false view of intention" (Wollheim, 1971 p. 186), the conception of intention as prior planning, 'in the head' of the artist, and at best causally connected to his work. Further, Wollheim's view is not simply that the author's intentions must be retrieved. On the contrary, he stresses:

... the reconstruction of the creative process, where the creative process must ... be thought of as something not stopping short of, but terminating on, the work of art itself. (Wollheim, 1980 p. 187)

And he grants that "[t]he creative process ... is a more inclusive phenomenon than the artist's intention" (Wollheim, 1980 p. 200) because it "... includes many background beliefs, conventions, and modes of artistic production against which the artist forms his intentions" (Wollheim, 1980 p. 201). And the appropriate perspective here must be that of the spectator (or critic) since he/she "... is justified in using both theory and hindsight unavailable to the artist" (Wollheim, 1980 p. 201).

17. NB this is idealised, not ideal — see Chapter Ten.

18. Levinson (1996 pp. 188-189) distinguishes *categorial intentions* from *semantic intentions*. But, in fact, both are relevant here: see McFee, 2005 pp. 85-87.

19. Computer-generated 'stuff', and so on, can be set aside here.

20. Compare Mozart's letter of 20th April, 1782 to his sister Konstance: "... I had already composed the fugue and was writing it down while I worked out the prelude in my head" (Spaethling, 2000 p. 308).

21. This is the CB version, first performed by Fernando Grillo at the Rioyan Festival, France on 26th March 1976: there are also versions for 'cello and for 'cello and 'percussion' [1st performance 15th October 1978] — my thanks to Michael Finnissy for information; and more generally.

22. The key text here is Hirsch, 1966. (The expression "intentionalist backlash" is from Beardsley, 1970 p. 17.)

23. This is how Levinson's requirement (quoted earlier) for "a complete grasp" and "a full knowledge" (Levinson, 1996 p. 218) is met even though there are no such finite totalities.

Chapter Six

1. My thanks to Michael Finnissy for discussion of this example.

2. In effect, case (c) may differ from case (b) precisely in viewing the event from the perspective of the performer.

3. Compare Sparshott (1995 p. 136) on the notion of "musical coherence" as a requirement for musical improvisation.

4. A worry here: might two works have the same 'authorial instruction'? [What are the criteria for identity here?]

5. When Danto (2003 p. 46) calls this "a mild obscenity", he is surely understating.

6. Danto (2003 p. 46) suggests that, "[l]ike everything by Duchamp, this work is a field of fiercely contested interpretation ...". But all begin from the 'non-art' *tone* of this title: whatever Duchamp was doing here, it certainly involves a

rejection of some of the past of art — or, perhaps, of some past reactions to (central) artworks from the canon, such as the *Mona Lisa*.

7. I owe this example to Terry Diffey, from his PhD thesis: *Aesthetic Judgements and Works of Art*, University of Bristol, 1966.

Chapter Seven

1. On the idea that our everyday lives are circumscribed by *talk*, see EKT pp. 49-52.

2. See Austin 1962 p. 2:

> ... strange though the doctrine looks, we are sometimes told to take it easy — really it's just what we've all believed all along. (There's the bit where you say it and the bit where you take it back.)

3. Perhaps *some* of Gautier's comments should be seen as about the dancer viewed as a *person*. But, to that degree, his interest was in the 'real thing', not the artwork.

4. Petipa choreography, first danced by Legnani! See Brinson and Crisp, 1980 pp. 62-63.

5. Quoting Goethe, *Faust I*, opening scene in the *Studierzimmer*.

6. No doubt, here there is always *some* causal story describing the causal basis — or physical substrate — of one's judgement; but (as we will see in Chapter Eight) that story can never be explanatory of the normativity of that judgement.

7. Julian Dodd (2007), for instance, might dispute this: see Appendix.

8. Here, I am running together both what I called "performance traditions" and "traditions of performance" (McFee, 2003b pp. 121-143); and see Chapter Ten §10.

Chapter Eight

1. An award winning play, first shown in the UK on BBC 1 television, on 14th September, 1976.

2. Not just visual: clearly there is also the aural, as for instance in hearing the music — moreover, a fuller account would comment on exceptional cases, such a deaf dancers, for whom sound operates as a kind of projective tactile modality.

3. As Barbara Montero did in "Practice Makes Perfect: The Effects of Dance Training on the Aesthetic Judge" — a paper presented to the American Society for Aesthetics Pacific Division meeting in Asilomar California, March 2007, as made available to participants.

4. I said much the same thing in UD (p. 266) in stressing that, at least in typical cases, only "projective" perceptual modalities could be involved in artistic appreciation.

5. The quotation is from Montero "Practice Makes Perfect: ...".

6. My thanks to the authors for discussion of this paper, kindly sent to me in typescript.

7. Carroll & Moore, 2008 pp. 424-425: "... the mirror reflexes that manifest themselves in outward behaviour probably have a physiological substrate in what cognitive scientists have labelled *mirror neurons.*"

It is suggested (Carroll & Moore, 2008 p. 425 note 24) that:

> [n]ot only would this claim [about the role of mirror neurons] demystify the phenomenon of kinaesthetic communication, but it would also account for the similarity of responses by providing material grounds for claims of intersubjectivity.

Would these really be stronger claims than saying, for instance, "We are human beings with similar backgrounds"? I doubt it!

8. They continue: "The feedback from our own muscles stirs our own autonomic nervous system in a way that is roughly parallel to what is happening in him ..." !!!! [The reference for this is A. N. Meltzoff & A. K. Moor "Imitation of Facial and Manual Gestures by Human Neonates", *Science*, Vol. 198 (October) 1977 pp. 75-78.]

9. In reprinting this paper, Noel Carroll (2010 p. 506) explicitly responds to my alter-ego, Grahman McPhee, on this point: he suggests that choreographers may "... intend to communicate feelings to spectators by means of their movement while at the same time they do not understand all of the mechanisms that make the transmission possible." But this reply precisely conceeds that the mirror reflex is simply part of the *mechanism* of the communication — on a parallel with, say, the muscle-movements in one's face — and not something specifically intended. Hence the expression "critical channel of communication" *is* misleading: at best, one intends facial expressions not their mechanism (in muscular movements).

10. There are debates among neuro-scientists as to the ascription of mirror neurons to humans: in humans, *the mirror system* might be a more traditional description — let my comments be shorthand for that.

11. There were ostensibly discovered by Rizzolatti (Legrenzi & Umiltà, 2011 p. 29).

12. It continues with the references: "M. A. Umiltà, E. Kohler, V. Gallese, L. Fogassi, L. Fadiga, C. Keysers, and G. Rizzolatti, "I Know What You are Doing: A Neorophysiological Study", *Neuron*, Vol. 31, pp. 155-165; V. Gallese, L. Fadiga, L. Fogassi, and G. Rizzolatti "Action Recognition in the Premotor Cortex", *Brain*, Vol. 119 pp. 593-609; G. Rizzolatti, L. Fadiga, V. Gallese, and L. Rogassi, "Premotor Cortex and Recognition of Motor Actions", *Cognitive Brain Research*, Vol. 3, pp. 131-141." [In a sense, this is just one reference, round in a circle; the doctrine is something each paper 'tells' the next! So they *appear* to support one another; and do so *psychologically.*]

13. And perhaps "... neuroimaging studies suggest that mirror neurons are also present in the human brain" (Legrenzi & Umiltà, 2011 p. 34).

14. It is much easier here to recognise (and explain) failures: thus, it is "... suggested that the malfunctioning of the mirror neurons is fundamental to pathologies characterised by difficulty in forming relationships with others, such as autism" (Legrenzi & Umiltà, 2011 p. 35).

15. Compare for example Danto. 1987 *passim* (discussed Chapter Eleven below); as Danto (1987 p. 61) appropriate quotes from Wölfflin, "Not everything possible at every time".

16. The quotations are from Montero "Practice Makes Perfect: ...". But see also Montero, 2006b p. 156.

17. Montero "Practice Makes Perfect: ...": see also Montero, 2006b p. 156: "... a significant increase in activity in various motor areas" of the brain.

18. For an estimate of neuroscience congruent with mine, but expressed (if somewhat over-emphatically) by self-proclaimed neuropsychologists who, while more optimistic than I am concerning the current state of brain research, share similar reservations about the application of that research to the cultural context, see Legrenzi & Umiltà, 2011 pp. 41-90.

19. However, Searle's own use of this point differs from mine. Compare Robinson, 2007 pp. 176-183.

20. Montero "Practice Makes Perfect: ...".

21. Some material in this paragraph and the next four derive from EKT pp. 129-130.

22. And I have merely stated his conclusions here, not argued for them.

Chapter Nine

1. Its first appearance piece was credited to Renee *Conway* — here, and in the bibliography, its correction follows the later erratum notice.

2. Also quoted Conroy, 2007 p. 2(a). My interest here differs from that Renee is pursuing in her paper (Conroy, 2007) — some of its ideas aid me in elaborating my points.

Also (see below) extensive use is made of "Dancework Reconstruction: Charting the Philosophical Terrain", Conroy's contribution to the American Society for Aesthetics Pacific Division meeting in Asilomar, California 2007, circulated for the meeting. As Conroy intended, this text accurately summarises many of the major claims concerning dance reconstruction. Since I am not criticising the formulations, this use is not unfair. [I thank Renee for her permission to draw on this unpublished work.]

3. Kivy there discusses reasons why this expression should be preferred to "historically authentic performance".

4. As noted above, I quote extensively from Renee Conroy's unpublished "Dancework Reconstruction: Charting the Philosophical Terrain" (citing it as "Conroy, unpub") both because it clarifies key points and to acknowledge my general debt to Conroy for sustained discussion of these topics. I have also

benefitted from reading with interest her PhD thesis, "The Art of Re-making Dances: A Philosophical Analysis of Dance Reconstruction", University of Washington, 2009; for which, again, I thank her. (Its first chapter covers much the same ground as the unpublished paper cited.)

5. Its assumption of a finite totality gives us theoretical reasons to suspect it!

6. From Kivy, 1995 p. 4; elaborated in Kivy, 1995 Chapters Two, Three and Four.

7. A fourth is the *personally* authentic, such that "[g]reat performers usually have styles all their own: styles that emanate from *them*, and, therefore, their performances are correctly characterised as 'personally authentic'." (Kivy, 2007 p. 99). Although at first this seems another problem, appearing "... inimical to the historical authenticity concept" (Kivy, 2007 pp. 97-98) and pointing away from the plausibility of the historically authentic, it recurs in ways we will come to: see next note.

8. Here, *personal authenticity* may be important: performers who are constrained absolutely by past performances cannot make the contribution to the piece usually given through its under-determination by (say) the score; and which the choreographer intended that the performers should supply. In this sense, "... the personally authentic performance is supposed to be an original, imaginative creation ..." (Kivy, 2007 p. 99).

9. See Chapter Five §1 for the case of the expression "plastic arm".

10. This may be one use of Kivy's lions (one-eyed, and otherwise), in UD pp. 108-109, as well as illustrating the normativity of artistic judgement.

11. On my institutionalism, see Chapter Eleven §§4-6; also AJ Chapter Six; McFee, 2008.

12. As we benefit when the philosophy of the past shows that there are *other* ways of doing/thinking than those we standardly know/use: see FW pp. 152-153.

Chapter Ten

1. For a defeasible relation, like *contract* in law, if certain conditions are fulfilled, that relation holds *unless* ... That is, it represents a nearly universal generalisation that, when the conditions are fulfilled, the relation holds; and the burden of proof is on any *objector* who must appeal to the satisfaction of *recognised heads of exception*: see Chapter Three §5; Chapter Four §2; also AJ pp. 33-34.

2. To understand the idea of an *intentional object*, one can begin from an account of experiencing emotions, also often conceived as cognitive (Kivy, 2002 pp. 25-27). Then, in standard cases of someone feeling (say) *fear*, experiencing the emotion involves an implicit knowledge-claim: such-and-such is taken as a suitable object of fear (the mad axeman, the escaped leopard). And the intentional object of one's fear specifies what one is frightened *of*. So "... fear is tethered to the apprehension of harmfulness" (Carroll, 2009 p. 31) — this is not quite right, since some fears are non-specific (UD pp. 171); but assuming such

specificity for artworks seems right. And hence seeing the work itself as the *intentional object* of our responses to it. See also Scruton, 1997 pp. 227-228; McFee, 1997 p. 37.

3. As Travis (2004 pp. 247-248) points out, this argument imports a particular view of what is open to perception.

4. Although regarding evaluation as central, Carroll (2009) highlights correctly a number of other functions of criticism, and discusses their contribution to the overall evaluative project.

5. A personal experience of mine: see also Polanyi, 1973 p. 101.

6. The pass/fail asymmetry might reflect the need to grant the historical character of art, in my sense (see McFee, 1992b; AJ pp. 119-145) — we might be far less certain of the negative judgement's future.

7. The following two paragraphs are reworked from McFee 2004b pp. 124-125.

8. As raised by Bob Sharpe, 2004.

9. And, of course, our idealisation here cannot imply *complete* mastery of *all* aspects since, throughout, we have been at pains to dent the reality of such finite totalities in the human — and especially artistic — realm.

10. An example of some of the required detail occurs earlier in this important text.

11. Gracyk (1997 p. 141) notes the view (from Thomas Godlovitch) that authenticity is "... a feature of performances, not merely of sounds": his point is that sounds alone must be transfigured (that is, heard transfigured) to become the musical work — and it is that work that is performed.

12. In correspondence — but his comments also reflect Alban Berg's view that recognition of structure, and such like, for music must typically be aural (one must *hear* it); but this can be problematic. Indeed, Berg ([1924] 1965 p. 189) specifically identified, as an issue for Schönberg's music, the need:

> ... to recognize the beginning, course and ending of all melodies, to hear the sounding-together of the voices not as a chance phenomenon but as harmonies and harmonic progressions, to trace smaller and larger relationships and contrasts as what they are — to put it briefly: to follow a piece of music as one follows the words of a poem in a language that one has mastered through and through means the same — for one who possesses the gift of thinking musically — as understanding the work itself.

13. With music by Peter Maxwell Davis.

14. Here, we should remind ourselves thast this is not Collingwood's sense of the term "craft": see Chapter Seven §2.

15. There *are* questions about historicity here: when is the case like "plastic" in Akenside's 18th century poem, when like transformed answers? See McFee, 1992b esp. p. 313; McFee, 1995 esp. pp. 281-282; AJ pp. 119-145.

16. My thanks to Renee Conroy for reminding me of this passage.

17. Although Mackrell was writing specifically about male dancers, the point still holds for today's female dancers.

18. My thanks to Anna Pakes for reminding me of this.

Chapter Eleven

1. Indeed, Suits (1978 p. x) claims that, had Wittgenstein followed through on his injunction to "Look and see" (PI §66), he would have found roughly the definition of games that suits develops.

2. Feyerabend, 1987 p. 272; also UD p. 307. The parallel here is with (a) [as practitioners] the scientists who say that Einstein is right, Newton wrong on some topic and (b) the philosophers who find the views incommensurable.

3. Sharpe (2004 p. 36: original italics) explains institutionalism as follows:
A work of art is an artifact presented to the public for their appreciation by a representative of the art-world or an agent for it.

This seems at least a first approximation to an acceptable institutionalist account of art.

4. Some standard epistemic constraints, such as a principle of total evidence (see Carnap, 1950 p. 211), also apply.

5. Also, early work by Morris ("Songs that Tell a Story": 1982) actually follow the storyline of the Country-&-Western songs that were its source — just the sort of thing dancers-in-training were told was unforgivable. (When I put the point to Morris [in Brussels, in 1990], he remarked that it was just as well, then, that he had not received that training!)

6. This study should be undertaken in detail: anecdotally, I'd say that the highly trained dancer from today's dance-school is more *versatile* than his/her forebear from the 1970s — yes to ballet, tap, jazz, contemporary-as-Graham, contemporary-as-Cunningham, Contact Improvisation, Bharata Natyam. But these are not 'instruments' well-designed for any *particular* danceworks: they can do *anything* — but, for me, typically nothing *well*. So, like most people, I prefer my Kathak in Kathak-trained dancers, not those struggling to break the bonds of classical ballet. But I also prefer my Graham in dancers whose bodies fall 'naturally' (that is, as a result of training) into the style of Graham, neither those who think that all contemporary dance is the same, nor those whose bodies fall easily into the characteristic shapes of Cunningham. Of course, this is just an impression I have. But it is a strong impression.

7. Interestingly, the work Banes (2007 p. 112) identifies as her favourite from the event, entitled "Almost Dance", that she was reviewing is presented as "... a clever, biting parody of socialist realist ballet": that is, as apparently fitting a central dance category!

8. Of course, this is not strictly evidence — in the ideal case, it is logically related to the conclusion drawn from it.

Appendix

1. Aubrey, 1982 p. 161: "... had ... [Descartes] kept himself to geometry he had been the best geometer in the world but that his head did not lie with philosophy."

2. Julian Dodd certainly put it this way to me in conversation.

3. Interestingly, Dodd's introduction of the type-token distinction does not discuss Peirce's remarks: he simply assumes (a) that we well understand the distinction — except, as we shall see, much of that 'understanding' is misplaced; and (b) that it is equivalent to other platonising notions.

4. Dodd (2007 p. 31) takes exception to Wollheim's remark taking the type as *definitive* of the token.

5. Compare EKT, especially pp. 180-182: saying "A cheetah can outrun a man" is not discussing *all* cheetahs, nor any particular ones.

6. Are these the same thing? Perhaps one might think such-and-such was outside of time in one sense, in that destroying all the tokens does not destroy the type (at least automatically). So the type exists in potentiality at times when there is no token. Yet all of this is compatible with both having a beginning and (even) an end in time — say, with an artwork no longer performable because completely forgotten, the scores or script lost, and so on.

7. Does the following *crazy* thought lurk here: that Chomskian creativity is to be explained by our matching the new token-sentence to some prior-existing type-sentence? Let us hope a more sophisticated account of mind prevails!

8. Further, there is no finite totality here; no *all*.

9. For elaboration, see Travis, 2008 passim; AJ pp. 36-41; EKT pp. 36-38.

10. See Dancy, 1998 p. 32:

> [Berkeley] holds that a perfectly non-abstract idea, the idea of a particular man, can stand for all men whatever ...

See also Intro §§19-20 (pp. 99-100).

11. Note that Kivy (1993 p. 52) too quotes Wolterstorff on "norm kinds".

12. Interestingly, something similar might be said of Collingwood's introduction of *art proper* by highlighting features of *musical* appreciation (Collingwood, 1938 pp. 130-141).

13. Note here the rejection of this kind of idealism even by Frege, a Platonist: see Travis, 2004.

14. The expression, and the thesis, is Gombrich's: see Wollheim, 1987 p. 16.

15. Austin (1962 p. 2) notes: "There's the bit where you say it and the bit where you take it back."

16. I am what Julian Dodd (2007 p. 127) calls "a contextualist" — self-avowedly!

Bibliography

Acocella, Joan *Mark Morris*. New York: Farrar, Strauss, Giroux, 1993.

Adair, Christy *Woman and Dance: Sylphs and Sirens*. London: Macmillan Press, 1992.

Alvarez, Al *The Shaping Spirit: Studies in Modern English and American Poets*. London: Chatto & Windus, 1958.

—— *The Savage God*. London: Heinemann, 1971.

Anscombe, G. E. M. *Intention*. Oxford: Blackwell, 1957.

—— "On Sensations of Position", *Metaphysics and the Philosophy of Mind* (Collected Papers Volume Two). Oxford: Blackwell, 1981 pp. 71-74.

Arbeau, Thoinot [1589] *Orchesography* (trans. Mary E. Stuart). New York: Dover, 1967.

Archer, Kenneth & Hodson, Millicent "Confronting Oblivion", in Stephanie Jordan (ed.) *Preservation Politics: Dance Revived Reconstructed Remade*. London: Dance Books, 2000 pp. 1-12

Aubrey, John *Brief Lives* (ed. Richard Barber). Woodbridge: Boydell, 1982.

Austin, J. L. *Sense and Sensibilia*. Oxford: Clarendon Press, 1962

—— *Philosophical Papers* (Second Edition). Oxford: Clarendon Press, 1970.

—— *How To Do Things With Words*. Oxford: Clarendon Press, 1975.

Austin, Richard *Birth of a Ballet*. London: Vision Press 1976.

Baker, Gordon *Wittgenstein's Method: Neglected Aspects*. Oxford: Blackwell, 2004.

Baker, Gordon & Hacker, Peter *Frege: Logical Excavations*. Oxford: Blackwell, 1984a.

—— *Language, Sense and Nonsense*. Oxford: Blackwell, 1984b.

Bambrough, Renford *Reason, Truth and God*. London: Methuen, 1969.

Banes, Sally *Terpsichore in Sneakers: Post-Modern Dance* (with a new introduction). Hanover, NH: Wesleyan University Press, 1987.

—— *Democracy's Body: Judson Dance Theatre 1962-1964*. Ann Arbor, MI: Duke University Press, 1993.

—— *Writing Dancing in the Age of Postmodernism*. Hanover, NH: University Press of New England, 1994.

—— *Dancing Woman*. London: Routledge, 1998.

—— *Before, Between, and Beyond: Three Decades of Dance Writing*. Madison, WI: University of Wisconsin Press, 2007.

Battin, Margaret et al. *Puzzles about Art: An Aesthetics Casebook*. New York: St. Martins, 1989.

Beardsley, Monroe *Aesthetics: Problems in the Philosophy of Criticism*. New York: Harcourt, Brace, 1958.

────── *The Possibility of Criticism*. Detroit: Wayne State University Press, 1970.

Beardsmore, R. W. *Art and Morality*. London: Macmillan, 1971.

Beckett, Samuel "Jack B. Yates", in his *Disjecta: Miscellaneous Writings and a Dramatic Fragment* (ed. Ruby Cohn) New York: Grove Press, 1984 pp. 89-90.

Bennett, Tony *Formalism and Marxism*. London: Methuen, 1979.

Berg, Alban [1924] "Why is Schoenberg's Music so Difficult to Understand?" reprinted in Willi Reich *The Life and Work of Alban Berg*. London: Thames & Hudson, 1965 189-204.

Best, David *Expression in Movement and the Arts*. London: Henry Kimpton, 1974.

────── *Philosophy and Human Movement*. London: Allen and Unwin, 1978.

────── *The Rationality of Feeling*. London: Falmer Press, 1992.

Blacking, John "Movement, Dance, Music, and the Wenda Girls' Initiation Cycle" in Paul Spencer (ed.) *Society and the Dance*. Cambridge: Cambridge University Press, 1985 pp. 64-91.

Borges, Jorge Luis "Pierre Menard, author of *Don Quixote*" in his *Fictions* [trans. A. Kerrigan]. New York: Grove Press, 1962 pp. 42-51.

Brinson, Peter & Crisp, Clement *Ballet and Dance: A Guide to the Repertory*. London: David & Charles, 1980.

Buchanan, Bruce G., Davis, Randall, & Feigenbaum, Edward A. "Expert Systems: A Perspective from Computer Science" in N. Charness, R. Hoffman & K. Anders Ericsson (eds) *Cambridge Handbook of Expertise and Expert Performance*. Cambridge: Cambridge University Press, 2006 pp. 87-104.

Calvo-Merino, Beatriz, Glaser, D. E., Haggard, P., & Passingham, R. E. "Action Observation and Acquired Motor Skills: an fMRI Study with Expert Dancers", *Cerebral Cortex*, Vol 15, No. 8, 2005 pp. 1243-1249.

Caplan, Ben "Review of Julian Dodd *Works of Music*", *British Journal of Aesthetics*, Vol. 47 No.4, 2007 pp. 445-446.

Carnap, Rudolf *Logical Foundations of Probability*. London: Routledge & Kegan Paul, 1950.

Carr, David "Thought and Action in the Art of Dance", *British Journal of Aesthetics*, Vol. 27, 1987 pp. 345-357.

────── "Meaning in Dance", *British Journal of Aesthetics*, Vol. 37, 1997 pp. 349-366.

Carroll, Noël *Beyond Aesthetics*. Cambridge: Cambridge University Press, 2001.

———— *The Philosophy of Motion Pictures*. Oxford: Blackwell, 2008.

———— *On Criticism*. London: Routledge, 2009.

———— *Art in Three Dimensions*. Oxford Clarendon Press, 2010.

Carroll, Noël & Moore, Margaret "Feeling Movement: Music and Dance" *Revue Internationale de Philosophie*, Vol. 62 No. 246, 2008 pp. 413-435.

Cavell, Stanley *Must We Mean What We Say?*. New York: Scribners, 1969.

———— *The Senses of Walden (An Expanded Edition)*. San Francisco: North Point Press, 1981.

Challis, Chris "Dancing Bodies: Can the Art of Dance be Restored to Dance Studies?" in G. McFee (ed.) *Dance, Education and Philosophy*. Aachen: Meyer and Meyer, 1999 pp. 143-153.

Chapman, John "XXX and the Changing Ballet Aesthetic", *Dance Research*, Vol. 2 No. 1, 1984 pp. 35-47.

Cioffi, Frank "Intention and Interpretation in Criticism" in Cyril Barrett (ed.) *Collected Papers on Aesthetics*. Oxford: Blackwell, 1965 pp. 161-183.

Collingwood, R. G. *The Principles of Art*. London: Oxford University Press, 1938.

Conroy, Renee "Dance Reconstruction: Kinesthetic Preservation or Danceworld Kitsch?", *ASA Newsletter*, Vol. 27, No. 1, Spring 2007 pp. 1-3.

———— "Dancework Reconstruction: Charting the Philosophical Terrain" presented to the American Society for Aesthetics Pacific Division meeting in Asilomar, California 2007 (unpublished typescript — cited as "Conroy, unpub").

———— "Review of Banes *Before, Between, and Beyond*" in *Journal of Aesthetics and Art Criticism*, Vol. 66 No. 7 2008 pp. 312-314.

———— "Dance" in Anna C. Ribeiro (ed.) *Continuum Companion to Aesthetics*. London: Continuum, 2011, pages forthcoming.

Croce, Arlene *Afterimages*. London: A. & C. Black, 1978.

———— *Going to the Dance*. New York: Alfred A. Knopf, 1982.

Cunningham, Merce *The Dancer and the Dance: Merce Cunningham in Conversation with Jacqueline Lesschaeve*. New York: Scribners, 1984.

Dancy, Jonathan "Editor's Introduction", George Berkeley *Principles of Human Knowledge*. Oxford: Oxford University Press, 1998 pp. 5-69.

Danto, Arthur *The Transfiguration of the Commonplace*. Cambridge, MA: Harvard University Press, 1981.

———— "De Kooning's Three-Seater", in his *The State of the Art*. New York: Prentice Hall, 1987 pp. 58-61.

———— *Embodied Meanings*. New York: Farrar, Strauss, Giroux, 1994.

———— *After the End of Art: Contemporary Art and the Pale of History*. Princeton, NJ: Princeton University Press, 1997.

———— "Art and Meaning" in Noël Carroll (ed.) *Theories of Art Today*. Madison, WI: University of Wisconsin Press, 2000 pp. 130-140.

———— *The Abuse of Beauty*. Chicago: Open Court, 2003.

———— *Unnatural Wonders: Essays from the Gap between Art and Life*. New York: Columbia University Press, 2005.

Davies, Stephen *Musical Meaning and Expression*. Ithaca, NY: Cornell University Press, 1994.

———— *Themes in the Philosophy of Music*. Oxford: Clarendon Press, 2003

———— "Author's Intentions, Literary Interpretation, and Literary Value" *British Journal of Aesthetics* Vol. 16 No. 3 July, 2006 pp. 223-247.

Derrida, Jacques *Limited Inc.* Evanston, Il: Northwestern University Press, 1988.

Dickie, George *Art and The Aesthetic: An Institutional Analysis*. Ithaca, NY: Cornell University Press, 1974.

———— "The Institutional Theory of Art" in Noël Carroll (ed.) *Theories of Art Today*. Madison, WI: University of Wisconsin Press, 2000 pp. 93-108.

Diffey, Terry *The Republic of Art*. New York: Peter Lang, 1992.

Dodd, Julian *Works of Music: An Essay in Ontology*. Oxford: Clarendon Press, 2007.

Dunn, Douglas (and Trisha Brown) "Dialogue on Dance", in Jean Morrison Brown, Naomi Mindlin & Charles Woodford (eds) *The Vision of Modern Dance* (Second Edition). London: Dance Books, 1998 pp. 177-186.

Durrell, Lawrence *A Key to Modern Poetry*. London: Peter Nevill, 1952. [American edition: *A Key to Modern British Poetry*. Norman: University of Oklahoma Press, 1952.]

Dworkin, Ronald *Law's Empire*. Cambridge, MA: Belknap/Harvard University Press, 1986.

———— *Freedom's Law: The Moral Reading of the American Constitution*. Cambridge, MA: Harvard University Press, 1996.

Easton, Carol *No Intermissions: A Life of Agnes de Mille*. Cambridge, MA: Da Capo Press, 1996/2000.

Feyerabend, Paul K. *Farewell to Reason*. London: New Left Books, 1987.

Foster, Susan Leigh *Reading Dancing*. Berkeley: University of California Press, 1986.

———— *Choreography and Narrative: Ballet's Staging of Story and Desire*. Bloomington: Indiana University Press, 1996.

———— "Dancing Bodies" in Jane C. Desmond (ed.) *Meaning in Motion: New Cultural Studies of Dance*. Durham: Duke University Press, 1997 pp. 235-257.

Franko, Mark "Repeatability, Reconstruction and Beyond" *Theatre Journal*, Vol. 41 No. 1, March 1989 pp. 56-74.

Frege, Gottlob [1918] "Thoughts" in his *Collected Papers on Mathematics, Logic, and Philosophy*. Oxford: Blackwell, 1984 pp. 351-372.

Fry, Roger "The Grafton Gallery: An Apologia" [1912] reprinted in Christopher Reed (ed.) *A Roger Fry Reader*. Chicago: University of Chicago Press, 1996 pp. 112-116.

Fuller, Peter *Beyond the Crisis in Art*. London: Writers & Readers, 1981.

Gautier, Théophile *Gautier on Dance* (ed. Ivor Guest). London: Dance Books, 1986.

Goodman, Nelson *Languages of Art*. Indianapolis: Bobbs-Merrill, 1968.

—— *Problems and Projects*. Indianapolis: Hackett, 1972.

—— "Comments on Wollheim's paper", *Ratio*, Vol. 20, 1978 pp. 49-51.

—— "Predicates without Properties" in Peter French, Theodore Uehling, Jr., & Howard Wettstein (eds) *Contemporary Perspectives in the Philosophy of Language*. Minneapolis: University of Minnesota Press, 1979 pp. 347-348.

—— *Of Mind and Other Matters*. Cambridge, MA: Harvard University Press, 1984.

Goodman, Nelson & Elgin, Catherine Z. *Reconceptions in Philosophy*. London: Routledge, 1988.

Gracyk, Theodore "Listening to Music: Performances and Recordings", *Journal of Aesthetics and Art Criticism*, Vol. 55 No 2, 1997 pp. 139-150.

Grice, Paul "Reply to Richards" in Richard E. Grandy & Richard Warner (eds) *Philosophical Grounds of Rationality: Intentions, Categories, Ends*. Oxford: Clarendon Press, 1986 pp. 45-106.

—— *Aspects of Reason*. Oxford: Clarendon Press, 2001.

Ground, Ian *Art or Bunk?* Bristol: Bristol Classical Press, 1989.

Hamilton, Jim "Theatre" in Berys Gaut & Dom Lopes (eds) *Routledge Companion to Aesthetics*. London: Routledge, 2001 pp. 557-568.

—— *The Art of Theatre*. Oxford: Blackwell, 2007.

Hanna, Judith L. *Dance, Sex and Gender*. University of Chicago Press, 1988.

Hirsch, E. D. *Validity in Interpretation*. New Haven: Yale University Press, 1966.

Hockney, David *David Hockney: My Early Years*. London: Thames and Hudson, 1976.

Jordan, Stephanie *Striding Out*. London: Dance Books, 1992.

—— "Preface", in Stephanie Jordan (ed.) *Preservation Politics: Dance Revived Reconstructed Remade*. London: Dance Books, 2000 (no page numbers).

Jowitt, Deborah *Jerome Robbins: His Life, His Theatre, His Dance*. New York: Simon & Schuster, 2004.

Kenner, Hugh (ed.) *Seventeenth Century Poetry: The Schools of Donne and Jonson*. New York: Holt, Rinehart & Winston, 1964.

Kenyon, Nicholas "Editorial" in *Early Music* (Early Dance Issue), Vol. 14 No. 1 February, 1986 p. 2.

Kivy, Peter "What Makes Aesthetic Terms *Aesthetic?*", *Philosophy and Phenomenological Research*, Vol. 36, 1975 pp. 197-211.

——— *Music Alone: Philosophical Reflections on the Purely Musical Experience.* Ithaca, NY: Cornell University Press, 1990.

——— *The Fine Art of Repetition.* Cambridge: Cambridge University Press, 1993.

——— *Authenticities: Philosophical Reflections on Musical Performance.* Ithaca, NY: Cornell University Press, 1995.

——— *New Essays on Musical Understanding.* Oxford: Clarendon Press, 2001a.

——— *The Possessor and the Possessed.* New Haven: Yale University Press, 2001b.

——— *Music, Language and Cognition.* Oxford: Clarendon Press, 2007.

Kripke, Saul [1972] *Naming and Necessity.* Oxford: Blackwell, 1980.

Kristeller, P. O. "The Modern System of the Arts" in his *Renaissance Thought II: Papers on Humanism and the Arts.* New York: Harper and Row, 1965 pp. 163-227.

Kustow, Michael *Peter Brook: A Biography.* New York: St. Martins Press, 2005.

Lamarque, Peter "Literature" in B. Gaut & D. Lopes (eds) *The Routledge Companion to Aesthetics.* London: Routledge, 2000 pp. 449-461.

——— *The Philosophy of Literature.* Oxford: Blackwell, 2009.

Legrenzi, Paolo & Umiltà, Carlo *Neuromania: On the Limits of Brain Science.* Oxford: Oxford University Press, 2011.

Levine, Debra "An American Turn at British 'Cinderella'", *Los Angeles Times Calendar*, 24th January, 2010, p. E8.

Levinson, Jerrold *Music, Art and Metaphysics.* Ithaca, NY: Cornell University Press, 1990.

——— *The Pleasures of Aesthetics: Philosophical Essays.* Ithaca, NY: Cornell University Press, 1996.

——— "Hypothetical Intentionalism: Statement, Objections and Replies" in M. Krausz (ed.) *Is There a Single Right Interpretation?* University Park, Pennsylvania: University of Pennsylvania Press, 2002 pp. 309-318.

——— *Contemplating Art.* Oxford: Clarendon, 2006.

Lidbury, Clare "The Preservation of the Ballets of Kurt Jooss" in Stephanie Jordan (ed.) *Preservation Politics: Dance Revived Reconstructed Remade.* London: Dance Books, 2000 pp. 89-96.

Livingstone, Paisley *Art and Intention: A Philosophical Study.* Oxford: Clarendon, 2005.

Lyas, Colin "Wittgensteinian Intentions" in Gary Iseminger (ed.) *Intention and Interpretation*. Philadelphia: Temple University Press, 1992 pp. 132-151.

Lyons, John *Chomsky*. London: Fontana, 1970.

McAdoo, Nick "Kant and the Problem of Dependent Beauty" *Kant-Studien* Vol. 93 No. 4, 2002 pp. 444-452.

McFee, Graham *Much of Jackson Pollock is Vivid Wallpaper*. New York: University Press of America, 1978.

———— *Understanding Dance*. London: Routledge, 1992a.

———— "The Historical Character of Art — A Re-Appraisal", *British Journal of Aesthetics*, Vol. 32 No. 4, 1992b pp. 307-319.

———— "Was that *Swan Lake* I saw You at Last Night?: Dance-identity and Understanding", *Dance Research*, Vol. XII No. 1, 1994 pp. 20-40.

———— "Back to the Future: A Reply to Sharpe", *British Journal of Aesthetics*, Vol. 35. No 3, 1995 pp. 278-283.

———— "Meaning and the Art-Status of *Music Alone*" *British Journal of Aesthetics* Vol. 37 No. 1, 1997 pp. 31-46.

———— "Dance, Aesthetics of", in E. Craig (ed.) *Routledge Encyclopedia of Philosophy* Volume 2. London: Routledge, 1998a: pp. 774-777.

———— "Dance: Contemporary Themes", in M. Kelly (ed.) *Encyclopedia of Aesthetics* Volume 1, London: Oxford University Press, 1998b: pp. 494-497.

———— "The Aesthetics of Dance", in B. Gaut & D. Lopes (ed.) *Routledge Companion to Aesthetics*. London: Routledge, 2000a pp. 545-556.

———— *Free Will*. Teddington: Acumen, 2000b.

———— "Wittgenstein, Performing Art and Action" in M. Turvey & R. Allen (eds) *Wittgenstein, Theory and the Arts*. London: Routledge, 2001 pp. 92-117.

———— "Art, Essence and Wittgenstein" in S. Davies (ed.) *Art and Essence*. Westport, CT: Praeger, 2003a pp. 17-38.

———— "Cognitivism and the Experience of Dance" in A. C. Sukla (ed.) *Art and Experience*. Westport, CT: Praeger, 2003b pp. 121-143.

———— *The Concept of Dance Education* (Expanded Edition). Eastbourne: Pageantry Press, 2004a.

———— "Wittgenstein and the Arts: Understanding and Performing" in Peter Lewis (ed.) *Wittgenstein, Aesthetics and Philosophy*. Aldershot: Ashgate, 2004b pp. 109-136.

———— *Sport, Rules and Values*. London: Routledge, 2004c.

———— "The Artistic and the Aesthetic", *British Journal of Aesthetics* Vol. 45 No 4, 2005 pp. 368-387.

———— "The Friends of Jones' Painting: A Case of Explanation in the Republic of Art", *Contemporary Aesthetics*, Vol. 6, 2008.

———— *Ethics, Knowledge and Truth in Sports Research: An Epistemology of Sport*. London: Routledge, 2010a.

———— "Danse, Identité, Exécution" (in French: Trans J. Beauquel) in Julia Beauquel & Roger Pouivet (eds) *Philosophie de la Danse*. Rennes: Presses Universitaire de Rennes, 2010b pp. 143-166.

———— "Dance, Dancers and Subjectivity: Some Questions about Subjectivity and the Performing Arts" in Inma Alvarez, Hector Perez and Francisca Perez-Carreno (eds) *Expression in the Performing Arts*. Newcastle Upon Tyne: Cambridge Scholars Publishing, 2010c pp. 118-150.

———— *Artistic Judgement: A Framework for Philosophical Aesthetics* (Philosophical Studies Series Vol. 115). Dordrecht, NL: Springer Verlag, 2011.

Mackrell, Judith *Out of Line: The Story of British New Dance*. London: Dance Books, 1992.

———— *Reading Dance*. London: Michael Joseph, 1997.

Malcolm, Norman "The Privacy of Sensations" in his *Thought and Knowledge*. Ithaca: Cornell University Press, 1977 pp. 104-132.

Margolis, Joseph "Introductory Materials" in J. Margolis (ed.) *Philosophy Looks at the Arts*. New York: Scribners, 1978 pp. 289-292.

Meskin, Aaron "Productions, Performances and their Evaluation" in G. McFee (ed.) *Dance, Education and Philosophy*. Aachen: Meyer and Meyer, 1999 pp. 45-61.

Montero, Barbara "Proprioception as an Aesthetic Sense" *Journal of Aesthetics and Art Criticism*, Vol. 62 No. 2 Spring, 2006a pp. 231-242.

———— "Proprioceiving Someone Else's Movement", *Philosophical Explorations*, Vol. 9 No. 2, June 2006b pp. 149-161.

Morris, Desmond *Manwatching: A Field Guide to Human Behaviour*. London: Jonathan Cape, 1977.

Newman, Ernest *The Life of Richard Wagner*. London: Cassell, 1945.

Nikolais, Alwin "Excerpts from 'Nik: A Documentary'", in Jean Morrison Brown, Naomi Mindlin & Charles Woodford (eds) *The Vision of Moderrn Dance* (Second Edition). London: Dance Books, 1998 pp. 113-121.

Parry, Jann "Let Them Eat Doughnuts" *The Observer Review* 13th January, 2002 p. 14.

Pasles, Chris "Getting to the Root of Dance Rights", *LA Times Calendar*, 6th August, 2006 p. E35.

Peirce, C. S. *The Simplest Mathematics: The Collected Papers of Charles Sanders Peirce Volume IV* (ed. Charles Hartshorne & Paul Weiss) Cambridge, MA: Harvard University Press [1934], 1960.

Polyani, Michael *Personal Knowledge* London: Routledge, 1973.

Quinton, Anthony "Tragedy" in his *Thoughts and Thinkers*. New York: Holmes & Meier, 1982 pp. 94-107.

Quirey, Belinda *May I Have The Pleasure?* London: BBC Publications, 1976.

Redfern, Betty "The Child as Creator, Performer, Spectator", in *Dance and The Child: Keynote Addresses and Philosophy Papers*, Canadian Association of Health, Physical Education and Recreation, 1979, pp. 3-24.

———— *Dance, Art and Aesthetics*. London: Dance Books, 1983.

Reid, Thomas [1785] *Essays on the Intellectual Powers of Man*. Edinburgh: Edinburgh University Press, 2002.

Rhees, Rush *Without Answers*. London: Routledge & Kegan Paul, 1969.

Richards, I. A. *Principles of Literary Criticism*. London: Routledge & Kegan Paul, 1924.

Robinson, Daniel (ed.) *Neuroscience and Philosophy: Brain, Mind and Language*. New York; Columbia University Press, 2007.

Rowell, Bonnie *Dance Umbrella: The First Twenty-One Years*. London: Dance Books, 2000.

Rubidge, Sarah "Identity and the Open Work" in Stephanie Jordan (ed.) *Preservation Politics: Dance Revived Reconstructed Remade*. London: Dance Books Ltd., 2000 pp. 205-211.

Russell, Bertrand *The Problems of Philosophy*. Oxford: Home University Library, 1912.

———— *Logic and Knowledge* [Marsh (ed)] London: George Allen & Unwin, 1956.

Ryle, Gilbert *The Concept of Mind*. London: Hutchinson, 1949.

Schapiro, Meyer *Mondrian: On the Humanity of Abstract Painting*. New York: George Brazille, 1995.

Schön, Donald *The Reflective Practitioner*. New York: Basic Books, 1983.

———— *Educating the Reflective Practitioner*. San Francisco: Jossey-Bass, 1987.

Scruton, Roger *The Philosopher on Dover Beach*. Manchester: Carcanet Press, 1990.

———— *The Aesthetics of Music*. Oxford: Clarendon Press, 1997.

Searle, John *The Rediscovery of the Mind*. Cambridge, MA: MIT Books, 1992.

——— *Freedom and Neurobiology: Reflections on Free Will, Language, and Political Power*. New York: Columbia University Press, 2007a.

——— "Putting Consciousness Back in the Brain" in Daniel Robinson (ed.) *Neuroscience and Philosophy: Brain, Mind and Language*. New York; Columbia University Press, 2007b pp. 97-124.

Segal, Lewis, "Five Things I Hate about Ballet", *Los Angeles Times Calendar* (Part Two) Sunday , 6th August 2006 p. E31, E36.

———— "Bausch Sidesteps Talk of Intention", *Los Angeles Times Calendar*, Wednesday, 7th November, 2007 pp. E1, E9.

———— "An Art of Stolen Glances", *Los Angeles Times Calendar*, Sunday, January 6th 2008 p. F9.

Sharpe, R. A. "Type, Token, Interpretation, and Performance," *Mind* Vol. 86, 1979 pp. 437–40.

———— *Contemporary Aesthetics: A Philosophical Analysis*. New York: St Martin's Press, 1983.

———— *Music and Humanism: An Essay in the Aesthetics of Music*. Oxford: Clarendon, 2000.

———— *Philosophy of Music: An Introduction*. Chesham: Acumen, 2004.

Siegel, Marcia *At the Vanishing Point*. New York: Saturday Review Press, 1972.

———— *Watching the Dance Go By*. Boston: Houghton Mifflin, 1977.

———— *The Shapes of Changes*. Boston: Houghton Mifflin, 1979.

Smith, Adam [1795] "On the Affinity between Music, Dancing and Poetry" in his *Essays on Philosophical Subjects*. Oxford: Oxford University Press, 1980 pp. 210-213.

Spaethling, Robert (ed.) *Mozart's Letters, Mozart's Life: Selected Letters*. New York: Norton & Co, 2000.

Sparshott, Francis *A Measured Pace: Towards a Philosophical Understanding of the Arts of Dance*. University of Toronto Press, 1995.

———— *The Future of Aesthetics*. Toronto: University of Toronto Press, 1998.

Stokes, Adrian *Tonight the Ballet*. London: Faber and Faber, 1935.

Storer, T. "Miniac: World's Smallest Electronic Brain", *Analysis* Vol. 22 1962 pp. 151-152.

Suits, Bernard *The Grasshopper: Games, Life and Utopia*. Edinburgh: Scottish Academy Press, 1978.

Syed, Matthew *Bounce: The Myth of Talent and the Power of Practice*. London: Fourth Estate, 2010.

Taylor, Roger *Art: An Enemy of the People*. Hassocks: Harvester Press, 1978.

———— *Beyond Art: What Art Is and Might Be if Freed from Cultural Elitism*. Brighton: Harvester, 1981.

Tharp, Twyla *The Collaborative Habit: Life Lessons for Working Together* (with Jesse Kornbluth). New York: Simon & Schuster, 2009.

Tolstoi, Leo [1895] *What is Art?* (trans A. Maude). Oxford: Oxford University Press, 1930.

———— *Anna Karenina*. London: Everyman's Library, 1939.

Travis, Charles "The Twilight of Empiricism" *Proceeding of the Aristotelian Society*, Vol. CIV 2004 pp. 245-270.

———— *Occasion-Sensitivity: Selected Essays*. Oxford: Clarendon Press, 2008.

Urmson, J. O. "The Performing Arts" in H. D. Lewis (ed.) *Contemporary British*

Philosophy (Fourth Series). London: George Allen & Unwin, 1976 pp. 239-252.

Walton, Kendall "Categories of Art" reprinted in J. Margolis (ed.) *Philosophy Looks at the Arts* (Second Edition). Philadelphia, PA: Temple University Press, 1978 pp. 88-114; and in his *Marvelous Images: On Values and the Arts*. Oxford: Oxford University Press, 2008 pp. 195-219.

Weidman, Charles "Random Remarks", in Jean Morrison Brown, Naomi Mindlin & Charles Woodford (eds) *The Vision of Modern Dance* (Second Edition). London: Dance Books, 1998 pp. 65-69.

Wieand, Jeffrey "Perceptually Indistinguishable Objects" in Robert J. Yanal (ed.) *Institutions of Art: Reconsiderations of George Dickie's Philosophy*. University Park, PA: Pennsylvania State University Press, 1994 pp. 39-49.

Wiggins, David *Sameness and Substance Renewed*. Cambridge: Cambridge University Press, 2001.

Williams, Bernard *Truth and Truthfulness*. Princeton, NJ: Princeton University Press, 2002.

Williams, Drid *Ten Lectures on Theories of the Dance*. Metuchen, NJ: Scarecrow Press, 1991.

Williams, Drid *Anthropology and the Dance: Ten Lectures*. (Second Edition) Urbana: University of Illinois Press, 2004.

Wimsatt, W. K. & Beardsley, Monroe [1954] "The Intentional Fallacy" in J. Margolis (ed.) *Philosophy Looks at the Arts*. New York: Scribners, 1978 pp. 293-306.

Wisdom, John *Philosophy and Psycho-Analysis* Oxford: Blackwell, 1953.

——— *Paradox and Discovery*. Oxford: Blackwell, 1965.

Wittgenstein, Ludwig *Philosophical Investigations*. (trans. G. E. M. Anscombe). Oxford: Basil Blackwell, 1953/2001.

——— *On Certainty*. (trans. D. Paul & G. E. M. Anscombe). Oxford: Blackwell, 1969.

——— *Culture and Value*. (trans. Peter Winch) [Second Edition: 1998]. Oxford: Basil Blackwell, 1980.

———*Philosophical Occasions 1912-1951*. (eds James Klagge & Alfred Nordmann). Indianapolis, IN: Hackett, 1993.

Wollheim, Richard "Philosophy and the Arts" in Bryan Magee (ed.) *Modern British Philosophy*. London: Secker & Warburg, 1971 pp. 178-190.

——— *On Art and the Mind*. Harmondsworth: Allen Lane, 1973.

——— "Are the Criteria of Identity that Hold for a Work of Art in the Different Arts Aesthetically Relevant?" *Ratio* Vol. 20 No. 1 (June) 1978 pp. 29-48.

——— *Art and Its Objects* (Second Edition). Cambridge: Cambridge University Press, 1980.

———— *The Thread of Life*. Cambridge: Cambridge University Press, 1984.

———— "Imagination and Pictorial Understanding" *Proceedings of the Aristotelian Society Supplementary Volume* No 40 1986 pp. 45-60.

———— *Painting as an Art*. London: Thames and Hudson, 1987.

———— *The Mind and Its Depths*. Cambridge, MA: Harvard University Press, 1993a.

———— "Danto's Gallery of Indiscernibles" in Mark Rollins (ed.) *Danto and His Critics*, Oxford: Blackwell, 1993b pp. 28-38.

————"On Pictorial Representation" in Rob Van Gerwen (ed.) *Richard Wollheim on the Art of Painting*. Cambridge: Cambridge University Press, 2001 pp. 13-27.

Wolterstorff, Nicholas *Works and Worlds of Art*. Oxford: Clarendon, 1980 pp. 54-58.

Youngerman, Suzanne "Movement Notation Systems as Conceptual Frameworks: the Laban System," in M. Sheets-Johnstone (ed.) *Illuminating Dance: Philosophical Explorations*. Associated University Presses, 1984: pp. 101-123.

Ziff, Paul *Understanding Understanding*. Ithaca, NY: Cornell University Press, 1972.

———— *Antiaesthetics: An Appreciation of the Cow with the Subtile Nose*. Dordrecht, NL: Reidel Publishing, 1984.

Index